PATENT LAW
IN A NUTSHELL®

FOURTH EDITION

RANDALL R. RADER
The Rader Group PLLC
Retired Chief Judge
United States Court of Appeals
for the Federal Circuit
Professorial Lecturer in Law
George Washington University

BENJAMIN J. CHRISTOFF
Fish & Richardson P.C.

WEST
ACADEMIC
PUBLISHING

860 Blue Gentian Road, Suite 350
Eagan, MN 55121
1-877-888-1330

Printed in the United States of America

ISBN: 978-1-64708-840-8

The authors thank Elizabeth Richardson and Aaron Johansen for their assistance in preparing the first edition of this Nutshell and I-Chu Wang for her assistance in preparing the second edition. We also appreciate the dedication and diligence of the editors at West Academic.

OUTLINE

TABLE OF CASES

References are to Pages

PATENT LAW
IN A NUTSHELL®

FOURTH EDITION

CHAPTER 1
FOUNDATIONS OF PATENT LAW

I. FOUNDATIONS OF PATENT LAW

While historians occasionally refer to earlier precursors in Italy or Greece, the modern patent system began with an exception to the English 1624 Statute of Monopolies. Martin J. Adelman, Randall R. Rader & John R. Thomas, *Cases & Materials on Patent Law 9* (5th ed. 2018) (ART). From that starting point, the various American colonies imported the patent tradition. The origins of U.S. patent law thus antedate the Republic itself. From those roots, scholars have set forth various justifications for the patent law regime.

Modern economic theorists, for instance, opine that patents promote an efficient use of a scarce resource—namely technical knowledge. Indeed, a scarcity of knowledge about rats, fleas, and hygiene in 1340s, for example, cost the lives of one-third of the inhabitants of Europe in the black plague epidemic. In modern times, the plagues of AIDS or cancer illustrate that some forms of knowledge remain far too scarce.

Historians attribute the rise of patent law to the antiquation of trade guilds. At the end of the feudal era, patents began to replace the trade secret scheme of the guilds as the optimal protection for intellectual property. The key reason was public disclosure: trade guilds generally did not disclose their best ideas to the public—just the opposite.

Natural law theory posits that an innovator is entitled to enjoy the fruits of his inventive labor—and under the patent laws he can do so by temporarily excluding others from using his invention. A corollary of this school of thought is that patent law converts the conceptual and theoretical invention into property rights capable of valuation and trading in the marketplace. The transferability of patents encourages the efficient conversion of those property rights into useful products and technology. Even more recent theories recognize patent law as a beneficial monopoly based on the public utility model. John F. Duffy, Rethinking the Prospect Theory of Patents, 71 U. Chi. L. Rev. 439 (2004).

Other rationales underlying the patent system exist but cannot receive full attention in this brief overview. As two examples, certain academics have offered rent dissipation and races to invent as justifications for aspects of patent law. Mark F. Grady & Jay I. Alexander, Patent Law and Rent Dissipation, 78 Va. L. Rev. 305 (1992); Robert P. Merges & Richard R. Nelson, On the Complex Economics of Patent Scope, 90 Colum. L. Rev. 839 (1990).

II. ECONOMICS (INCENTIVE TO INVENT)

The majority of modern patent literature emphasizes economic justifications. An essential function of the patent system is to incentivize invention while minimizing free-riding. *See, e.g.*, Rebecca S. Eisenberg, Patents and the Progress of

Science: Exclusive Rights and Experimental Use, 56 U. Chi. L. Rev. 1017 (1989).

The patent system incentivizes investment in research, which speeds the advance of technology. Often technological advances consume millions or even billions of dollars in research and development costs. Without some form of protection, free-riders would swiftly reverse-engineer and copy the innovator's technology. The innovator would lose its vast investment in an instant. In the short run, prices would decline because the market would ignore the R&D cost component of every inventive product.

But the long-term result would be a drastic chilling effect on research investment. Because marginal prices for an inventive product or service would drop below the average cost (which includes both the marginal cost and the per-unit development cost), investors would have little economic incentive to fund expensive development projects. Without patent protections, no rational participant in the marketplace would incur research investments—instead they would wait for others to innovate, then quickly copy. And ultimately, innovations that are extremely research intensive, *e.g.*, cures for cancer, might slow or never be achieved.

Moreover, a rational innovator in a non-patent system would hide his advances as long as possible as a trade secret in order to boost his head-start advantage in the market. Even without patent rights, an innovator enjoys some benefit as the market's first mover. But this head start, by itself, does not adequately protect inventions demanding vast research investments. And while trade secrets might impede copying, they also impede future development by avoiding any enabling public disclosure of the new technology.

Assume, for example, that an inventor finds the cure for AIDS or cancer. No doubt that invention would only be accomplished after the expenditure of billions of dollars in research investments. Without patent protection, a copyist might easily reverse engineer that product within a few weeks. The inventor could never hope to recoup the costs of discovery.

Further, without protection, the rational investor would seek more dependable investments. Patents thus protect research investment by giving the inventor control over the economic benefits from the technology for a limited time. Put differently, the patent system gives the inventor a reward (temporary exclusive rights) for the successful conclusion of what is often rigorous and expensive research. Using patent protections, the inventor may both recover research costs and accumulate capital for other projects.

Of course, consumers pay the differential between strict marginal pricing and accurate, investment-inducing pricing that compensates for research and development costs. Inevitably this price differential means that, at first, perhaps a smaller group of consumers can enjoy the product at the increased price during the limited period of exclusive rights. In a price-sensitive market, the higher price invariably reduces the demand for the good or service. This price elasticity restricts the use of inventions to those consumers willing (or able) to pay the exclusive-right price. Particularly in health care products (where the market is nearly inelastic), this economic reality creates a moral concern.

The limited period of exclusivity, however, substantially reduces those moral issues. Every invention in or before 2002 (assuming a 20-year exclusive right) is free after 2022. Thus each generation effectively funds a gift of technology to the next, asking only that their children do the same for their grandchildren. In essence, the patent system allows each generation to gift inventive solutions to future generations. As each generation speeds life-saving or life-enhancing technology into use, the long-term benefits of early production of new technology outweigh the costs of patents in the short term.

III. HISTORY: ANTIDOTE TO TRADE SECRETS (INCENTIVE TO DISCLOSE)

Historians often trace the rise of the patent system to the time when trade guilds began to fade as the conventional protectors of sensitive technology. As noted earlier, without a patent system, inventors guarded their advances as trade secrets. At the close of the feudal period, trade guilds required years of apprenticeship to earn access to proprietary secrets. Although this practice prevented free-riding, the high barrier to entry (that is, completion of an apprenticeship) discouraged competition and impeded scientific advance. Only those within the guild had the incentive and know-how to make technological advances. Simply put, trade guilds shrank the pool of potential inventors. But the public patent grant removed those artificial barriers: In exchange for full, public disclosure in the patent application, the inventor received a limited period of exclusive rights.

Trade secrets remain an option to protect innovations. Although secrecy may not protect inventions that can be understood once in use, a widespread secrecy practice would impede advances in many technology fields. Patents, in contrast, encourage rapid disclosure and give other innovators access to the most recent enhancements in technology. With this wealth of information available, each advance often spurs further improvements.

A race to disclose, however, can come at a cost. Some have argued that the profit incentive can concentrate scarce research resources on projects with the greatest potential economic rewards. For example, researchers might invest more in the search for curing universal heart-burn maladies than for curing a rare cancer. This academic complaint, however, ignores the economic realities of limited resources and distrusts the market to efficiently allocate scarce research resources.

The race to disclose might also complicate research efforts by creating a patent thicket that can increase research costs. While theoretically plausible, this so-called tragedy of the anti-commons, if it exists at all, is rare. In the first place, the patent system does not permit the scope of exclusive rights to exceed the scope of disclosure. This requirement (enforced largely by the enablement and obviousness doctrines) ensures that patents do not preempt more than they contribute to the useful arts. Accordingly, each patent delineates both its contribution and the prospect for further patentable improvements on the same technology. That is, patents document the state of current technology and thus facilitate further research to extend the horizons of technology.

Moreover, the market generally licenses technology at a value commensurate with its contribution to the sciences. For example, multiple minor patents in a crowded area of technology will likely be made available for "rent or purchase" at lower rates. Competitors also often thin-out the patent thicket through cross-licensing or "pooling" patents that cover the various aspects of a technology. Market forces thus reduce the tragedy of the anti-commons to an academic concern.

Nonetheless, in the crowded information technology industry with its heavy reliance on semiconductor and software technology, major corporations have argued that patent "trolls" (an undefined pejorative most often referring to patentees seeking royalties without producing a product) use litigation strategies to obtain royalties beyond the economic contribution of the invention to the technology. Still, beyond anecdotal evidence, no authoritative and comprehensive study has yet documented that patents somehow prevent technological advance by complicating research in a field preempted by multiple intellectual property rights.

IV. HISTORY: TECHNOLOGY TRANSFER

At the advent of the patent era, a sovereign would often use the promise of an exclusive right to lure technology into its domain. The inventor-turned-entrepreneur could thus obtain an exclusive right by merely relocating innovative technology.

In the modern world, intellectual property is still a central component of international technology transfer policy. The 1995 treaty on the Trade Related Aspects of Intellectual Property (TRIPS) made membership in the World Trade Organization (WTO) conditional on adoption of intellectual property institutions. Every signatory nation had an incentive to adopt a patent system that meets basic international standards. Functional patent-granting and patent-enforcing institutions became every nation's ticket to enjoy minimal tariffs and other WTO trade benefits. In simple terms, protecting advanced technology became the means of acquiring advanced technology.

But even before TRIPS, patent protection influenced technology transfer. Most developed nations have had some form of patent protection for decades, if not centuries. Developing nations, on the other hand, have generally lacked robust patent systems. Patent owners have often declined to transfer their technology to such nations without adequate enforcement. National patent policy and institutions have thus consistently influenced technology transfer.

Of course, even without an inventor's consent, copyists may nonetheless acquire access to patented technology available in other parts of the world. In a sense, the inventor is no worse off because he was not counting on remuneration from countries where he would hold no patent rights. But on the other hand, nations without a vigorous patent system, at a minimum, discourage legitimate research investments and technology transfer within their borders. Often an inadequate patent system may also create incentives for a nation's own inventors, with their ability to develop a technology that may lift the economy of their entire nation, to do their work in other locations, where it will be protected. Any potential for this kind of "brain drain" may have the long-term consequence of transferring technology even before its development.

V. NATURAL RIGHTS (ENTITLEMENT THEORY)

Patents are a form of property. 35 U.S.C. § 261 even provides that "patents shall have the attributes of personal property." As a species of property, patents share the philosophical origins of real property. Under John Locke's fundamental justification for property rights, a divine being created the world as a universal common in which individuals possess an equal right. *See* John Locke, The Second Treatise of Government ¶ 27 (1690), in Two Treatises of Government (Peter Laslett ed.

1960). Within that universal common, each individual personally owns the products of his labor.

In a related but distinct theory, Georg Wilhelm Friedrich Hegel proffered that property results not from the fruit of one's labor but from the exercise of free will. *See* Hegel's Philosophy of Right (T.M. Knox trans. 1952). The interaction of human will with the corporeal world creates enduring objects, or property. These objects, a natural part of their creator's personality, deserve protection from unauthorized use.

Under either Locke's labor theory or Hegel's moral rights theory, invented knowledge belongs to its creator or discoverer. But these labor-based rights are not limitless: an individual cannot take from the universal common without leaving enough for others to use and enjoy. To some degree, knowledge as a form of private property is counterintuitive. Most cultures view knowledge as something to be freely shared. On the other hand, technical knowledge, often the product of expensive research ventures, must be generated. Patent rights provide the requisite "fuel of interest," in the words of Abraham Lincoln, to stimulate inventive labor or the "fire of genius."

Entitlement theories also show that patents serve the larger economic service of converting inchoate knowledge into useful technology for public consumption. The incentives of patent law do some of their best work after invention, disclosure, and issuance of a patent. At that point, the patent system enables an inventor to raise capital to market and manufacture the invention.

Private ownership of those valuable property rights can generate capital and incentives to convert the concepts into usable products. Invention only starts the process of creating useful technology. The further work of conversion to useful products, manufacturing, and distribution also requires capital. Patents can generate that investment. In addition, patents solve the inventor's dilemma by creating a way to obtain development capital without compromising the idea. The owner of the idea, additionally, must use the knowledge efficiently or the market will transfer that ownership to better uses. In simple terms, private is more efficient than collective ownership.

A modern corollary of this principle, the prospect theory, suggests that patents promote efficient use of a scarce resource like knowledge. Edmund W. Kitch, The Nature and Function of the Patent System, 20 J.L. & Econ. 265 (1977). The prospect theory opines that the owner/inventor can efficiently direct future research to refine and improve the new technology.

VI. PATENTS AND PUBLIC UTILITY THEORY

Many economists criticize the patent system for eliminating the "surplus" otherwise enjoyed by the consumer. That is, the consumer would get the benefit of lower prices without patents recapturing the costs of research and development. The usual economic proposal to retain the consumer surplus emphasizes rewards in lieu of patents. A leading scholar, Professor Duffy, made a frontal assault on this chorus by pointing out that there is a similar loss of consumer surplus in the field of public utilities—an example where economists almost universally praise the benefits of pricing above marginal cost. John F. Duffy, Rethinking the Prospect Theory of Patents, 71 U. Chi. L. Rev. 439 (2004).

Under this reasoning, public utilities, like electricity generation, have very low marginal costs once the infrastructure of dams and power lines are in place. These utilities, however, require a monopoly to both promote efficiency in generation and distribution and to recover over time the vast investment in infrastructure. Similarly patents engender a beneficial monopoly that allows the innovator to recover research and development costs over the life of the patent. The international patent system is more efficient than an international reward system (which the governments of the world are not likely to create or administer anyway).

VII. CONCLUSION

In spite of some defects, the patent system is one of the greatest inventions of Western civilization. With manageable costs of administration, the system stimulates inventive activity that facilitates economic expansion while simultaneously encouraging conversion of theoretical science into useful technology. Finally, the system achieves moral benefits by its limited terms with each generation providing a gift of innovation to its successors.

CHAPTER 2

PATENT ACQUISITION

I. THE UNITED STATES PATENT AND TRADEMARK OFFICE

A. EXAMINATION

As the administrative agency in charge of granting patents, the United States Patent and Trademark Office—typically abbreviated as USPTO, PTO, or simply Patent Office—examines all patent applications to ensure compliance with substantive and procedural requirements.[1] In particular, § 131 requires the Patent Office to examine patent applications:

> The Director shall cause an examination to be made of the application and the alleged new invention; and if on such examination it appears that the applicant is entitled to a patent under the law, the Director shall issue a patent therefor.

The Patent Office examines patent applications on a first-come-first-served basis, absent compelling or

---

[1] To fund its operations, the Patent Office charges fees for performing various functions, including those related to examining applications. *See* 35 U.S.C. § 41; 37 C.F.R. §§ 1.16–1.28. In fact, the revenue collected from these fees historically has exceeded the amount Congress appropriates to the Patent Office, and there is a Patent and Trademark Reserve Fund for fees collected in excess of the appropriated amount. 35 U.S.C. § 42. Of course, the Patent Office may only access the Reserve Fund with the permission of Congress through its appropriation Acts.

unusual circumstances requiring accelerated examination.

The Patent Office examines applications for compliance with formal requirements as well as perform a search for prior art. Should the application fail to conform with either procedural or substantive requirements, § 132(a) provides:

> Whenever, on examination, any claim for a patent is rejected, or any objection or requirement made, the Director shall notify the applicant thereof, stating the reasons for such rejection, or objection or requirement, together with such information and references as may be useful in judging of the propriety of continuing the prosecution of his application; and if after receiving such notice, the applicant persists in his claim for a patent, with or without amendment, the application shall be reexamined. No amendment shall introduce new matter into the disclosure of the invention.

Upon rejection or objection, the Patent Office issues an Office Action identifying the inadequacies of the patent application. 37 C.F.R. § 1.104. An applicant typically has three months to respond to an Office Action (in unusual circumstances, just one month). But the applicant may extend this period up to 6 months total. 35 U.S.C. § 133. The applicant responds to the Office Action with argument in either a Reply or an Amendment (this nomenclature depends on whether the applicant contests the action or amends the application in light of the rejection or objection) that the rejection or objection was either factually or legally improper. 37 C.F.R. §§ 1.111, 1.121. This back-and-forth continues until the Patent Office allows the application or issues a Final Office Action under 37 C.F.R. § 1.113, at which point the applicant must either appeal, request continued examination, or abandon the application.

The Patent Office plays an important gatekeeping function. It facilitates an efficient and trustworthy patent system by preventing the issuance of undeserving patents. Without rigorous examination, so-called scarecrow patents would raise costs of doing business, either by allowing their owners to extract preventable royalty payments or by forcing litigation to invalidate the worthless patents. During examination, the Patent Office applies the substantive requirements of patent law: eligibility, utility, novelty, non-obviousness, adequate disclosure, and definiteness. Importantly, even if a patent issues, the mere fact of issuance does not preclude future challenges based on these substantive requirements. For example, an affected party can assert invalidity defenses in litigation or challenge validity through post-grant procedures at the Patent Office.

The following chart outlines the usual pre-examination, examination, and post-examination procedures for obtaining a U.S. patent. Two common paths toward a patent grant are marked by solid lines; other possibilities are marked with dashed lines. One solid line shows an allowance issued directly by the examiner. The other leads to an appeal to the Patent Trial and Appeal Board, which may affirm, reject, or modify the examiner's rejections. The chart does not show all possible permutations, and the specific path of an individual case's prosecution may vary. For example, post-grant proceedings such as reexamination, *inter partes* review, post-grant review, and reissue are not shown. Similarly, petitions and pre-grant publications are not shown.

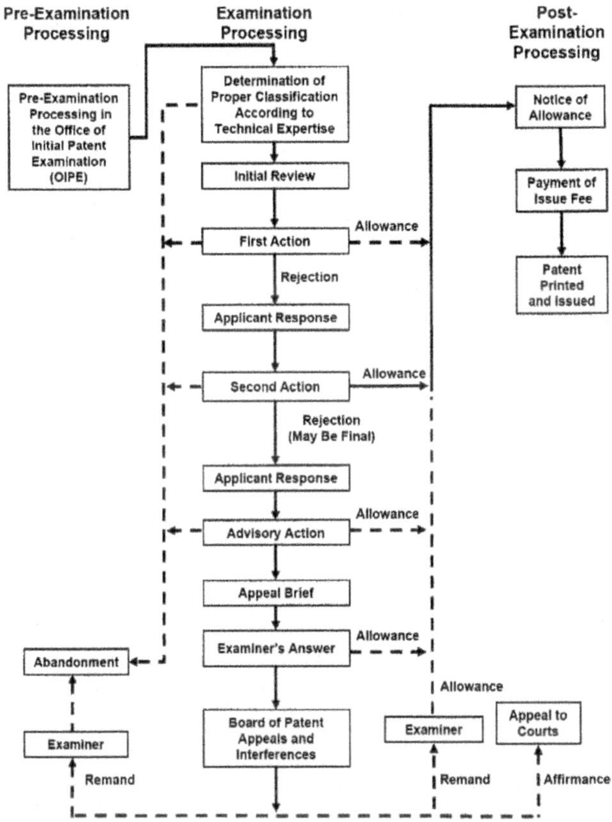

B. HISTORICAL DEVELOPMENT

The evolution of the Patent Office parallels the convolution of the patent system as a whole. The Constitution sets forth the primary authority underlying the patent laws: "The Congress shall have Power . . . To promote the Progress of Science and useful Arts, by securing for limited Times to Authors and Inventors the exclusive Right to their respective Writings and Discoveries." U.S. CONST. art. I, § 8, cl. 8. Like other grants of power in the Constitution, this clause merely gives Congress the power to shape the substantive and procedural requirements of patents. *See, e.g., In re Bergy,* 596 F.2d 952, 958–59 (CCPA 1979).

Swiftly utilizing this power, Congress enacted the first Patent Act in 1790, which authorized the first three examiners—the Secretary of State, the Secretary of War, and the Attorney General—to grant patents. Patent Act of 1790, 1 Stat. 109 (Apr. 10, 1790). Congress soon realized that the many competing responsibilities of these cabinet members prevented substantive examination of patent applications.

The next iteration of the Patent Act eliminated the three-person board in favor of a pure registration system. *See* Patent Act of 1793, 1 Stat. 318 (Feb. 21, 1793). Even though the Department of State maintained a registry of all patents under this act, patents received no substantive examination. Litigation was the sole means of detecting and invalidating unpatentable subject matter. Ultimately this registration system proved inefficient. Under the 1793 Act, two parties could even acquire patents on the same invention, which may have been actually unpatentable for both of them when a court finally litigated validity issues.

In 1836, the next Patent Act reinstated an examination system. Patent Act of 1836, 5 Stat. 117

(Jul. 4, 1836). This act created a Patent Office within the Department of State and set forth procedural and substantive requirements for patentability.

The 1870 Act followed with important changes, including establishing the modern practice of peripheral claims to define the outer bounds of the invention. Patent Act of 1870, 16 Stat. 198 (July 8, 1870). Before 1870, central claiming described inventions in more general terms. In any event, judicial interpretation of the 1836 and 1870 Acts resulted in the common law origins of many doctrines familiar to current patent practitioners, including non-obviousness, enablement, and experimental use.

Aside from the creation of the Court of Customs and Patent Appeals (CCPA), which was granted jurisdiction over appeals from the Patent Office in 1929, statutory patent law remained largely untouched until the seminal Patent Act of 1952. This monumental achievement both codified much of the common law and also reoriented the law in important areas such as obviousness and functional claiming.

The modern obviousness requirement remains the crowning achievement of the 1952 Act. Before 1952, the judiciary struggled to articulate a neutral, objective standard to distinguish genuine "inventions" from mere minor technological improvements. Moreover, the advent of the antitrust era cast an unfavorable light on the patent "monopolies." *Transparent-Wrap Mach. Corp. v. Stokes & Smith Co.*, 329 U.S. 637, 644 (1947) (calling a patent a "legalized monopoly"); *see also* The Sherman Act, 15 U.S.C. § 2 (1890). The Supreme

Court had been requiring a "flash of creative genius" to prove an invention worthy of a patent. *See, e.g.*, *Cuno Eng'g. Corp. v. Automatic Devices Corp.*, 314 U.S. 84, 91 (1941). This inherently subjective test for non-obviousness relied on an after-the-fact assessment of the invention's ability to evoke a "gee-whiz" reaction. The fabled Judge Learned Hand protested openly that this test was "as fugitive, impalpable, wayward, and vague a phantom as exists in the whole paraphernalia of legal concepts." *Harries v. Air King Prods. Co.*, 183 F.2d 158, 162 (2d Cir. 1950).

As discussed later in Chapter 8, the modern test for obviousness that appeared in 1952 is *objective*—resting on factual considerations evaluated through the prism of a hypothetical person of ordinary skill in the particular technical art at the time of invention. This advance in evaluating inventive contributions transformed patent acquisition (also called prosecution) as well as litigation.

Nonetheless, even after the 1952 Act, the Supreme Court could not articulate and apply a uniform test for inventiveness. *See, e.g.*, *Anderson's-Black Rock, Inc. v. Pavement Salvage Co.*, 396 U.S. 57 (1969); *Sakraida v. Ag Pro, Inc.*, 425 U.S. 273 (1976). Some circuits followed the non-obviousness requirement in the 1952 Act, while others continued to apply the "flash of genius" test. Compare *Republic Indus., Inc. v. Schlage Lock Co.*, 592 F.2d 963 (7th Cir. 1979) and *Rengo Co. v. Molins Mach. Co.*, 657 F.2d 535 (3d Cir. 1981) with *Fred Whitaker Co. v. E.T. Barwick Indus., Inc.*, 551 F.2d 622 (5th Cir. 1977) and *Am. Seating*

Co. v. Nat'l Seating Co., 586 F.2d 611 (6th Cir. 1978). The vast differences between hospitable and inhospitable courts of appeals generated widespread forum shopping and undercut predictability in patent law.

This unseemly situation contributed to Congress's decision in 1982 to create the United States Court of Appeals for the Federal Circuit. This new circuit consolidated all patent appeals in a single court with exclusive subject matter jurisdiction over patent appeals from district courts and the Patent Office. The Federal Circuit promptly adopted the decisions of its predecessor court, the CCPA, as binding precedent. *South Corp. v. United States*, 690 F.2d 1368, 1370 (Fed. Cir. 1982). While the Federal Circuit normally has 12 active judges, appeals are typically heard and decided by a 3-judge panel. But occasionally the full court sits en banc, either to overrule precedent, *Newell Cos. v. Kenney Mfg. Co.*, 864 F.2d 757 (Fed. Cir. 1988), (en banc), or to settle important issues of law. *See, e.g., Cybor Corp. v. FAS Techs., Inc.*, 138 F.3d 1448 (Fed. Cir. 1998) (en banc).

The creation of the Federal Circuit disrupted the long-time system that distributed appeals amongst the various circuits according to geographic jurisdiction, regardless of subject matter. Congress and patent lawyers hoped that this dramatic disruption would bring certainty, uniformity, and predictability to the law. For the most part, the Federal Circuit has met these expectations. Some critics have contended, however, that the court's decisions vary depending on the composition of judges hearing the particular appeal, thus undermining predictability. R. Polk Wagner & Lee Petherbridge, *Is the Federal Circuit Succeeding?: An Empirical Assessment of Judicial Performance,* 152 U. Penn. L. Rev. 1105 (2004).

From 1952 to 1999, the basic structure of the patent system remained largely untouched, but a few legislative amendments deserve mention. For one, the 1995 amendments changed the statutory term of a patent from 17 years from the date of grant to 20 years from the date of filing. Uruguay Round Agreements Act, Pub. L. No. 103–465, 108 Stat. 4809 (1994).

The 1999 amendments, for the first time, seemed to reflect the value of harmonizing U.S. law with intellectual property standards around the world. American Inventors Protection Act, Pub. L. No. 106–113, 113 Stat. 1501 (1999). The most noteworthy changes harmonize U.S. law with European and Japanese standards, including a first user defense to infringement, the publication of pending applications 18 months from the priority date, and *inter partes* reexaminations of issued patents. The publication of pending applications marks a significant departure from the prior policy of maintaining the secrecy of pending applications, which dated back to the Patent Act of 1790. Moreover, *inter partes* reexamination, which provides an alternative to challenging a patent's validity in court, marked the first step towards an administrative opposition system.

Congress again moved in 2011 to harmonize U.S. law with the rest of the world and enacted the Leahy-

Smith America Invents Act (AIA). The AIA makes significant, fundamental changes to the patent statute. *See* Pub. L. No. 112–29, 125 Stat. 284 (2011). The amendment that received perhaps the most public attention at the time was the change from a "first-to-invent" regime to a "first-inventor-to-file" regime. All applications with an effective filing date on or after March 16, 2013, would be examined under a new version of 35 U.S.C. § 102.

Other notable amendments included: prioritizing examination of certain applications; allowing pre-issuance submission of prior art; allowing post-grant review proceedings based on any ground of invalidity (i.e., not simply patents and printed publications); permitting supplemental examination; removing the penalties for failing to disclose the best mode; expanding the first user defense to infringement based on prior commercial use; revising the fee structure and intending to allow the Patent Office proper levels of funding commensurate with the user-fee-based revenue; authorizing multiple physical locations for the Patent Office's employees across the country; changing the prohibition against falsely marking a good with a patent; and setting forth the appropriate conditions for joinder of unrelated parties in a multi-defendant patent litigation.

The AIA's provisions have multiple effective dates, and U.S. patent law and patent practitioners will live with parallel statutes and rules for the next few decades.

C. ORGANIZATION

Like any massive institution, the Patent Office has a well-organized structure to promote efficiency. With respect to examining applications, the Office of Patent Application Processing receives patent applications, labels them with unique application numbers, and forwards them along for examination (so long as they are complete enough for examination). The Patent Office divides applications between nine Technology Centers, each dedicated to its own technical area. Technology Centers are subdivided into Art Units. Generally, the Art Units, each of which comprises multiple primary and assistant examiners, have great expertise with—and repeated exposure to—applications pertaining to similar subject matter. As the front-line representatives for the interests of the Patent Office (and thus the public), the primary and assistant examiners review patent applications and issue official actions.

II. PROSECUTION PROCEDURES

Three sources provide the procedures governing the prosecution of a patent: the Patent Act as codified in 35 U.S.C. § 1 *et seq.*, administrative rules as set forth in 37 C.F.R. § 1.1 *et seq.*, and the Manual of Patent Examining Procedure (MPEP). Although the MPEP is a publication of the Patent Office, it does not set out binding law, even if courts sometimes cite its provisions as persuasive authority. Compare *In re Recreative Techs.*, 83 F.3d 1394 (Fed. Cir. 1996) with *Litton Sys., Inc. v. Whirlpool Corp.*, 728 F.2d 1423

(Fed. Cir. 1984). Patent examiners and applicants routinely rely upon the MPEP during prosecution.

A. APPLICATION TYPES

Under 35 U.S.C. § 111, an application falls into one of two categories: a provisional application under subsection (b) or a non-provisional application under subsection (a). Aside from originally filed applications, non-provisional applications include continuing applications, such as divisional, continuation, and continuation-in-part applications. An applicant may now request continued examination of an application after a final rejection—this procedure mimics the filing of a continuation application.

1. Provisional Applications

A provisional application is essentially a temporary placeholder for an application to follow. This type of application thus has streamlined requirements. It must have a disclosure complying with the requirements of § 112(a)[2] and a drawing where necessary to understand the subject matter. Notably, a provisional application need not include claims. 35 U.S.C. § 111(b)(2). The provisional does not undergo substantive examination; rather the Patent Office merely records and stores it. Unless the applicant converts it into a non-provisional

---

[2] The AIA amends § 112 to refer to alphabetic subsections (i.e., subsections (a)–(f)). Thus, traditional references to § 112, first paragraph, should be understood as referring to § 112(a), which was not substantively amended.

application within 12 months, the Patent Office will deem it abandoned.

The provisional application serves the purpose of setting a priority date for the disclosed subject matter. A non-provisional application claiming an invention described in a provisional application receives the benefit of the provisional application's earlier filing date, so long as the two applications share at least one inventor and the provisional application's written description adequately supports the non-provisional application's claims. *See, e.g.*, *New Railhead Mfg., L.L.C. v. Vermeer Mfg. Co.*, 298 F.3d 1290, 1294 (Fed. Cir. 2002). But a provisional application cannot claim priority to any earlier application. Importantly, the provisional application, because not examined, does not reduce the term of any patent that arises from its initial filing. In other words, a provisional application does not trigger the start of the issued patent's 20-year term.

2. Non-Provisional Applications

The Patent Office substantively examines each non-provisional application. Filing a non-provisional starts the 20-year patent term clock. These applications must contain a specification with a disclosure, at least one claim, a drawing if necessary to understand the subject matter, and an oath by an applicant. 35 U.S.C. § 111(a)(2). Even if initially missing the oath or any requisite fees, the filing date of the application is the date of receipt of the specification and drawings (if any). Although not mandatory, 37 C.F.R. § 1.77 strongly recommends a particular arrangement for the contents of the specification. A specification should generally have, among other things, a background of the invention, a short summary of the invention, a brief description of the drawings, a detailed description of the invention, at least one claim, and an abstract of the disclosure.

3. Continuing Applications

A patent application may claim priority to another non-provisional application, as well as a provisional application. As a matter of convenience, patents claiming priority are said to be "related," and have genealogical designations, such as "parent," "grandparent," "child," "sibling," and so on. Descendent applications, which include continuations, continuations-in-part (CIP), and divisional applications, fall under the general heading of "continuing applications." Continuing applications allow an inventor to prolonging the prosecution process and modify the focus of the claimed inventions. To get the benefit of the original filing and priority date, the descendant application must claim subject matter that is sufficiently supported or described in the ancestor application, share at least one inventor with the prior application, originate (*i.e.*, be filed) while the prior application is still pending, and expressly refer to the prior application. *See* 35 U.S.C. § 120; 37 C.F.R. §§ 1.53(b), 1.78. There is no limit to the number of continuing applications that can claim priority to an earlier ancestor application.

The Federal Circuit has explained the differences between the types of continuing applications:

> "Continuation" and "divisional" applications are alike in that they are both continuing applications based on the same disclosure as an earlier application. They differ, however, in what they claim. A "continuation" application claims the same invention claimed in an earlier application, although there may be some variation in the scope of the subject matter claimed. A "divisional" application, on the other hand, is one carved out of an earlier application which disclosed and claimed more than one independent invention, the result being that the divisional application claims only one or more, but not all, of the independent inventions of the earlier application. A "CIP" application is a continuing application containing a portion or all of the disclosure of an earlier application together with added matter not present in that earlier application.

Transco Prods. Inc. v. Performance Contracting, Inc., 38 F.3d 551, 555–56 (Fed. Cir. 1994) (citations omitted). By noting that a CIP application contains new matter, the court implicitly acknowledged that it may have more than one priority date. That would be true where certain claims are supported by one ancestor application and other claims are supported by another. Subject matter not expressly or inherently disclosed in the parent application is not entitled to the benefit of that parent's filing date. *See, e.g.*, *Litton Sys., Inc. v. Whirlpool Corp.*, 728 F.2d 1423 (Fed. Cir. 1984).

a) Restriction Requirements and Divisionals

The Patent Office creates a divisional application using a "restriction requirement" under § 121, which states:

> If two or more independent and distinct inventions are claimed in one application, the Director may require the application to be restricted to one of the inventions. If the other invention is made the subject of a divisional application which complies with the requirements of section 120 it shall be entitled to the benefit of the filing date of the original application. . . . The validity of a patent shall not be questioned for failure of the Director to require the application to be restricted to one invention.

35 U.S.C. § 121. Under this provision, the Patent Office can require the applicant to separate an application that discloses multiple inventions into distinct applications.

The Patent Office uses restriction requirements to block applicants' attempts to circumvent the fee structure by prosecuting multiple separate inventions in a single application. Restriction requirements also increase the efficiency of examination by sending different inventions to their most appropriate Art Units.

The statute also exempts patents that were subject to a restriction requirement from later being deemed unpatentable for "double patenting"—*i.e.*, improperly claiming the same subject matter as another patent owned by the patentee:

> A patent issuing on an application with respect to which a requirement for restriction under this section has been made, or on an application filed as a result of such a requirement, shall not be used as a reference either in the Patent and Trademark Office or in the courts against a divisional application or against the original application or any patent issued on either of them, if the divisional application is filed before the issuance of the patent on the other application.

35 U.S.C. § 121. Double patenting is discussed further in Chapter 10. But in essence, § 121 shields claims that were withdrawn to comply with a restriction requirement from a double patenting rejection in light of the initial application. *See, e.g.*, *Geneva Pharms., Inc. v. GlaxoSmithKline PLC*, 349 F.3d 1373 (Fed. Cir. 2003). So long as the "independent and distinct inventions" remain separated in subsequent continuing applications—*i.e.*, there is "consonance" between originally restricted claims and their descendants—the applicant retains a statutory shield against invalidity for double patenting. If the applicant breaks consonance or if the Patent Office does not unambiguously issue a restriction requirement, the statutory shield disappears.

b) Requests for Continued Examination

An applicant may file a request for continued examination (RCE) under 37 C.F.R. § 1.114 to continue prosecuting a pending application under a final rejection (or where prosecution is otherwise closed). Such a request must include a submission showing that an RCE would be appropriate, such as an information disclosure statement that lists additional references for consideration by the Patent Office, an amendment to any portion of the specification, or new evidence in support of patentability. If there is an outstanding Office Action, the request for continued examination must address each ground of rejection and objection contained in the Office Action. 37 C.F.R. § 1.114(c). An applicant must also make an effort to advance prosecution.

B. PUBLICATION RULE

Until 1999, the Patent Act protected the secrecy of all patent applications. To harmonize U.S. practice with international standards, Congress amended the Patent Act to order publication of most applications 18 months after their earliest filing date. But a notable exception provides that if the subject matter claimed in the application is not the subject of a foreign application filed in accordance with an international agreement (like the Paris Convention or the Patent Cooperation Treaty), then an applicant may request at the time of filing the application that the Patent Office refrain from publishing the application. 35 U.S.C. § 122.

In exchange for eliminating the secrecy of the pending application, the Patent Act grants provisional rights in limited circumstances. Specifically, a patent owner may obtain a reasonable royalty from infringers accruing from the date of Patent Office publication, so long as two conditions are met: the published application must contain claims substantially identical to the claims in the patent maturing from that application, and the patentee must have given actual notice of the published application to the infringer. 35 U.S.C. § 154(d). In practice, however, these provisional rights have nominal value because most patent applications are amended during prosecution.

C. INTERFERENCES & DERIVATION PROCEEDINGS

In addition to *ex parte* prosecution of a patent application, the Patent Office has historically examined pending applications in an *inter partes* setting where a patent or patent application claims the same invention as, that is, "interferes" with, a pending application. A so-called interference—a deceptively intricate administrative proceeding traditionally governed by pre-AIA 35 U.S.C. §§ 135 & 102(g) and 37 C.F.R. § 1.601 *et seq.*—determines which applicant (or patentee) has priority over the invention.

Prior to 2011, the statute provided that an interference occurs when "an application is made for a patent which . . . would interfere with any pending application, or with any unexpired patent." 35 U.S.C.

§ 135 (2002). The Patent Office could declare an interference between two conflicting applications *sua sponte*, without any prompting by (or even knowledge of) either applicant. Alternatively, a patent applicant could provoke an interference upon discovering a newly-issued patent or published pending application that claims the same invention. Importantly, a party to an interference who expected to lose the priority contest could nonetheless prevent the winner from obtaining a patent by successfully arguing that the subject matter is not patentable.

Under the AIA, derivation proceedings replaced interferences for patents or applications having an effective filing date on or after March 16, 2013. To initiate a derivation proceeding, a patent applicant petitions the Patent Office for a "finding that an [inventor] named in an earlier application . . . derived the claimed invention from an [inventor] named in the petitioner's application . . . and, without authorization, the earlier application claiming such invention was filed." 35 U.S.C. § 135 (2012). Derivation proceedings have a narrower, but similar, scope in comparison to interferences—whose result did not hinge on whether the first applicant had *derived* information from the second applicant.

Chapter 11 examines interferences and derivation proceedings in greater detail.

D. PETITION AND APPEAL RIGHTS

Upon a final rejection or objection, an applicant may either appeal to the Patent Trial and Appeal Board (PTAB or Board) under 35 U.S.C. § 134, in the case of a rejection, or petition the Patent Office Director under 37 C.F.R. § 1.181, in the case of an objection. The CCPA distinguished these separate courses as follows:

> Decisions of the examiner directly relating to the rejection of claims are subject to appeal. These questions generally deal with the merits of the invention, involving factual determinations and the legal conclusions drawn therefrom regarding the application disclosure, the claims and the prior art. The examiner's rulings dealing with procedural matters, such as whether an affidavit or amendment is untimely, and formal requirements, such as whether a new application title will be required, are reviewable upon petition.

In re Searles, 422 F.2d 431, 435 (CCPA 1970). The Board hears all internal appeals, as well as interferences (now derivations). This administrative body consists of administrative patent judges who are typically former examiners or patent attorneys with both scientific and legal credentials. 35 U.S.C. § 6. Three administrative patent judges hear each appeal. The entire Board may rehear any case decided by a three-judge panel. The Board delivers opinions supported by "substantial evidence"—that is, evidence that a reasonable person would accept as adequate to support a conclusion. *See, e.g., In re Gartside,* 203 F.3d 1305, 1312 (Fed. Cir. 2000). Notably, the Board is not wholly independent from the Patent Office:

> Even though Board members serve an essential function, they are but examiner-employees of the PTO, and the ultimate authority regarding the granting of a patent lies with the Commissioner. . . . [T]he Board is merely the highest level of the Examining Corps, and like all other members of the Examining Corps, the Board operates subject to the Commissioner's overall ultimate authority and responsibility.

In re Alappat, 33 F.3d 1526, 1535 (Fed. Cir. 1994) (en banc) (footnotes omitted). If the Board changes or modifies the examiner's rejection—even if relying on the same statutory ground and same references—the application is then remanded to the examiner for further proceedings.

A patent applicant who unsuccessfully appeals to the PTAB may seek judicial review. Most often, an applicant will appeal to the Court of Appeals for the Federal Circuit under 35 U.S.C. § 141. Alternatively, an applicant may file a civil action in district court under 35 U.S.C. §§ 145 or 146. This second route, although less common due to the additional expense and time, offers an advantage: the applicant may introduce additional evidence (or the same evidence in a separate form, such as live testimony) beyond the Patent Office record.

A patent applicant who unsuccessfully petitions the Commissioner may also seek judicial review. These challenges, which occur rarely, invoke a number of different statutes, including the Administrative Procedure Act, 5 U.S.C. § 701 *et seq.*, the All Writs Act, 28 U.S.C. § 1651, or a civil suit under 28 U.S.C. § 1338(a) against the highest-ranking Patent Office official. The Federal Circuit hears appeals from these suits as well as from actions under § 145 or § 146.

III. POST-GRANT PROCEDURES

Once the Patent Office issues a patent, the agency may revisit the patent grant in a variety of circumstances.

A. CERTIFICATES OF CORRECTION

If the Patent Office makes an error in printing a patent, a patentee may request the Patent Office to correct the mistake, so long as the mistake is evident in the publicly available prosecution history file. 35 U.S.C. § 254. This commonsense provision permits a blameless patentee to undo the Patent Office's inadvertent mistakes at no additional cost. Even if the patentee is responsible for the error, he may nevertheless petition to correct the mistake:

> Whenever a mistake of a clerical or typographical nature, or of minor character, which was not the fault of the Patent and Trademark Office, appears in a patent and a showing has been made that such mistake occurred in good faith, the Director may, upon payment of the required fee, issue a certificate of correction, if the correction does not involve such changes in the patent as would constitute new matter or would require re-examination.

35 U.S.C. § 255.

Section 255 contains a few salient points. First, the provision only permits corrections of a typographical or minor character—a patentee may not make substantive changes to a patent with a certificate of correction. A patentee thus may not add new matter or make changes that would require reexamination. A patentee may seek correction only "where it is clearly evident from the specification, drawings, and prosecution history how the error should appropriately be corrected." *Superior Fireplace Co. v. Majestic Prods. Co.*, 270 F.3d 1358, 1373 (Fed. Cir. 2001). Second, the mistake must have occurred in good faith, i.e., patentee may not mislead the Patent Office during prosecution to obtain allowance then later attempt to correct that deception through a certificate of correction. Finally, a certificate of correction is only effective against subsequently filed litigations. It does not have retroactive effect with respect to litigation pending at the time the certificate of correction issues. *Southwest Software, Inc. v. Harlequin Inc.*, 226 F.3d 1280, 1294 (Fed. Cir. 2000).

An alleged infringer may invalidate a certificate of correction as part of a defense to infringement: "Invalidating a certificate of correction for impermissible broadening therefore requires proof of two elements: (1) the corrected claims are broader than the original claims; and (2) the presence of the clerical or typographical error, or how to correct that error, is not clearly evident to one of skill in the art." *Cent. Admixture Pharmacy Servs., Inc. v. Advanced Cardiac Solutions, P.C.*, 482 F.3d 1347, 1353 (Fed. Cir. 2007). If the correction is invalidated, the patent simply reverts to its unamended form, and the litigation proceeds under the originally issued, uncorrected claims.

A patentee may choose to enforce a patent containing insignificant errors without first petitioning the Patent Office for a certificate of correction. Indeed, a court has inherent authority to correct minor errors through, for example, claim construction, so long as "(1) the correction is not subject to reasonable debate based on consideration of the claim language and the specification and (2) the prosecution history does not suggest a different interpretation of the claims." *Novo Indus., L.P. v. Micro Molds Corp.*, 350 F.3d 1348, 1354 (Fed Cir. 2003).

B. REISSUE

1. Error Correction

Unlike the minor corrections permitted by a certificate of correction, reissue permits significant revisions affecting the scope, validity, and even enforceability of an issued patent. The Patent Act provides:

> Whenever any patent is, through error, deemed wholly or partly inoperative or invalid, by reason of a defective specification or drawing, or by reason of the patentee claiming more or less than he had a right to claim in the patent, the Director shall, on the surrender of such patent and the payment of the fee required by law, reissue the patent for the invention disclosed in

> the original patent, and in accordance with a new and amended application, for the unexpired part of the term of the original patent. No new matter shall be introduced into the application for reissue.

35 U.S.C. § 251(a).[3] To qualify for reissue, a patentee must declare that the patent is wholly or partly inoperative or invalid either due to a defective specification or due to the failure of a patentee to claim more or less than he had a right to claim. *See* 37 C.F.R. § 1.175.

Before the AIA, the reissue statute also required that the error arose "without any deceptive intention." The deletion of this requirement may lower the standard for successful initiation of prosecution for a reissue application.

Reissue focuses on two prongs: an error in the patent and error in conduct that caused the error in the patent. *Hewlett-Packard Co. v. Bausch & Lomb Inc.*, 882 F.2d 1556, 1564 (Fed. Cir. 1989). In *Hewlett-Packard*, the court ruled that a reissue patent that added claims of narrower scope than the original claims was invalid. Without deciding that a failure to include narrower claims is correctable through a reissue application, the court held that the reissue oath did not assert an error in conduct. In particular, the prosecuting attorney's affidavits had mischaracterized the circumstances that caused the

---

[3] The AIA amends § 251 to refer to alphabetic subsections (i.e., subsections (a)–(d)). Thus, traditional references to § 251, first paragraph, should be understood as referring to § 251(a).

error in patent claim scope. In other circumstances, though, the court has explained that an "attorney's failure to appreciate the full scope of the invention is one of the most common sources of defects in patents." *In re Wilder*, 736 F.2d 1516, 1519 (Fed. Cir. 1984). The *Wilder* court further stated that the "fact that the error could have been discovered at the time of prosecution with a more thorough patentability search or with improved communication between the inventors and the attorney does not, by itself, preclude a patent owner from correcting defects through reissue." *Id.* The Federal Circuit later reaffirmed that an applicant may seek reissue solely due to the failure to include dependent claims that more narrowly define the inventive subject matter. *See In re Tanaka*, 640 F.3d 1246, 1248–49 (Fed. Cir. 2011)

Once the Patent Office accepts a reissue application, the prosecution starts anew with the typical back-and-forth of Office Actions and responses. 37 C.F.R. § 1.176. Indeed, an applicant may even file continuing applications, such as divisional applications, as necessary. *See In re Staats*, 671 F.3d 1350 (Fed. Cir. 2012); *In re Graff*, 111 F.3d 874, 876 (Fed. Cir. 1997). But because § 251 includes the express prohibition that "[n]o new matter shall be introduced into the application for reissue," the patentee cannot file a continuation-in-part claiming priority to the reissue application. If the Patent Office reissues the patent, the amended claims will have only prospective application while reissue claims that are substantially identical to the original claims will have both retrospective and prospective application. 35 U.S.C. § 252 para. 1. Reissue proceedings are open to the public.[4]

As the statute implies, a patentee may seek to broaden the scope of the claimed subject matter. The patentee may only do so within a relatively short period of time (two years) after issuance: "No reissued patent shall be granted enlarging the scope of the claims of the original patent unless applied for within two years from the grant of the original patent." 35 U.S.C. § 251(d). This window enables a patentee to claim subject matter within the scope of the patent that was erroneously omitted from the original version of the patent.

2. Intervening Rights

Because the public is entitled to reasonably rely upon the scope of an issued patent and because that patent might undergo revision during reissue proceedings, the Patent Act grants the public limited rights to the originally claimed subject matter. 35 U.S.C. § 252 para. 2. In particular, the statute provides for absolute intervening rights and equitable intervening rights. *See, e.g., Shockley v. Arcan, Inc.*, 248 F.3d 1349, 1359 (Fed. Cir. 2001).

The distinction between the two types of intervening rights focuses on the status of the goods at issue. Absolute intervening rights permit an entity that made, purchased, used, offered, sold, or

---

[4] The Patent Office maintains a website called the Patent Application Information Retrieval system (PAIR) that hosts documents relating to public communications to and from the Office.

imported a particular thing covered by the reissue patent to continue using that particular thing—unless the activity would have infringed the original patent. Absolute intervening rights therefore only apply to things already in existence when the reissue patent issues. *See id.* at 1360. These rights are automatic and do not require judicial intervention.

Equitable intervening rights are broader than absolute intervening rights. A court has discretion, when "equitable for the protection of investments made or business commenced before the grant of the reissue," to allow an accused infringer to "(1) continue the manufacture, use, offer for sale, and sale of additional articles made before the reissue; and (2) continue to manufacture, use, offer to sell, or sell articles for which substantial preparations for manufacture or use was made before the grant of the reissue." *Id.* at 1361. As with absolute intervening rights, there are no equitable intervening rights if the infringing activity fell within the original claim scope.

3. Recapture

If a patentee attempts to correct the failure to appreciate the full scope of an invention by seeking broader claims within two years, the law contains an important safeguard beyond intervening rights—namely the prohibition of subject matter recapture. Not all errors are correctable. The "reissue statute was not enacted as a panacea for all patent prosecution problems, nor as a grant to the patentee of a second opportunity to prosecute *de novo* his original application." *In re Weiler,* 790 F.2d 1576, 1582 (Fed. Cir. 1986). Accordingly, the patentee may not use reissue to erase a clear intent to exclude certain subject matter from the scope of the claimed invention. This recapture rule "bars the patentee from acquiring, through reissue, claims that are of the *same* or of *broader scope* than those claims that were canceled from the original application." *Ball Corp. v. United States,* 729 F.2d 1429, 1436 (Fed. Cir. 1984) (emphasis in original).

The contours of the recapture rule have been explained by the Federal Circuit:

> [I]f the reissue claim is broader in some aspects, but narrower in others, then: (a) if the reissue claim is as broad as or broader in an aspect germane to a prior art rejection, but narrower in another aspect completely unrelated to the rejection, the recapture rule bars the claim; (b) if the reissue claim is narrower in an aspect germane to prior art rejection, and broader in an aspect unrelated to the rejection, the recapture rule does not bar the claim, but other rejections are possible.

In re Clement, 131 F.3d 1464, 1470 (Fed. Cir. 1997).

The recapture rule may also apply in instances beyond incorporating canceled subject matter into the scope of a reissue claim. In particular, a patentee may not attempt to delete limitations that he emphasized during the prosecution, even if those limitations may not have been essential to the patentability of the original claims. *Hester Indus.,*

Inc. v. Stein, Inc., 142 F.3d 1472, 1481 (Fed. Cir. 1998).

C. REEXAMINATION, SUPPLEMENTAL EXAMINATION & INTER PARTES REVIEW

Reexamination is an administrative proceeding that—as its name suggests—involves a secondary examination of patented subject matter. Reexam, in theory, provides an alternative to judicial resolution of validity in a faster, less costly manner. The statute only permits a reexamination when the Patent Office determines, either on its own or on request, that there is a "substantial new question of patentability" based solely on prior art patents and printed publications. 35 U.S.C. §§ 301–303. Furthermore, the "existence of a substantial new question of patentability is not precluded by the fact that a patent or printed publication was previously cited by or to the Office or considered by the Office." *See id.* § 303(a); *In re Swanson,* 540 F.3d 1368, 1379 (Fed. Cir. 2008). In the relatively short period since its inception only a few decades ago, reexamination expanded from a purely *ex parte* scheme to include an *inter partes* proceeding more akin to civil litigation, though still before the Patent Office. *Inter partes* reexamination has since been replaced with complementary proceedings called *inter partes* review and post-grant review, which are discussed in detail in Chapter 11.

1. *Ex Parte* Reexamination

Any individual—a competitor, a patentee, a licensee, or any other third-party—may file a request for *ex parte* reexamination of a patent. The requester must cite prior art patents or printed publications to the Patent Office along with a statement of their relevance to at least one the claim of the patent. 35 U.S.C. §§ 301–02. If ordered, reexamination follows the same procedures as the prosecution of any other application. The patentee may "propose any amendment to his patent and a new claim or claims thereto, in order to distinguish the invention as claimed from the prior art cited . . . or in response to a decision adverse to patentability of a claim of a patent." 35 U.S.C. § 305.

The patentee does not have free reign to amend unrelated aspects of the claims; any amendment must concern some aspect related to the reexamination proceedings. *See In re Freeman*, 30 F.3d 1459, 1468 (Fed. Cir. 1994). The statute also specifies that "[n]o proposed amended or new claim enlarging the scope of a claim of the patent will be permitted in a reexamination proceeding." 35 U.S.C. § 305. This means that claim scope after amendment cannot exceed the broadest claim scope of the issued patent. That is, an amended claim cannot include any subject matter not within the scope of any unamended claim, even if the amended claim is narrower in other aspects. Unsurprisingly, this determination involves a dual claim construction and then comparison of the initial claims and amended claims. *See, e.g., Hockerson-Halberstadt, Inc. v.*

Converse Inc., 183 F.3d 1369, 1374 (Fed. Cir. 1999). If there is any broadening of scope—even changing "at least" to "at least approximately"—the broadened claim does not revert to its unamended form. Instead, the claim is invalid. *Quantum Corp. v. Rodime, PLC*, 65 F.3d 1577, 1580–83 (Fed. Cir. 1995).

In fact, even a narrowing amendment may limit a patentee's ability to enforce a patent surviving reexamination. Under 35 U.S.C. § 307(b), the statute provides for intervening rights identical to those for reissue patents. Section 307(b), like § 252, provides at least some protection to a person who would not have been liable for infringing the initial claims, even if liable for infringing the reexamined claims. *See Bloom Eng'g Co. v. N. Am. Mfg. Co.*, 129 F.3d 1247, 1250 (Fed. Cir. 1997).

2. Supplemental Examination

Rather than expressly request *ex parte* reexamination of an issued patent, a patent owner may request that the Patent Office "consider, reconsider, or correct information believed to be relevant to the patent." 35 U.S.C. § 257. Notably, this provision is not limited to patents and printed publications and instead includes any information bearing on the patentability of the issued patent. If the Patent Office concludes that information cited in the request for supplemental examination raises a substantial new question of patentability, the Patent Office will order *ex parte* reexamination of the patent. When requested in advance of litigation, supplemental examination may allow for an avenue to prevent a determination of unenforceability based upon information that had not been considered, was inadequately considered, or was incorrect during original examination.

3. *Inter Partes* Reexamination & *Inter Partes* Review

One of the criticisms of *ex parte* reexamination stemmed from the absence of an adversary rebutting the arguments of patentability proffered by the patentee. Even after the proceedings began, an interested party would be relegated to the sidelines and prohibited from participation. To alleviate this problem, Congress provided for a limited *inter partes* reexamination (pre-AIA) or *inter partes* review (post-AIA), both of which permit a third-party requestor to present arguments regarding an issued patent's invalidity. These optional alternatives to *ex parte* reexamination are, in effect, a limited opposition system. Although initially scarcely used, *inter partes* reexamination became an attractive surrogate for—and, at times, supplement to—expensive and protracted litigation.

Beginning on September 16, 2012, *inter partes* review largely replaced the *inter partes* reexamination procedures. Because of *inter partes* review proceedings' vast importance to the modern U.S. patent system, these proceedings are discussed in detail in Chapter 11. But it suffices here to point out a few of the defining characteristics of *inter partes* review. For example, a party requesting an *inter partes* review must establish that there is a reasonable likelihood that it will prevail with respect to at least one of the claims challenged in the petition. The grounds for *inter partes* review are limited to anticipation and obviousness based upon prior art patents and publications. *Inter partes* review may only be filed after the later of the termination of a post-grant review (if initiated) or the expiration of the period of time during which a post-grant review could have been initiated (i.e., 9 months after grant or reissuance of a patent). If a patent owner serves an alleged infringer with a complaint, the alleged infringer has only one year to file for *inter partes* review of a patent named in the complaint. There is an important check on *inter partes* review (referred to as estoppel): a losing petitioner cannot assert any ground of invalidity in an infringement case that was raised or reasonably could have been raised during the post-grant review. Further, the patent owner has the right to cancel any challenged claim or to propose a reasonable number of substitute claims for any challenged claim. But any amendment cannot enlarge the scope of the claims of the patent or introduce new matter.

D. POST-GRANT REVIEW

Congress recently authorized post-grant review of patents in a limited opposition-type scheme. Like *inter partes* review, these are discussed in detail in Chapter 11 dealing with PTAB practice. This short discussion will only point out a few highlights regarding post-grant review proceedings. Specifically, a post-grant review petitioner may request to cancel as unpatentable the claims of a patent on any ground of invalidity, such as anticipation, obviousness, inadequate disclosure, and indefiniteness. The petition for post-grant review must be filed within nine months following patent issuance. The Patent Office will institute the post-grant review if the petition establishes that it is more likely than not—a higher standard than the "reasonable likelihood" standard that applies in *inter partes* reviews—that at least one claim challenged in the petition is unpatentable. The same estoppel check on *inter partes* review also applies to post-grant review, but with potentially greater effect: because post-grant review offers a broader array of invalidity grounds to assert, more invalidity grounds could later be deemed waived. Further, as in *inter partes* review, the patent owner has the opportunity to cancel claims and propose substitute claims, with the caveat that substitute claims may not enlarge the claim scope.

IV. CONCLUSION: THE WORLD'S MOST LIBERAL SYSTEM

The United States has the most liberal system in the world for obtaining patents. For instance, it permits inventors to broaden their claims using the reissue process in the first two years after grant and to achieve essentially the same result with a continuing application perhaps for the life of the continuation. In general, other major patent systems such as those in Europe and Japan do not permit inventors to broaden their claims after grant. The details of the prosecution of patent applications in other major systems such as at the European Patent

Office and the Japanese Patent Office are otherwise generally similar to USPTO practices. But, as will be discussed later in Chapter 11, the PTAB has gained significant new power under the AIA to invalidate issued patents, which has tended to make enforcement more challenging.

CHAPTER 3
PATENT ELIGIBILITY

I. INTRODUCTION

The patent statute's framework suggests that patent eligibility is best understood as a threshold issue before examining other requirements of "patentability," such as whether the claimed invention is useful, novel, nonobvious, adequately described, and properly claimed. Although many discoveries are eligible for patenting, some subject matter cannot be patented even if meeting the other requirements. Historically, the mutually exclusive categories of eligible and ineligible subject matter have been well defined. At least in the United States, almost every invention with a useful, real-world application was eligible for patenting. However, in recent history the U.S. Supreme Court has raised the bar for patent eligibility by broadening its judicially-created exceptions to eligibility. Eligibility now plays a prominent role in patent validity analysis, notwithstanding the plain language and structure of the statute.

The historic common law standard for determining eligibility flows from the very inclusive words of the famous Statute of Monopolies—"manner of new manufacture." The United States broke away from the common law tradition in 1790, followed by Canada in the 19th century. This U.S. approach defines eligibility positively. The European Patent Office, in contrast, takes a different approach with a lengthy list of subject matter that cannot be patented rather than what can be patented.

A. THE CONSTITUTION & LAWS OF NATURE

The Constitution's patent and copyright clause grants Congress the authority to enact laws that "promote the progress of science and useful arts." U.S. CONST. art. I, § 8, cl. 8. Because this constitutional requirement provides a minimal constraint, the general rule had typically been that all useful subject matter is eligible for patenting. The Supreme Court, however, has carved-out some (probably unnecessary) exceptions to that general rule: "laws of nature, natural phenomena, and abstract ideas." *Diamond v. Diehr*, 450 U.S. 175, 185 (1980). Each of these categories would also fail to present new, inventive and fully-disclosed inventions, but the Supreme Court preferred nevertheless to create some general categories of banned subject matter. Under later Supreme Court expansion, these general categories grew to encompass many subject matter areas that have at least some utility.

Patent law has other, more precise, doctrines to separate esoteric scientific theory from usable technology—notably the enablement requirement—but over the past decade the Supreme Court has preferred its own philosophical eligibility doctrine over the more statutorily grounded patent law filters. As a result, eligibility has taken on monumental proportions with a similarly monumental unpredictability.

Returning to a search for a doctrine to ensure the development of usable technology, the Supreme Court's eligibility test (in broad terms) seeks an application for every claim of every invention. In other words, the inquiry shifted from assessment of subject matter categories to assessment of each claim's sufficiency. In that latter context, even a nominal practical application may not be sufficient to pass the eligibility test. Indeed, the Supreme Court requires something beyond a practical, real-world application: "The question before us is whether the claims do significantly more than simply describe these natural relations. To put the matter more precisely, do the patent claims add *enough* to their statements of the correlations to allow the processes they describe to qualify as patent-eligible processes that *apply* natural laws?" *Mayo Collaborative Servs. v. Prometheus Labs., Inc.,* 566 U.S. 66, 77 (2012). *Mayo* therefore seems to require an analysis of the inherent value of inventive concepts without any analysis of prior art as a measuring standard.

Under *Mayo*, even though an inventive concept exhibits a concrete and practical application and may "promote the progress of science and useful arts," that subject matter may nevertheless be ineligible as not adding "enough" to a law of nature. It is worth noting that *Mayo* seems to follow the analysis espoused in *Funk Brothers Seed Co. v. Kalo Inoculant Co.*, 333 U.S. 127 (1948), even though that case and its reasoning was later effectively overruled and discredited by *Diamond v. Diehr*, 450 U.S. 175 (1981). Apparently making a committed return to its earlier, discrediting reasoning, the Court further entrenched its *Mayo* analysis in two subsequent eligibility decisions. *See Ass'n for Molecular Pathology v. Myriad Genetics, Inc.*, 569 U.S. 576 (2013); *Alice Corp. Pty. v. CLS Bank Int'l*, 573 U.S. 208, 2360 (2014).

B. THE LANGUAGE OF § 101

Beginning with the Patent Act of 1790, the statute embraced broad categories of subject matter that seemed to include nearly any inventive endeavor. *See* Patent Act of 1790, 1 Stat. 109, 110 (Apr. 10, 1790) (setting forth the eligible subject matter as "any useful art, manufacture, engine, machine, or device, or any improvement therein"). In subsequent enactments, the categories expanded further to explicitly include processes—formerly included as an "art"—and compositions of matter. Section 101 of the Patent Act currently recites: "Whoever invents or discovers any new and useful process, machine, manufacture, or composition of matter, or any new and useful improvement thereof, may obtain a patent therefor, subject to the conditions and requirements of this title."

Thus, the statute sets forth in positive terms four general categories of patent-eligible subject matter: processes, machines, manufactures, and compositions of matter. A new and useful process refers to the use of any "process, machine, manufacture, composition of matter, or material." 35 U.S.C. § 100(b). For example, a patent-eligible process can be a treatment of certain materials to achieve a desired result. *Cochrane v. Deener*, 94 U.S. 780 (1877).

A new and useful machine refers to "a concrete thing, consisting of parts, or of certain devices and combination of devices." *Burr v. Duryee*, 68 U.S. 531, 570 (1864). A new and useful manufacture refers to "the production of articles for use from raw or prepared materials by giving to these materials new forms, qualities, properties, or combinations, whether by hand-labor or by machinery." *Diamond v. Chakrabarty*, 447 U.S. 303, 308 (1980) (quoting *Am. Fruit Growers, Inc. v. Brogdex Co.,* 283 U.S. 1, 11 (1931)).

And lastly, a new and useful composition of matter refers to "all compositions of two or more substances and . . . all composite articles, whether they be the results of chemical union, or of mechanical mixture, or whether they be gases, fluids, powders or solids." *Id.* (quoting *Shell Dev. Co. v. Watson,* 149 F. Supp. 279, 280 (D.D.C. 1957)). Although the statute divides eligible subject matter into four categories, these categories are not mutually exclusive. An inventor may claim an invention as subject matter falling in more than one category. *Bandag, Inc. v. Al Bolser's Tire Stores, Inc.*, 750 F.2d 903 (Fed. Cir. 1984).

In sum, it is difficult to imagine any invention that would not fit into one or more of these broad categories of eligible subject matter as set forth in the patent statute. The statute's broad embrace of eligible subject matter, however, has become largely irrelevant under the new judge-made rules for eligibility. The eligibility inquiry has ironically become dominated by the Supreme Court's *exceptions* to § 101, rather than plain language of § 101 itself.

II. CATEGORIES OF ELIGIBILITY CASES

A. PROCESS VERSUS PRODUCT CLAIMS

As mentioned above, the four statutory categories eligible for patenting are processes, machines, manufactured objects, and compositions of matter. While the latter three categories are physical and relatively easy to deem tangible, processes present more difficulties. In fact, processes are the only category that the patent statute attempts to define, albeit somewhat reflexively: "The term 'process' means process, art or method, and includes a new use of a known process, machine, manufacture, composition of matter, or material." 35 U.S.C. § 100(b). While not removing all ambiguity, this definition at least strongly suggests that most processes are eligible for patenting. Though more conceptually difficult, processes are eligible unless falling within the excluded categories (laws of nature, natural phenomena, and abstract ideas). Thus, processes must engage or produce something tangible. In fact, the statutory definition clarifies that the use of physical entities qualifies as eligible.

For example, a metallic alloy is eligible as a physical composition of matter. A man-made process for forging that alloy on an industrial scale would similarly be eligible, as would a process for using that alloy in the body of a car. In short, any process related to the use or production of that alloy should be eligible—so long as (under recent Supreme Court precedent) it adds "*enough*" to any underlying ideas, natural laws, or natural raw materials.

B. COMPUTER-RELATED INVENTIONS

Processes incorporated into an electronic device, like a computer or other machine, have spawned the greatest amount of litigation (and uncertainty) over eligibility. The current state of the law dominated by the Supreme Court's exceptions has been called a "swamp of verbiage." *MySpace, Inc. v. GraphOn Corp.*, 672 F.3d 1250, 1260 (Fed. Cir. 2012). Courts have struggled mightily to understand the tangible aspects of hardware and software. Early in the computer age, software processes, for instance, often received treatment in courts as just ethereal algorithms. In reliance on the broad statute, the United States reached a consensus that these processes are indeed eligible for patenting, so long as the claims are formatted properly. *Classen Immunotherapies, Inc. v. Biogen IDEC*, 659 F.3d 1057, 1073–75 (Fed. Cir. 2011) (Rader, C.J., additional views). In Europe, "computer programs as such" are not patent eligible, but, once again, when formatted properly, they also achieve protection at the European Patent Office.

Underlying the early U.S. consensus was an understanding that hardware and software are generally interchangeable. That is, the computer defines and uses processes as either software or hardware. *In re Alappat*, 33 F.3d 1526, 1545 (Fed. Cir. 1994) ("[P]rogramming creates a new machine, because a general purpose computer in effect becomes a special purpose computer once it is programmed to perform particular functions pursuant to instructions from program software."). Thus, while a computer program containing a theory-based software algorithm may seem abstract, at the same time that algorithm in hardware is an eligible machine or an article of manufacture.

Before the U.S. reached this consensus, however, the Supreme Court—in the very earliest days of computer technology—struggled with this dichotomous relationship. In *Gottschalk v. Benson*, 409 U.S. 63 (1972), the Court encountered a claimed method related to a conversion of numbers from a pure binary format to a binary-coded decimal. While computers typically understand and encode numbers in binary format, human beings prefer viewing numbers in the familiar decimal format. Thus, the invention seemed to have real application and value, as it made the computer's binary processes accessible to humans. In simple terms, a customer wants to see the price on a soft drink dispensing machine in familiar decimal numbers, not as an indecipherable binary array.

Nonetheless, the Court in *Benson* held that the claims recited subject matter ineligible for patenting. Instead of finding a statutory "process," the Court imposed its own "physical transformation" requirement. Because the claimed binary transformation was easily accomplished by "head and hand," the Court held that the claimed method was merely an abstract mathematical formula.

Perhaps the nascence of the computer technology and a failure to foresee its importance influenced the Court's opinion. The Court did, however, grant claim 8, which covered the same method using a reentrant shift register, a fairly standard electronic component.

The *Benson* decision is laced with self-impeaching reasoning. For instance, the Court states, "It is conceded that one may not patent an idea." 409 U.S. at 71. But *all* patents embody and claim ideas. The Supreme Court either confused patent law with copyright law or meant to say "one may not patent an *abstract* idea." At another point, the Court (alarmingly) opined, "The mathematical formula involved here has no substantial practical application except in connection with a digital computer . . . ." *Id.* The Court seems to belittle the invention as limited to improving a mere digital computer—which may, of course, qualify as the most revolutionary advance of the 20th century.

Whatever its basis, the Court's unfavorable treatment of computer-related claims came to an end nearly a decade later in *Diamond v. Diehr*, 450 U.S. 175 (1981). *Diehr* is credited with bringing the U.S. to its consensus in favor of software eligibility. In *Diehr*, the claims recited a method for operating a rubber-molding press that incorporated a well-known scientific principle, the Arrhenius equation, for calculating the reaction time of polymers. Distinguishing *Benson*, the Court characterized the claims as a process of curing synthetic rubber, not a mathematical algorithm. Specifically, the Court focused on the claims as a whole with an emphasis on limitations that recited a physical transformation. If the Arrhenius equation were a theory applicable only to polymeric reactions, the Supreme Court's logic would be suspect. In that circumstance, the use of the equation and the physical transformation would be redundant. The equation would only apply to a machine for curing polymers like rubber. In truth, however, the Arrhenius equation derives from generalized thermodynamics and predicts the rate of chemical reactions beyond just polymerization.

Diehr realigned the law of patent eligibility to more accurately reflect the breadth of the patent statute and ushered in nearly three decades of settled reliance on that statutory standard. Importantly, *Diehr* precluded an analysis that subtracts patent ineligible components from the claim before measuring patentability. Instead, a claim may qualify as patentable when the inventive advance in the claim is the part that standing alone would not be patent eligible. Even though Sir Isaac Newton's laws of mechanics would be abstract and ineligible, their application to make new machines or technical processes would therefore qualify as patentable because the claim as a whole would be nonobvious.

But when the Supreme Court in *Mayo Collaborative Services. v. Prometheus Laboratories, Inc.*, 566 U.S. 66 (2012), later returned to the uncertainties of the *Benson* era, it backtracked from *Diehr* and disallowed claims that recited newly discovered natural phenomena or laws combined with otherwise known elements. *Mayo* has therefore once again made suspect any claim with a single feature that may be abstract or natural.

During the *Diehr* era, the Federal Circuit decided a case referred to (often pejoratively) as opening the floodgates to patenting of business methods, namely *State Street Bank & Trust Co. v. Signature Financial Group, Inc.*, 149 F.3d 1368 (Fed. Cir. 1998). *State Street Bank* is best understood as the case that explicitly confirmed the patent eligibility of computer-implemented inventions. In that case, the Federal Circuit examined the patent eligibility of a computer system to reallocate investment income to maximize tax benefits. The Federal Circuit decision relied primarily on basic statutory construction. The Circuit reasoned that the only possible exclusion for a mathematical algorithm or a computer process is abstractness. But an invention is not abstract, the famous Judge Giles Rich reasoned, if it is concrete and useful. The claimed invention had a strong practical utility and therefore overcame any abstractness.

In this straightforward analysis, the court refocused the eligibility inquiry onto the essential characteristics of the subject matter, namely concreteness and utility. Because a machine programmed with the claimed financial system undeniably produced a useful, concrete, and tangible result, the claims were eligible. Beyond limiting the ineligible subject matter to that which is merely abstract mathematical algorithm, the *State Street Bank* court noted that a *per se* exception excluding business methods found no support in the legal precedents of the Federal Circuit or its predecessors.

Although the *State Street Bank* court could not rule on the eligibility of method claims, it paved the way for *AT&T Corp. v. Excel Communications, Inc.*, 172 F.3d 1352 (Fed. Cir. 1999). In that case, the only claims at issue were process claims directed to a method of inserting data into a long-distance call record to facilitate billing—solely an exchange of information, not a physical transformation. The Federal Circuit held that these claims recited eligible subject matter. The complementary decisions of *State Street Bank* and *AT&T* quieted most challenges to the patent eligibility of computer programs and so-called business methods.

The Supreme Court eventually reacted to these Federal Circuit decisions by revisiting its own eligibility standards. The Court's first case on the topic, *Bilski v. Kappos*, 561 U.S. 593 (2010), involved claims related to hedging against the risk of price fluctuations in a commodity market. Without significant explanation or any definition of "abstractness," the *Bilski* Court ruled that these claims are not a statutory "process" but instead are abstract.

Perhaps due to the enduring controversial nature of business method patents, Congress also created a special post-grant review proceeding for an eight-year period of time, starting on September 16, 2012. This procedure (called "Covered Business Method" or "CBM" review) was only available to persons who have been sued for infringing a business method patent, i.e., a patent that claims a method or corresponding apparatus for performing data processing or other operations used in the practice, administration, or management of a financial product or service—except that the term does not include patents for technological inventions. By the sunset of CBM reviews, business method review petitions accounted for about 5% of the total number of AIA post-issuance review petitions that have been filed.

The Supreme Court did not stop with *Bilski*, but returned to its abstractness preclusion in the case of *Alice Corp. Pty. v. CLS Bank Int'l*, 573 U.S. 208 (2014). In *Alice*, the Court addressed whether a computerized method for intermediated settlement was patent eligible. The claims used escrow principles in the context of emerging e-commerce markets to facilitate internet transactions. Relying on *Mayo* and *Benson*, and distinguishing *Diehr*, the Court held the claim was abstract because it "simply recite[d] the concept of intermediated settlement as performed by a generic computer." *Alice*, at 2359. Implementing the claimed function using a generic computer, according to the Court, was not the sort of "additional feature" that rendered the claim eligible. *Id.* at 2358.

Again the Supreme Court supplied no definition or standard for "abstractness," but sought to "distinguish between patents that claim the 'building block[s]' of human ingenuity and those that integrate the building blocks into something more," according to the *Mayo* rule. Like the risk hedging in *Bilski*, the concept of intermediated settlement is "a fundamental economic practice long prevalent in our system of commerce." Therefore, intermediate settlement, like hedging, is an "abstract idea" beyond the scope of 35 U.S.C. § 101.

After *Mayo* and *Alice*, the following diagram depicts the Supreme Court's new eligibility rules:

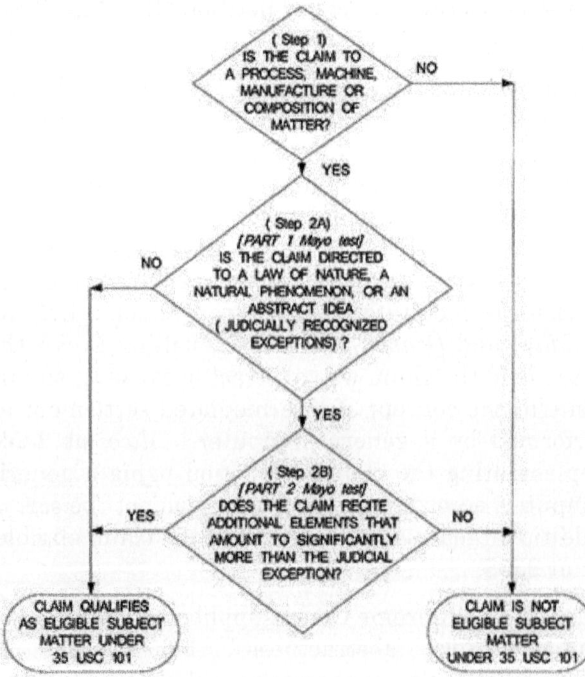

Even *Alice* has not been the high point of the storm created by the Supreme Court's new eligibility rules. Instead, the winds have blown even more fiercely in the Federal Circuit. According to publicly available statistics, the court has invalidated claims as ineligible in approximately 80% of cases since 2014. In one influential case, *Electric Power Grp., LLC v. Alstom S.A.*, 830 F.3d 1350, 1353–54 (Fed. Cir. 2016), the court synthesized its prior case law and announced the principle that a claim is ineligible if it covers "a process of gathering and analyzing information of a specified content, then displaying the results." This simplification has tended to downplay the importance of how information is gathered, processed and displayed: if the invention involves those basic steps, they are likely ineligible.

But on a few notable occasions, the Federal Circuit has dampened the effect of *Alice*. For example, it has decided that a computer-related invention was not directed to an abstract idea within the meaning of *Alice*—the first step of the *Mayo* test. *See, e.g.*, *Enfish, LLC v. Microsoft Corp.*, 822 F.3d 1327, 1336 (Fed. Cir. 2016) (data storage and retrieval system); *McRO, Inc. v. Bandai Namco Games Am. Inc.*, 837 F.3d 1299, 1316 (Fed. Cir. 2016) (lip synchronization of three-dimensional characters); *Thales Visionix Inc. v. United States*, 850 F.3d 1343, 1349 (Fed. Cir. 2017) (inertial system for tracking motion of objects relative to a moving reference frame).

On a few other occasions, the Federal Circuit found that an invention added "enough" beyond well-understood, routine or conventional activities—the second step of *Mayo* analysis. *See e.g.*, *Bascom Glob. Internet Servs., Inc. v. AT&T Mobility LLC*, 827 F.3d

1341, 1349–50 (Fed. Cir. 2016) (website filtering); *Amdocs (Israel) Ltd. v. Openet Telecom, Inc.*, 841 F.3d 1288, 1300 (Fed. Cir. 2016) (system for processing network accounting information).

Additionally, certain Federal Circuit decisions since *Alice* have perhaps made it more difficult for district courts to find a patent ineligible early in the case. In *Aatrix Software, Inc. v. Green Shades Software, Inc.*, 882 F.3d 1121 (Fed. Cir. 2018), the court held that the district court had improperly dismissed the case under Rule 12(b)(6) for patent ineligibility because the district court had not resolved factual disputes raised by the complaint. In particular, the plaintiff's proposed second amended complaint alleged that the patent claims solved particular "improvements and problems" in the technical field. This allegation meant that the claims might contain "unconventional" elements and therefore pass muster under *Alice*. And because at the dismissal stage such allegations must be accepted in favor of the plaintiff, dismissal was inappropriate.

The court applied similar reasoning in *Berkheimer v. HP Inc.*, 881 F.3d 1360 (Fed. Cir. 2018), holding that the district court had erroneously granted summary judgment in favor of the defendant that the asserted claims were ineligible without resolving factual issues raised by the specification. The specification included allegations that raised certain factual issues about eligibility—namely that the claimed invention stored parsed data in an unconventional way. If taken as true, the claims might meet the *Alice* test. The court explained that "[t]he question of whether a claim element or combination of elements is well-understood, routine and conventional to a skilled artisan in the relevant field is a question of fact" and thus must be proven by clear and convincing evidence. *Id.* at 1368. Because the plaintiff had raised the factual issue of whether the claimed invention was indeed "conventional," summary judgment was improper.

In sum, the *Mayo/Alice* regime suggests some ways to draft claims to improve their chances of evading the storm. For instance, system claims are often preferred over method claims. A claim should also include more technical and detailed titles and descriptions, as well as recitations of pertinent hardware, in order to escape the accusation of "preempting" a broad field or idea. Further, likelihood of eligibility is enhanced when the claims recite an improvement to computer functionality itself, rather than, for example, a long-existent task being accomplished using a computer. Finally, the best chance for a process to survive is to claim a method that never previously existed in any form, and can therefore be distinguished from processes already in use.

Although the Supreme Court cautioned lower courts to "tread carefully in construing this exclusionary principle [of ineligibility] lest it swallow all of patent law," *Alice*, 573 U.S. at 2354, the *Alice* decision inevitably brought eligibility challenges to vast numbers of software and computer-related claims. With the statutory language largely out of the picture, the new court-made eligibility rules have changed the face of patent law—injecting unprecedented uncertainty and putting U.S. law in conflict with most of the rest of the world on the eligibility of computer-related inventions and software.

C. TAX STRATEGIES

A strategy to minimize or avoid taxes is, as a hyper-technical matter, not excluded from eligibility under § 101. Yet, "[f]or purposes of evaluating an invention under section 102 or 103 of title 35, United States Code, any strategy for reducing, avoiding, or deferring tax liability, whether known or unknown at the time of the invention or application for patent, shall be deemed insufficient to differentiate a claimed invention from the prior art." *Leahy-Smith America Invents Act*, Pub. L. No. 112–29, § 14(a) (2011). But this treatment of deeming all tax strategies as anticipated and obvious does not apply to "a method, apparatus, technology, computer program product, or system, that is used solely for preparing a tax or information return or other tax filing, including one that records, transmits, transfers, or organizes data related to such filing; or . . . is a method, apparatus, technology, computer program product, or system used solely for financial management, to the extent that it is severable from any tax strategy or does not limit the use of any tax strategy by any taxpayer or tax advisor." *Id.* at § 14(c). Congress thus effectively made tax strategies ineligible for patenting.

D. METHODS OF MEDICAL TREATMENT

Methods of medical treatment often present patent eligible subject matter in the United States. Almost invariably such methods have a practical and beneficial result. Surgical methods may thus be eligible for patenting. For example, U.S. Patent No. 6,761,724 (issued July 13, 2004) claims methods for inserting a medical device (a new lens) into the subretinal region of an eye.

Methods of diagnosing a disease are similarly often patent-eligible. As an example, U.S. Patent No. 4,940,658 (issued July 10, 1990) claims methods for detecting a cobalamin or folate deficiency, which if untreated could cause a serious illness, such as vascular disease, cognitive dysfunction, birth defect and cancer. As discussed further below, however, eligibility trouble can arise when a diagnostic method uses gene sequences, which the Supreme Court has held to constitute excluded "natural phenomena"—despite the arduous process of locating, isolating, and using them. *Ass'n for Molecular Pathology v. Myriad Genetics, Inc.*, 569 U.S. 576, 590 (2013).

Methods of treating a disease using a particular dosing regimen may also be patent-eligible. For instance, U.S. Patent No. 5,994,329 (issued Nov. 30, 1999) claims methods of treating and preventing osteoporosis by administering a compound according to a specific dosing regimen. But again, many of these types of methods will have to pass the stricter standards of the *Mayo* decision.

Even before *Mayo*, physicians objected to the patenting of surgical procedures. They raised a chorus of concern about potential threats to public health in the event of an injunction on a medical procedure, about potential effects on ethical obligations of physicians to publicize medical advances, about potential increases in the cost of health care, about potential interferences with peer-reviewed medical procedures, and about potential invasions of privacy during enforcement of a medical method patent. In response, Congress added paragraph (c) to 35 U.S.C. § 287, a section of the patent statute related to remedies (discussed in Chapter 16), and eliminated any remedy, including injunction, damages, and attorney fees, due to a medical practitioner's performance of a medical activity.

Specifically, § 287(c) defines "medical activity" as "the performance of a medical or surgical procedure on a body," excluding "(i) the use of a patented machine, manufacture, or composition of matter in violation of such patent, (ii) the practice of a patented use of a composition of matter in violation of such patent, or (iii) the practice of a process in violation of a biotechnology patent." In essence, medical practitioners may infringe a patent claiming a medical activity as such with impunity, which effectively removes many medical methods from patent protection.

Other countries apply far more restrictive reservations regarding the propriety of patenting methods of medical treatment. For example, both

Article 1709 of NAFTA and Article 27 of the TRIPS agreement permit the exclusion of diagnostic, therapeutic and surgical methods for the treatment of humans or animals from the subject matter eligible for patenting. The European Patent Convention takes advantage of that option, and contains Article 53(c), which states:

> (c) methods for treatment of the human or animal body by surgery or therapy and diagnostic methods practised on the human or animal body; this provision shall not apply to products, in particular substances or compositions, for use in any of these methods.

Despite that provision, Article 54(4) permits patenting of a medical use of a compound not previously used as a medicament by torturing the meaning of prior art: "Paragraphs 2 and 3 [relating to novelty] shall not exclude the patentability of any substance or composition, comprised in the state of the art, for use in a method referred to in Article 53(c), provided that its use for any such method is not comprised in the state of the art." That is, an old compound is not to be treated as old.

Thus exclusions on medical methods have led creative lawyers to circumvent the exceptions. Ironically at least in the European Patent Office, a first medical use claim of an old compound gives the inventor all pharmaceutical uses for that known compound, whereas the United States provides protection only for the medical indication disclosed by the inventor.

E. COMPOSITIONS OF MATTER AND BIOTECHNOLOGY

Compositions of matter, one of the four enumerated categories explicitly set forth in the statute, did not create problems related to patent eligibility until the era of genetic engineering and biotechnology. These technologies manipulate genes to create novel organisms, such as pest-resistant crops, or to produce complex proteins to regulate the human body. For example, genetic engineering produced the "oncomouse," a type of mouse susceptible to cancer that facilitates oncological research.

Unlike the tortuous path taken towards settling the eligibility of computer-related inventions in the 20th century, the Supreme Court quickly put an end to the question of the eligibility of living organisms in *Diamond v. Chakrabarty*, 447 U.S. 303 (1980). In that case, the patent claimed a bacterium genetically modified to consume oil. The Court treated the issue as a narrow question of statutory interpretation: whether the claimed organism was either an article of manufacture or a composition of matter within § 101. On that point, the Court determined that the modified bacterium did not appear in nature. The new organism was a product of human ingenuity. Accordingly, it qualified as patent-eligible. Even though the case only decided that the organism itself was patent eligible, it signaled that patent law's doors were open for biotechnology in general.

While the *Chakrabarty* decision facilitated the patenting of any genetically modified organism in the

U.S., the Supreme Court of Canada interpreted the exact same statutory eligibility language to reach the opposite conclusion for the oncomouse invention. That court held that the genetically engineered oncomouse was neither a "manufacture" nor a "composition of matter." *Harvard College v. Canada*, 2002 SCC 76. This decision diverged from the worldwide consensus on the patentability of life forms. Even the Council of the European Union and the European Parliament finally adopted the *Directive on the Legal Protection of Biotechnological Inventions* (the *Biotech Directive*) on July 6, 1998 to provide broad protection of life forms within the European Community.

Even though *Chakrabarty* firmly established the eligibility of man-made, living subject matter, the Supreme Court revisited a related issue—whether a man-made plant was eligible for patenting under § 101 and also for protection under either the Plant Protection Act or the Plant Variety Protection Act. *J.E.M. Ag Supply, Inc. v. Pioneer Hi-Bred International, Inc.*, 534 U.S. 124 (2001). Again focusing on the broad language of § 101, the Court ruled that an engineered plant qualifies as patent-eligible. In essence, the Court held that more than one statute may supply protection to plant inventions.

Following *Mayo*, however, another Supreme Court decision, *Ass'n for Molecular Pathology v. Myriad Genetics, Inc.*, 569 U.S. 576 (2013), drastically narrowed the scope of eligibility in biotech by excluding isolated gene segments. Before *Myriad*, careful patent drafters would claim the "isolated" or "purified" version of the gene in order to steer clear of the judicial exception for natural phenomena. *See Ass'n for Molecular Pathology v. United States Patent & Trademark Office*, 653 F.3d 1329, 1354 (Fed. Cir. 2011) ("[A] portion of a native DNA molecule—an isolated DNA—has a markedly different chemical nature from the native DNA. It is, therefore, patentable subject matter."). Indeed, the genetic sequence is not likely found in an isolated or purified state in nature. But the Supreme Court rejected that argument, upending established PTO practice, and held that "a naturally occurring DNA segment is a product of nature and not patent eligible merely because it has been isolated." *Myriad*, at 2111. The Supreme Court did affirm, however, the eligibility of complementary DNA (cDNA)—a synthetic form of DNA that omits portions within DNA that do not code for proteins. *Id.* At a minimum, this decision has reduced the protection available for investment in genetic research.

F. MECHANICAL INVENTIONS

Rather than rein in the Supreme Court's *Alice* analysis to provide certainty for stakeholders in the patent system, the Federal Circuit has seemingly further expanded the judicially-created exceptions to eligibility. In some cases, the court has held that even mechanical inventions with concrete, physical limitations and apparent real-world uses fall short of eligibility. For example, in *American Axle & Mfg., Inc. v. Neapco Holdings LLC*, 967 F.3d 1285, 1289–90 (Fed. Cir. 2020), the court held ineligible a claim covering a method for manufacturing a driveline propeller shaft having a liner designed to attenuate vibrations through the shaft assembly. The court determined that the claim was directed to a law of nature, namely Hooke's law relating frequency to mass and stiffness. *Id.* at 1293–94. The court ultimately faulted the claim for being too broad: "This case would be significantly different, if, for example, specific [finite element analysis] models were included in claim 22. But they are not." *Id.* at 1295.

In another case, *Chamberlain Group, Inc. v. Techtronic Indus. Co.*, 935 F.3d 1341, 1349 (Fed. Cir. 2019), the court held that a claim covering a "movable barrier," i.e., a garage door, was an ineligible abstract idea. Despite the physical nature of the invention, the court concluded at *Alice* step one that the asserted claims were "drawn to the abstract idea of wirelessly communicating status information about a system." *Id.* at 1348. Cases such as *American Axle* and *Chamberlain* illustrate, if nothing else, that the prevailing eligibility analysis has strayed from the text of the statute, and that ascertaining the boundaries of the Supreme Court's eligibility exceptions can prove challenging. They also show that broad claims—even if they contain physical, real-world limitations—may nevertheless be at risk of being deemed ineligible on the grounds that they preempt too much territory under the *Alice* framework.

III. TRIPS

Article 27 of the TRIPS Agreement, an agreement that has been entered into by most of the countries of the world, defines subject matter eligible for patenting:

> 1. Subject to the provisions of paragraphs 2 and 3, patents shall be available for any inventions, whether products or processes, in all fields of technology, provided that they are new, involve an inventive step and are capable of industrial application.[1] Subject to paragraph 4 of Article 65, paragraph 8 of Article 70 and paragraph 3 of this Article, patents shall be available and patent rights enjoyable without discrimination as to the place of invention, the field of technology and whether products are imported or locally produced.

This vital international treaty makes any invention capable of an industrial application (which may be reminiscent of *State Street Bank's* utility-based reasoning) subject matter eligible for patenting. Member countries, however, retain the discretion to exclude certain subject matter specified in paragraphs 2 and 3:

> 2. Members may exclude from patentability inventions, the prevention within their territory of the commercial exploitation of which is

---

[1] For the purposes of this Article, the terms "inventive step" and "capable of industrial application" may be deemed by a Member to be synonymous with the terms "non-obvious" and "useful" respectively.

necessary to protect *ordre public* or morality, including to protect human, animal or plant life or health or to avoid serious prejudice to the environment, provided that such exclusion is not made merely because the exploitation is prohibited by their law.

3. Members may also exclude from patentability:

(a) diagnostic, therapeutic and surgical methods for the treatment of humans or animals;

(b) plants and animals other than micro-organisms, and essentially biological processes for the production of plants or animals other than non-biological and microbiological processes. However, Members shall provide for the protection of plant varieties either by patents or by an effective *sui generis* system or by any combination thereof. The provisions of this subparagraph shall be reviewed four years after the date of entry into force of the WTO Agreement.

Many countries experience difficulties in defining the scope of these exceptions. Perhaps the best course to providing proper incentives for investment and research might be to maintain a broad scope for patent eligibility and instead vigorously scrutinize applications under the requirements for patentability—novelty, inventive step, enablement, and so forth.

CHAPTER 4

UTILITY

I. INTRODUCTION

A. § 101

In addition to the categories of patent eligible subject matter, 35 U.S.C. § 101 sets forth the "usefulness" requirement for patent protection. Section 101 states:

> Whoever invents or discovers any new and useful process, machine, manufacture, or composition of matter, or any new and useful improvement thereof, may obtain a patent therefor, subject to the conditions and requirements of this title.

The utility requirement is common sense—and so much so that a formal utility requirement might not even be necessary. A rational inventor would not invest in research and development and then pour more resources into prosecuting or enforcing a patent if the invention has no use. Even if an irrational inventor undertook those expenses, enforcing an exclusive right to useless subject matter would bring no damages. It is thus no surprise that the utility requirement has not often proven important in patent case law. When utility does appear in litigation or policy disputes, it generally entails some purpose other than preventing inventors from acquiring and enforcing useless patents on useless technology.

The "use" of an invention does play an important role in patent jurisprudence, but not in the sense of the ultimate usefulness of the innovation, which, as suggested above, is a requirement enforced more by market realities than by judicial intervention. Patent law's important utility requirement appears in 35 U.S.C. § 112(a). This provision (discussed in Chapter 9) ensures that each patent contains sufficient description to enable a person of ordinary skill in the art to make and use the invention. It thus presumes that every invention worthy of a patent has some describable use.

Nonetheless, because § 101 uses the word "useful," this requirement has presented a few questions. For instance, how useful must a new invention be? Must an invention improve on existing technology or merely serve some practical purpose? Should the invention's social, economic, or environmental impact affect patentability? And, perhaps most importantly, should utility replace obviousness as a measure of patentability for biotechnological inventions?

B. HISTORICAL DEVELOPMENT OF THE DOCTRINE

The venerable Justice Story inaugurated the commentary on utility. Apparently recognizing the self-enforcing character of utility, he sought a purpose for the requirement that restricted the patentability of nefarious or immoral inventions:

> All that the law requires is, that the invention should not be frivolous or injurious to the well-

> being, good policy, or sound morals of society. The word "useful," therefore, is incorporated into the act in contradistinction to mischievous or immoral. For instance, a new invention to poison people, or to promote debauchery, or to facilitate private assassination, is not a patentable invention. But if the invention steers wide of these objections, whether it be more or less useful is a circumstance very material to the interests of the patentee, but of no importance to the public. If it be not extensively useful, it will silently sink into contempt and disregard.

Lowell v. Lewis, 15 F. Cas. 1018, 1019 (No. 8568) (C.C.D. Mass. 1817). Justice Story's remarks acknowledge that the patent system does not require that an invention improve on prior art. Thus the utility doctrine does not involve a subjective search for "better" uses. Instead, as first articulated by Justice Story, utility generally lets the market decide if an invention carries "importance to the public" or "sink[s] into contempt and disregard." With the market policing usefulness in the sense of economic worthiness and the obviousness requirement policing usefulness in the sense of worthiness for a patent, Justice Story finds moral concerns the only role remaining for the statutory "usefulness" requirement.

Perhaps for this reason, utility produced little case law until the rise of biotechnology. The leading treatise on patent law at the end of the 19th century had little to say about the usefulness requirement. This treatise reached for some general language that utility means more than "a mere curiosity, a scientific process exciting wonder yet not producing physical results, or [a] frivolous or trifling article not aiding in the progress nor increasing the possession of the human race." 1 W. ROBINSON, TREATISE ON THE LAW OF PATENTS FOR USEFUL INVENTIONS 463 (1890).

II. THREE TYPES OF UTILITY

At various times in history, utility has taken three separate forms, discussed in turn below.

A. BENEFICIAL UTILITY

The first category, beneficial utility, arose from Justice Story's recitation of the utility requirement. Based on the Justice's reasoning, 19th century courts would invalidate patents on inventions considered immoral, such as gambling devices. *See, e.g.*, *Brewer v. Lichtenstein*, 278 F. 512, 513–14 (7th Cir. 1922); *Schultze v. Holtz,* 82 F. 448 (N.D. Cal. 1897); *Nat'l Automatic Device Co. v. Lloyd*, 40 F. 89, 90 (N.D. Ill. 1889). With little to justify patent law as a moral arbiter, this fleeting impulse has long since disappeared. Novel and nonobvious gambling devices are indeed patentable, regardless of subjective moral considerations. *WMS Gaming, Inc. v. Int'l Game Tech.,* 184 F.3d 1339 (Fed. Cir. 1999); *In re Murphy,* 200 USPQ 801 (BPAI 1977).

Another iteration of beneficial utility received some attention in the 20th century, specifically, the use of patented devices to deceive consumers. As noted, this consideration fell within early applications of beneficial utility. *See Rickard v. Du*

Bon, 103 F. 868, 870–73 (2d Cir. 1900); *Scott & Williams, Inc. v. Aristo Hosiery Co.*, 7 F.2d 1003 (2d Cir. 1925). The Federal Circuit has held more recently, however, that even deceptive devices do not lack utility.

In *Juicy Whip, Inc. v. Orange Bang, Inc.*, 185 F.3d 1364 (Fed. Cir. 1999), the patentee asserted infringement of a patent on a device that dispensed beverages. In particular, the invention mixed a beverage from separate ingredients after the consumer ordered a drink. This last-second mixing kept drinks more germ-free. The invention, however, also attracted customers by displaying some luscious-appearing liquid sloshing about in a large transparent globe. Of course, the display liquid was not the beverage actually dispensed to the buyer. The aspects of the invention that displayed a liquid solely for visual appeal raised the issue of consumer deception. The Federal Circuit did not evaluate these moral concerns. In rejecting the outdated formulation of utility, the court stated:

> The fact that one product can be altered to make it look like another is in itself a specific benefit sufficient to satisfy the statutory requirement of utility.
>
> It is not at all unusual for a product to be designed to appear to viewers to be something it is not. For example, cubic zirconium is designed to simulate a diamond, imitation gold leaf is designed to imitate real gold leaf, synthetic fabrics are designed to simulate expensive natural fabrics, and imitation leather is

> designed to look like real leather. In each case, the invention of the product or process that makes such imitation possible has "utility" within the meaning of the patent statute, and indeed there are numerous patents directed toward making one product imitate another.

Juicy Whip, 185 F.3d at 1367. The court then explained that the patent laws do not serve to prevent deceptive trade practices. Accordingly, deceptive or fraudulent inventions do not *per se* lack utility. Beneficial utility simply does not apply anymore in patent cases.

B. GENERAL UTILITY

General utility, the next rare category of usefulness, requires that the invention actually work. This aspect of usefulness does not mean that the invention must work as well as expected or even function better than the prior art. Rather, general utility is more fundamental: does the invention purport to violate scientific truths? For example, a perpetual motion machine (or any device allegedly creating more energy than it consumes) lacks general utility because it violates the laws of thermodynamics. *See, e.g.*, *Newman v. Quigg*, 877 F.2d 1575, 1581–82 (Fed. Cir. 1989).

C. SPECIFIC UTILITY

Specific utility, the third category, requires that the invention work for its intended purpose. Most subject matter clearly satisfies this requirement—a new fastener, for example, by its very nature fastens one thing to another. Specific utility, however, is the branch of usefulness that has become significant in the modern world of chemical and biotechnological inventions. These types of inventions are often developed long before researchers can discover their specific purpose or purposes. A protein, for instance, does not inherently designate its biological activity. Indeed, an inventor may develop a new chemical composition or biotechnological sequence without a definitive grasp of its potential uses. Often the inventor can only guess about those potential uses based on similar compositions or sequences already in use.

In *Brenner v. Manson,* 383 U.S. 519 (1966), the Supreme Court inaugurated a heightened scrutiny of chemical inventions under the specific utility doctrine. The technology at issue related to steroids, a class of compounds having a backbone of carbon rings. The positioning of particular atoms on these rings dictates the use and application of a specific steroid. The Court invalidated a process patent, because the patentee did not yet know the specific purpose of the chemical entities resulting from the process. It explained:

> The basic quid pro quo contemplated by the Constitution and the Congress for granting a patent monopoly is the benefit derived by the public from an invention with substantial utility. Unless and until a process is refined and developed to this point—where specific benefit exists in currently available form—there is insufficient justification for permitting an

> applicant to engross what may prove to be a broad field. . . .
>
> This is not to say that we mean to disparage the importance of contributions to the fund of scientific information short of the invention of something "useful," or that we are blind to the prospect that what now seems without "use" may tomorrow command the grateful attention of the public. But a patent is not a hunting license. It is not a reward for the search, but compensation for its successful conclusion.

Brenner, 383 U.S. at 534–36 (footnotes omitted). The Court's holding was particularly harsh because a utility had been disclosed to the public by another inventor before Manson's filing date. That utility, however, did not appear in Manson's own application. Because the useful property was certainly inherent in the compound, perhaps a more correct application of utility in *Brenner*, consistent with much of its language, is that a failure to *disclose* utility renders the subject matter unpatentable under § 112, first paragraph (a lack of enablement)—not § 101. Nonetheless, the Supreme Court refocused the utility requirement on some showing in the specification of a benefit to the public.

The Federal Circuit—no doubt recognizing the difficulty of a judicial assessment of benefit to the public when even science itself often does not recognize an inherent benefit for years—attempted to cabin *Brenner*. For instance, calling on other precedents, the Federal Circuit explained in one case that an invention need not be more effective than prior art devices: "Finding that an invention is an 'improvement' is not a prerequisite to patentability. It is possible for an invention to be less effective than existing devices but nevertheless meet the statutory criteria for patentability." *Custom Accessories, Inc. v. Jeffrey-Allan Indus., Inc.*, 807 F.2d 955, 960 n.12 (Fed. Cir. 1986).

Another case, *In re Brana,* 51 F.3d 1560 (Fed. Cir. 1995), epitomized the Federal Circuit's attempt to narrow the application of *Brenner*. In that case, the Federal Circuit considered a specification's description of certain antitumor compounds. The court upheld as an adequate utility a designation of some *specific* biological activity, even if not conclusively proven safe and efficacious in humans. The court explained: "Usefulness in patent law, and in particular in the context of pharmaceutical inventions, necessarily includes the expectation of further research and development. The stage at which an invention in this field becomes useful is well before it is ready to be administered to humans." *Brana*, 51 F.3d at 1568.

But *Brana* did not put an end to the *Brenner* utility requirement. Instead, the Patent and Trademark Office promulgated examination guidelines based on *Brenner*, under which "[a]n invention has a well-established utility if (i) a person of ordinary skill in the art would immediately appreciate why the invention is useful based on the characteristics of the invention (e.g., properties or applications of a product or process), and (ii) the utility is specific, substantial, and credible." MPEP § 2107; see also id. § 2107.01.

The requirements of specificity, substantiality, and credibility had little statutory basis, but served another purpose relating to biotechnology.

Applying these guidelines, the PTO rejected a claim to a gene fragment—an "expressed sequence tag" (EST)—within a variety of corn with natural herbicidal properties for lack of a recitation of a "substantial" utility. Although the applicant protested that it had disclosed several uses, including use of the fragment as a probe to identify the valuable genetic properties of the new corn variety, the Federal Circuit, relying on *Brenner*, upheld the rejection and the PTO guidelines:

> Essentially, the claimed ESTs act as no more than research intermediates that may help scientists to isolate the particular underlying protein-encoding genes and conduct further experimentation on those genes. The overall goal of such experimentation is presumably to understand the maize genome—the functions of the underlying genes, the identity of the encoded proteins, the role those proteins play during anthesis, whether polymorphisms exist, the identity of promoters that trigger protein expression, whether protein expression may be controlled, etc. Accordingly, the claimed ESTs are, in words of the Supreme Court, mere "object[s] of use-testing," to wit, objects upon which scientific research could be performed with no assurance that anything useful will be discovered in the end.

In re Fisher, 421 F.3d 1365, 1373 (Fed. Cir. 2005) (citing *Brenner*, 383 U.S. at 535).

The PTO's utility guidelines support rejecting inventions (in the *Fisher* example, a biotechnological research tool) that purportedly contribute "insubstantially" to the advance of technology. This substantiality test really amounts to an assessment of the state of the prior art and the contributions of the claimed advance. For most branches of technology, the proper tool for assessing "substantiality" and "credibility" of inventive contributions is the non-obviousness requirement of 35 U.S.C. § 103 *(analogous to the inventive step requirement in other countries)*. Thus, the PTO guidelines and the *Fisher* case upholding them are best understood as compensating for the easily-met standard of non-obviousness for biotech inventions that existed before the Supreme Court, in *KSR Int'l Co. v. Teleflex Inc.*, 550 U.S. 398, 403 (2007), emphasized an "expansive and flexible approach" to finding obviousness. *See, e.g., In re Deuel,* 51 F.3d 1552, 1559 (Fed. Cir. 1995) (" 'Obvious to try' has long been held not to constitute obviousness. . . . The fact that one can conceive a general process in advance for preparing an undefined compound does not mean that a claimed specific compound was precisely envisioned and therefore obvious."). After more recent Federal Circuit cases restored a meaningful non-obviousness test for ESTs, *see, e.g., In re Kubin,* 561 F.3d 1351, 1359 (Fed. Cir. 2009) (explaining that the Supreme Court implicitly overruled *Deuel*), the PTO guidelines on "substantiality" are likely to have less application. Nonetheless the *Brenner* version of the utility doctrine appears to have been revived and continues to arise in some cases. *See, e.g.*, *Grunenthal GMBH v. Alkem Lab'ys Ltd.*, 919 F.3d 1333, 1345–46 (Fed. Cir. 2019) (explaining that "a patent must have specific and substantial utility" and holding that the claimed compound met the utility requirement based on the specification's statement that it could be used to treat pain or urinary incontinence).

III. INDUSTRIAL APPLICATION

Many of the world's patent systems have a requirement of industrial application rather than utility. Both Europe and Japan require industrial application as a prerequisite for patentability. The importance of this requirement varies depending on other features of the patent system.

The European standard for industrial application was explained in *Human Genome Sciences Inc. v. Eli Lilly & Co.*, [2011] UKSC 51. In that case, the Supreme Court of the United Kingdom reviewed U.S. decisions relating to § 101 as well as those of the European Patent Office in deciding the requirement for "industrial application" under the European Patent Convention. The court ruled that a claim to a nucleic acid for encoding a specific polypeptide met the industrial application requirement, even though the application did not disclose its usefulness with respect to any problem, disease, condition, or diagnosis.

CHAPTER 5
ANTICIPATION

I. INTRODUCTION

Novelty, the most fundamental characteristic of patentability, ensures that an inventor has truly created something new. An inventor has invented nothing if the "new creation" already exists elsewhere. In patent parlance, to gain a patent, knowledge in the prior art cannot anticipate the claimed subject matter. Thus, this basic rule prevents anyone from obtaining an exclusive right to technology already in the public domain.

This rule also achieves the policy objective of promoting efficient research. Novelty encourages an inventor to investigate already-existing solutions before undertaking expensive research—i.e., libraries before laboratories, and investigation before investment. Novelty thus helps inventors avoid "reinventing the wheel."

The novelty rule requires that a single prior art reference contain, expressly or inherently, each and every feature of the claimed invention. Application of this rule requires a definition of prior art. Thus, the statutory provisions governing novelty also are the sections that set forth the types of prior knowledge—that is, prior art—that will preclude a patent. These statutory categories of prior art generally provide reliable and verifiable descriptions of the state of public knowledge.

Anticipation requires two discrete steps. First, assess the state of public knowledge at the time of invention. This step requires identification of the information available in the statutory categories of prior art. Until the Leahy-Smith America Invents Act of 2011 (AIA), the patent laws gave a different geographical reach to the various prior art categories. For instance, patents or printed publications anywhere in the world qualified as prior art references. Unwritten historical information also qualified as prior art—for example, a public use or sale of the claimed subject matter—but the statute formerly limited these less verifiable sources to the United States.

Under the new "first-inventor-to-file" regime applicable to all applications having an effective filing date on or after March 16, 2013, there is no territorial restriction on prior art. Rather § 102 states that patent claims are barred if "patented, described in a printed publication, or in public use, on sale, or otherwise available to the public before the effective filing date of the claimed invention." Public uses or sales outside the United States are just as trustworthy as uses or sales within the United States.

After identifying the most relevant prior art, the test involves examination of each reference individually to find, expressly or inherently, each and every aspect of the claimed invention. If any single prior art reference contains every claim limitation, then the claim has been anticipated.

Although a patentable invention must be new, the statutory intricacies of novelty and other patent-barring events were traditionally among the more dense and complex. The governing provision for all patents and applications having a priority date before March 16, 2013 (i.e., pre-AIA), states:

> A person shall be entitled to a patent unless—
>
> (a) the invention was known or used by others in this country, or patented or described in a printed publication in this or a foreign country, before the invention thereof by the applicant for patent, or
>
> (b) the invention was patented or described in a printed publication in this or a foreign country or in public use or on sale in this country, more than one year prior to the date of the application for patent in the United States, or
>
> (c) he has abandoned the invention, or
>
> (d) the invention was first patented or caused to be patented, or was the subject of an inventor's certificate, by the applicant or his legal representatives or assigns in a foreign country prior to the date of the application for patent in this country on an application for patent or inventor's certificate filed more than twelve months before the filing of the application in the United States, or
>
> (e) the invention was described in (1) an application for patent, published under section 122(b), by another filed in the United States

before the invention by the applicant for patent or (2) a patent granted on an application for patent by another filed in the United States before the invention by the applicant for patent, except that an international application filed under the treaty defined in section 351(a) shall have the effects for the purposes of this subsection of an application filed in the United States only if the international application designated the United States and was published under Article 21(2) of such treaty in the English language; or

(f) he did not himself invent the subject matter sought to be patented, or

(g)(1) during the course of an interference conducted under section 135 or section 291, another inventor involved therein establishes, to the extent permitted in section 104, that before such person's invention thereof the invention was made by such other inventor and not abandoned, suppressed, or concealed, or (2) before such person's invention thereof, the invention was made in this country by another inventor who had not abandoned, suppressed, or concealed it. In determining priority of invention under this subsection, there shall be considered not only the respective dates of conception and reduction to practice of the invention, but also the reasonable diligence of one who was first to conceive and last to reduce to practice, from a time prior to conception by the other.

35 U.S.C. § 102 (2002).

For ease of understanding, this dense section creates two different categories that bar patentability (and also define prior art). The novelty subsections—(a), (e), (f), and (g)—preclude a patent based on preexisting knowledge. These categories become "prior art" if they occur before the date of the claimed invention. The barring subsections—(b), (c), and (d)—have a different cut-off, keyed to the date of application. The priority cut-off is commonly called the "critical date." These barring provisions—particularly the very important subsection (b)—operate much like the prior art provisions of the replacement first-inventor-to-file system, except that the critical date is one year before the actual U.S. filing date.

The main difference between these two categories is the triggering timing. The date of invention usually differs from the date of application. But in some cases, the law can operate to merge the invention date and the filing date.

Under the traditional first-to-invent system, the novelty sections award a patent to the first inventor of a technology, irrespective of whether a later inventor filed an earlier application on the same subject matter. This first-to-invent priority system was unique to the United States. When multiple persons claimed the right to a patent on a given technology, only the United States would allow the later filers to prove that their inventive acts occurred before those of the earlier filer. Even after the AIA, in some rare instances, a second U.S. filer may still win the patent under the new first-inventor-to-file regime.

Every other patent system in the world has instead chosen the efficiency and ease of a first-to-file priority system. A strict priority system awards the patent to the first applicant, even if another actually invented the technology first. Although simple to administer, this rule, according to proponents of the U.S. rule, lacks fairness to, for example, less-sophisticated inventors who may be slower to file.

In an international market, invention protection will require careful attention to the differences between a U.S. first-to-invent rule and the world's first-to-file system. In an abundance of caution, most large multinational corporations typically file for patent protection before any potential public disclosure.

Depending on effective filing date, the USPTO will examine a patent application under either the new first-inventor-to-file rule or the old rule. The new scheme will slowly replace the old first-to-invent regime as fewer and fewer patents and applications claim a filing date before March 16, 2013. Until totally replaced, however, practitioners must understand both regimes.

As mentioned above, the first-to-invent system's statutory bars under subsections (b), (c) and (d) preclude patentability based on certain events taking place before the "critical date" (keyed to the filing date). Specifically, the statutory bars of § 102(b) involve publications, public uses or sales occurring more than one year before the filing date. During the one-year grace period, the inventor may assess the merits of filing a patent application or carefully prepare an application. Inventors who publish an article in a scientific journal, for example, thus have one year to prepare an application on that inventive material. (A similar grace period persists under the first-inventor-to-file regime.)

Inventors must also remember that, in the first-to-invent system, events other than their own publications can create prior art. Publications, public uses or offers to sell by other parties more than a year before the actual U.S. filing date are also prior art. Such an occurrence might seem unlikely. Yet, the competitive atmosphere of modern-day progress, with many of the leading researchers attending the same conferences and pursuing the same new technology, makes inventive coincidence nearly a norm. Thus, even with the benefit of a one-year grace period, inventors have a strong incentive to file as soon as possible. Moreover, first-to-file systems in the rest of the world make the virtues of early filing very clear for foreign patent protection.

The statutory bars in §§ 102(c) and (d) of the first-to-invent regime preclude patenting of inventions that have been abandoned to the public or claimed in a foreign application filed more than a year before the domestic filing date. All of the statutory bars carry the attributes of a statute of limitations on a first inventor's entitlement to a patent. Chapter 6 examines the statutory bars in greater detail.

A. NOVELTY UNDER THE FIRST-TO-INVENT REGIME

Newness is an essential patentability requirement under any regime. The most important novelty provision, § 102(a), sets forth four patent-defeating events: (i) the invention was already known by others, (ii) the invention was already used by others, (iii) the invention was already patented, or (iv) the invention was already described in a printed publication. The first two categories only apply to domestic events; the other two have no geographic limitation.

The apparent simplicity of the terms "patented," "printed publication," and "in this country" mask complexities. For example, it is easy enough to determine whether a prior patent on the same invention exists, at least in the United States, by searching issued patents. But the "patented" category extends to every foreign country—some of which offer unique forms of intellectual property protection that do not correspond perfectly with a domestic patent. For example, in *In re Carlson*, 983 F.2d 1032 (Fed. Cir. 1992), the Federal Circuit determined that a design protected by a German Geschmacksmuster qualified as "patented." A Geschmacksmuster requires only registration of a design and lacks any substantive examination process (somewhat similar to copyright protection). The Federal Circuit emphasized the public availability of these German registrations in designating them as prior art. Even though only a local office in Germany provided access to the information, and the notice of publication in the Bundesanzeiger (i.e., Federal Gazette) did not contain a copy of the registered design, the court placed the Geschmacksmuster within the scope of § 102(a) prior art.

Similarly, a description of the claimed invention in a journal article disseminated in printed hardcopy obviously serves as a printed publication. But a description in an electronic document or other communication medium, on the other hand, might seem to lack the reliability of a "printed publication." Nevertheless, these electronic storage, retrieval, and dissemination devices qualify as printed publications. *In re Wyer*, 655 F.2d 221, 227 (CCPA 1981).

Courts have often described public access as the touchstone for qualification as prior art. But applying even this touchstone defies bright-line rules. For example, in *In re Hall*, 781 F.2d 897 (Fed. Cir. 1986), the prior art reference was a doctoral thesis for a graduate student at Freiburg University in Germany. Although a printed publication, the court, as expected, invoked public accessibility as the deciding factor. In measuring public access, the court held that a single, cataloged thesis in only one library provides sufficient access to the publication's teachings to reasonably diligent persons of ordinary skill in the art. Thus, an indexed or distributed publication apparently qualifies as sufficiently accessible to the interested public.

But other indicia of accessibility may also suffice. *In re Klopfenstein*, 380 F.3d 1345, 1348 (Fed. Cir.

2004); *Bruckelmyer v. Ground Heaters, Inc.*, 445 F.3d 1374, 1379 (Fed. Cir. 2006). Several factors generally guide the case-by-case inquiry to determine whether a printed publication is, in fact, prior art within the statutory meaning: (1) the duration of the reference's public availability; (2) the sophistication, expertise, and expected diligence of the reference's intended audience; (3) the likelihood of a reasonable expectation that the reference would or would not be copied; and (4) the ease of copying or duplication of the reference. *SRI Int'l, Inc. v. Internet Sec. Sys., Inc.*, 511 F.3d 1186, 1202 (Fed. Cir. 2008).

Under this rubric, merely listing a reference in a database with minimal searching capabilities might not suffice to establish public accessibility. In *In re Lister*, 583 F.3d 1307, 1315–16 (Fed. Cir. 2009), the Federal Circuit distinguished between database types: the U.S. Copyright Office's automated catalog did not establish a reference's public accessibility because the catalog "was not sorted by subject matter and could only be searched by either the author's last name or the first word of the title of the work"; however, two commercial databases were sufficient where the databases' users "could perform keyword searches of the titles, but not the full texts, of the works."

Further, the description of an invention in a patent or patent application often serves as a printed publication. The USPTO publishes all patents upon issuance, *see* 35 U.S.C. § 153, and it publishes most patent applications 18 months after filing, *id.* § 122. Foreign patent offices also typically publish all applications 18 months after filing. Even the pre-grant published application will serve as prior art, as patent issuance is not necessary for an application to constitute a printed publication.

The entire specification of an issued patent, regardless of the scope of the claims, becomes prior art. The prior art in a patent is not limited by the applicant's choice to claim less subject matter. For most intents and purposes, therefore, the "printed publication" category subsumes the "patented" category of § 102(a).

Lastly, the geographic location of the knowledge or use by someone other than the inventor can readily and easily be determined in most cases. In the modern world, however, the nature of research within multinational companies may make it difficult define the locus of uses and knowledge of an invention. For example, in *Ex Parte Thomson*, 24 USPQ2d 1618, 1992 WL 336793 (BPAI 1992), the Board sustained a rejection based on references that, alone, would not have permitted a person of ordinary skill in the art to make and use the subject matter on the ground that the claimed subject matter was also commercially available in Australia. The Board thus supplemented the disclosure in a domestic printed publication with a foreign use. Extraterritorial evidence may therefore help show that a printed publication in the United States contained sufficient disclosure (i.e., enabled an ordinarily skilled artisan) to anticipate the claimed subject matter. *See Thomson*, 1992 WL 336793, at *2; *see also In re Elsner*, 381 F.3d 1125, 1128 (Fed. Cir. 2004) (holding that, for purposes of the § 102(b) bar, "evidence of the foreign sale of a claimed reproducible plant variety may enable an otherwise non-enabled printed publication disclosing that plant").

B. SECRET PRIOR ART UNDER THE FIRST-TO-INVENT REGIME

The essential importance of prior art is its ability to reflect the state of knowledge in the public domain (remember that § 102 encourages library research ahead of laboratory research, with public accessibility as the touchstone). But pre-AIA §§ 102(e), (f), and (g) contain limited exceptions to even this fundamental feature of prior art. These sections together define secret prior art—a necessary but disfavored category.

The secret information defined in § 102(e) could appropriately be described as "inevitable" prior art. Prior art principles must accord protection to secret applications for patents. The Supreme Court firmly established this category of prior art in *Alexander Milburn Co. v. Davis-Bournonville Co.*, 270 U.S. 390 (1926). In that case, the Court held that disclosed (even if unclaimed) subject matter in an issued patent is prior art as of its filing date, not its issue date. The second paragraph of pre-AIA § 102(e) codified this rule, and thus defines as prior art "a patent granted on an application for patent by another filed in the United States before the invention by the applicant for patent." *See* 35 U.S.C. § 102(e) (2002).

The first paragraph of § 102(e) works similarly, but for applications filed in the United States: subject matter in a published patent application filed in the United States is prior art as of the filing date of the application. In connection with applications, § 102(e) also refers to the Patent Cooperation Treaty (PCT), which is partially codified at § 351(a). (The PCT is discussed in Chapter 17.) Specifically, § 102(e) provides that an international application filed under the PCT constitutes prior art as of its filing date only if it designated the United States and was published in English. Section 102(e) thus implicitly prohibits using the filing dates of other PCT applications, which instead will serve as prior art printed publications as of their publication dates. This rule in § 102(e) stems from *In re Hilmer*, 359 F.2d 859 (CCPA 1966), in which the CCPA attempted to narrow the category of secret prior art.

The first-inventor-to-file statutory scheme under the AIA retains a similar category of prior art in new § 102(a)(2). However, USPTO guidance identifies certain notable differences. For example, "[t]he documents upon which a prior art rejection under 35 U.S.C. § 102(a)(2) may be based are U.S. patent documents only." MPEP § 2152. The disclosures contemplated by this provision are also those that came before the invention's "effective filing date" rather than its invention date. *Id.* § 2152.01. The new § 102(b)(2) also enumerates certain types of disclosures that fall within the ambit of § 102(a)(2) but will nevertheless not qualify as prior art, such as disclosures that were "obtained directly or indirectly from the inventor or a joint inventor."

The secret prior art of pre-AIA § 102(f) also bars a patent on another's invention. Under this provision, an applicant cannot claim subject matter derived from someone else, the true inventor. *See Pannu v. Iolab Corp.*, 155 F.3d 1344, 1348–50 (Fed. Cir. 1998). The fairness principle behind § 102(f) survived the transition from first-to-invent to first-inventor-to-file: a person who derives the patented knowledge from an inventor should not be entitled to obtain a patent.

The final category of secret prior art under the first-to-invent scheme, § 102(g), prohibits the patenting of subject matter previously invented by another. This statutory language not only provides for interferences—administrative procedures involving priority fights—but also invalidates patents based on prior invention in certain circumstances. The brevity of § 102(g) hides its complexity. This section receives its own separate explanation in Chapter 7.

II. IDENTIFICATION OF PRIOR ART UNDER THE U.S. FIRST-INVENTOR-TO-FILE REGIME

Under the first-inventor-to-file system, § 102 has been drastically shortened and seemingly simplified. For all patents and applications having an effective filing date on or after March 16, 2013, § 102(a) now states:

> (a) NOVELTY; PRIOR ART.—A person shall be entitled to a patent unless—

(1) the claimed invention was patented, described in a printed publication, or in public use, on sale, or otherwise available to the public before the effective filing date of the claimed invention; or

(2) the claimed invention was described in a patent issued under section 151, or in an application for patent published or deemed published under section 122(b), in which the patent or application, as the case may be, names another inventor and was effectively filed before the effective filing date of the claimed invention.

These two categories now define the universe of prior art. The first resembles the traditional categories of previous § 102(a) and § 102(b), and the second resembles the traditional category of previous § 102(e).

The new statute does not include subsections analogous to the first-to-invent's §§ 102(c), (d) & (g). Thus, prior abandonment does not independently serve as a basis for prior art. Foreign filing more than 12 months before filing for a patent in the United States does not create an independent bar. And prior invention does not, by itself, bar a subsequent patenting by another, assuming of course that the first inventor never makes it public in the ways listed elsewhere in the new § 102(a). Specifically, a first inventor only creates prior art by disclosing or filing for patent protection.

A. NOVELTY UNDER THE FIRST-INVENTOR-TO-FILE REGIME

Similar to the pre-AIA § 102(a) and (b), the new § 102(a)(1) provides for familiar categories of prior art, such as patents and printed publications, a public use bar, and an on-sale bar. But unlike some other countries' pure first-to-file systems, the new § 102 statute gives the first inventor a personal grace period after making the following types of disclosures:

> (1) DISCLOSURES MADE 1 YEAR OR LESS BEFORE THE EFFECTIVE FILING DATE OF THE CLAIMED INVENTION.—A disclosure made 1 year or less before the effective filing date of a claimed invention shall not be prior art to the claimed invention under subsection (a)(1) if—
>
> > (A) the disclosure was made by the inventor or joint inventor or by another who obtained the subject matter disclosed directly or indirectly from the inventor or a joint inventor; or
> >
> > (B) the subject matter disclosed had, before such disclosure, been publicly disclosed by the inventor or a joint inventor or another who obtained the subject matter disclosed directly or indirectly from the inventor or a joint inventor.

35 U.S.C. § 102(b)(1). The scope of this personal grace period will likely be determined through years of future litigation.

B. SECRET PRIOR ART UNDER THE FIRST-INVENTOR-TO-FILE REGIME

Much like pre-AIA § 102(e), the current § 102(a)(2) sets the filing date (rather than the publication or issue date) as the date when a patent or published application operates as prior art. Section 102(b)(2), however, provides personal exceptions for applications that disclose subject matter obtained from the inventor or subject matter commonly owned by the same assignee:

> (2) DISCLOSURES APPEARING IN APPLICATIONS AND PATENTS.—A disclosure shall not be prior art to a claimed invention under subsection (a)(2) if—
>
> > (A) the subject matter disclosed was obtained directly or indirectly from the inventor or a joint inventor;
> >
> > (B) the subject matter disclosed had, before such subject matter was effectively filed under subsection (a)(2), been publicly disclosed by the inventor or a joint inventor or another who obtained the subject matter disclosed directly or indirectly from the inventor or a joint inventor; or
> >
> > (C) the subject matter disclosed and the claimed invention, not later than the effective filing date of the claimed invention, were owned by the same person or subject to an obligation of assignment to the same person.

35 U.S.C. § 102(b)(2). For subsection (b)(2)(C) immediately above, the statute then defines, in § 102(c), the circumstances when the disclosed subject matter and a claimed invention will be deemed "owned by the same person or subject to an obligation of assignment to the same person":

> (c) COMMON OWNERSHIP UNDER JOINT RESEARCH AGREEMENTS.—Subject matter disclosed and a claimed invention shall be deemed to have been owned by the same person or subject to an obligation of assignment to the same person in applying the provisions of subsection (b)(2)(C) if—
>
> (1) the subject matter disclosed was developed and the claimed invention was made by, or on behalf of, 1 or more parties to a joint research agreement that was in effect on or before the effective filing date of the claimed invention;
>
> (2) the claimed invention was made as a result of activities undertaken within the scope of the joint research agreement; and
>
> (3) the application for patent for the claimed invention discloses or is amended to disclose the names of the parties to the joint research agreement.

35 U.S.C. § 102(c).

One way to understand these new provisions is to examine the circumstance when a second filer can nonetheless ultimately acquire the patent grant.

This happens because the second filer was actually the first to disclose the invention.

In a hypothetical, assume Mary discloses her invention in a public conference. Under § 102 (b)(1)(A), that event begins the one-year grace period. James files the first patent application on that invention six months later (still within Mary's one-year grace period). Mary files herself two months later. The result is that, under § 102(b)(1)(A), even though James was the first to file, Mary will prevail because of her earlier disclosure. That is the case even if James independently invented the technology. Also observe that, under § 102(b)(2)(B), Mary's prior disclosure insulates her from the publication of James' patent application. Thus, the first discloser and the second filer, Mary, prevails over the first filer because she disclosed first and filed within her grace period. This example untangles some important aspects of the new § 102.

III. ANTICIPATION

Although parsing the text of § 102—whether under the traditional first-to-invent or under the new first-inventor-to-file—can present challenges, the actual test for anticipation is straightforward and strict: each and every element of the claimed subject matter must be disclosed inherently or expressly in a single, enabling reference. Anticipation presents the mirror image of infringement: "That which infringes if later anticipates if earlier." *Polaroid Corp. v. Eastman Kodak Co.*, 789 F.2d 1556, 1573 (Fed. Cir. 1986) (citing *Peters v. Active Mfg. Co.*, 129 U.S. 530, 537 (1889)).

A. EACH AND EVERY ELEMENT

The identification of each and every element of the claimed subject matter turns on the proper construction of the claims themselves. As discussed in later chapters, the claims define the scope of the invention.

The interesting case of *Titanium Metals Corp. v. Banner*, 778 F.2d 775 (Fed. Cir. 1985), shows the importance of the claims to all aspects of patent law, including anticipation. This case also shows that the discovery of a new property in an old device or composition does not entitle the discoverer to a new patent on the prior art. In *Titanium Metals*, the patent at issue related to a titanium-nickel-molybdenum alloy and recited three claims:

> 1. A titanium base alloy consisting essentially by weight of about 0.6% to 0.9% nickel, 0.2% to 0.4% molybdenum, up to 0.2% maximum iron, balance titanium, said alloy being characterized by good corrosion resistance in hot brine environments.
>
> 2. A titanium base alloy as set forth in claim 1 having up to 0.1% iron, balance titanium.
>
> 3. A titanium base alloy as set forth in claim 1 having up to 0.8% nickel, 0.3% molybdenum, up to 0.1% maximum iron, balance titanium.

The patent applicant stressed that these compositions resisted corrosion in hot brine environments. The most relevant piece of prior art was a minor three-page article in the Russian language showing data generated by various titanium-nickel-molybdenum alloys. One dot on one of many graphs in the Russian article showed a titanium base alloy containing 0.25% molybdenum by weight and 0.75% nickel by weight—a composition clearly falling within the percentages recited in claims 1 and 2. By the way, the dot is the third dot from the left on the graph marked Figure 1c.

The article did not, however, disclose superior resistance to corrosion in hot brine environments. Nevertheless, the court held that the Russian article anticipated claims 1 and 2, because the alloy was not new, even if the applicants for the patent discovered properties of the alloy (corrosion resistance) unspecified by the article. Of course, this result would not have prevented the applicant from acquiring a method patent on the use of the old alloy for corrosion resistance. *Perricone v. Medicis Pharm. Corp.*, 432 F.3d 1368, 1378 (Fed. Cir. 2005).

Titanium Metals also sets forth an important anticipation rule: a prior art reference that discloses a single composition anticipates a broader range containing the single composition. That is, a prior art disclosure of a species anticipates a claimed genus. The inverse, however, is not necessarily true. Prior disclosure of a genus does not automatically anticipate a single species within that genus. The reason is that a claimed species within a prior art genus may have properties not shared by the rest of the genus. This genus/species problem arises most often with chemical compounds.

The test for anticipation is sometimes called the four-corners test. If the claimed subject matter can be found within the ambit of a single prior art reference, the subject matter is anticipated. The anticipation inquiry does not combine references (though one or more additional references may be consulted to flesh out the disclosed subject matter by evidencing the inherent knowledge or understanding of ordinarily skilled artisans without, however, supplying an otherwise missing element). Similarly, the inquiry does not consider elements analogous to the disclosure of a reference.

The four-corners test also requires that the single reference disclose the subject matter as arranged or combined in the same way as the claim. *Net MoneyIN, Inc. v. VeriSign, Inc.*, 545 F.3d 1359, 1371 (Fed. Cir. 2008). In *Net MoneyIN*, the Federal Circuit reversed a judgment of invalidity because it was necessary to mix and match different parts of two different protocols within the same prior art document. If the claim had recited subject matter of one or the other protocol, it would have been anticipated. But it was improper to combine the separate protocols in finding anticipation.

B. ENABLEMENT REQUIREMENT

The test for sufficient disclosure of each and every element within a single reference is enablement. The disclosure must contain sufficient disclosure to enable one of skill in the art to make (or in this case, identify) each and every element of the claimed subject matter. This echoes the enablement rule in Chapter 9, even though an anticipatory reference need not teach how to use the subject matter. *See Rasmusson v. SmithKline Beecham Corp.*, 413 F.3d 1318, 1325 (Fed. Cir. 2005). Nor is proof of efficacy required for a prior art reference to be enabling. *Id.* at 1326.

For example, in *Titanium Metals*, the Russian article did not disclose a method to make the claimed alloy. Nonetheless the article showed that manufacture of the alloy was well within the knowledge of one of ordinary skill in the art. In fact, even the patent applicant's expert admitted that, given the disclosure of the Russian article, he knew multiple methods of preparing the alloys. Thus, the article contained sufficient enabling disclosure of each and every element and thus qualified as an anticipatory reference.

C. INHERENCY

The most difficult portion of the test for anticipation relates to inherency. The prior art may disclose inherently, rather than expressly, some aspect or all of the claimed subject matter. Under this rule, the prior art disclosure must *necessarily* include the inherent (unexpressed) subject matter. That is, the inherent subject matter must not be only occasionally present or accidentally present; the inherent subject matter must be inevitable from the prior art reference's disclosure. *Tilghman v. Proctor*,

102 U.S. 707, 711 (1880). Probabilities and possibilities do not suffice.

Inherent disclosure requires resort to extrinsic evidence, meaning evidence beyond the four corners of the prior art reference. Therefore, the inherency rule poses a question about the kinds of extrinsic evidence that suffice for inherent disclosure. As a general matter, inherency requires recognition by one of ordinary skill in the art that the disclosure contains the non-express subject matter. This rule does not, however, temporally fix the types of evidence to show inherent disclosure. For example, technology may progress and reveal previously unknown (or even unknowable) features and properties of the prior art. Yet, if necessarily present, the previously-unknown element inherently anticipates. Thus, the inherent subject matter need not be recognized at the time of the anticipatory reference or even before the date of invention or filing. *EMI Group of N. Am., Inc. v. Cypress Semiconductor Corp.*, 268 F.3d 1342, 1351 (Fed. Cir. 2001).

The case of *Schering Corp. v. Geneva Pharmaceuticals, Inc.*, 339 F.3d 1373 (Fed. Cir. 2003), illustrates this complex doctrine of inherent anticipation. The prior art was a non-drowsy antihistamine compound, loratadine or CLARITIN®. When a patient ingested loratadine, the body changed it (i.e., metabolized it) into a metabolite, DCL or CLARINEX®. The patent-at-issue claimed this metabolite. Researchers did not identify or isolate the metabolite outside a patient's body until several years later. Nonetheless, the loratadine reference anticipated the application for the metabolite, even though the earlier patent on loratadine made no mention of metabolites.

The Federal Circuit noted that the metabolite was necessarily present upon ingestion of loratadine. The metabolite was therefore inherent in the ingestion of the prior art CLARITIN® compound and anticipated by the corresponding reference. Notably, the prior art inherently anticipated the new metabolite compound even though no one recognized or knew of the metabolite until years later. The court also noted, however, that the prior reference would not anticipate a carefully-crafted claim to an isolated and purified metabolite outside the body. The isolated and purified form of DCL outside the body was a worthy invention when properly claimed.

A more recent example of inherency arose in a case involving the use of an enzyme, phytase, to prevent ethanol processing equipment from accumulating insoluble byproduct deposits (i.e., fouling). *U.S. Water Servs., Inc. v. Novozymes A/S*, 843 F.3d 1345 (Fed. Cir. 2016). The issue was whether two prior art references, Antim and Veit, necessarily disclosed "adding phytase *for the purpose of reducing deposits*." The district court had found that this claim limitation was inherently met on the grounds that Antim and Veit disclosed the presence of phytase. *Id.* at 1351. But it improperly ignored U.S. Water's expert testimony that practicing Antim and Veit will not *always* result in deposit reduction. *Id.* Because that material question of fact remained unanswered and disputed, the Federal Circuit vacated the district court's grant of summary judgment of inherent disclosure.

D. ANTICIPATION VS. OBVIOUSNESS

A final note of comparison and caution: novelty, of course, is the rarer of the two primary conditions for patentability based on prior art. The more common condition, non-obviousness, does not mandate absolute newness. Instead, non-obviousness carves out an area of unpatentable subject matter around preexisting knowledge. "[D]ifferences between the prior art reference and a claimed invention, however slight, invoke the question of obviousness, not anticipation." *Net MoneyIN, Inc. v. VeriSign, Inc.*, 545 F.3d 1359, 1371 (Fed. Cir. 2008).

Although their functions are very similar, novelty and non-obviousness are quite distinct, despite the rote incantation that "anticipation is the epitome of obviousness." *Jones v. Hardy*, 727 F.2d 1524, 1529 (Fed. Cir. 1984). Novelty is judged by a single reference; obviousness, on the other hand, is judged by any number of references. Obviousness also requires analysis of secondary considerations of non-obviousness; these secondary considerations are irrelevant to anticipation. *Cohesive Techs., Inc. v. Waters Corp.*, 543 F.3d 1351, 1364 (Fed. Cir. 2008). Thus, as Chapter 8 discusses later, obviousness requires the collective knowledge in the prior art to contain a motivation to combine individual pieces of knowledge to arrive at the claimed subject matter.

This axiomatic distinction, at times, becomes blurred. For example, a second reference may aid in determining novelty when it more fully explicates a feature inherent in the primary reference. Similarly, subject matter may be unpatentable in view of a single reference where it would have been obvious at the time of the invention to modify the teachings of the single reference to arrive at the claimed invention, so long as a person of ordinary skill in the art would have followed common-sense reasoning in making the modification.

Even though novelty and non-obviousness are separate statutory requirements, the provisions that guide a novelty inquiry provide evidence of the knowledge at the time of the invention, which in turn guides a non-obviousness inquiry. The prior art used to judge obviousness arises from the novelty provisions.

CHAPTER 6
STATUTORY BARS

I. INTRODUCTION

The first-to-invent version of 35 U.S.C. § 102 that applies to patents and applications having an effective filing date before March 16, 2013, contains provisions that create statutory bars, namely subsections (b), (c), and (d). Of these, § 102(b) provides the most common, yet most difficult to grasp, bar. This section bars a patent for any invention "in public use or on sale in this country, more than one year prior to the date of the application for patent in the United States." If the invention was used publicly or offered for sale in the United States more than one year before the application was filed, that invention cannot receive a patent. In contrast, the first-inventor-to-file version of 35 U.S.C. § 102 neither limits uses and sales geographically to the United States nor allows for any period of time between the public disclosure and another's filing of an application, except in limited circumstances.

The statutory bars under both regimes have one simple goal: to encourage timely filing and disclosure of an invention. Under former § 102(b), an inventor must file within one year of any public use of, or offer to sell, the invention. The date corresponding to one year before the filing of the patent application is therefore often called the "critical date." Statutorily barred activities, such as publishing an invention in a scientific journal or offering it for sale, even one day before the critical date, negates patentability.

The one-year delay following publication or commercialization provides an inventor with a "grace period," during which the inventor can perfect the invention and prepare a patent application. An inventor can control the critical date by choosing when to publicize or commercialize an invention. Of course, a third party may also trigger the one-year period, and thus catch an unwary inventor off guard. Accordingly, despite the grace period, an astute inventor will file an application as quickly as possible.

The purpose for the statutory bars becomes apparent by comparing the world's first-to-file systems with the former U.S. first-to-invent system. Under a first-to-file system, an inventor who files a patent application first is awarded the patent, even if someone else previously invented the technology. This system, of course, encourages a race to the patent office. In the U.S.'s pre-America Invents Act (AIA) system (first-to-invent), on the other hand, the first inventor obtained the patent even if someone else had already filed an application on the same invention. The old system therefore tolerated—or even encouraged—an inventor's delay in filing a patent application. Indeed, a first inventor might benefit from waiting for others to perfect the invention and build a market only to file at a later, more profitable point. This flaw in the first-to-invent system could slow the pace of disclosure and innovation. Therefore, to ensure that inventors do not delay disclosure and defeat the objectives of the patent system, the patent laws include statutory bars.

A hypothetical might clarify the rationale for the statutory bars under former § 102(b). Assume that an inventor creates a pill that grows new cartilage. This invention, as may often occur, has unanticipated side-effects, such as growing cartilage where it is not needed: protruding noses and drooping earlobes. In a pure first-to-invent system, the inventor would wait until a third party independently created the same invention and corrected the side-effects. Then, the initial inventor would step in and claim the exclusive right. In the process, the inventor might gain the benefits of the third party's work. Even without the side-effects wrinkle in the hypothetical, an inventor would have an incentive to let someone else undertake the expense of manufacturing and marketing the invention before stepping in to claim an exclusive right to the technology and a share of the profit.

Without the statutory bars, an inventor could publicize and commercialize an invention for years, reaping monetary benefits and intangible goodwill, all while waiting to file an application until a competitor attempted to enter the market. An inventor could thus effectively prolong the term of the exclusive right indefinitely—or at least until a competitor penetrated the market. Under a pure first-to-invent system, nothing would discourage an inventor from keeping the invention secret and filing a patent only when a competitor enters the same market.

But the statutory bars prevent that strategy and encourage inventors, under peril of losing their rights as inventors, to file and disclose their invention earlier rather than later. Because of the statutory bars, the United States patent system was never really a pure first-to-invent system.

A grace period between publication and filing can also serve important objectives under the first-inventor-to-file regime. In a first-to-file regime, an inventor can lose all patent rights by inadvertently disclosing the invention before filing. Thus, an inventor who publishes the invention at a scientific convention has created prior art against his own later filing of a patent application. A grace period prevents this kind of forfeiture and offers the inventor an opportunity to prepare an application after initial publication. The AIA thus allows for a one-year grace period that is personal to the first inventor.

The operation of the statutory bars and grace period under the former § 102(b) produced a surprising benefit before the AIA: it ameliorated the differences between the non-U.S. first-to-file systems and the U.S. first-to-invent system. The difference could have been vast because the rest of the world defined "prior" art based on the filing date. However, for patents with a priority date before March 16, 2013, the U.S. often uses the date of invention to determine the art that qualifies as "prior" for validity determinations. This difference narrows, though, because any art in existence more than a year before the filing date (i.e., the critical date) will be "prior" art under both systems. Because the first-to-invent § 102(b) makes everything more than a year before filing "prior" art, the world and U.S. systems in fact had almost always recognized and relied upon the same references when considering validity. The pre-AIA U.S. system therefore operated much like a first-to-file (or more precisely, first-inventor-to-file). The AIA's change to a first-inventor-to-file simply represents a step further towards a first-to-file system.

The legal implications of the "public use" and "on-sale" statutory bars depend on the character of the barring activities. The barring activities in the first-to-invent § 102(b) fall into two categories: activities performed by the applicant and activities performed by a (often unknown) third party. The latter activities further divide into three subcategories: informing, non-informing, and secret activities. Accordingly, a third party's secret use may differ in implications from an inventor's own non-informing use, and so forth.

II. PUBLIC USE UNDER THE FIRST-TO-INVENT REGIME

Pre-AIA § 102(b) precludes a patent for any invention in public use in this country more than one year before its filing date (i.e., before the critical date).

A. DEFINITIONS

When is a use considered "public"? Public use under former 35 U.S.C. § 102(b) includes any use of the claimed invention by an applicant in a public setting, as well as any use by a person other than the applicant who is under no limitation, restriction or obligation of secrecy to the inventor. The "public" nature of a use or disclosure thus depends on the informing, non-informing, and secret categories. Informing uses reveal the very nature of the invention and so put the public in possession of the invention. For example, mere disclosure of a new shape for a tennis racquet frame or a new stringing pattern would place those inventions in the possession of the observing public.

Non-informing uses do not reveal the nature of the invention. In a non-informing use, the public can have and enjoy the benefits of the invention without observing its inventive features. For example, a new water purification process may benefit the public without any public awareness of the inventive features.

Secret uses similarly do not reveal the nature of the invention, but they differ from non-informing uses with respect to the intent of the inventor or owner of the invention. In a secret use, the inventor adopts a deliberate policy of keeping the invention as a trade secret and refuses to disclose it to the public.

B. ACTIVITIES OF THE APPLICANT

An applicant can be barred from a patent because of his own past actions. An applicant's own informing, non-informing and secret uses all bar the patentability of an invention, so long as the use occurred before the critical date.

The critical date is determined based on the effective filing date of the patent or application. An effective filing date before March 16, 2013, creates a critical date one year before the effective filing date. An effective filing date on or after March 16, 2013, creates a critical date concurrent with the effective filing date.

1. Informing

Informing activities are those uses that reveal the very nature of the invention and, thus, put the public in possession of the invention. An informing use by the inventor before the critical date will bar a patent. For example, in *Pennock v. Dialogue*, 27 U.S. 1 (1829), a patentee sold substantial amounts of patented hose to several hose companies for public use in fighting fires. The patent claimed a process for joining hose sections together to resist pressure at the joints. The public could gain possession of the invention upon use or careful observation. When the patentee sued for infringement, the accused party asserted that the patent was invalid because the patentee had openly used the invention for over seven years before filing an application.

Justice Story aptly described this flaw in a pure first-to-invent system:

> If an inventor should be permitted to hold back from the knowledge of the public the secrets of his invention; if he should for a long period of years, retain the monopoly, and make and sell his invention publicly and thus gather the whole profits of it, relying upon his superior skill and knowledge of the structure; and then, and then only, when the danger of competition should force him to procure the exclusive right, he should be allowed to take out a patent, and thus exclude the public from any farther use than what should be derived under it during his fourteen years; it would materially retard the progress of science and the useful arts, and give a premium to those who should be least prompt to communicate their discoveries.

Pennock, 27 U.S. at 19.

To correct this flaw, Justice Story in *Pennock* invalidated the patent and created the first statutory bar to encourage timely filing. Following that precedent, the Patent Act—under both the first-to-invent and first-inventor-to-file regimes—now permits only a single year during which an inventor may perfect the invention before filing.

2. Non-Informing

Non-informing uses do not reveal the nature of the invention and, thus, do not easily put the public in possession of the invention. Nevertheless, non-informing uses by the inventor before the critical date bar patent protection.

The Supreme Court discussed a non-informing use in *Egbert v. Lippmann*, 104 U.S. 333 (1881). In *Egbert*, Samuel Barnes invented an improved corset spring. In 1855 and 1858, Barnes gave his female friend a pair of the improved corset springs, which she wore over a long period of time. In 1863, Barnes explained to his visitor, Joseph Sturgis, how the corset springs worked. Three years later, Barnes filed a patent application for the improvement, which matured into a patent.

The Supreme Court, in deciding whether Mr. Barnes' single, "private," invisible—and therefore non-informing—use was public, enunciated three important principles. First, a single use may be "public." Second, the public to whom the inventor reveals the invention can be a single person. The number of persons privy to the use does not make it public or private. Indeed, disclosure to a single person without any obligation of confidentiality can constitute a public use. Finally, the Court explained that an invisible use may still be public. So, for example, a part embedded deep in a machine and beyond view may still be a barring public use vis-à-vis the inventor.

The Court ultimately decided that Barnes had made a public use of the invention at least two years before the date of filing. (In 1881, when *Egbert* was decided, the grace period lasted two years, which Congress reduced to one year in 1939.) In particular, Barnes had given the corset springs to his friend, without any restriction on their use, and she had worn them for several years before he filed his application. Moreover, he had waited eleven years after his invention to file a patent application. He had enjoyed the full use of his invention for many years before seeking a patent and, therefore, could not retrieve patent rights to the springs from the public domain. But all was not lost. His intimate friend became Mrs. Barnes.

3. Secret

Secret activities neither reveal the nature of the invention nor put the public in possession of the invention. But secret uses differ from the non-informing uses in that the inventor carrying out a secret use intends to avoid the patent system by keeping the invention as a trade secret.

For example, in *Metallizing Engineering Co. v. Kenyon Bearing & Auto Parts Co.*, 153 F.2d 516 (2d Cir. 1946), the Second Circuit held that an inventor's secret exploitation of his invention constituted a "public use." The patentee created a novel process for creating a shiny metal coating. He used this method in his facility but kept it a trade secret. The finished products were sold—but the products themselves gave no indication of the secret process. He used the invention secretly for more than a year before he filed his patent application.

Encouraging prompt filing, Judge Learned Hand held that the inventor, by selling a product secretly made using the inventive method more than one year before the inventor's filing date, had erected a public use bar. It was irrelevant that the consumers had not learned the details of the secret method.

C. ACTIVITIES OF THIRD PARTIES

Third parties' activities can also bar an invention's patentability. In particular, a third party's informing and non-informing uses before the critical date bar patentability, but a third party's secret use does not. It is worth noting that such secret uses can give rise to a defense to infringement under § 273 for any patent issued after September 16, 2011, but they still do not invalidate a patent.

1. Informing

Informing uses by third parties invoke the statutory bar—even though the third party initiates the use without the knowledge of the inventor. The informing use gives the public the expectation that the invention is in the public domain, regardless of the identity of the user.

For instance, in *Electric Storage Battery Co. v. Shimadzu*, 307 U.S. 5 (1939), Shimadzu invented a method of forming a lead powder with increased reactivity. The defendant in this case, Electric Storage Battery, defended by asserting that it had used a machine that involved both the claimed methods and claimed apparatus more than two years before Shimadzu's U.S. filing date. The Court held that the defendant's use of the machine, which was open to the employees of the plant where it was used and was not shielded or kept secret, invalidated the patents at issue.

2. Non-Informing

A non-informing use by a third party may also create a statutory bar to patentability. In *Abbott Laboratories v. Geneva Pharmaceuticals, Inc.*, 182 F.3d 1315 (Fed. Cir. 1999), the Federal Circuit decided that a third party's sale of a composition that—even unbeknownst to the third party—contained the patented compound invoked the statutory bar.

Abbott invented and marketed a hypertension medicine that was a Form IV anhydrate of a chemical compound. A third party, Byron Chemical, sold a small amount of the patented Form IV prior to the critical date. At the time of the sales, Byron did not even know that the composition it sold included trace amounts of Form IV. Three years after the sale and one year after the filing date of the patent application, Abbott discovered that Byron's sale included the Form IV anhydrate. One year later the defendant whom Abbott had sued for infringement discovered this fact as well.

The Federal Circuit held that the Form IV anhydrate was on sale even though no one knew that the compound was sold in Form IV. Therefore, even though the public had no reason to believe that it had received the invention, the court held that the non-informing sale invoked the statutory bar to Abbott's patent.

3. Secret

A secret use by a third party, on the other hand, does not bar patentability of an invention. In *W.L. Gore & Associates, Inc. v. Garlock, Inc.*, 721 F.2d 1540 (Fed. Cir. 1983), the involved a method of processing polytetrafluorethylene, commonly known as PTFE or TEFLON®. Making PTFE required stretching the basic composition. Unfortunately, PTFE broke easily when it was stretched, even when stretched very slowly. Contrary to the prevailing wisdom in the art, the patentee learned to make PTFE by stretching it very *quickly*. He filed a patent application claiming the process and the composition.

But years earlier, John Cropper of New Zealand had developed and constructed a machine for stretching PTFE quickly to make a special tape. Cropper sold his machine to Budd Company in the United States. Budd began selling the tape but kept the machine and process a trade secret.

The Federal Circuit concluded that the sale of the tape made by the secret method did not disclose the invention publicly. Like non-informing uses, the public would never learn the claimed process by examining the tape. But the key difference here was that the third party, Budd, deliberately concealed its invention. Simply put, the third party had chosen trade secret protection over patent protection. The court held that, under these circumstances, Budd's secret use could not invalidate Gore's patent. Perhaps for this reason, the public today often refers to PTFE as "GORE-TEX®," not "BUDD-TEX."

III. ON SALE BAR UNDER THE FIRST-TO-INVENT REGIME

The on-sale bar prevents an inventor from obtaining a patent where he commercially exploits the invention after it was ready for patenting and more than a year before filing. The Patent Act traditionally provided an inventor a one-year grace period during which the inventor could sell the invention or offer it for sale. The first-inventor-to-file might also allow for a similar grace period, but the courts would need to interpret the statutory language, such as whether placing the invention on sale qualifies as an excepted "disclosure."

The threshold inquiry in an on-sale bar case under the first-to-invent system is often whether the product or process is complete and ready for sale. Inventions rarely, if ever, spring fully operational out of the head of their creator. Rather the inventive process typically progresses from day to day towards a solution to a problem. During this development phase, events may transpire that place a new technology in the public domain. For example, a company may separate the engineering department from the marketing department and yet ask that the marketers determine demand for a product while the engineers continue development.

The Federal Circuit struggled with different factual situations to set forth a test for determining when the invention is sufficiently complete to invoke the on-sale bar. *Compare UMC Elecs. Co. v. United States*, 816 F.2d 647, 656 (Fed. Cir. 1987) (stating that "the subject matter of the sale or offer to sell fully anticipated the claimed invention or would have rendered the claimed invention obvious by its addition to the prior art") *with Seal-Flex, Inc. v. Athletic Track & Court Construction*, 98 F.3d 1318, 1322 (Fed. Cir. 1996) (stating that "the issue is not how much development had already been done, but whether the invention was in fact complete and was known to work for its intended purpose").

In *Pfaff v. Wells Electronics, Inc.*, 525 U.S. 55 (1998), the Supreme Court finally ventured to resolve the confusion with a two-part test for the on-sale bar. First, the invention must be the subject of a commercial offer for sale. Second, the invention must be ready for patenting at the time of that offer. The two parts of the Supreme Court's test are considered in detail below.

A. COMMERCIAL OFFER FOR SALE

The first element of the on-sale bar under the first-to-invent regime is whether the invention was the subject of a commercial offer for sale. A commercial offer for sale is typically measured by general rules of contract law, that is, an offer must be sufficiently firm and definite to permit immediate acceptance to form a binding contract (assuming consideration supports both ends of the bargain). *Group One, Ltd. v. Hallmark Cards, Inc.*, 254 F.3d 1041, 1046–48 (Fed. Cir. 2001).

In *Pfaff*, for example, the Supreme Court was asked to determine whether certain activity by the inventor of a simple mechanical invention—a semiconductor chip socket—was sufficient to invoke the on-sale bar. The inventor had shown drawings to a customer and subsequently received an order for the invention from the customer. The Court held that the inventor's acceptance of the purchase order evinced a commercial offer before the critical date. The on-sale bar does not require an actual sale. A sufficiently definite offer that *could* be accepted (even if not actually accepted) suffices to invoke the bar. In fact, even a single unrestricted offer for sale precludes patentability.

B. READY FOR PATENTING

The second element of the on-sale bar requires the invention to be ready for patenting. The ready-for-patenting standard does not require that the inventor reduce the invention to practice (e.g., by performing experiments or otherwise showing that it will actually work for its intended purpose). However, a reduction to practice establishes that the invention is ready for patenting. An invention can be ready for patenting before the final tests and trials that reduce the invention to practice are completed.

The enablement test governs the "ready for patenting" requirement. *Scaltech, Inc. v. Retec/ Tetra, L.L.C.*, 269 F.3d 1321, 1331 (Fed. Cir. 2001). An invention may thus be ready for patenting if, for example, the inventor prepares a drawing or other description of the invention that is sufficiently specific to enable a person skilled in the art to practice the invention. In some simple technologies, even conception can signify that an invention is ready for patenting. In *Pfaff*, as an example, the inventor sent engineering drawings to a manufacturer to begin making the invention. Those drawings satisfied the second portion of the test because the drawings enabled the manufacturer to make the invention as claimed.

To conclude this section on the on-sale bar, the bar remains in-tact following the AIA. *Helsinn Healthcare S.A. v. Teva Pharm. USA, Inc.*, 855 F.3d 1356, 1369–71 (Fed. Cir. 2017). The *Helsinn* case involved a treatment for chemotherapy-induced nausea. Nearly two years before applying for a patent, patentee Helsinn entered into a contract with pharmaceutical distributor MGI Pharma, in which Helsinn agreed to supply MGI with its patented treatment. Helsinn argued that this agreement constituted a secret sale—and that secret sales no longer bar patentability under the AIA. According to Helsinn, Congress's addition to § 102 of the catch-all phrase, "or otherwise available to the public," implied a new requirement of the on-sale bar that sales must be accompanied by a public disclosure about the details of the invention. Put differently, Helsinn argued that the catch-all phrase implied the exclusion of secret sales, like those in *Egbert*, from the patentability bar. But the court disagreed, holding that the new catch-all phrase did not affect the on-sale bar's operation.

IV. EXPERIMENTAL USE NEGATION UNDER THE FIRST-TO-INVENT REGIME

A. EXCEPTION VERSUS NEGATION

The experimental use negation operates to expand the grace period laid out in § 102(b). As a negation instead of an exception, experimental use is not an independent test. That is, the experimental use negation is merely the application of the standard statutory bar test but without a concomitant indication or suggestion that the pre-critical date use was public or that the offer for sale was commercial. In *Pfaff*, the Supreme Court reaffirmed the experimental use (or sale) negation, stating that "an inventor who seeks to perfect his discovery may conduct extensive testing without losing his right to obtain a patent for his invention—even if such testing occurs in the public eye. The law has long recognized the distinction between inventions put to experimental use and products sold commercially." *Pfaff*, 525 U.S. at 64.

The Court in *Pfaff* also reaffirmed the primary precedent for experimental uses, namely *City of Elizabeth v. American Nicholson Pavement Co.*, 97 U.S. 126 (1878). *See Pfaff*, 525 U.S. at 64 ("In 1878, we explained why patentability may turn on an inventor's use of his product."). In *City of Elizabeth*, the invention was a wooden pavement for a road. The inventor put the wooden pavement surface on a road in Boston, Massachusetts, more than six years before filing a patent application. After receiving the patent, the inventor sued Elizabeth, New Jersey, for infringement.

The city defended by arguing that the inventor violated the public use bar because the road was in use long before the critical date. While acknowledging that the inventor used the invention in public, the Supreme Court did not agree that the inventor's use triggered the patentability bar. Rather, it fashioned a doctrine allowing an inventor (including a person acting under his directions or orders) to perfect the inventive subject matter through experimentation, even openly, without using it "publicly." The Court reasoned that, although the inventor laid his road in a public area and the public gained some benefit from it, he laid the road in order to test the features rather than to abandon his invention or donate it to the public. In addition, the inventor installed the road at his own expense, with the consent of the owner of the road, and he carefully monitored the conditions of the roadway.

The Court emphasized the toll-collector's testimony that the inventor had visited the road daily, asked frequent questions about the drivers' reactions as they traversed the road, and closely examined the pavement by repeatedly striking it with his cane. This evidence convinced the Court that the inventor used the road not publicly but experimentally to test its usefulness and durability.

A century later, the Federal Circuit emphasized the singular nature of the experimental use negation to the public use bar:

> [I]t is incorrect to impose on the patent owner, as the trial court in this case did, the burden of proving that a "public use" was "experimental." These are not two separable issues. It is incorrect to ask: "Was it public use?" and then, "Was it experimental?" Rather, the court is faced with a single issue: Was it public use under § 102(b)?

TP Lab'ys, Inc. v. Pro. Positioners, Inc., 724 F.2d 965, 971 (Fed. Cir. 1984). Thus, the same facts should be examined for both public use and the experimental negation to the public use bar.

B. SALES OF THE INVENTION

An inventor may also sell an invention for experimental purposes without running afoul of the on-sale bar doctrine. For example, in *Manville Sales Corp. v. Paramount Systems, Inc.*, 917 F.2d 544 (Fed. Cir. 1990), the Federal Circuit held that an inventor's sale of his highway lighting system to the State of Wyoming was experimental, not commercial. The inventor did nothing to lead the public to believe that the new lighting system was in the public domain. To the contrary, he conveyed to the state that its use in this single, remote location was experimental, and he marked the design drawing as confidential. Further, the rest stop chosen for the experimental sale was closed to the public at the time.

Under these circumstances, the inventor did nothing improperly to extend the term of his patent by commercially exploiting the invention before filing. Rather, he retained ownership of the invention throughout the testing, only subsequently receiving compensation for the invention. He also waited to market the invention until after he knew it worked for its intended purpose. Before he had actually tested it, the court held, he had "no proven invention to disclose." *Manville*, 917 F.2d at 550.

V. PATENTS AND PRINTED PUBLICATIONS

Under pre-AIA § 102(b), a patent is anticipated if "the invention was patented or described in a printed publication in this or a foreign country . . . more than one year prior to the date of the application for patent in the United States." This provision makes the United States' former first-to-invent system analogous to a first-to-file system for any invention patented or described in a printed publication before the critical date. That is, the provision triggers a kind of statute of limitations when an invention is disclosed in a printed publication anywhere in the world. *In re Foster*, 343 F.2d 980, 987–88 (CCPA 1965). The AIA's first-inventor-to-file system eliminates this grace period, except for disclosures based on the inventor's own work.

The difficulty here lies in determining what constitutes a printed publication. Let us revisit the case *In re Hall*, 781 F.2d 897 (Fed. Cir. 1986), also summarized in the previous chapter. There a doctoral thesis published before the critical date invoked the printed publication bar even though the publication was in a foreign language and resided solely at Freiburg University in Germany. The

Federal Circuit explained that " 'public accessibility' has been called the touchstone in determining whether a reference constitutes a 'printed publication' bar." *Hall*, 781 F.2d at 899. To invalidate a patent, the "proponent of the publication bar must show that prior to the critical date the reference was sufficiently accessible, at least to the public interested in the art, so that such a one by examining the reference could make the claimed invention without further research or experimentation." *Id.* Because the doctoral thesis was accessible through indexing and cataloging, the publication invalidated Mr. Hall's patent.

VI. OTHER STATUTORY BARS UNDER THE FIRST-TO-INVENT REGIME

Pre-AIA §§ 102(c) and 102(d) erect additional bars to patentability, discussed in the sections below.

In addition, in the AIA, Congress added a catch-all phrase to § 102, so that the provision now excludes from patentability "[any] invention [that] was patented, described in a printed publication, or in public use, on sale, *or otherwise available to the public* before the effective filing date of the claimed invention." 35 U.S.C. § 102(a)(1) (emphasis added). Future litigation will have to clarify what new activities, if any, fall within the new catch-all language in § 102.

A. ABANDONMENT

Under pre-AIA § 102(c), an inventor is not entitled to a patent for an invention if he abandoned the invention. For example, in *Kendall v. Winsor*, 62 U.S. 322 (1858), Winsor asserted a patent for a harness-making machine. The defendants argued that Winsor had abandoned his invention by expressly informing them that he did not want to obtain a patent on it, but rather preferred to keep the technology as a trade secret. The jury, however, disagreed and concluded that Winsor had not in fact abandoned the patented technology.

On appeal, the Supreme Court explained that "[i]t is the unquestionable right of every inventor to confer gratuitously the benefits of his ingenuity upon the public, and this he may do either by express declaration or by conduct equally significant with language." *Kendall*, 62 U.S. at 329. The Court provided three examples of abandonment: (i) acquiescing to others' use of the invention, (ii) forfeiting rights by a willfully or negligently postponing protection of the invention, and (iii) attempting to keep the improvement as a trade secret until another introduces it. The latter two of these three scenarios are largely redundant of other patent-defeating sections in the first-to-invent regime—namely §§ 102(b) and 102(g). The abandonment defense therefore typically arises only where the inventor consciously and intentionally dedicates the invention to the public. Notably, only the inventor may abandon his invention. A third party may not effect an abandonment by surreptitiously pirating the invention and communicating it to the public. *Id.* at 330–31.

The first-inventor-to-file regime under the AIA eliminates abandonment as a separate category of prior art.

B. DELAY

Under pre-AIA § 102(d), an inventor is not entitled to a patent for an invention if

> the invention was first patented or caused to be patented, or was the subject of an inventor's certificate, by the applicant or his legal representatives or assigns in a foreign country prior to the date of the application for patent in this country on an application for patent or inventor's certificate filed more than twelve months before the filing of the application in the United States.

That is, applicants are barred if (i) they file for patent protection in a foreign country more than a year before filing a U.S. patent application, and (ii) the foreign application matured into a patent before the U.S. filing date. *Bayer AG v. Schein Pharms., Inc.*, 301 F.3d 1306, 1312 (Fed. Cir. 2002).

For example, in *In re Kathawala*, 9 F.3d 942 (Fed. Cir. 1993), the inventor filed patent applications in the United States, Greece, and Spain. The United States application was filed on April 11, 1985, more than one year after the Greek and Spanish applications were filed on November 21, 1983. The Greek application issued as a patent on October 2, 1984, and the Spanish application issued on January 21, 1985, both prior to the United States filing date.

The Federal Circuit upheld the bar. Because the inventor had the opportunity to file an application for patent in the United States before the issuance of the foreign patents, but instead delayed filing, the court held that the inventor was not entitled to a patent in the United States.

CHAPTER 7

NOVELTY: PRIOR INVENTION

I. INTRODUCTION

This chapter discusses the novelty requirements set forth in the first-to-invent § 102, paragraphs (a), (e), (f), and (g), which were introduced in Chapter 5. These paragraphs all concern ways to ascertain whether the claimed subject matter had already been invented.

First-to-invent's § 102(a) straightforwardly states the essential first-to-invent rule that was fundamental to novelty in the United States. In particular, an inventor was entitled to a patent unless "the invention was known or used by others in this country, or patented or described in a printed publication in this or a foreign country, before the invention thereof by the applicant for patent." Or in short form, a public disclosure will preclude a later patent on the same subject matter. The four categories—known by another in the United States, used by another in the United States, patented, and described in a printed publication—are examined in greater detail in Chapter 5.

First-to-invent's § 102(e) relates to a special category of secret, non-public disclosure that nonetheless precludes a patent for the disclosed subject matter, namely an earlier patent application. To preempt a later patent application on the same subject matter under this section, the earlier application must have appeared publicly as a published application or as an issued patent.

First-to-invent's § 102(f) prevents a putative inventor from patenting subject matter that he did not truly invent. An imposter may not receive a patent for subject matter derived from another's work. In a real sense, this non-derivation requirement is different from the prior art generating provisions of first-to-invent's §§ 102(a), (e) and (g). Nonetheless its emphasis on novelty correlates sufficiently with those other paragraphs to warrant joint consideration.

First-inventor-to-file's § 102(b) and § 135 create limited exceptions to the general rule that a prefiling disclosure negates patentability. First-inventor-to-file's § 135 creates derivation proceedings to prevent an earlier filer from obtaining a patent on information learned from another, and new § 102(b) excludes certain prior disclosures made by the inventor (or joint inventor) from prior art.

The statutory framework applicable to patents obtained under the new first-inventor-to-file regime retains certain aspects of first-to-invent's §§ 102(a), 102(e), and 102(f). The courts, however, have not yet decided the extent to which previous principles and concepts are imported into the new statutory scheme.

Perhaps the most critical and complex category of secret prior art under the first-to-invent regime, § 102(g) generally prevents the patenting of subject matter already invented by another. Section 102(g) contains two paragraphs. The first paragraph provides the statutory basis for an interference—an administrative proceeding before the Patent Office for determining which of two pending patent applications (or which of a pending application and an issued patent) represents the work of the first inventor. The second paragraph provides the statutory basis to invalidate a patent based on another's prior invention of the same subject matter. The relatively terse statutory language conceals the complexity of determining priority or validity based on prior invention.

In contrast to Chapter 6 discussing statutory bars, the novelty requirements in this chapter are not universally applicable across the world. Instead, these rules are unique to the United States' first-to-invent system. These provisions add complexity to domestic patent law and increase the transaction costs of worldwide patenting, although the complexity should decrease as the United States transitions to the first-inventor-to-file system.

II. PRIOR INVENTION UNDER FIRST-TO-INVENT'S § 102(a)

A. "KNOWN OR USED"

One of the earliest U.S. patent cases set forth the first-to-invent requirement embodied in pre-America Invents Act § 102(a). In *Woodcock v. Parker*, 30 F. Cas. 491 (D. Mass. 1813), the court explained that only the first inventor receives a patent even if a second person independently invented the same subject matter. In fact, once the subject matter becomes public, it does not even matter that the first inventor abandoned it and thereby allowed the second inventor to be the person who actually benefitted society. To repeat the central principle, the event that defeats novelty is the prior invention, not simply the prior disclosure of inventive subject matter. After *Woodcock*, the patent statute began explicitly prohibiting the award of a patent to subject matter "known or used" before the applicant's date of invention (as opposed to the applicant's filing date).

Even though the important date is the date of invention, an applicant is not generally required to identify that precise date. Rather, for ease of administration, the inventor typically relies on his filing date and only specifies an earlier invention date when prior art arises that necessitates that specificity. Thus, if an examiner discovers prior art that renders the claimed subject matter unpatentable under first-to-invent's § 102(a), the applicant may then file an affidavit under 37 C.F.R. § 1.131 (called a Rule 131 affidavit) establishing an invention date before the reference.

Chapter 5 goes over the territorial limitations of knowledge or use by others in first-to-invent's § 102(a) as well as the meaning of "patented or described in a printed publication." This chapter's examination of the phrase "known or used by others" thus completes the discussion of § 102(a). Unlike the "public use" bar of first-to-invent's § 102(b), the phrase "known or used by others" limits the patent-defeating knowledge to persons other than the inventor. Inventors' own use or knowledge does not create prior art against themselves. (But inventors can, of course, publish, exploit, or sell their work and thus create a statutory bar under § 102(b).) First-inventor-to-file's § 102(a)(1), however, creates prior art based on information "available to the public" without exclusion of the inventor's own work.

In any event, another's prior use or knowledge of the subject matter does not defeat a later patent application if that prior use was kept secret, that is, never made public. *Gillman v. Stern*, 114 F.2d 28, 31 (2d Cir. 1940). To qualify as the first and original inventor, a third party must have enriched the art. Accordingly, a private and deliberately undisclosed use does not anticipate a later invention of the same subject matter because the public never received the benefit of the initial invention. This rule corresponds well with the rule that a third party's deliberately secret use cannot erect a statutory bar under first-to-invent's § 102(b). Again similar to § 102(b)'s scheme, a third party's public, non-informing uses do not follow the same rule. These non-informing uses preclude the patentability of the subject matter.

Subject matter is "known" within the meaning of first-to-invent's § 102(a) if reasonably accessible to the interested public. For example, in *National Tractor Pullers Association v. Watkins*, 205 USPQ 892 (N.D. Ill. 1980), the alleged infringer asserted that the patent-in-suit, which covered a resistance sled used in tractor pulling contests, was invalid under § 102(a). The infringer produced evidence that a putative earlier inventor had sketched the invention on the underside of a kitchen tablecloth.

Because that earlier inventor had neither reproduced the drawings before their destruction nor commercialized the depicted device, the court correctly determined that this evidence was not anticipatory prior art because the interested public did not have reasonable access to it. This rule also sounds familiar because it correlates with the public accessibility requirement for printed publications, such as through indexing and cataloguing. *See e.g.*, *In re Klopfenstein*, 380 F.3d 1345 (Fed. Cir. 2004).

B. FIRST-TO-INVENT'S § 102(a) BEFORE THE PATENT AND TRADEMARK OFFICE

Because the important date under first-to-invent's § 102(a) is the date of invention, the Patent and Trademark Office permits patent applicants to show a date of invention that pre-dates the prior art. But because a rejection under § 102(a) alone is not made in every application, an applicant usually does not specify a date of invention until it becomes necessary to "swear behind" or antedate a reference. The date of filing serves as the presumptive invention date, until an inventor needs to show an earlier date of invention with a Rule 131 affidavit. Notably, once a patent applicant or patentee antedates a reference, the inquiry ends. That is, the PTO does not seek out an earlier date of invention for the prior art reference, which makes sense because those inventive activities are not publicly accessible. The current administrative rule, 37 C.F.R. § 1.131—which is substantively similar to the same rule before the AIA—provides:

(a) When any claim of an application or a patent under reexamination is rejected, the applicant or patent owner may submit an appropriate oath or declaration to establish invention of the subject matter of the rejected claim prior to the effective date of the reference or activity on which the rejection is based. . . . Prior invention may not be established under this section if either:

(1) The rejection is based upon a U.S. patent or U.S. patent application publication of a pending or patented application naming another inventor which claims interfering subject matter as defined in § 41.203(a) of this chapter, in which case an applicant may suggest an interference pursuant to § 41.202(a) of this chapter; or

(2) The rejection is based upon a statutory bar.

(b) The showing of facts for an oath or declaration under paragraph (a) of this section shall be such, in character and weight, as to establish reduction to practice prior to the effective date of the reference, or conception of the invention prior to the effective date of the reference coupled with due diligence from prior to said date to a subsequent reduction to practice or to the filing of the application. Original exhibits of drawings or records, or photocopies thereof, must accompany. . . the affidavit . . . .

Rule 131 allows inventors to establish a date of invention using inventive activities in certain foreign countries as well as the United States. Further, the Rule specifies two categories where an affidavit cannot antedate a reference: interferences to determine priority over the same subject matter and statutory bars. Under the second category, if a printed publication precedes the filing date of a patent by more than a year, that printed publication serves as a bar under § 102(b) regardless of the applicant's or patentee's ability to show an earlier date of invention.

A Rule 131 affidavit must possess sufficient content to antedate a reference. For example, in *In re Stryker*, 435 F.2d 1340 (CCPA 1971), the court considered whether an uncorroborated affidavit had to substantiate prior invention of the entire claimed subject matter or just the subject matter disclosed in the prior art reference. The court decided the latter: the affidavit did not need to substantiate prior invention of claimed features not found in the reference. Instead, an antedating affidavit need only show prior invention of the features disclosed in the reference. Otherwise, broad claims whose features matched those of both the reference and affidavit would escape unpatentability, while narrower claims with features not mentioned in the same affidavit would be invalid. The *Stryker* rule prevents this anomaly.

III. PRIORITY UNDER FIRST-TO-INVENT'S § 102(g)

A. § 102(g)

Perhaps the most complicated prior art section of the pre-AIA patent laws, § 102(g) recites:

> (1) during the course of an interference conducted under section 135 or section 291, another inventor involved therein establishes, to the extent permitted in section 104, that before such person's invention thereof the invention was made by such other inventor and not abandoned, suppressed, or concealed, or
>
> (2) before such person's invention thereof, the invention was made in this country by another inventor who had not abandoned, suppressed, or concealed it. In determining priority of invention under this subsection, there shall be considered not only the respective dates of conception and reduction to practice of the invention, but also the reasonable diligence of one who was first to conceive and last to reduce to practice, from a time prior to conception by the other.

The first paragraph provides a mechanism for resolving interferences. Under the first paragraph, a party seeks more than a mere denial of another's entitlement to a patent on the claimed subject matter; it seeks to secure a patent for itself. Put differently, the first paragraph determines priority of invention. As innovators across the world compete to develop new and valuable technologies, they will often arrive at similar or even identical inventions at approximately the same time. Where two inventive entities claim the same invention, the United States patent system has a winner-take-all approach: the first inventor obtains the exclusive right to the subject matter and the second inventor gets nothing, not even a right to continue to practice his independent development.

The second paragraph serves a purpose distinct from, yet related to, interferences: it permits an alleged infringer to invalidate an issued patent based on either his own or a third party's prior invention (but only if "in this country").

B. STATUTORY FRAMEWORK

Although both paragraphs recite slightly different language, the stepwise procedure of resolving priority is the same. In § 102(g)(2), the statute sets forth the general rule of priority: "A person shall be entitled to a patent unless . . . before such person's invention thereof, the invention was made in this country by another inventor." But there is an important and complicating exception: if the first inventor "abandoned, suppressed, or concealed" the subject matter, the second inventor has priority. In the case of an interference under this scenario, the second inventor would receive a patent covering the subject matter. In the case of a challenge to validity, the first inventor's patent is invalid, and the second inventor is not awarded a patent.

Further, the last sentence of § 102(g) informs that a date of invention requires an examination of "not only the respective dates of conception and reduction to practice of the invention, but also the reasonable diligence of one who was first to conceive and last to reduce to practice, from a time prior to conception by the other." Thus the priority rule awards a patent to the first to reduce to practice unless the second person to reduce the invention to practice was the first to conceive of the invention and diligently worked to reduce the subject matter to practice. That basic rule, however, is subject to the abandonment, suppression, or concealment requirement.

1. Interferences

As noted, first-to-invent's § 102(g) serves not only as a category of prior art but also as the source for interferences. An interference is a very complex administrative proceeding, and interference practitioners could easily devote their entire career to learning the intricacies of these priority contests. An interference may occur between two pending applications or between a pending application and an issued, unexpired patent. The Patent and Trademark Office would declare an interference when "an application is made for a patent which . . . would interfere with any pending application, or with any unexpired patent." 35 U.S.C. § 135 (2002). An interference may arise between two conflicting applications without any prompting by (or even knowledge of) either applicant. Alternatively, a patent applicant may provoke an interference upon discovery of a newly issued patent or published pending application that claims the same invention.

In fact, an interference may even be declared between a reissue application and an issued patent.

Even a basic understanding of interference procedures requires knowledge of a certain vocabulary. To begin with, the two parties have uniform names: "Senior party means the party entitled to the presumption . . . that it is the prior inventor. Any other party is a junior party." 37 C.F.R. § 41.201. The presumption that a party is the prior inventor arises based on the date of that party's proper constructive reduction to practice (i.e., application filing date). *See* 37 C.F.R. § 41.201. These senior and junior designations are not just names—they establish procedural and evidentiary burdens. For this reason, the senior party enjoys a greater probability of winning an interference than a junior party. With respect to other nomenclature, a "count" corresponds to the claimed invention over which both parties seek exclusive rights. The count defines the parameters of the dispute.

Importantly, the Patent and Trademark Office will only declare an interference in some circumstances, namely "the subject matter of a claim of one party would, if prior art, have anticipated or rendered obvious the subject matter of a claim of the opposing party and vice versa." 37 C.F.R. § 41.203. This rule sets forth a two-way test that judges the patentability of each invention vis-à-vis the other. *Eli Lilly & Co. v. Bd. of Regents of the Univ. of Wash.*, 334 F.3d 1264, 1268–69 (Fed. Cir. 2003).

The AIA replaced interference proceedings with a new regime of derivation proceedings that echoes elements of interferences. Derivation proceedings, however, are limited to scenarios in which an applicant of an earlier-filed application claims subject matter derived, without authorization, from the inventor of a later-filed application.

2. Conception

The touchstone of invention is conception, that is, the completion of the mental portion of the process of inventing. *Burroughs Wellcome Co. v. Barr Labs., Inc.*, 40 F.3d 1223, 1227–28 (Fed. Cir. 1994). An inventor conceives of an invention upon formation of "a definite and permanent idea of the complete and operative invention." *Hybritech Inc. v. Monoclonal Antibodies, Inc.*, 802 F.2d 1367, 1376 (Fed. Cir. 1986) (quoting 1 ROBINSON ON PATENTS 532 (1890)). An idea is complete when a person having ordinary skill in the art would be able to reduce the invention to practice, including every claimed feature, without extensive research or experimentation. *Burroughs*, 40 F.3d at 1228. A general goal or research plan is not enough; the inventor must have a specific idea or particular solution firmly in mind, even if knowledge that the invention will actually work is still lacking. Reduction to practice requires the inventor to make the invention work; conception occurs before the operative invention has actually worked.

Chemical compounds have an even more stringent conception rule. For example, in *Oka v. Youssefyeh*, 849 F.2d 581 (Fed. Cir. 1988), the court encountered a priority dispute over a count reciting a particular genus of chemical compounds, specifically 2-indanyl and 5-indanyl classes. The court divided conception for chemical compounds into two parts: (i) the idea of a structure or formula and (ii) the possession of an operative method of synthesizing that structure. Where the second step is within the knowledge of one of ordinary skill in the art, the standard rule for conception governs, namely the formation of a complete idea constitutes conception.

In *Oka*, however, the junior party, Youssefyeh, attempted to show an earlier conception with two distinct sets of corroborated activities. First, Youssefyeh attempted to show that he had the idea of the 2-indanyl compounds along with the belief that those compounds could be synthesized according to conventional techniques. The court discounted that belief because the evidence showed that a person of ordinary skill in the art took over six months to formulate those compounds. The court explained that conception occurred only when Youssefyeh had both the idea of the chemical structure and an operative method of synthesis.

Because conception can be entirely mental, the inventor's challenge is often to produce contemporaneous evidence that corroborates the conception. The corroboration requirement compensates for the often ethereal nature of conception by requiring particular proof beyond the inventor's mere recollection. *Singh v. Brake*, 317 F.3d 1334, 1340–41 (Fed. Cir. 2003). A rule of reason governs this corroborating evidence. *See, e.g.*, *Linear Tech. Corp. v. Impala Linear Corp.*, 379 F.3d 1311, 1327 (Fed. Cir. 2004).

3. Reduction to Practice

An inventor may reduce an invention to practice in two ways: constructively, by filing a patent application, or actually, by building and testing a physical embodiment of the invention. If the inventor relies on a constructive reduction to practice, the filed application must fully disclose the invention. As noted in *Travis v. Baker*, an application "must be for the same invention as that defined in the count in an interference, and it must contain a disclosure of the invention sufficiently adequate to enable one skilled in the art to practice the invention defined by the count, with all the limitations contained in the count, without the exercise of the inventive faculties." 137 F.2d 109, 111 (CCPA 1943).

An actual reduction to practice must show that the invention works for its intended purpose in the actual environment of its use. Once again, a rule of reason governs the sufficiency of the proof. The case of *Scott v. Finney*, 34 F.3d 1058 (Fed. Cir. 1994), illustrates these principles at work. The invention was a penile prosthesis. The inventor sought to show an actual reduction to practice but had not tested the prosthesis in intercourse. Instead the inventor presented a videotape of the prosthesis inducing an erection during surgery to install the device. The court held that the junior party had sufficiently tested the relatively simple medical device. The court explained:

> When reviewing the sufficiency of evidence of reduction to practice, this court applies a reasonableness standard. Complex inventions

> and problems in some cases require laboratory tests that accurately duplicate actual working conditions in practical uses. . . . Less complex inventions and problems do not demand such stringent testing.

Scott, 34 F.3d at 1061–62 (quotations and citations omitted).

In some circumstances, conception and reduction to practice occur simultaneously. For example, an inventor does not conceive of a gene until identification of the gene's structure (and not just the principal biological property). Thus, conception and reduction to practice occur simultaneously upon discovery of the gene's sequence. *Amgen, Inc. v. Chugai Pharm. Co.*, 927 F.2d 1200, 1205–06 (Fed. Cir. 1991).

Similar to conception, a reduction to practice requires corroboration with contemporaneous evidence. Again, this rule prevents fraud, and in some circumstances can be quite stringent. In one case, a witness testified that he had read and understood a notebook entry on a specific date. The court rejected this proof of an earlier reduction to practice:

> Those affiants' statements that by a certain date they had "read and understood" specified pages of [the junior party's] laboratory notebooks did not corroborate a reduction to practice. They established only that those pages existed on a certain date; they did not independently

corroborate the statements made on those pages.

Hahn v. Wong, 892 F.2d 1028, 1033 (Fed. Cir. 1989). In another case, the court upheld an inventor's offer of his lab notebook showing his practice of the claimed invention. As corroboration, the inventor proffered testimony of a co-worker from whom the inventor acquired supplies for the invention, testimony of another co-worker that he had seen the product produced by the claimed method, and general evidence that the company followed a program to record inventive activity. *Lacotte v. Thomas*, 758 F.2d 611 (Fed. Cir. 1985).

Also similar to conception, the court measures the sufficiency of evidence under a rule of reason. *Holmwood v. Sugavanam*, 948 F.2d 1236, 1238–39 (Fed. Cir. 1991) (citation omitted). Various factors guide the rule of reason analysis. *See Price v. Symsek*, 988 F.2d 1187, 1195 & n.3 (Fed. Cir. 1993).

4. Diligence

As noted earlier, an inventor who diligently pursues a reduction to practice after an early conception may win priority over the first reducer to practice. While diligence naturally depends on the factual circumstances, it requires persistent, dogged work from conception to reduction to practice. The classic case in this area is *Gould v. Schawlow*, 363 F.2d 908 (CCPA 1966). From that case, a clear rule emerged: "The party chargeable with diligence must account for the entire period during which diligence is required." *Id.* at 919. Gordon Gould, now in the

Inventor's Hall of Fame, spent about a thousand hours over a 14-month period pursuing a reduction to practice of his conception of a laser, but he was not diligent enough. Specifically, Gould could not show work in a few gaps of several weeks.

A general averment of the number of days spent reducing the invention to practice does not show diligence without a concomitant showing of the specific work accomplished on each day. That is, the junior party must provide very specific evidence of diligence. The corroboration requirement also applies to diligence and makes overcoming the senior party's bid very difficult.

Diligence is *only* relevant where one party claims an earlier date of conception and a later date of reduction to practice. That is, only one party's diligence ever affects the outcome of a priority contest: the first to conceive but second to reduce to practice. The inventor who is both first to conceive and first to reduce an invention to practice wins the priority contest outright without any showing of diligence.

The required period of diligence for the inventor who was first to conceive and last to reduce to practice begins "prior to the conception by the other" and extends to that inventor's own reduction to practice (constructive or actual). Diligence outside of those bounds is irrelevant.

5. Abandoned, Suppressed, or Concealed

A first inventor does not always win a priority contest under the first-to-invent regime. Indeed, a first inventor may lose by abandoning, suppressing, or concealing the invention. Section 102(g) thus provides an impetus to promptly file a patent application describing the subject matter (or otherwise publicly disclose it). Although abandoning, suppressing, and concealing all relate to the general idea that an inventor must somehow enrich the public knowledge soon after finalizing the invention, they are slightly different conceptually. When establishing abandonment, suppression, or concealment, the second inventor does not need to prove the category within which the first inventor's activities belong.

An inventor may abandon, suppress, or conceal the invention either actively or passively. That is, an inventor may actively conceal the invention as a trade secret. Or the inventor may abandon or suppress the invention by unreasonably delaying its public disclosure. *E.g.*, *Fujikawa v. Wattanasin*, 93 F.3d 1559 (Fed. Cir. 1996); *Shindelar v. Holdeman*, 628 F.2d 1337 (CCPA 1980). Abandonment, suppression, or concealment most often appear in cases involving "spurring," that is, where the first inventor is spurred into filing a patent application by learning of second inventor's competing application or commercial activity. To avoid forfeiture, the first inventor must publicly disclose the invention within a reasonable amount of time after reducing it to practice by filing a patent application, describing it in a publicly available publication, or commercializing it in an informing way that enables the public to learn of the invention. *Dow Chem. Co. v. Astro-Valcour, Inc.*, 267 F.3d 1334 (Fed. Cir. 2001). The method of public disclosure impacts the types of activities that negate an inference of forfeiture. Although occasionally (and erroneously) called "diligence," the level of activity negating an inference of abandonment, suppression, or concealment is far less onerous than the diligence requirement.

An inventor who abandons, suppresses, or conceals the invention may still prevail in a priority fight. To win in that situation, the first inventor must "demonstrate that he renewed activity on the invention and that he proceeded diligently to filing his patent application, starting before the earliest date to which [the second inventor] is entitled." *Paulik v. Rizkalla*, 760 F.2d 1270, 1273 (Fed. Cir. 1985) (en banc). If that were not the rule, inventors would never return to projects that had been ignored for an extended period of time. Accordingly, an inventor may partially minimize the consequences of abandoning, suppressing, or concealing an invention if no one began work on the same invention prior to the inventor's return to the inventive project.

6. The Second Paragraph of First-to-Invent's § 102(g)

To a large extent, the legal standards under first-to-invent's § 102(g) are the same under both paragraphs. One difference is that § 102(g)(2) applies only if the prior invention was in this country.

Another is that § 102(g)(2) applies to an earlier invention that is secret (so long as it was not abandoned, suppressed, or concealed). Because the second paragraph permits invalidation of a presumptively valid patent, the procedure entails a different burden of proof. *See, Apotex USA, Inc. v. Merck & Co.*, 254 F.3d 1031, 1037–38 (Fed. Cir. 2001).

7. Examples

The following examples provide a helpful guide—or crib sheet—to who would win a priority dispute under § 102(g). In each of the examples, assume the events occur in chronological order.

A files; B files.	A prevails, because its reduction to practice predates B's. Note that both reductions to practice are constructive.
B reduces to practice; A files; B files.	B prevails, because its reduction to practice predates A's reduction to practice. Note that B's earliest reduction to practice is actual, while A's reduction to practice is constructive and B files within his grace period.

A reduces to practice; B reduces to practice; A files; B files.	A prevails, because its reduction to practice predates B's.
B conceives and proceeds with requisite diligence; A files; B files.	B prevails, because although it was the second to reduce to practice, it conceived first and diligently worked until reduction to practice.
A conceives and proceeds with requisite diligence; B conceives and proceeds with requisite diligence; A reduces to practice; A files; B files.	A prevails, because both its conception (with diligence) and its reduction to practice predates B's.
B reduces to practice; A reduces to practice; B abandons, suppresses, or conceals; A files; B files.	A prevails, because although B was the first to reduce to practice, B subsequently abandoned, suppressed, or concealed and did not resume activities prior to A's inventive activity.

B conceives and proceeds with requisite diligence; A reduces to practice; A files; B publicly discloses the invention; A obtains a patent.	A's patent is invalid, because B conceived first and diligently worked until publicly disclosing the invention.

IV. PRIOR INVENTION UNDER PRE-AIA § 102(e) & POST-AIA § 102(a)(2)

Although related to a priority fight under first-to-invent's § 102(g), first-to-invent's § 102(e) prevents the patenting of subject matter described in an earlier application, so long as that earlier application either matures into a patent or is published prior to grant. Thus, while pre-AIA § 102(g) focuses on the claimed invention, pre-AIA § 102(e) focuses on the disclosure of a patent or patent application. Pre-AIA § 102(e) proscribes a patent grant where

(e) The invention was described in—

> (1) an application for patent, published under section 122(b), by another filed in the United States before the invention by the applicant for patent or
>
> (2) a patent granted on an application for patent by another filed in the United States before the invention by the applicant for patent, except that an international application filed under the treaty defined in section 351(a) shall have the effects for the purposes of this subsection of an application

> filed in the United States only if the international application designated the United States and was published under Article 21(2) of such treaty in the English language [.]

As first established by the Supreme Court in *Alexander Milburn Co. v. Davis-Bournonville Co.*, 270 U.S. 390 (1926), this section fixes the date of an issued patent or published application as its filing date, even though its contents remain secret until issuance or publication. While the secret prior art discussed in this section may negate novelty, it may negate non-obviousness as well. That is, the novelty requirement defined by § 102(e) also established prior art that can be combined or modified in an obviousness analysis. *Hazeltine Research, Inc. v. Brenner*, 382 U.S. 252, 255–56 (1965).

These same principles reappear under first-inventor-to-file's § 102(a)(2), which states that a person is entitled to a patent, unless "the claimed invention was described in a patent issued under section 151, or in an application for patent published or deemed published under section 122(b), in which the patent or application, as the case may be, names another inventor and was effectively filed before the effective filing date of the claimed invention." The substantive differences, if any, between first-to-invent's § 102(e) and first-inventor-to-file's § 102(a)(2) will likely be resolved through future litigation.

V. DERIVATION UNDER FIRST-TO-INVENT'S § 102(f)

Because a patent should issue to only the correct inventor, § 102(f) negates the patentability of subject matter if the applicant or patentee "did not himself invent the subject matter sought to be patented." Thus, one cannot file a patent application claiming subject matter that another invented. For instance, a corporation cannot establish a policy whereby the president is always named the sole inventor regardless of the actual inventors' identities. The Supreme Court explained this commonsense rule in *Agawam Woolen Co. v. Jordan*, 74 U.S. (7 Wall.) 583, 602–03 (1868):

> Suggestions from another, made during the progress of such experiments, in order that they may be sufficient to defeat a patent subsequently issued, must have embraced the plan of improvement, and must have furnished such information to the person to whom the communication was made that it would have enabled an ordinary mechanic, without the exercise of any ingenuity and special skill on his part, to construct and put the improvement in successful operation.

The Court indicated that the prior inventor must have disclosed the subject matter to the person seeking to patent the subject matter. It is not enough that the disclosure rendered the subject matter obvious; rather, the strict anticipation test governs this rule, just like the other subparagraphs in § 102.

Gambro Lundia AB v. Baxter Healthcare Corp., 110 F.3d 1573, 1577–78 (Fed. Cir. 1997).

Like prior disclosure in a patent or published patent application under § 102(e), the non-derivation requirement of § 102(f) may also operate in an interference under § 102(g). In fact, parties in a priority fight will occasionally assert that the opposing parties derived the subject matter of the count from them. In such a circumstance, "the person attacking the patent must establish prior conception of the claimed subject matter and communication of the conception to the adverse claimant." *Price v. Symsek*, 988 F.2d 1187, 1190 (Fed. Cir. 1993). This standard applies equally to all inquiries under § 102(f), even where § 102(g) is not at issue.

VI. DERIVATION PROCEEDINGS UNDER FIRST-INVENTOR-TO-FILE'S § 135

The first-inventor-to-file regime includes "derivation proceedings," which retain elements of first-to-invent's § 102(g) and § 102(f). Post-AIA § 135 states that a petition to institute a derivation proceeding "shall set forth with particularity the basis for finding that an individual named in an earlier application as the inventor or joint inventor derived such invention from an individual named in the petitioner's application as the inventor or joint inventor and, without authorization, the earlier application claiming such invention was filed." This petition must be filed within one year of patent issuance or publication of the application claiming the invention, whichever is earlier. Derivation proceedings are discussed at greater length in Chapter 11.

VII. EXCEPTIONS TO FIRST-INVENTOR-TO-FILE'S NOVELTY REQUIREMENT

The first-inventor-to-file regime retains a one-year grace period. The new § 102(b) setting forth exceptions to § 102(a)'s patent prohibition based on prior art has been explained a bit earlier. Section 102(b) has two categories. The first relates to direct or indirect disclosures by the inventor (or a joint inventor) not more than one year prior to the effective filing date. The second category of exceptions relates to direct or indirect disclosures by the inventor (or a related party) in published applications and issued patents, which are deemed prior art under § 102(a)(2).

CHAPTER 8
NON-OBVIOUSNESS

I. INTRODUCTION

In addition to being novel, an invention must be non-obvious, that is, a sufficient advance beyond the collective knowledge in the art to warrant an exclusive right. Novelty mandates that the invention cannot already be expressly or inherently disclosed to the public. An invention, however, might be strictly new in the sense that it did not exist in its entirety before the invention, but still be essentially the same as prior technology. Exclusive rights are not necessary nor offered to encourage the creation of obvious variations. Obviousness, therefore, compares the invention to the prior art to determine whether a single or, most often, multiple references would have led a person of ordinary skill in the art to formulate the claimed invention at the time of invention.

Some combinations of old prior art are very inventive and worthy of an exclusive right. In fact, inventions are very often combinations of elements already in the prior art. These combinations are not necessarily obvious. Rather the obviousness inquiry requires a factual assessment of the prior art compared to the invention as a whole. Pre-AIA § 103(a) sets forth the traditional statutory test:

> A patent may not be obtained though the invention is not identically disclosed or described as set forth in section 102 of this title, if the differences between the subject matter

> sought to be patented and the prior art are such that the subject matter as a whole would have been obvious at the time the invention was made to a person having ordinary skill in the art to which said subject matter pertains. Patentability shall not be negatived by the manner in which the invention was made.

Although the Leahy-Smith America Invents Act (AIA) altered the language, the changes primarily relate to amending the statute's focus on the "claimed invention" as well as the "effective filing date." The practical differences, if any, will likely be sorted out in the coming years.

Each phrase of this statute contains a vital part of the obviousness test. To begin with, the statute refers to inventions that are "not identically disclosed or described as set forth in section 102." This phrase clarifies that non-obviousness is a requirement beyond novelty. Accordingly, an innovation may be novel yet still unpatentable because it is obvious.

The statute next refers to "the differences between the subject matter sought to be patented and the prior art." (Again, the AIA language is that "the differences between the *claimed invention* and the prior art.") This passage requires a factual comparison between the claimed invention, that is, "the subject matter sought to be patented," and the prior art. As discussed earlier, a printed publication, patent, or any other form of information specified in § 102 defines the prior art categories. Although failing to anticipate a claimed invention, these prior art references nonetheless count as part of the ongoing patentability equation as the critical components of an obviousness analysis.

After identification of the prior art, the obviousness inquiry weighs, as a factual matter, the *differences* between the claimed invention and the prior art. Assessing the significance of these differences requires great judgment. With some inventions, a very slight difference—a slight shift in the angle of entry or in molecular structure—can greatly distinguish the invention from the prior art and greatly advance the scientific field. *See Eibel Process Co. v. Minn. & Ontario Paper Co.*, 261 U.S. 45 (1923). With other inventions, seemingly large changes—such as the key to triggering a gene to express itself or the isolation and sequencing of a gene for encoding a particular protein—still do not distinguish the invention from the prior art because the significant advance was expected by an artisan of ordinary skill. *See In re Kubin*, 561 F.3d 1351 (Fed. Cir. 2009); *In re O'Farrell*, 853 F.2d 894 (Fed. Cir. 1988). Thus, application of the obviousness test, though easily explained in a paragraph or two, may only be applied confidently after years of scientific and legal experience.

The statute specifically requires application of the obviousness test to the claimed invention "as a whole." This instruction ensures that, for new combinations of old elements, an invention cannot be broken down into its constituent parts when comparing it to the scope and content of the prior art. For example, an invention claiming the combination of A, B, and C is not necessarily rendered obvious by finding references showing that A, B, and C were individually known. Without this simple statutory phrase, the value in combining the elements—often a central creative feature—would be inappropriately negated. Simply, "at the time of invention, the inventor's insights, willingness to confront and overcome obstacles, and yes, even serendipity, cannot be discounted." *Ortho-McNeil Pharm., Inc. v. Mylan Lab'ys., Inc.*, 520 F.3d 1358, 1364 (Fed. Cir. 2008).

Very often inventive genius lies in recognizing that a combination of old elements will advance the art. For instance, the best antacid in its class, the billion-dollar pharmaceutical named famotidine and sold under the trademark Pepcid®, was the combination of three molecular elements known in the prior art. *Yamanouchi Pharm. Co. v. Danbury Pharmacal, Inc.*, 231 F.3d 1339 (Fed. Cir. 2000). Although each element of this marvelous invention was already in the prior art, it took researchers many years, great expense, and counterintuitive inventiveness to discover this unique new combination. Without the "as a whole" requirement, the Patent Office and courts would be tempted to parse the invention into its three known molecular components, use the invention as a retrospective "recipe" or "blueprint" for obviousness, locate each component in the prior art, and consequently reject the advance as obvious.

The statute next provides the succinct legal test for patentability in this section, reciting that the inquiry turns on whether the claimed invention "would have been obvious." This legal test sounds simple but is difficult to apply. Sometimes the non-obviousness is referred to "inventiveness," and other countries often have an analogous test called the "inventive step" requirement. The non-obviousness requirement creates an unpatentable zone around the state of the art, proscribing persons in the art from obtaining exclusive rights to routine or trivial improvements to an art.

Finally, the statute evaluates obviousness "at the time the invention was made." Like the "as a whole" requirement, this aspect of the test is both difficult and essential. This temporal rule prevents hindsight—a particularly insidious phenomenon that uses the inventor's own work and disclosure as a blueprint or roadmap against its own validity. As noted earlier, inventions very often combine existing elements in new and productive ways. After the invention, this combination may appear self-evident because the constituent elements were already known. This type of analysis, however, evinces hindsight, or using the new combination to identify its preexisting components.

To prevent hindsight from threatening the patentability of almost every invention, the legal test deliberately propels the evaluator back to the time before the invention. The Patent Office examiner or court must forget that claimed invention took place when evaluating and comparing the scope and content of the prior art with the claimed invention. Casting oneself back to before the invention—a self-induced amnesia—is hardly easy. The invention often colors our perception of the art field and sometimes even the vocabulary of the new area.

Lastly, the obviousness inquiry relies upon the objective lens of a hypothetical person, much like the reasonable and prudent person in tort law. This hypothetical person is "a person having ordinary skill in the art to which said subject matter pertains" (or, in the AIA vernacular, "a person having ordinary skill in the art to which the claimed invention pertains"). This objectivity prevents the obviousness inquiry from being clouded with the decision maker's own knowledge, skill, and intellect. Notably, the ordinarily skilled artisan is neither the inventor, who may have extraordinary skill in the art, nor a novice, who may have only minimal technical knowledge. Obviousness is thus an objective test to assess the worthiness of the technical advance to receive a patent. The inquiry depends on factual differences between the claimed invention and prior art at the time of the invention as understood by one of ordinary skill in the art.

Fields populated with the highly skilled practitioners—such as the satellite communications industry—thus might require a more stringent standard for patentability. *See In re Rouffet*, 149 F.3d 1350, 1356–57 (Fed. Cir. 1998) (noting the "lofty skill level for ordinary artisans" in that field). While courts generally speak of the need for determining the skill in the art, even the plentiful case law of the Federal Circuit does not routinely produce cases that turn solely on the level of skill in the art. Nonetheless, at least in theory, nearly everything would be patentable in a field where everyone is a dullard, while almost nothing would be patentable in a field where the ordinary level of skill requires a

Nobel prize. In fact, Albert Einstein worked in the Swiss patent office. If he had performed examinations using his own understanding as the standard, it would be easy to imagine him tossing a week's worth of applications over his shoulder as obvious in a few minutes and then returning to writing his theory of relativity.

II. HISTORY OF PATENT LAW'S "CROWN JEWEL"

The lengthy historical development of the "novelty-plus" test suggests the difficulty in framing the right measure of inventiveness sufficient to warrant an exclusive right. During the first 60 years, patentability rested principally on novelty and utility. In fact, the 1952 Patent Act established the first statutory requirement for patentability beyond novelty and utility. Prior to 1952, courts developed "negative rules" for determining patentability, which prevented patent protection for mere changes in material, proportion, or form over existing technology or mere combinations of known mechanisms.

The first recognition of a need for a measure of inventiveness—as well as its doctrinal moorings—came in *Hotchkiss v. Greenwood*, 52 U.S. (11 How.) 248 (1851). Dealing with a purported invention that merely fashioned a common door knob out of a material (ceramics) that had recently become more amenable to new applications, the Court stated that only "inventions" were patentable. The Court then elaborated that new technology only constituted an invention when it transcends the everyday or routine efforts of a skilled mechanic. The ceramic doorknob did not qualify.

Although foreshadowing the objective person of ordinary skill in the art, the early *Hotchkiss* decision focused on the ingenuity or "inventiveness" of the subject matter without a neutral standard to distinguish the unpatentable improvements of a skilled mechanic from the patentable advances of an inventor. With the focus on the invention, this test invited courts to use hindsight. If the inventive subject matter impressed the court, it received approval as being the "product of an inventor." If the subject matter did not evoke a "gee whiz" reaction, it was merely a mechanic's handiwork. By its very nature, this test invited insidious hindsight.

After percolating for roughly a century, the *Hotchkiss* test for patentability evolved to embrace slightly different terminology: did the subject matter exhibit "a flash of creative genius"? *Cuno Eng'g Corp. v. Automatic Devices Corp.*, 314 U.S. 84, 91 (1941). This verbal construct was just the hindsight reaction analysis in slightly more demanding terminology. This stringent patentability standard caused Justice Jackson to comment: "[T]he only patent that is valid is one which this Court has not been able to get its hands on." *Jungersen v. Ostby & Barton Co.*, 335 U.S. 560, 572 (1949) (Jackson, J., dissenting).

The hindsight-reaction test reached its high-water mark in *Great A. & P. Tea Co. v. Supermarket Equipment Corp.*, 340 U.S. 147 (1950). The invention was a supermarket counter that combined several features to improve the efficiency and speed of the check-out counter, including a conveyor belt. Beyond a "flash of genius," the Supreme Court required some synergistic effect in the invention. The invention had to surprise or amaze beyond the sum of its parts. Otherwise the new technology was merely the combination of known elements. The Supreme Court did not seem to acknowledge that nearly every invention would be a combination or reconstruction of available and known elements. If characterized as a "mere combination," a great deal of inventive subject matter in this era lacked sufficient "genius" or "synergy."

In desperation, the Patent Office and the patent bar turned to Congress. The result was the 1952 Patent Act. The 1952 Act sets forth the objective test for obviousness. Patentability hinged on factual evidence about the likelihood that a person of ordinary skill in the art would have found the subject matter as a whole obvious at the time of the invention.

The Supreme Court did not interpret that Act until nearly a decade and a half later. *Graham v. John Deere Co.*, 383 U.S. 1 (1966); *Calmar, Inc. v. Cook Chem. Co.*, 380 U.S. 949 (1965); *United States v. Adams*, 383 U.S. 39 (1966). Then, after upholding the objective factual analysis of the new § 103, the Supreme Court slipped again into its hindsight reaction methodology in *Anderson's-Black Rock, Inc. v. Pavement Salvage Co.*, 396 U.S. 57 (1969), and *Sakraida v. Ag Pro, Inc.*, 425 U.S. 273 (1976). These cases reinvigorated the synergism test employed prior to the 1952 Act, bringing along with it the use of hindsight reasoning to find patents invalid as a matter of course.[1]

With the various circuits unable to discern the uniform test for inventiveness, Congress again stepped in. This time, in 1982, the legislature created the United States Court of Appeals for the Federal Circuit. The Federal Circuit quickly opted to follow the Supreme Court's more responsible *Graham* test. *See, e.g., Chore-Time Equip., Inc. v. Cumberland Corp.*, 713 F.2d 774 (Fed. Cir. 1983). The objective standard for obviousness thereafter prevailed nationwide.

In its obviousness jurisprudence, the Federal Circuit placed a particular emphasis on the "teaching, suggestion, motivation" (TSM) test to prevent hindsight, *In re Rouffet*, 149 F.3d 1350 (Fed. Cir. 1998), and secondary considerations as part of the obviousness test, *Hybritech, Inc. v. Monoclonal Antibodies, Inc.*, 802 F.2d 1367 (Fed. Cir. 1986) (secondary considerations are not merely "icing on the cake"). Over time, some Federal Circuit opinions applied the motivation to combine test rigidly to require reference to a specific prior art teaching that suggested the combination without taking into account the creativity and common sense of a person having ordinary skill in the art. *See, e.g., In re Lee*, 277 F.3d 1338 (Fed. Cir. 2002). One of these instances, *KSR Int'l Co. v. Teleflex, Inc.*, 550 U.S. 398

---

1 The Supreme Court's decision in *KSR Int'l Co. v. Teleflex, Inc.*, 550 U.S. 398 (2007), attempted to reconcile *Anderson's-Black Rock* and *Sakraida* with the traditional *Graham* test for obviousness.

(2007), brought the issue of obviousness back to the Supreme Court. In *KSR*, the Supreme Court reversed the Federal Circuit. In its lengthy unanimous opinion, the Court reaffirmed the basic principles enunciated by *Graham* and urged an "expansive and flexible approach" to obviousness in general. 550 U.S. at 415.

III. PRIOR ART

The obviousness test rests on the foundation of an accurate and complete picture of the prior art. Section 102 usually—but not exclusively—defines the categories that supply that art. Statements and admissions by the patentee or applicant, for instance, provide another less common, even if potent, source of knowledge. The broad categories of "printed publications" and "patents," however, do not narrow the range of prior art to the knowledge most pertinent to the claimed invention. Thus, beyond the simple qualification of falling within a § 102 category, a prior art candidate for the obviousness calculus must also be "analogous" to the claimed subject matter. A prior art candidate is "analogous" if it is sufficiently related to the claimed invention to fairly count as part of the obviousness equation.

A. § 102

With only two exceptions (the analogous art requirement and the joint venture exclusion), the rule defining prior art is simple: art that applies to the novelty determination also applies for obviousness. Thus, the same references relevant for determining novelty often apply as well in an obviousness inquiry. For example, a patent or printed publication commonly serves as a reference for obviousness.

The first-to-invent regime includes a limited exception, however: a reference under § 102(a) does not constitute prior art under § 103 if the applicant had earlier possessed an obvious variation of the reference. *In re Stryker*, 435 F.2d 1340, 1341–42 (CCPA 1971). On the other hand, consistent with the general rule, a patent filed but not issued before the filing of another patent may serve as so-called "secret" prior art under first-to-invent's § 102(e) and § 102(g). *Hazeltine Research, Inc. v. Brenner*, 382 U.S. 252, 255–56 (1965); *In re Bass*, 474 F.2d 1276, 1286–87 (CCPA 1973). Thus, a prior invention—even if unpatented and not disclosed until after the priority date of a patent—may serve as an obviousness reference under pre-AIA's § 102(g)(2). Left unchecked, this would even mean that related work by inventors employed by the same company could render subsequent work obvious. Because of this clear inequity, first-to-invent's § 103—discussed below—prevents some provisions of § 102 from creating prior art in limited circumstances.

Pre-AIA § 102(f) presents another situation in which prior art for obviousness purposes is not necessarily public. This section bars a patent on subject matter obtained, that is, derived, from someone else. Section 102(f) notably applies not only to public disclosures but also to private communications. *See OddzOn Prods., Inc. v. Just Toys, Inc.*, 122 F.3d 1396, 1401–02 (Fed. Cir. 1997).

The transition of § 102 to a first-inventor-to-file regime retains some of these doctrines. For example, § 102(a) defines prior art as including patents, printed publications, public uses, sales, and other publicly available information. The AIA's §§ 102(b) & 102(c) evoke the protections to applicants formerly provided by pre-AIA's § 103(c).

1. Analogous Art

The general § 102 categories are broader than the prior art genuinely relevant to the obviousness equation. The applicable prior art, however, must come from the "analogous art"—a technical area judged sufficiently germane to the claimed invention's field. An applicant or inventor is really only presumed to have access to all technical knowledge within a field reasonably related to the inventive subject matter. Thus, prior art is analogous (and thus available for obviousness) if it is either in the same field of endeavor as the inventive subject matter (regardless of the problem addressed by the invention) or reasonably pertinent to the particular problem addressed by the invention. *In re Clay*, 966 F.2d 656, 658–59 (Fed. Cir. 1992).

In *Clay*, a case illustrating the analogousness requirement, the Federal Circuit found prior art non-analogous to the claimed invention. The claimed invention recovered residual oil in storage tanks when the outlet port was located above the bottom of the tank. The invention filled the tanks with gel to bring the oil up to the drainage pipe level. The prior art extracted more oil from *natural* rock formations by filling formation anomalies with a gel to improve oil flow and production. The Federal Circuit defined the problem addressed by the invention narrowly. If the Federal Circuit had defined the problem as filling dead spaces to improve petroleum extraction, then the similarities between the prior art and the invention might have resulted in obviousness. The Federal Circuit, however, confined the problem to extracting oil from man-made tanks. Thus, despite similarities between the claims and the prior art, the rock formation prior art was not pertinent to the oil tank inventive problem.

Another picture of analogousness comes in *Innovention Toys, LLC v. MGA Entertainment, Inc.*, 637 F.3d 1314 (Fed. Cir. 2011). In that case, the Federal Circuit vacated the district court's conclusion of non-analogousness. The claim covered a laser-based strategy board game. The players moved and rotated mirrored pieces, deflecting laser beams in an effort to strike the opponent's key playing piece with the beam. The asserted prior art was a video game called "Laser Chess," which, as the name suggests, depicts a virtual board game that involved moving pieces and lasers, and whose goal is to win by striking the opponent's king piece with a laser beam. The Federal Circuit held that, because the claims were directed to a "board game"—without specifying the physical or electronic nature of the game—Laser Chess could be analogous prior art even though in electronic (not physical) form. Indeed, "the "[b]asic game elements remain the same regardless of the medium in which they are implemented." *Id.* at 1322–23.

The analogous art test is really a court-created fairness doctrine. The law will not hold an inventor accountable for prior art far removed from the inventive subject matter either by field or by pertinence. With "libraries before laboratories" as the governing principle, the analogous art test ensures that only relevant sections of the library apply for obviousness.

In reality, the analogousness requirement rarely limits the scope of prior art. This threshold requirement for prior art is probably best understood as a corollary of the § 103 principle that only knowledge accessible to one of ordinary skill in the inventive field renders subject matter obvious. *See In re Klein*, 647 F.3d 1343, 1348 (Fed. Cir. 2011).

2. Joint Research Exception

As briefly described above, first-to-invent's § 103(c) states:

> Subject matter developed by another person, which qualifies as prior art only under one or more of subsections (e), (f), and (g) of section 102 of this title, shall not preclude patentability under this section where the subject matter and the claimed invention were, at the time the invention was made, owned by the same person or subject to an obligation of assignment to the same person.

Accordingly, pre-AIA § 103(c) exempts § 102(e), (f), and (g) art from an obviousness inquiry where the inventions were subject to a common assignment. In practice, the assignment condition usually means that the inventions and the prior art were the product of the same research team or facility. Subsection (c) contains narrow limits: If, for instance, a reference is otherwise available as prior art, such as under § 102(a) or (b), it remains available for obviousness.

This subsection addresses a specific problem involving research teams. Any corporate or university research team likely features several different scientists working together. A team might make several inventions over a period of years. The applications for the various team inventions, however, may list in each case a different combination of inventors. Thus, although the entire team contributed to the advances, the team's first inventions will serve as prior art against the team's later inventions because each invention technically lists a different "inventor." Without first-to-invent's § 103(c), the rules of prior art would discourage collaborative research. *See In re Bass*, 474 F.2d 1276 (CCPA 1973). Under this section, the team—in essence, the inventor—does not create prior art against itself. The AIA's § 102(b) espouses a similar principle to exclude certain prior art under § 102(a)(2).

B. PRIOR ART BY ADMISSION

A second, less common, category for prior art occurs when the patent applicant (or patentee) identifies the work of another as prior art, regardless of whether it actually falls within a statutory category. This non-statutory category—admissions—also contains a limited exception analogous to, but narrower than, the pre-AIA's § 103(c). Under that exception, work by the same inventive entity does not qualify as prior art unless falling within one of the categories enumerated in § 102. *Riverwood Int'l Corp. v. R.A. Jones & Co.*, 324 F.3d 1346 (Fed. Cir. 2003).

In the absence of that limited exception, if the specification (including the drawings) identifies some technology as prior art, that admitted prior art is eligible for consideration in an obviousness determination. Similarly, a claim drafted in *Jepson* format—a format that recites the invention as an improvement on the subject matter identified in the preamble—sweeps the subject matter in the preamble into the prior art.

IV. THE SUPREME COURT TRILOGY

While the 1952 Act codified the ultimate patentability test now called non-obviousness, the proper understanding of § 103 remained unclear until Supreme Court examined it in a trilogy of cases in 1966: *Graham v. John Deere*, *Cook Chemical*, and *Adams*. These long-awaited cases—it took an eternity of 13 years before the Court addressed the new statute—are the most important to understanding obviousness. In fact, they are among the most important patent cases of the modern era. Certainly the Federal Circuit deserves praise for elevating the trilogy to that lofty status, and the Supreme Court similarly acknowledged that prominence for these cases: "*Graham* . . . set out a framework for applying the statutory language of § 103." *KSR*, 550 U.S. at 406.

In *Graham v. John Deere Co.*, 383 U.S. 1 (1966), the Supreme Court explained that obviousness is a legal conclusion buttressed by four factual inquiries. The Court specified these factual underpinnings:

(1) the scope and content of the prior art;

(2) differences between the prior art and the claims at issue;

(3) the judgment of obviousness to a person of ordinary skill in the pertinent art at the time of invention examining the invention as a whole; and

(4) objective indicia of non-obviousness (also called secondary considerations), such as commercial success, long felt but unsolved needs, and failure of others.

Although giving prominence to the first three as the background for determining obviousness, the Court also explained that the secondary considerations are relevant indicators of non-obviousness. The Court recognized, furthermore, the inherent difficulties in determining obviousness:

> What is obvious is not a question upon which there is likely to be uniformity of thought in every factual context. The difficulties, however, are comparable to those encountered daily by the courts in such frames of reference as negligence and scienter, and should be amenable to a case-by-case development.

Graham, 383 U.S. at 18.

The *Graham* case began when Graham sued the John Deere Company for infringing the '798 patent on a plow with a spring clamp. The defendant questioned the validity of the patent in light of an earlier patent, the '811 patent, to the same inventor, Graham. The prior art patent was the same plow with one variation—a hinge plate was moved from one side of the shank to the other. This seemingly slight change, however, meant that the shank would not break when it hit a stone—a significant improvement in the performance of the plow. Graham had successfully weathered validity challenges, including a prior appeal to a regional circuit, and had asserted his patent against other infringers before this case. Nonetheless the Supreme Court upheld a determination that the '798 was invalid.

In reaching this conclusion, the Court applied, for the first time in Supreme Court jurisprudence, the objective test of § 103 with its factual underpinnings. After examining the differences over prior art carefully, the Court rather abruptly skips some other factual underpinnings and reaches a conclusion of obviousness: "Certainly a person having ordinary skill in the prior art, given the fact that the flex in the shank could be utilized more effectively if allowed to run the entire length of the shank, would immediately see that the thing to do was what Graham did, i.e., invert the shank and the hinge plate." 383 U.S. at 25. Although quick to resolve some factual issues on appeal (such as the level of ordinary skill and the likelihood that an artisan would even recognize the problem, let alone "immediately" see the solution) and perhaps too hesitant to examine the secondary considerations, the Court still set a landmark standard for neutral application of the obviousness test.

In *Calmar v. Cook Chemical*, the Court similarly invalidated the Scoggin '943 patent on a leak-proof cap for a pump-sprayer insecticide dispenser. The prior art that the Supreme Court found most important to the obviousness inquiry, the Livingstone '480 patent, had not been considered by the patent examiner who granted Scoggin's patent. After noting that the '943 patent involved only "small and quite non-technical mechanical differences," the Court observed that those "differences were rendered apparent" by the Livingstone prior art patent. 383 U.S. at 36. The Court, however, emphasized that obviousness depended on "prior art as it stood at the time of the invention," *id.*, thus eschewing the history of hindsight that bedeviled prior validity determinations at the Court.

After *Cook Chemical*, the Court wisely considered a third case that upheld an important patent under the new standard. The United States used the battery technology featured in this case during World War II, and Adams, the inventor, sued for infringement. In *United States v. Adams*, the patent claimed a battery whose electrolyte, or battery fluid, was water. Adams did not, however, claim this important distinguishing feature of his invention. Reading the claims in light of the specification, the Court nonetheless determined "the stated object" of the invention included a "water-activated cell." 383 U.S. at 49.

In fact, this feature plays the central role in one of the great stories of patent litigation lore: Adams's attorney arose before the Supreme Court, took a drink from his glass of water, and then dropped a tiny Adams battery into the glass. The inventive battery immediately lit a tiny light, and it continued to shine throughout the argument. Adams's attorney later said that he knew he had won the case when the Justices kept their eyes on the tiny light throughout the remainder of the argument.

The Supreme Court's *Adams* opinion invokes several secondary considerations in favor of non-obviousness. In particular, the Court observed that the record disclosed the skepticism of experts before the invention, the endorsement of experts after disclosure, and unexpected results. In a case that featured a great deal of prior art very close to the invention, these secondary considerations evidently played an important, perhaps even dispositive, role.

The Supreme Court's more recent *KSR* pronouncement adds significance to *Graham* and the rest of the trilogy. A review of the Federal Circuit's obviousness jurisprudence brings *KSR* into better focus.

V. THE FEDERAL CIRCUIT

While *Graham* set forth the basic test for obviousness, the Federal Circuit refined that test in its later evolution of the doctrine. In particular, the Federal Circuit focused the test on evidence suggesting or motivating the combination or modification of prior art to render an invention obvious. While increasing vigilance against hindsight bias, the Federal Circuit also placed an emphasis on objective indicia of non-obviousness. A flexible, nonrigid application of the teaching, suggestion, or motivation test remains an important tool in determining non-obviousness. *See, e.g.*, *Examination Guidelines Update: Developments in the Obviousness Inquiry After KSR v. Teleflex*, 75 Fed. Reg. 53,643 (Sept. 1, 2010).

A. TEACHING, SUGGESTION, OR MOTIVATION TO COMBINE

Under § 103, the comparison of the prior art with the claimed invention must be done "as a whole." Thus, the analysis cannot be done piecemeal by parsing the claimed invention into its constituent parts and finding an analog for each separate feature of the new combination. In *KSR*, the Supreme Court reiterated the importance of this "as a whole" methodology: "[A] patent composed of several elements is not proved obvious merely by demonstrating that each of its elements was, independently, known in the prior art." 550 U.S. at 418.

This essential "as a whole" provision suggests a methodology that focuses on the factors that would have motivated one of ordinary skill in the art at the time of the invention to make the new combination as a routine or obvious next step in the relevant art. This method distills to an essential finding supported by concrete evidence that an ordinarily skilled artisan confronted with the same problems as the inventor would have selected the elements from the most relevant prior art and combined them to create the claimed invention. In practical terms, therefore, this test seeks concrete evidence of some teaching, suggestion, or motivation to modify or combine prior art elements without using the inventor's own disclosure or patent claim as a blueprint. This point has special significance. If that evidence is to remain untainted by hindsight, it must date back to a time before the invention.

Although a finding of motivation was often coterminous or synonymous with the legal conclusion of obviousness, this tool was just an identification of the types of evidence that apply in the obviousness calculus. Indeed, the Federal Circuit treated the inquiry for a motivation or suggestion to combine or modify the prior art as a question of fact. This evidence of teachings, suggestions, or motivations to combine references appears in three different forms: the nature of the problem may itself suggest a combination, *Ruiz v. A.B. Chance Co.*, 357 F.3d 1270, 1276 (Fed. Cir. 2004); the teachings of the pertinent references may suggest a combination, *In re Rouffet*, 149 F.3d 1350, 1355 (Fed. Cir. 1998); or the customary knowledge of those ordinarily skilled in the art may suggest a combination. *National Steel Car v. Canadian Pacific Railway, Ltd.*, 357 F.3d 1319, 1337 (Fed. Cir. 2004). The Federal Circuit cautioned, however, against unsupported use of the customary knowledge category. In reversing the PTO's conclusion of obviousness, the court explained:

> [The Board] relied upon the high level of skill in the art to provide the necessary motivation. The Board did not, however, explain what specific understanding or technological principle within the knowledge of one of ordinary skill in the art would have suggested the combination. Instead, the Board merely invoked the high level of skill in the field of art. If such a rote invocation could suffice to supply a motivation to combine, the more sophisticated scientific fields would rarely, if ever, experience a patentable technical advance.

Rouffet, 149 F.3d at 1357. Thus to ensure relevant, accurate, and reliable TSM evidence, the Federal Circuit in some cases discounted the customary knowledge category and instead required some actual reference from before the invention to support the suggestion. *See, e.g.*, *In re Lee*, 277 F.3d at 1343–44. In fact, the Federal Circuit in its *KSR* opinion had adopted this strict type of reasoning.

B. *KSR*

KSR featured rather simple technology—an adjustable throttle pedal for an automobile. Teleflex owned U.S. Patent No. 6,237,565 (Engelgau), which combined an adjustable pedal with an electronic sensor to measure the pedal depression. Adjustable pedals, of course, make the throttle more accessible to drivers of different heights. Electronic sensors on those pedals measure movement without cumbersome mechanical cables. Both of these features were in the prior art: the Asano patent described an adjustable pedal, and the Rixon patent (as modified by the Smith reference) described the particular electronic calibration features of the Engelgau patent. Asano incidentally was not before the PTO when it granted the Engelgau patent.

When Teleflex sued KSR for infringement, the District Court invalidated the Engelgau patent on summary judgment. The Federal Circuit reversed because the trial court had not made specific findings to identify specific evidence of teachings, suggestions, or motivations to combine. The Supreme Court, in turn, reversed the Federal Circuit: "A person having ordinary skill in the art could have combined Asano with a pedal position sensor in a fashion encompassed by claim 4, and would have seen the benefits of doing so." *KSR*, 550 U.S. at 422.

On one level, *KSR* may have only corrected a rather fundamental and simple error by the Federal

Circuit. The error appears right before footnote 3 in the Federal Circuit's opinion:[2]

> In this case, the Asano patent does not address the same problem as the [Engelgau] patent. The objective of the [Engelgau] patent was to design a smaller, less complex, and less expensive electronic pedal assembly. The Asano patent, on the other hand, was directed at solving the "constant ratio problem."

Teleflex, Inc. v. KSR Int'l, Co., 119 Fed. Appx. 282, 288 (Fed. Cir. 2005). This passage shows that the Federal Circuit overlooked the fundamental proposition that obvious variants of prior art references are themselves part of the public domain. A British case makes this point forcibly:

> Anything which is obvious over what is available to the public cannot subsequently be the subject of valid patent protection even if, in practice, few would have bothered looking through the prior art or would have found the particular items relied on. Patents are not granted for the discovery and wider dissemination of public material and what is obvious over it, but only for making new inventions.

Lilly Icos LLC v. Pfizer Ltd., [2000] EWHC Patents 49 at ¶ 62.

---

[2] The error appeared in a nonprecedential opinion that would not have been reviewed, or even seen, by any judges on the Federal Circuit except the three on the panel.

In the context of *KSR*, the Asano teachings and its obvious variants were in the prior art, even if that patent did address a different problem. Therefore the Federal Circuit erred by dismissing Asano. The Supreme Court identified that error in its opinion:

> The second error of the Court of Appeals lay in its assumption that a person of ordinary skill attempting to solve a problem will be led only to those elements of prior art designed to solve the same problem. The primary purpose of Asano was solving the constant ratio problem; so, the court concluded, an inventor considering how to put a sensor on an adjustable pedal would have no reason to consider putting it on the Asano pedal. Common sense teaches, however, that familiar items may have obvious uses beyond their primary purposes, and in many cases a person of ordinary skill will be able to fit the teachings of multiple patents together like pieces of a puzzle.

KSR, 550 U.S. at 420 (citations omitted).

The Supreme Court also condemned the Federal Circuit's "rigid and mandatory" TSM test as a primary source of error: "The obviousness analysis cannot be confined by a formalistic conception of the words teaching, suggestion, and motivation, or by overemphasis on the importance of published articles and the explicit content of issued patents." *KSR*, 550 U.S. at 419. Instead the Supreme Court repeatedly advised that "common sense" would broaden the use of customary knowledge in the obviousness equation. The Court observed, "A person of ordinary skill is also a person of ordinary creativity, not an automaton." *Id.* at 421. Thus, at a minimum, the Supreme Court's decision overruled instances of "rigid" application of the TSM test and broadened use of customary knowledge as an ingredient for obviousness.

At one point in its analysis, the Court observed that the Federal Circuit had also "elaborated a broader conception of the TSM test than was applied" in the decision it reversed. *See id.* Specifically the Court referred to the *DyStar* decision, wherein the Federal Circuit had opined: "Our suggestion test is in actuality quite flexible and not only permits, but *requires*, consideration of common knowledge and common sense." *Id.* at 421 (citing *DyStar Textilfarben GmbH & Co. v. C.H. Patrick Co.*, 464 F.3d 1356, 1367 (Fed. Cir. 2006)). The Court did not expressly endorse this formulation of the TSM test, but hinted that it would be "more consistent" with the Supreme Court's requirements. *Id.* at 422. In sum, the TSM test in its more flexible and expansive form has survived the correction of the *KSR* mistake.

Moreover, with respect to obviousness in general, the Supreme Court rejected any "rigid rule." As the Court counseled, "a court can take account of the inferences and creative steps that a person of ordinary skill in the art would employ." *Id.* at 418.

C. SCRUTINY OF HINDSIGHT

The key reason for the TSM categories of evidence was to ensure that obviousness focuses on events before the time of invention. Hindsight can take many forms. Because an inventor is charged with the knowledge of all prior art, even the venerable Judge Rich once pictured the obviousness decision as engaging the inventor working in his shop with the prior art references hanging on the walls around him. *See In re Winslow*, 365 F.2d 1017, 1020 (CCPA 1966). While this depiction of a hypothetical event is vivid and compelling, it creates an opportunity for a certain form of dangerous hindsight—namely hindsight in selecting the prior art that might hang on the laboratory walls. For example, this image cannot convey that the most pertinent prior art would in fact be hidden and obscured by voluminous amounts of irrelevant art. To visualize inventors with only the most relevant art hanging before their eyes invites insidious hindsight that effectively plucks out the most applicable references from those which are inapplicable or even misleading. The Federal Circuit has abandoned this antiquated visual, relying on the facts and evidence in each case to discern a suggestion or motivation to combine or modify references.

KSR did not ignore the dangers of hindsight: "A factfinder should be aware, of course, of the distortion caused by hindsight bias and must be cautious of arguments reliant on *ex post* reasoning." 550 U.S. at 421. This caution, however, cannot lead to "[r]igid preventative rules." *Id.* Thus, the legal prevention of hindsight, such as rejecting the *Winslow* formulation, also survives *KSR*. "[A] flexible approach to the TSM test prevents hindsight and focuses on evidence before the time of invention without unduly constraining the breadth of knowledge available to one of ordinary skill in the art during the obviousness analysis." *In re Translogic Tech.*, 504 F.3d 1249, 1260 (Fed. Cir. 2007) (citation omitted); *see also Rolls-Royce, PLC v. United Techs. Corp.*, 603 F.3d 1325, 1338 (Fed. Cir. 2010).

D. OBJECTIVE CRITERIA (SECONDARY CONSIDERATIONS)

Objective or so-called secondary considerations remain, of course, germane to the ultimate conclusion of obviousness. Although the legal test of obviousness does not differ between prosecution and litigation, the methodology used by the Patent and Trademark Office provides a useful example of how secondary considerations can affect an obviousness determination. Before reevaluating obviousness by including secondary considerations, a *prima facie* case of obviousness should exist based solely on the first three *Graham* factors. The Federal Circuit explained the dance between applicant and the Office:

> The *prima facie* case is a procedural tool of patent examination, allocating the burdens of going forward as between examiner and applicant. The term "*prima facie*" case refers only to the initial examination step. As discussed in *In re Piasecki*, [745 F.2d 1468, 1472 (Fed. Cir. 1984),] the examiner bears the initial burden, on review of the prior art or on any other ground, of presenting a *prima facie* case of unpatentability. If that burden is met, the burden of coming forward with evidence or argument shifts to the applicant. . . .

> If examination at the initial stage does not produce a *prima facie* case of unpatentability, then without more the applicant is entitled to grant of the patent.
>
> In reviewing the examiner's decision on appeal, the Board must necessarily weigh all of the evidence and argument. An observation by the Board that the examiner made a *prima facie* case is not improper, as long as the ultimate determination of patentability is made on the entire record.

In re Oetiker, 977 F.2d 1443, 1445 (Fed. Cir. 1992) (citations omitted). Thus, obviousness before the Patent Office divides into two phases—one with and one without secondary considerations. Importantly, in the latter phase (post-*prima facie* case) with secondary considerations, the inquiry mandates that all evidence, including the differences between the scope and content of the prior art, be reevaluated before concluding that the claimed invention is in fact obvious.

These secondary considerations are secondary in name only; the Federal Circuit often views them as essential to the obviousness inquiry. *See Crocs, Inc. v. Int'l Trade Comm'n*, 598 F.3d 1294, 1310 (Fed. Cir. 2010). As such, the more apt nomenclature is to call them "objective indicia." Empirical evidence, such as the reaction of the marketplace and competitors, provides much firmer ground than a purely hypothetical exercise in the courtroom.

In fact, objective indicia of non-obviousness can successfully overcome a *prima facie* case of obviousness. *Transocean Offshore Deepwater Drilling, Inc. v. Maersk Drilling USA, Inc.*, 699 F.3d 1340, 1354–55 (Fed. Cir. 2012). In *Transocean*, the claims covered a "dual-activity" drilling rig equipped with two stations that performed complementary functions to improve drilling efficiency. The Federal Circuit had already held—in a previous appeal in the same case—that two prior art references, Horn and Lund, together established a *prima facie* case of obviousness.

In this appeal, however, the Federal Circuit considered whether the record supported the jury's finding of non-obviousness. The court explained, "Few cases present such extensive objective evidence of non-obviousness." *Id.* at 1354. "This [ ] is precisely the sort of case where the objective evidence establishes that an invention appearing to have been obvious in light of the prior art was not." *Id.* at 1355 (citation and quotation marks omitted). The objective evidence was detailed and persuasive and related to six separate types of objective indicia. *See id.* at 1349–54.

Objective indicia must bear some relationship to the claimed invention, that is, there must be a nexus between the claimed invention and the proffered objective evidence. In the case of commercial success, for example, the applicant or patentee must show that the success is the result of innovative claims, not merely the result of effective marketing strategies or general popularity of like products in the prior art.

Although the Supreme Court identified a few examples of objective indicia, creative litigants over the years have added a few more. As would be expected, not all objective indicia are equal, because some show non-obviousness to a greater extent than others. The following is a non-exhaustive list in approximate order of the strongest to the weakest evidence showing non-obviousness: skepticism, unexpected results, long-felt need, prior failure, licenses, copying, and commercial success. Note that the most potent, relevant indicia occur less frequently and share a greater connection to the claimed invention than the least potent.

First, skepticism of experts in the art expressed before the inventor's work bolsters the case for non-obviousness. *Burlington Indus., Inc. v. Quigg*, 822 F.2d 1581, 1582–83 (Fed. Cir. 1987). Because this evidence typically arises before the invention, it has particular persuasive value, but it is extremely rare that experts will "rule out" or criticize a line of research or inventive concept that later revolutionizes their field.

Second, unexpected results—in one form similar to the now-defunct synergism test for non-obviousness—can include evidence of surprise and commendation by those skilled in the art upon learning of the invention. *Specialty Composites v. Cabot Corp.*, 845 F.2d 981, 991 (Fed. Cir. 1988). In another form, unexpected results can be documentary evidence that exceeds the expectations of skilled artisans. This evidence can suffer from hindsight, because it may appear after the invention, which perhaps changed expectations. Expectations are inherently subjective, and litigation can influence the nature and intensity of those expectations. Still, unexpected results play such an important role in chemical obviousness cases that they remain near the top of the list.

Third, a long-felt need for a solution to a particular problem also supports non-obviousness. *Tex. Instruments, Inc. v. U.S. Int'l Trade Comm'n*, 988 F.2d 1165 (Fed. Cir. 1993). Often, however, the expressions of long-felt need do not correlate exactly with the problem solved by the invention. An invention can sometimes create its own market, meaning that the invention identified a problem which others had not recognized at all. In any event, the nexus requirement, of course, assures that the long-felt need correlates with the problem solved by the invention.

Fourth, prior failures by other inventors certainly supplement the case for non-obviousness. *Heidelberger Druckmaschinen AG v. Hantscho Commercial Prods. Inc.*, 21 F.3d 1068, 1071–72 (Fed. Cir. 1994). But prior failures are not helpful if the person who allegedly failed was actually working on a slightly different problem or had little motivation or desire to succeed due to satisfaction with the extant technology. *In re Sneed*, 710 F.2d 1544, 1550 (Fed. Cir. 1983). Evidence of other failures rarely relates to exactly the same problem addressed by the invention. Again the nexus requirement tries to assure this correlation.

Fifth, extensive licensing supports non-obviousness, because it shows that the industry respects the invention. At the same time, however, a long period of no infringement may show that the licenses are truly motivated by a desire to avoid the costs of litigation, rather than by respect for the non-obviousness of the invention. *Pentec, Inc. v. Graphic Controls Corp.*, 776 F.2d 309, 316 (Fed. Cir. 1985). In a healthy market, moreover, many licenses are part of a larger cross-licensing arrangement that undermines the nexus between a particular license in a large package and the claimed features it licenses.

Sixth, copying—particularly when done by the accused infringer without concomitantly copying other subject matter—also can show that the invention is non-obvious. *Advanced Display Sys., Inc. v. Kent State Univ.*, 212 F.3d 1272, 1285–86 (Fed. Cir. 2000). But copying is not persuasive in all contexts. For example, copying is not reliable evidence of non-obviousness where the accused product is not identical to the claimed invention and the accused infringer vigorously denies infringement. While copying is a high form of flattery, it may have been done solely because the copyist reasonably believes that the patent is not infringed, invalid or unenforceable.

And seventh, commercial success may, in some cases, show non-obviousness. *Hybritech Inc. v. Monoclonal Antibodies, Inc.*, 802 F.2d 1367, 1382 (Fed. Cir. 1986). In fact, commercial success includes the sales of infringers as well as those of the patentee and its licensees. *Syntex (U.S.A.) Inc. v. Paragon Optical Inc.*, 7 USPQ2d 1001 (D. Ariz. 1987). But the commercial success could be due to any number of market factors, including superior business acumen or marketing. Accordingly, the nexus requirement serves as an effective check on evidence of commercial success. Even though it is often viewed with some skepticism and has problems with causation, commercial success is often presented to show non-obviousness, because sales data are easy to acquire.

While those are the categories most commonly invoked to show non-obviousness, an accused infringer may introduce an objective criterion of its own to support a case of obviousness. Evidence of contemporaneous independent—that is, not based on derivation—invention shows that other could (and did) invent the same subject matter. It provides real evidence showing persons of ordinary skill in the art would have found the claimed subject matter obvious at the time of invention.

KSR does not disturb the role of secondary considerations, but instead reaffirms that "Graham set forth a broad inquiry and invited courts, where appropriate, to look at any secondary considerations that would prove instructive." 550 U.S. at 415. In the context of that case, the Court noted that "Teleflex has shown no secondary factors to dislodge the determination that claim 4 is obvious." 550 U.S. at 426.

E. OBVIOUSNESS "TRAPS"

Because obviousness is an exceptionally slippery doctrine that proves elusive to master, there are a few admonitions that, if heeded, aid one's understanding of the requirement.

1. Standard of Proof

The standard of proof of invalidity is higher for an issued patent being litigated in federal district court in comparison to the standard that applies for a pending patent application or a patent at issue in a PTAB post-grant proceeding (*see* Chapter 11). Prior to issuance (or during PTAB post-grant proceedings), the factual predicates need only be established by a preponderance of evidence.

But once a patent issues, that patent enjoys a presumption of validity in litigation under 35 U.S.C. § 282. *Microsoft Corp. v. i4i Ltd. P'ship*, 564 U.S. 91, 100–01 (2011). Accordingly, in litigation the patent's invalidity must be proven by clear and convincing evidence. This heightened standard of proof stems from respect for the administrative and scientific expertise of the PTO. *Am. Hoist & Derrick Co. v. Sowa & Sons, Inc.*, 725 F.2d 1350, 1359–60 (Fed. Cir. 1984). Even so, this rationale does not apply to questions or prior art that were not considered by the examiner.

The Supreme Court's *KSR* decision seemed to call into question the presumption's universal application: "We nevertheless think it appropriate to note that the rationale underlying the presumption—

that the PTO, in its expertise, has approved the claim—seems much diminished here." *KSR*, 550 U.S. at 426. But this should only result in an appropriate jury instruction, not the total elimination of the statutory requirement:

> Simply put, if the PTO did not have all material facts before it, its considered judgment may lose significant force. And, concomitantly, the challenger's burden to persuade the jury of its invalidity defense by clear and convincing evidence may be easier to sustain. In this respect, although we have no occasion to endorse any particular formulation, we note that a jury instruction on the effect of new evidence can, and when requested, most often should, be given. When warranted, the jury may be instructed to consider that it has heard evidence that the PTO had no opportunity to evaluate before granting the patent.

Microsoft Corp., 564 U.S. at 111 (citation omitted).

2. Manner of Invention Irrelevant

The final sentence of pre-AIA § 103(a) indicates that "[p]atentability shall not be negatived by the manner in which the invention was made." (Under the new § 103, this requirement is changed slightly to "[p]atentability shall not be negated by the manner in which the invention was made.") This language overruled the "flash of genius" test. One of the weaknesses of the old Supreme Court regime was that it discounted a methodical, yet plodding, path of exhaustive research and development. The "shall not be negatived" phrase placed the plodding research effort on a level footing with inventions inspired by a "flash." Thus, the statute offers its awards to accidental or lucky inventors, even though such incentives had nothing to do with the development of the invention. Thus, the inventor's motivation and path to the claimed invention are simply irrelevant to the judgment of a person of ordinary skill in the art at the time of the invention.

A corollary to this statutory prohibition suggests no special rule for combination inventions. New combinations neither enjoy an advantage nor suffer heightened obstacles to obviousness. Rather, obviousness of combinations depends, to a large extent, on the presence or absence of a teaching, motivation, or suggestion to combine bits and pieces of the prior art (as flexibly applied) to create the claimed invention. Moreover, this portion of the statute guards against finding all "easy" inventions obvious; sometimes the "easy" solution is the hardest to achieve.

3. Obvious to Try

An inquiry that does not find an invention obvious will often state that the evidence only shows that the invention was "obvious to try." This terminology suggests that the obviousness analysis is incomplete or short of the necessary factual finding of a motivation or suggestion to combine or modify the teachings of prior art references. The "obvious to try" label emphasizes that it is not correct "to pick and choose among individual parts of assorted prior art references 'as a mosaic to recreate a facsimile of the claimed invention.' " *Akzo N.V. v. U.S. Int'l Trade Comm'n*, 808 F.2d 1471, 1481 (Fed. Cir. 1986) (quoting *W.L. Gore & Assoc., Inc. v. Garlock*, 721 F.2d 1540, 1552 (Fed. Cir. 1983)). Thus, an "obvious to try" test may point to hindsight. Prior to *KSR*, the Federal Circuit clearly rejected an "obvious to try" approach to obviousness:

> The admonition that "obvious to try" is not the standard under § 103 has been directed mainly at two kinds of error. In some cases, what would have been "obvious to try" would have been to vary all parameters or try each of numerous possible choices until one possibly arrived at a successful result, where the prior art gave either no indication of which parameters were critical or no direction as to which of many possible choices is likely to be successful. In others, what was "obvious to try" was to explore a new technology or general approach that seemed to be a promising field of experimentation, where the prior art gave only general guidance as to the particular form of the claimed invention or how to achieve it.

In re O'Farrell, 853 F.2d 894, 903 (Fed. Cir. 1988) (citations omitted); *see also In re Kubin*, 561 F.3d 1351, 1358–61 (Fed. Cir. 2009).

KSR also made a passing reference to the "obvious to try" concept: "That it might have been obvious to try the combination of Asano and a sensor was likewise irrelevant." *KSR*, 550 U.S. at 414. Actually any discussion of "obvious to try" had no place in the

KSR case. The movable pedal technology only provided two places to put the electronic sensor—on the car or on the movable unit. The prior art had always chosen the car. Therefore the invention's choice to locate the sensor on the car was obvious wholly irrespective of "obvious to try" principles.

Nevertheless, the Supreme Court explained that the Federal Circuit erred in concluding "that a patent claim cannot be proved obvious merely by showing that the combination of elements was 'obvious to try.'" *KSR*, 550 U.S. at 421. The Supreme Court further explained:

> When there is a design need or market pressure to solve a problem and there are a finite number of identified, predictable solutions, a person of ordinary skill has good reason to pursue the known options within his or her technical grasp. If this leads to the anticipated success, it is likely the product not of innovation but of ordinary skill and common sense. In that instance the fact that a combination was obvious to try might show that it was obvious under § 103.

Id.

An example illustrates the distinction between obviousness and "obvious to try." Suppose that a prior art sporting magazine suggested that some alloy of aluminum and titanium would produce a light-weight baseball bat that would hit balls farther than any other metal bat. If the evidence shows only three possible alloys of aluminum and titanium, the prior art article will no doubt (absent objective indicia for instance) render all three possible alloys obvious. After all, the prior art clearly suggested that one of ordinary skill could make the combination easily. On the other hand, if the evidence shows 5,000 possible alloys and only one of them sends a ball 20 feet beyond all the others, then the article has probably only made it obvious to try to make the invention. The article did not render the inventive combination obvious. *Compare Rolls-Royce, PLC v. United Techs. Corp.*, 603 F.3d 1325, 1339 (Fed. Cir. 2010) *with Perfect Web Techs., Inc. v. InfoUSA, Inc.*, 587 F.3d 1324, 1331 (Fed. Cir. 2009).

This Supreme Court's change of direction on the traditional use of the term "obvious to try" had particular implications for chemical and biotechnological inventions. That story comes a little later.

4. Patentability vs. Validity

The procedures to obtain a patent invariably involve the obviousness test, as obviousness is a central patentability doctrine at the Patent Office. During infringement litigation, a defendant may also put up a defense of patent invalidity. Obviousness is a central doctrine of patent validity in court proceedings. Patentability, however, differs in important respects from validity.

In patentability, the obviousness inquiry begins with the *prima facie* test for obviousness (the first three steps) and only proceeds to objective criteria if necessary. With validity challenges, obviousness does not usually subdivide in this manner, although the defendant will often present a *prima facie* case of obviousness that the patent owner can rebut with evidence of objective criteria supporting the patentability of the claimed invention. *See In re Sullivan*, 498 F.3d 1345, 1351 (Fed. Cir. 2007).

During patentability proceedings at the Patent Office, the examiner will give the claims of the invention the "broadest reasonable interpretation." *In re Morris*, 127 F.3d 1048, 1053–54 (Fed. Cir. 1997). During validity proceedings, a court will conduct proceedings to determine the precise bounds of the claims. In any event, differences between patentability and validity proceedings often explain the different applications of the obviousness test. *In re Dillon*, 919 F.2d 688 (Fed. Cir. 1990) (en banc).

F. CHEMISTRY AND BIOTECHNOLOGY

Although the Federal Circuit has stated that "the requirement for non-obviousness in the case of chemical inventions is the same as for other types of inventions," *In re Johnson*, 747 F.2d 1456, 1460 (Fed. Cir. 1984), obviousness in the context of chemical and biotechnological technologies presents a distinct set of issues. Patenting in the chemical and biotechnological areas focuses to a large extent on claiming "new entities," such as new molecules in chemistry and new chains of amino acids or genetic materials in biotechnology.

For many years, the obviousness of chemical compounds was judged primarily by the proximity of the structure or nomenclature of the claimed compound to the prior art. This emphasis on "structural obviousness" dominated the *prima facie* obviousness inquiry and discounted any objective indicia of non-obviousness, such as a showing of unexpected results.

1. Chemistry

While historically "structural obviousness" may have controlled patentability, the Federal Circuit's predecessor rightfully differentiated a compound's formula from the compound itself, including all of its properties. *In re Papesch*, 315 F.2d 381, 391 (CCPA 1963). Nevertheless, structural similarity in the prior art will nearly always erect a *prima facie* case of obviousness against a new chemical which the applicant may attempt to rebut with evidence of unexpected results. *In re Dillon*, 919 F.2d 688 (Fed. Cir. 1990) *(*en banc*)*. The applicant may not rebut a *prima facie* case of obviousness based on structural similarities by identifying a property shared by the prior art, even if unknown. Obviousness in chemical compounds takes on heightened importance when viewed in the setting of the Hatch-Waxman Act, which regulates the interplay between generic drug companies and research-based drug companies.

2. Biotechnology

Even though chemistry and biotechnology share many aspects, they do not share the same emphasis on structure. Rather, many biotechnological inventions relate to genetic material composed of four building blocks (the nucleotide bases—adenine, guanine, cytosine, and thymine) that predictably pair up. Chemistry's emphasis on structure—remember there is an infinite number of molecules made from over a hundred elements—may have limited applicability to biotechnology. Even so, the body of law regarding obviousness in chemical cases had been imported to biotechnology prior to *KSR*, as explained for example in *In re Deuel*, 51 F.3d 1552, 1557–60 (Fed. Cir. 1995). But the Federal Circuit corrected this mistake in *In re Kubin*, 561 F.3d 1351, 1358–61 (Fed. Cir. 2009). The *Kubin* case used the Supreme Court's reversal of the usage of "obvious to try" to overrule the *Deuel* case.

Kubin held that biotech-related inventions, such as those related to isolated nucleic acids for encoding a known protein are subject to the same obviousness standards as other inventions. In particular, this case discards a pure structural comparison and allows the use of cloning methods and a high level of ordinary skill in the art to influence the obviousness of a DNA sequence or protein claim.

VI. NON-OBVIOUSNESS (INVENTIVE STEP) IN FOREIGN PATENT SYSTEMS

As one might expect, the verbal formulas used to determine obviousness (or inventive step) varies somewhat from system to system. Yet all of them require an identification and understanding of the teachings of the prior art and a comparison of that prior art with the claimed advance.

In Europe and systems that follow its methods, the well-known "problem and solution" approach to determining inventive step fails in cases where at least part of the invention lies in understanding the problem. In such cases, the solution is easy or obvious once the problem is understood. This approach exhibits another weakness as well, namely a predisposition to identify the problem as that associated with the closest prior art reference. This defect may divert attention away from other art that might render the claimed invention obvious. The U.S. obviousness test avoids these defects. In addition, most inventive step systems use some, but not all, of the secondary considerations that are very important to the U.S. non-obviousness test.

Nevertheless, as suggested earlier, obviousness and inventive step analyses invariably demand considerable legal and technical judgment. Any judgment call of this magnitude will produce reasonable disagreements. Thus any patent system relies heavily on the knowledge and wisdom of the inherently human (and therefore faulty) vessels charged with its administration. The legal formulas for the obviousness/inventive step test are important, but equally important are the institutional arrangements that affect the judgment calls. Thus, the efficiency and operation of patent offices around the world greatly affect the quality of patents and the success of the patent system in general.

CHAPTER 9
ADEQUATE DISCLOSURE

I. INTRODUCTION

In one sense, patents are contracts between the public and inventors. In exchange for an exclusive right, the inventor agrees to disclose new and non-obvious technology. For the public to get its part of the bargain, the inventor must fully disclose the invention. In other words, the inventor's primary obligation in the deal is to adequately disclose the technology to ensure that, at the end of the patent term, others can make and use the invention, and that, at the time of the disclosure, others may study and improve upon the invention. The statutory language governing the disclosure requirement appears in § 112(a) (pre-AIA § 112, first paragraph):

> The specification shall contain a written description of the invention, and of the manner and process of making and using it, in such full, clear, concise, and exact terms as to enable any person skilled in the art to which it pertains, or with which it is most nearly connected, to make and use the same, and shall set forth the best mode contemplated by the inventor or joint inventor of carrying out the invention.

The courts have interpreted this important (and cryptic) section to contain three requirements: enablement, written description, and best mode.

The AIA amended § 112 to refer to alphabetic subsections (i.e., subsections (a)–(f)). Thus, traditional references to § 112, first paragraph, should be understood as referring to § 112(a). Similarly, traditional references to § 112, second paragraph, correspond to § 112(b), and § 112, sixth paragraph, to § 112(f). The nomenclature has changed, even if the statutory text remains largely the same.

Enablement is the core doctrine that ensures adequate disclosure. This doctrine requires that the patent, when filed, includes sufficient technical information to enable a person of ordinary skill in the relevant art to make and use the claimed invention without undue experimentation. Enablement thus requires disclosure beyond a simple description or laconic explanation. An inventor must genuinely enrich the public's technical knowledge.

Beyond disclosure of inventive details, enablement serves two other vital purposes. Enablement polices the boundary between abstract theoretical science and actual technical contributions. This patent law principle thus ensures a technical solution to a real problem, not just visionary theories and hypotheses. In addition, and of vital importance, enablement polices the scope of the claims and prevents an inventor from overreaching. This principle accordingly ensures that the scope and content of the inventor's claimed exclusive right is commensurate with the actual invention. Stated otherwise, the boundary of the exclusive right granted by the patent cannot be more expansive than the inventor's technical contribution.

Case law has generated a separate disclosure doctrine to complement enablement. This doctrine, the written description requirement, emerges from the same phrases in § 112. This doctrine has its origins in preventing a patent applicant from adding new subject matter to his specification—either in the claims or the description—once filed. The written description doctrine thus polices priority by ensuring that an inventor may not improperly amend a pending application to claim later technological advances. In § 132, the patent statute expressly proscribes the addition of new matter to a pending application. The courts initially used § 112, first paragraph, as the mechanism to enforce § 132.

This traditional written description/new matter requirement, however, has since morphed into a separate substantive disclosure requirement for patentability. That is, at the risk of invalidity, a patent specification, which already includes the claim, must nonetheless describe the subject matter of the claim in other terms as well. Although the doctrine appears to lack precise enforcement standards, with time it seems to be merging with enablement, the long-standing and universal rule governing the scope of the claims.

The third requirement—best mode—is unique; it may no longer be presented as a defense in litigation. According to the last clause of § 112(a), the inventor must "set forth the best mode . . . of carrying out the invention." This requirement mandates disclosure in the patent specification of any specific instrumentalities or techniques that the inventor recognized at the time of filing as the best way of carrying out the invention. That is, inventors cannot obtain an exclusive right without disclosing to the public their would-be trade secrets for practicing the invention. For example, if an inventor invents a new configuration for a bookshelf that bears the load of texts more efficiently and knows of a particularly beneficial material for the new bookshelf, he must disclose that material as part of the application. The AIA removes violation of the best mode requirement as a defense to patent infringement.

II. ENABLEMENT

A. PURPOSE

Enablement, the other core validity doctrine alongside obviousness, ensures that the patent specification serves as an instruction manual teaching those of ordinary skill in the art to make and use the invention. Of course, the specification need not contain an overly exhaustive description. Rather, the description need only contain those details that, when combined with the baseline knowledge of a person of ordinary skill in the art, provide an understanding of the invention's use and fabrication.

The primary function of enablement is to ensure that the public receives useful information, not just theoretical hopes. Accordingly, enablement demarks the boundary between science fiction or visionary hopes and real technological advance. Jules Verne postulated and hypothesized about submarines and space ships decades before these became real technology. Had he attempted to patent these unspecific, incomplete ideas, he would not have been able to enable them. The knowledge of a person of ordinary skill in the art could not have filled out a purely hypothetical disclosure. Enablement, therefore, provides an objective test setting the boundary between a pioneering invention and a visionary hypothesis.

Enablement also ensures that claim scope does not exceed the inventor's actual technological contribution to the art. *See, e.g.*, *O'Reilly v. Morse*, 56 U.S. (15 How.) 62 (1854). An inventor thus cannot assert rights to an invention without sufficiently supporting the full scope of that assertion with enabling disclosure. Armed with the inventor's instruction in the patent's disclosure, other inventors can devise further improvements on the invention to advance technological progress in that area. By delineating the accurate boundary of the invention, enablement facilitates and encourages additional discoveries by creating incentives for subsequent improvements in the field. Enablement thus promotes further patentable improvements on patented inventions. *See, e.g.*, *Consol. Elec. Light Co. v. McKeesport Light Co.*, 159 U.S. 465 (1895).

B. TEST

Enablement requires that the specification, when filed, contain disclosure sufficiently clear and complete to enable one of ordinary skill in the art to make and use the full scope of the invention, as claimed, without undue experimentation. This test can be parsed into three critical portions. First, enablement is judged at the time of filing, preventing later developments from validating an inventor's prophetic guess about the progression in the art. Second, the disclosure must be clear and complete enough to enable the claimed invention, ensuring that the scope of the disclosure is commensurate with the scope of the claims. Third, a person of ordinary skill in the art must be able to make and use the invention without undue experimentation, permitting some (but not excessive) additional testing or research to make an operative embodiment of the invention.

1. At the Time of Filing

The first portion of the enablement test ensures that inventors have a complete idea before filing a patent application. Once again, Gordon Gould, the laser scientist, provides the classic example. In *Gould v. Hellwarth*, 472 F.2d 1383 (CCPA 1973), the court adjudicated an interference over a count concerning a "Q-switched" laser. By filing in April of 1959, Gould became the senior party. The junior party, Hellwarth, filed in August of 1961. Gould should have won the interference except for one problem: no one anywhere in the world built an operative laser until 1960. Accordingly, the court ruled that Gould could not have enabled a person of ordinary skill in the art to make an operable laser when neither he, nor anyone else, did it until later.

The court's opinion also noted that several renowned scientists testified years later at the trial that Gould's disclosure enabled a sodium mercury laser. Yet, as of 1968, no one had built an operative sodium mercury laser. How could they testify contrary to scientific history? Their testimony reveals another aspect of enablement: the as-filed disclosure cannot simply prophesy accurately about the development of new technology, rather it must enable operative technology at the time of filing.

Evidently Gould, as these noted scientists confirmed, predicted the fabrication and operation of a sodium mercury laser many years before it occurred. In the years after his basic disclosure, engineers learned the details necessary to make an operable laser, including (later) a sodium mercury laser. Prediction, even accurate prediction, however, is not enablement. Gould in fact did not adequately detail the making of a complete laser or he would have done it himself. Even though later developments confirmed his inadequate disclosure was "on the right track," it was still inadequate to enable. Enablement proceeds according to the state of the art at the time of filing. This classic *Gould* case illustrates that this rule precludes a patent on visionary, even if accurate, theoretical science that cannot produce operable technology.

As an aside, the court probably erred in awarding priority to Hellwarth over Gould. The court's fundamental error was in its reading of Gould's claims. The court read Gould's claims to cover lasers in general. In reality, Gould did not claim lasers in general, but an improvement, Q switching, on operable lasers. An inventor of an improvement may await the development of the basic technology before incurring the obligation to reduce the improvement to practice by showing it works for its intended purpose in the basic technology. *See, e.g., Columbia Broadcasting Sys. v. Sylvania Elec. Prods., Inc.*, 415 F.2d 719 (1st Cir. 1969) (noting that certain well-known techniques did not have to be disclosed in a patent relating to advances in color television). In this case, Gould should have received a chance to reduce his narrow invention to practice (and enable it) upon invention of the operable laser. Of course, Gould may well not have wished to claim this narrow victory when he instead wanted his disclosure to make him the father of all laser technology. In that context, the court was certainly correct to bar a broad claim to the laser in general for lack of enablement. In any event, enablement requires and encourages an operable technology, not merely an academic theory (even if later proved workable).

2. Scope of Disclosure

The second portion of the enablement test matches the scope of the disclosure to the scope of the claims. This requirement often depends on the state of knowledge in the scientific field of the invention. Thus, inventions in unpredictable fields require far more disclosure than inventions in more conventional fields. The necessary level of detail, however, never requires instruction on mass-producing the claimed invention. *Christianson v. Colt Indus. Operating Corp.*, 822 F.2d 1544, 1562 (Fed.

Cir. 1987) (commenting that it is not "an objective of the patent system to supply, free of charge, production data and production drawings to competing manufacturers"). Rather, the disclosure must be as detailed and revelatory as necessary to enable the full breadth of the claims.

An early biotechnology case provides an illustration. In *In re Wright*, 999 F.2d 1557 (Fed. Cir. 1993), Dr. Stephen E. Wright claimed processes for producing vaccines against pathogenic RNA viruses, further claimed the vaccines themselves, and finally claimed methods of using those vaccines against RNA viruses. RNA viruses comprise a varied, genetically diverse group of submicroscopic infective agents that produce terrible maladies like HIV, some leukemias, and some sarcomas. Dr. Wright claimed, among other things, a process to produce vaccines against RNA viruses in general. However, Dr. Wright's specification disclosed and detailed only a single working example: the production of a vaccine that immunizes chickens against Prague Avian Sarcoma Virus, a particular type of RNA virus belonging to the Rous Associated Virus family. The USPTO granted Dr. Wright the claims to his chicken vaccine and the processes for making it. The USPTO declined to grant Dr. Wright a patent on general RNA viruses or methods of making them, so he appealed.

The Federal Circuit sustained the USPTO's rejections for lack of enablement. In classic understatement, the court noted that the physiological activity of RNA viruses was not sufficiently predictable even five years after Wright's priority date, let alone at the effective filing date. Accordingly, a person of ordinary skill in the art would not have reasonably believed that, as claimed by Wright, all living organisms could be immunized against infection by any RNA virus by following the generalized methods and processes disclosed in the application. In more direct terms, the court could have said: "You have not cured AIDS or leukemia! You do not deserve a patent on cures for all RNA viruses!" Wright's disclosure, at best, merely invited experimentation to develop vaccines for specific types of RNA viruses. In fact, Wright had invented little, if anything, beyond a chicken virus vaccine.

Apparently conceding the audacity of his broad claims in light of his incredibly thin disclosure, Wright offered to narrow his claims to vaccines for all avian RNA viruses. Wright was still vastly overreaching. He had not even cured other chicken viruses, let alone all potential viruses in all species of birds. Stated in more careful legal terms, the sophistication of the ordinary practitioner in this field would not permit extrapolation of the particular chicken RNA virus to all avian RNA viruses. The court, therefore, upheld the Patent Office's rejection of the overbroad claims.

If, purely hypothetically, Wright had been able to posit a scientific principle that governed all avian viruses and showed that results against one would apply with equal force to another, then his single working example might have enabled a broader claim to cover all avian RNA viruses. Or, again completely hypothetically, if Dr. Wright had shown scientific principles that linked the chicken genome to turkeys and produced the same results for both, then he might have enabled a turkey vaccine beyond the chicken vaccine. Of course, in the treatment of viruses, that kind of understanding and technological achievement still lies in the distant future.

The second portion of the enablement test may be thought of as a comparison of the scope of enabling disclosure with the scope of the claims. When coupled with the reasonable knowledge and expectations of a person of ordinary skill in the art at the time of application, the description—taking into account the specific examples as well as generalized statements—cannot cover and explain less subject matter than the scope of the claims. That is, patentees may not claim more than they have invented and taught others to replicate.

Returning to biotechnology for a moment, as the science of genetic manipulation progressed, it became apparent that biotechnological inventions, such as the microorganisms at issue in *Diamond v. Chakrabarty*, 447 U.S. 303 (1980), could not be effectively enabled through a lifeless description in the patent or application. Instead, an inventor enables such an invention by providing a publicly accessible sample—a deposit—and identifying the source of that deposit. *See In re Lundak*, 773 F.2d 1216, 1222 (Fed. Cir. 1985).

To minimize the transaction costs involved in depositing samples in each country, patent-savvy countries signed the Budapest Treaty on the International Recognition of Deposits of

Microorganisms for the Purposes of Patent Protection. The Budapest Treaty established a uniform certification process for depositing microorganisms. Under this international agreement, a patentee may refer to a single deposit in a single depository regardless of the country of application. But again, the scope of the claims cannot exceed the scope of enabled subject matter, even where the subject matter is enabled through a publicly accessible sample in a depository.

3. No Undue Experimentation

The third portion of the enablement test limits the amount of work or effort by a person of ordinary skill in the art that the patentee may reasonably rely upon to supplement the patent's disclosure. Because the enablement rule permits some, but not unduly excessive, experimentation, this part of the test is again influenced by the nature of the scientific field.

In *Atlas Powder Co. v. E.I. du Pont De Nemours & Co.*, 750 F.2d 1569 (Fed. Cir. 1984), the Federal Circuit reviewed a determination that claims directed to emulsion blasting agents (explosives detonated by a high strength explosive primer) were adequately enabled. The patent disclosed a large number of ingredients—salts, fuels, and emulsifiers—that combined to form thousands of potential emulsions. The patent, however, did not identify the operable, as opposed to the inoperable, combinations. Without specifying any working examples, this patent might seem to have a fatal flaw. However, the court determined that the patentee was not required to distinguish operable combinations for two reasons. First, a well-known principle of chemistry, "Bancroft's Rule," would have assisted a person of ordinary skill in the art in selecting operative combinations. Second, the claims may include inoperative embodiments so long as a person of ordinary skill in the art can identify the operable embodiments without undue experimentation. Indeed, the claims may also encompass embodiments that work poorly because patent law does not require disclosure of only the most effective subject matter (unless it is a best mode as appears later).

The patent also described several prophetic examples—that is, experiments that the inventor has not actually performed. These descriptions did not render the patent invalid, because the inventor reasonably believed that those examples would, in fact, enable the claimed invention.

To be specific, Du Pont, the party attacking Atlas Powder's patent, tested the combinations in the claims. Out of 300 tests, 40 percent failed outright and only two emulsions worked. Again, these results would seem to be fatal to a case for enablement. But the court explained that bulk statistical aggregations do not necessarily reflect the difficulty of the experimentation to reach the claimed results. In this case, a person of ordinary skill, using Bancroft's well-known rule, would have quickly eliminated inoperable combinations and derived the optimal explosives. The patent required experimentation, but even the multiple experiments required in this case were not overly burdensome or undue.

In recent years, however, the Federal Circuit has shifted direction by holding genus claims non-enabled on the ground that identifying the compounds within their scope would require too many experiments, quantitatively, even if those experiments are purely routine. In *Wyeth & Cordis Corp. v. Abbott Lab'ys*, 720 F.3d 1380 (Fed. Cir. 2013), the central issue was what compounds fell within a genus claim's term, "rapamycin." Under the proper construction of that term, the answer hinged on an identification of the compounds that exhibited immunosuppressive and antirestenotic effects. Even though that identification could have been made through routine experimentation, and skilled artisans would have been able to significant limit the number of potential candidates, the court held that the identification would have involved undue experimentation because it would have required the synthesis and screening of approximately tens of thousands of compounds. According to the court, that quantity of routine experimentation was excessive, and thus the claim term was non-enabled. The Federal Circuit later issued a similar ruling in *Idenix Pharms. LLC v. Gilead Scis. Inc.*, 941 F.3d 1149, 1162 (Fed. Cir. 2019), with respect to which the Supreme Court denied certiorari. Commentators have suggested that the line of reasoning reflected in *Wyeth* and *Idenix* could make it exceedingly difficult for innovators in the chemical, biotechnology, and pharmaceutical fields to obtain valid genus claims.

See, e.g., Dmitry Karshtedt et. al., *The Death of the Genus Claim*, 35 Harv. J.L. & Tech. 1 (2021).

Recently in *Amgen Inc. v. Sanofi*, 143 S. Ct. 1243 (2023), the Supreme Court adopted the Federal Circuit's more stringent view of enablement. Amgen asserted genus claims covering antibodies that inhibited PCSK9, which impairs the body from removing LDL cholesterol, known to cause heart attacks and strokes. The two patents-in-suit disclosed 26 working examples, their amino acid sequences and 3D structures, and two methods for identifying other antibodies that inhibit PCSK9. The jury found the asserted claims adequately enabled, and the district court at one point observed that Amgen's experts' enablement opinions were factually supported. But the reviewing courts disagreed, emphasizing the large number of potential antibody candidates (i.e., millions) and the "substantial" time and effort that would be needed to identify other effective antibodies—even though most of those candidates could be screened as irrelevant. The Supreme Court reasoned that "the specification must enable the full scope of the invention as defined by its claims," and deemed the patents' two methods of finding working antibodies as two inadequately-enabling "research assignments." The Amgen decision heightens the bar for patent applicants to adequately enable genus claims where the number of candidate molecules is "vast." By failing to mention the jury's verdict, it also tends to heighten the bar for litigants at trial to marshal evidence supporting enablement. In general, because the extent of experimentation depends on the facts of each case, courts have adopted an eight-factor test to discern the boundary of undue experimentation in a particular field. These factors, commonly known as the *Wands* factors, include:

(1) the quantity of experimentation necessary,

(2) the amount of direction or guidance presented,

(3) the presence or absence of working examples,

(4) the nature of the invention,

(5) the state of the prior art,

(6) the relative skill of those in the art,

(7) the predictability or unpredictability of the art, and

(8) the breadth of the claims.

In re Wands, 858 F.2d 731, 737 (Fed. Cir. 1988). Although universally applicable, these factors have particular relevance to biotechnological inventions. *See, e.g.*, *Enzo Biochem, Inc. v. Calgene, Inc.*, 188 F.3d 1362 (Fed. Cir. 1999).

C. RELATIONSHIP TO UTILITY

The § 112(a) requirement that a patentee must enable others to make and use the claimed invention is similar to the utility requirement in § 101. As discussed in Chapter 4, utility serves as an insubstantial hurdle to patentability in most instances, except with respect to chemical and biotechnological inventions. But even in those technologies, the utility requirement merely requires that the patentee designate some application for the claimed subject matter. Enablement complements this requirement by ensuring some description in the specification to teach the skilled artisan that application. In fact, a patent lacking utility is necessarily not enabled: no person of ordinary skill in the art could ever practice the invention. *In re Swartz*, 232 F.3d 862, 863 (Fed. Cir. 2000).

For example, in *In re Ziegler*, 992 F.2d 1197 (Fed. Cir. 1993), Ziegler, a patent applicant, attempted to claim the benefit of priority to a foreign application to avoid an anticipatory reference. The Federal Circuit, however, determined that the foreign application did not enable the polypropylene as claimed in his domestic patent application, because Ziegler's foreign application lacked a disclosure of a specific utility. Ziegler's foreign application had merely disclosed that polypropylene could be pressed into a flexible film. Notably, Ziegler had not disclosed any practical use. (Polypropylene, of course, has numerous uses, most notably as semi-rigid packaging.)

III. WRITTEN DESCRIPTION

A. PURPOSE

Related to the enablement requirement, written description primarily serves a complementary purpose: to ensure that an inventor does not obtain claims on subject matter not initially disclosed in the application as filed and, thus, to which he is not entitled under the earlier priority date. *Ariad Pharms., Inc. v. Eli Lilly & Co.*, 598 F.3d 1336 (Fed. Cir. 2010) (en banc). If the inventor was the first to invent the new matter, then he may deserve claims to those improvements, but that assessment would require an accurate assessment of invention dates for the improvement. Others may have actually made the improvement first. In any event, the written description/new matter requirement prevents an applicant from perpetually "updating" his original disclosure to claim later developments. Thus, the written description requirement polices priority.

Assume an inventor creates a new superconductive metal alloy that speeds electronic communications. He files a patent application that describes and claims his new alloy for electric wires. While that application is pending, the inventor discovers several other derivative alloys that work even better as a communication medium. The inventor, however, can neither amend his claims in the initial application to recite the newer alloys nor amend his initial specification to describe the more recent advances. Instead, he must file a continuation-in-part that discloses and claims the newer developments. This new application will, of course, receive a later filing date. (Alternatively but at great risk as shown in Chapter 14, the inventor may choose to rely solely upon the doctrine of equivalents to preclude others from using an insubstantially different form of his invention.) While the inventor obtains the benefit of the filing date of his initial application for the initial alloy, he may only enjoy the benefit of the filing date of his subsequent application for the derivatives.

Under the written description/new matter doctrine, the inventor may draft new claims for the new derivative alloys (even though the as-filed claims did not recite that subject matter) if, and only if, the original specification disclosed those alternative formulations. Under the written description doctrine, the applicant may add new claims only if the specification "supports" or "shows possession of" the subject matter in the new claims or amendments. *Vas-Cath Inc. v. Mahurkar*, 935 F.2d 1555, 1563 (Fed. Cir. 1991).

Section 132 expressly states: "No amendment shall introduce new matter into the disclosure of the invention." The CCPA opined that the word "disclosure" might only encompass the descriptive portions of the application instead of the claims. In a surfeit of caution, the CCPA thus decided to use section 112, first paragraph, to prohibit new matter in claims. *In re Ruschig*, 379 F.2d 990, 995 (CCPA 1967). Thus, although a separate provision of the patent statute (§ 132) precludes applicants from introducing new disclosures (including new claims, new amendments to old claims, or new additions to the specification), the CCPA decided to use the "written description" language of § 112 (somewhat out of context) to police priority. The CCPA repeatedly emphasized that its new written description test was "equivalent" to the former new matter test. *In re Rasmussen*, 650 F.2d 1212, 1214 (CCPA 1981).

After subsequent judicial expansion, the new written description requirement goes beyond policing priority to testing the sufficiency of claims. Although this new application of the written description doctrine appears to be more onerous than enablement, *e.g.*, *In re DiLeone*, 436 F.2d 1404 (CCPA 1971), the Federal Circuit rejects that characterization, pleading that the court's expanded doctrine is not a " 'super enablement' standard for chemical and biotechnology inventions." *Ariad Pharms., Inc. v. Eli Lilly & Co.*, 598 F.3d 1336, 1352 (Fed. Cir. 2010) (en banc).

B. "POSSESSION" OF THE CLAIMED SUBJECT MATTER

The test for written description is relatively succinct: there must be adequate disclosure to show possession of the claimed subject matter at the time the application was filed. *See, e.g.*, *Ralston Purina Co. v. Far-Mar-Co, Inc.*, 772 F.2d 1570, 1575 (Fed. Cir. 1985). This test requires "adequate support" in the as-filed application for the later-claimed subject matter.

The case of *Vas-Cath Inc. v. Mahurkar*, 935 F.2d 1555 (Fed. Cir. 1991), illustrates this test. In that case, Dr. Mahurkar had filed a utility patent on a soft double-lumen catheter that allowed simultaneous insertion and removal of blood. At trial the court encountered prior uses that antedated Mahurkar's filing date. To avoid this prior art, Dr. Mahurkar wished to claim priority back to a design patent containing the same drawings as his later utility patents. The trial court determined that Dr. Mahurkar could not date the utility patents back to the earlier date of the design patent and, thus, invalidated the patents under § 102(b).

The Federal Circuit reversed and set forth the test for the written description/new matter doctrine: "[T]he applicant must . . . convey with reasonable clarity to those skilled in the art that, as of the filing date sought, he or she was in possession *of the invention*." *Id.* at 1563–64. Because this test depends on a factual analysis of the earlier disclosure in light of the understanding of a person of ordinary skill in the art, the Federal Circuit remanded.

On remand, the trial court determined that the patentee was in possession of the later-claimed subject matter at the time of the design application in part because the "utility application simply lays out the details of what the design drawings show—to be precise, the utility claims narrate what features of the drawings are important, without adding anything." *In re Mahurkar Patent Litigation*, 831 F. Supp. 1354, 1362 (N.D.Ill. 1993), *aff'd*, 71 F.3d 1573 (Fed. Cir. 1995). Dr. Mahurkar then developed his patented invention into a billion-dollar industry.

The "possession" test often presents special problems in determining whether disclosure of a genus can show possession of a later-claimed subgenus or species. *See, e.g., In re Smith*, 458 F.2d 1389, 1395–96 (CCPA 1972). In most instances, a broad genus does not adequately describe, or show possession of, a species or subgenus. But if "there are specific facts which lead to a determination that a subgenus is implicitly described," *Ex parte Westphal*, 26 USPQ2d 1858, 1860 (BPAI 1992), then the earlier disclosure of the genus may adequately support claims directed solely to a subgenus or species. Conversely, a disclosure of a sufficient number of species may show possession of a genus encompassing those species. *See Utter v. Hiraga*, 845 F.2d 993 (Fed. Cir. 1988).

C. WRITTEN DESCRIPTION UNCHAINED

Despite the traditional confines of written description as a doctrine to police priority, the Federal Circuit has expanded its reach to invalidate claims, even if those claims were part of the as-filed specification. The case that initiated the application of written description as a substantive requirement for patentability was *Regents of the University of California v. Eli Lilly & Co.*, 119 F.3d 1559 (Fed. Cir. 1997). In *Eli Lilly*, the patents generally related to recombinant DNA technology and to microorganisms and plasmids that produce insulin, a treatment for diabetes. The patent was filed in 1977—during the nascency of biotechnology—and described the cDNA (a type of genetic material) sequences found in rats that controlled the chemical pathways to make insulin. The patent's claims recited, *inter alia*, procaryotic microorganisms containing vertebrate insulin-encoding cDNA. Other claims specifically recited human insulin cDNA.

In invalidating the originally filed claims, the Federal Circuit made it clear that the inventor had not enabled the creation of human DNA, only the rat sequence. Yet, rather than invalidate under the traditional disclosure doctrine, the Federal Circuit declared that the applicant had not satisfied the written description doctrine, even though priority was not at stake. Thus, with no explanation for the need to create a new disclosure doctrine, the Federal Circuit set forth a new validity doctrine. *Eli Lilly* emphasized that the new doctrine "requires a precise definition, such as by structure, formula, chemical name, or physical properties." 119 F.3d at 1566 (quoting *Fiers v. Revel*, 984 F.2d 1164, 1171 (Fed. Cir. 1993)).

The rigid *Eli Lilly* test for written description soon encountered problems. In *Enzo Biochem, Inc. v. Gen-Probe Inc.*, 285 F.3d 1013 (Fed. Cir. 2002), the court initially held that a deposit of genetic material could not satisfy the written description requirement. After all, the deposit did not recite the "structure, formula, chemical name, [etc.]" required under *Eli Lilly*. Upon petition for rehearing, the panel reversed itself but maintained the viability of the written description doctrine. *Enzo Biochem, Inc. v. Gen-Probe Inc.*, 323 F.3d 956 (Fed. Cir. 2002).

More recently the Federal Circuit has continued its retreat from the stringent *Eli Lilly* formulation of the written description test. In *Capon v. Eshhar*, 418 F.3d 1349 (Fed. Cir. 2005), the Federal Circuit reformulated the test to vary with the complexity of the technology. Once again, this very general formulation supplied no standard for application of the *Eli Lilly* doctrine. And it imposed on juries the cumbersome task of deciding, nonsensically, that the patent's disclosure can enable a skilled artisan to make and practice the entire invention, but still not inform that same artisan that the inventor was in possession of the invention. After all, this broad generality applies to nearly every patent case and doctrine.

More recently, Federal Circuit began to fold its experimental written description doctrine back into the traditional confines of the enablement test for adequate disclosure: "[W]ritten description and enablement often rise and fall together." *Ariad Pharms., Inc. v. Eli Lilly & Co.*, 598 F.3d 1336, 1352 (Fed. Cir. 2010) (en banc); *see also Moba, B.V. v. Diamond Automation, Inc.*, 325 F.3d 1306, 1322 (Fed. Cir. 2003) (Rader, J., concurring). Appreciating the difficulties and redundancy of the *Eli Lilly* rule, the Federal Circuit has apparently begun to convert the written description requirement into the enablement doctrine—using a different label. Although the written description validity doctrine still has considerable "teeth," *see, e.g., Univ. of Rochester v. G.D. Searle & Co.*, 358 F.3d 916 (Fed. Cir. 2004), the move to reunite the Federal Circuit's disclosure doctrines under the traditional enablement test promises to restore some predictability to the tests for adequacy of disclosure.

D. POTENTIAL IMPACT OF NON-OBVIOUSNESS FINDING ON WRITTEN DESCRIPTION

In a recent development, the Federal Circuit appeared to hold that a finding of non-obviousness might make it harder to prove written description. In *Nuvo Pharms. (Ireland) Designated Activity Co. v. Dr. Reddy's Lab'ys Inc.*, 923 F.3d 1368 (Fed. Cir. 2019), the claims at issue covered the use of an NSAID (non-steroidal anti-inflammatory drug) to control pain in combination with an uncoated PPI (proton pump inhibitor) to reduce the likelihood of lesions and ulcers in the stomach and upper small intestine. The invention contemplated using some amount of *uncoated* PPI for immediate release to raise the gastric pH to at least 3.5. The invention was deemed non-obvious because a person of ordinary skill in the art would have been discouraged from using uncoated PPI and would not have expected it to work. But the generic drug companies argued, and the Federal Circuit agreed, that those findings showed that the inventor lacked possession at the time of invention, especially given that the specification did not provide experimental data or analytical reasoning showing the effectiveness of uncoated PPI for that purpose. The court accepted that argument even though, as it acknowledged, its written description case law does not require experimental data, theory, or other explanation on a claimed compound's effectiveness. Nevertheless, the *Nuvo* court reasoned that a skilled artisan would not have believed the uncoated PPI to be effective, and this fact apparently triggered a requirement for specific showing of its effectiveness in the specification. In the absence of such a showing, the court held that the claims lacked adequate written description. After *Nuvo*, patent owners should be aware of the possibility that their non-obviousness arguments could have the unintended consequence of heightening their burden to prove written description.

IV. BEST MODE

A. PURPOSE

Beyond the requirement for adequate disclosure, § 112(a) further requires disclosure of "the best mode contemplated by the inventor of carrying out his invention." This heightened disclosure obligation assists competitors in discovering the most effective implementations of the patented invention. To some extent, best mode attempts to level the playing field between the patentee and its competitors. The best mode requirement, to the extent it still exists, prevents a patentee from keeping some valuable aspects of an invention as a trade secret.

B. TWO-PART TEST

The best mode requirement does not mandate disclosure of all trade secrets associated with a patented invention. Instead a patentee need only disclose any way of practicing the invention that he considered better than any other at the time of filing. This test has two components: (1) the subjective belief of the inventor of a better method of practicing the claimed invention at the time of filing, and (2) concealment (occasionally mere non-disclosure) of that better method. *Wellman, Inc. v. Eastman Chemical Co.*, 642 F.3d 1355, 1360 (Fed. Cir. 2011).

1. Inventor's Subjective Belief

The first prong introduces a peculiar subjective test into patent law. For the most part, the patent statute requires objectivity. The best mode requirement is a notable exception to that general rule. (The intent prong under inequitable conduct is another example, but in that instance, circumstantial evidence often suffices to prove subjective intent. See Chapter 10 for a more complete discussion.) Instead of assessing disclosure through the eyes of a hypothetical person of ordinary skill in the art, the best mode requirement assesses the subjective, even idiosyncratic, beliefs of a flesh-and-blood inventor. Accordingly, the best mode test rejects as irrelevant the perception of a person of ordinary skill in the art at the time that the invention could be tweaked to enhance its operability. Only the inventor's perceptions are relevant.

The knowledge of others associated with the inventor, such as his attorneys or coworkers, is not imputed to the inventor. For example, in *Glaxo Inc. v. Novopharm Ltd.*, 52 F.3d 1043 (Fed. Cir. 1995), the court addressed whether claims directed to an anti-ulcer medicament were invalid for failure to disclose the best mode. While the inventor was unaware of an improved process for forming the medicament into a pharmaceutically acceptable composition, even

Glaxo's patent attorney knew the better method. Glaxo was the inventor's employer. Without evidence that the inventor shared the rather wide-spread knowledge possessed within Glaxo, the court refused to enforce a best mode prohibition. Instead, the court applied the statutory language "contemplated by the inventor" quite literally and thus limited starkly the reach of best mode.

Also notable is that the best mode requirement fixes the inventor's knowledge at the filing date. Subsequent discoveries of preferred embodiments do not create an obligation to update the disclosure with additional best modes. Even continuing applications—including continuations, divisionals, and continuations-in-part—that claim priority to an earlier application do not require an update of the best mode disclosure. For those continuing applications, the best mode disclosure obligation is fixed on the date of the earliest effective filing date. *Transco Prods. Inc. v. Performance Contracting, Inc.*, 38 F.3d 551, 557 (Fed. Cir. 1994).

2. Concealment

Even though the first prong is undoubtedly subjective, the second prong reintroduces some objectivity to determine whether the inventor in fact disclosed his best mode. Whether the inventor concealed his best mode requires a comparison between his subjective belief and the patent's disclosure. This inquiry turns on whether a person of ordinary skill in the art at the time would recognize that the inventor disclosed his subjective best mode in the patent as filed. *Wellman, Inc. v. Eastman Chemical Co.*, 642 F.3d 1355, 1360 (Fed. Cir. 2011).

Although rare (the Federal Circuit has only struck down about a half-dozen patents for failure to disclose a best mode), the case law contains a few examples of clear concealment of a known best mode. For example, in *Chemcast Corp. v. Arco Industries Corp.*, 913 F.2d 923 (Fed. Cir. 1990), the court upheld a judgment that the patentee did not disclose the best mode of his invention—a grommet for attaching material to sheet metal that could be used, for example, when securing upholstery to an automobile interior.

The record in that case showed that the inventor knew that the locking portion of the grommet should be made from a polyvinyl chloride (PVC) composition sold under the trade name R-4467. R-4467 had a particular hardness measured at 75 on the Shore D scale known in this art. In fact, the inventor knew that 750 man-hours over several months were required to develop R-4467. The inventor had developed a single embodiment of the grommet's locking portion at the time of his application, namely R-4467 with a hardness of 75 Shore D. Yet the inventor did not disclose either R-4467 or its important rigidity properties. The inventor disclosed materials with a hardness of 70 Shore A or harder. This disclosure was technically correct—75 Shore D was much, much harder than 70 Shore A—but in fact misled other artisans due to the vast differences between the physical properties of the Shore A and D hardness scales. A generic reference to PVC did not disclose R-4467. Thus, the inventor improperly concealed, rather than disclosed, the best mode.

Despite the extreme situation in *Chemcast*, § 112 does not obligate an inventor to highlight what he believes is his best mode. Rather, a patentee may bury the best mode in a list of a large number of less preferable alternatives without offending the best mode requirement. *See, e.g.*, *Randomex Inc. v. Scopus Corp.*, 849 F.2d 585, 589 (Fed. Cir. 1988). Accordingly, inventors often choose the course of including many modes of performing the claimed invention to avert potential best mode challenges.

The invention as claimed generally sets forth the limit of the inventor's best mode disclosure obligation. Although the vast majority of case law limits the best mode requirement to features recited in the claims, *see, e.g.*, *DeGeorge v. Bernier*, 768 F.2d 1318 (Fed. Cir. 1985); *Teleflex, Inc. v. Ficosa N. Am. Corp.*, 299 F.3d 1313 (Fed. Cir. 2002), some cases have opened the door to best modes related to features just beyond the explicit recitation of claimed elements. For example, in *Bayer AG v. Schein Pharmaceuticals, Inc.*, the court applied a "material effects" test to expand the reach of the best mode requirement to "aspects of making or using the claimed invention . . . [that] materially affected the properties of the claimed invention." 301 F.3d 1306, 1319 (Fed. Cir. 2002).

Under this somewhat controversial application of the best mode requirement, an inventor must determine whether unclaimed features "materially affect" the claimed invention. If so, this case would require disclosure of the best modes for any such unclaimed features. But even this articulation of the best mode requirement does not require an inventor to disclose either routine details readily available to a person of ordinary skill in the art or production details relating solely to commercial considerations beyond the quality or nature of the invention as claimed. *Eli Lilly & Co. v. Barr Labs., Inc.*, 251 F.3d 955 (Fed. Cir. 2001); *Young Dental Mfg. Co. v. Q3 Special Prods., Inc.*, 112 F.3d 1137 (Fed. Cir. 1997).

C. UNNECESSARY VESTIGE?

Although firmly entrenched in the patent statute, the best mode requirement is a misfit for a number of reasons. To begin with, best mode is really a trap for the unwary. The best mode requirement is largely self-enforcing. Any inventor with even a passing knowledge of patent law would never fall into the best mode trap because non-disclosure of a critical trade secret within the best mode requirement places the value of the entire patented invention at risk—a risk beyond the requirements of § 112. After all, competitors can, and invariably will, discover the undisclosed trade secret and claim it in a separate patent application. When that application ripens into a patent, the competitor will have a blocking patent capable of compromising the value of the original patent. Therefore, the best mode requirement is unnecessary—an informed patent applicant will never withhold a genuine best mode.

Instead, informed patent applicants will either disclose the best mode in the original patent's specification (often as a dependent claim) or, if the trade secret is not part of the claimed invention, file a separate patent application on the separate innovation. Because informed patent applicants know to avoid best mode problems, this § 112 requirement is invariably little more than a trap for the uninformed applicant—perhaps a university or independent inventor without corporate legal resources.

In fact, not only universities and garage inventors fall into the best mode trap, but also foreign inventors, because the United States is one of the few countries with a best mode requirement. Therefore, a foreign inventor who intends to apply for a patent in his country must include information pertaining to the best mode in his foreign priority application. Although filing in a country without a best mode requirement, the foreign inventor risks losing priority if he changes his application upon entry into the U.S. (A foreign inventor may, of course, supplement his disclosure to conform with the best mode requirement prior to filing in this country, but then he would not be entitled to priority back to his foreign application under § 119.) United States patent law thus creates extra burdens or traps for foreign applicants.

Because this relic runs counter to basic patent law policy, commentators often recommended dropping this requirement. *See, e.g.*, THE ADVISORY COMMISSION ON PATENT LAW REFORM: A REPORT TO THE SECRETARY OF COMMERCE 102–03 (1992); *see also* AIPLA Response to the National Academies Report

Entitled, "A Patent System for the 21st Century" 42–44 (2005). Perhaps driven by those criticisms, the AIA "pulled the teeth" of the best mode invalidity doctrine. While the requirement remains in the text of the patent statute, it no longer has any remedy. Failure to disclose the best mode is no longer a defense to an allegation of patent infringement. 35 U.S.C. § 282(b)(3)(A).

CHAPTER 10
ISSUES IN PATENT ACQUISITION

I. INTRODUCTION

As discussed in Chapter 2, an inventor must apply for a patent with the Patent Office, which examines the inventor's application for compliance with both formal and substantive requirements. Various issues may arise in connection with patent acquisition, including correct inventorship, inequitable conduct, and double patenting.

Specifically, only an inventor (or in limited circumstances, an assignee) may apply for a patent. In the event that a patent has multiple inventors, this simple requirement becomes more complex. For instance, even if an inventor only contributes to a single claim in a patent with many claims, that "lesser" inventor is not "lesser" under the law and instead enjoys co-ownership of the entire patent.

During the application process, a patent applicant also has a duty of candor. Under that duty, the applicant must disclose particularly important information to the Patent Office. If an applicant intentionally withholds any such information, the patentee can lose the right to enforce the entire patent.

Finally, an inventor may only receive a single patent for each invention (or obvious variants of the invention). Thus, if an applicant attempts to claim the same invention in different applications, the doctrine of double patenting prevents the inventor from using this device to undeservedly extend the patent term.

II. INVENTORSHIP

Under U.S. law, only the actual inventor (or set of inventors) receives a patent on the invention. (The Leahy-Smith America Invents Act, though, does allow issuance of a patent to an assignee under certain circumstances.) Although a simple proposition, declaration of the inventors often gives rise to disputes in patent litigation. To avoid these problems, the application must name all of the true inventors—and only the true inventors. Even if the application lists incorrect inventors at the time of filing, the declaration of inventorship must be corrected upon discovery of the error. A patent derived from someone other than the named inventor is invalid.

A. TEST FOR INVENTORSHIP

The patent statute expressly provides that, in general, only true inventors may file for a patent. 35 U.S.C. § 111(a). In the case of multiple inventors, they must jointly apply for a patent, "even though (1) they did not physically work together or at the same time, (2) each did not make the same type or amount of contribution, or (3) each did not make a contribution to the subject matter of every claim of the patent." 35 U.S.C. § 116. Even though their contributions need not be concurrent, qualitatively equivalent, or quantitatively equivalent, it is pivotal that each inventor must contribute to the conception of the invention as claimed.

As discussed in Chapter 7, conception—not reduction to practice—is the touchstone of inventorship. Consider for a moment a research team led by an eminent scientist. The scientist may originate an idea and then instruct his assistants to make the idea work. The assistants would generally use well-known research or experimental techniques to comply with the instructions. These technicians help to reduce the invention to practice, but do not qualify as inventors. Even the talented technician who supplements the inventor's work with significant research skills does not become an inventor without conception. On the other hand, the talented technician may also modify the invention during the work. That modification, if reflected in the claims, makes the assistant a joint inventor. The technician or assistant must actually conceive of some part of the invention to qualify as an inventor.

These conception rules mean that an inventor must contribute to the conception of the claimed subject matter, not merely to the disclosure of the patent. The Federal Circuit applied these principles in *Board of Education of Florida State University v. American Bioscience, Inc.*, 333 F.3d 1330 (Fed. Cir. 2003). In that case, a group of researchers worked together on related projects. A smaller part of the team conceived of a new chemical compound. The full team then worked to produce the new product. None of the team members beyond the small inventive group were inventors. None of the rest contributed to the conception of the claimed invention. The claims recited a chemical compound. Therefore, no one beyond the originators conceived of the compound with all of its components, a requirement for conception in the chemical field. Even though several others had specific parts of the claimed compounds in mind at the time, they had not conceived of or contributed to the entire invention. *See* Chapter 7.

Once a patent issues, the law creates a presumption that the named inventors are the correct and only inventors. *Hess v. Advanced Cardiovascular Sys., Inc.*, 106 F.3d 976 (Fed. Cir. 1997). This presumption discourages frivolous inventorship disputes. In *Hess*, for instance, a laboratory assistant simply implemented the invention as conceived by another.

If the wrong inventor files and prosecutes the patent, the correct inventors may petition the Patent Office to issue a certificate of correction naming the proper inventors. 35 U.S.C. § 256. Alternatively, an omitted inventor may request that a court, under the same statutory provision, order the Patent Office to correct the patent's inventorship. Similar to proving inventorship elsewhere, an allegedly omitted inventor must corroborate any claims of conception with contemporaneous documents, oral testimony, or other circumstantial evidence. *See* Chapter 7. Notably, if inventorship can be corrected under either one of the provisions of § 256, the patent is not invalid.[1]

B. CONSEQUENCES OF INCORRECT INVENTORSHIP

Even though not invalidating, incorrect inventorship can render a patent practically worthless. The default rule is that "each of the joint owners of a patent may make, use, offer to sell, or sell the patented invention within the United States, or import the patented invention into the United States, without the consent of and without accounting to other owners." 35 U.S.C. § 262. Even though this section refers to "owners" and not inventors, an inventor is the first owner of a patent. That inventor may assign his rights in a patent (or a patent application) to another, 35 U.S.C. § 261, but "an invention presumptively belongs to its creator," *Teets v. Chromalloy Gas Turbine Corp.*, 83 F.3d 403, 407 (Fed. Cir. 1996). And a contributor to even one claim of a patent is a co-inventor on the whole patent. There is no such creature as a partial inventor on a patent; a person is either a full-fledged inventor or not. 35 U.S.C. § 116. A contributor to a single claim therefore can effectively erase the benefits of the entire patent to the primary inventor.

Ethicon, Inc. v. United States Surgical Corp., 135 F.3d 1456 (Fed. Cir. 1998), tells the chilling story of

---

1 A change in inventorship under § 256 may also affect inventorship for a nondomestic patent application, such as a PCT application. *See Chou v. Univ. of Chicago*, 254 F.3d 1347, 1360 (Fed. Cir. 2001).

an inventing relationship gone awry. In a common scenario, this case featured an eminent scientist and an assistant. The eminent scientist, Dr. InBae Yoon, was a physician and noted leader in the field of surgical devices. Yoon already had many patents on trocars, the sharp instruments that open a small hole for endoscopic surgery.

Yoon hired an assistant, Young Jae Choi, to help with the mechanics of a new safety trocar that would detect penetration past tough muscle tissue and thus prevent stab wounds to the organs beyond. Choi, an electronics technician without even a college degree, collaborated with Yoon on the safety trocars. Choi and Yoon worked together for about a year and a half before Choi left the relationship. Soon thereafter Yoon filed a patent application disclosing and claiming safety trocars with himself as the sole inventor.

Yoon and his exclusive licensee asserted two claims of the patent against U.S. Surgical. Meanwhile, U.S. Surgical obtained a license from Choi (for a relatively small fee) and asserted that Choi was a co-inventor of the safety trocars. The district court, with the Federal Circuit's concurrence, found that Choi contributed to a few limitations in two claims (out of the patent's 55). In fact, Yoon had not even asserted those claims against U.S. Surgical. Choi corroborated his contributions to those few claims with some contemporaneous sketches depicting the subject matter.

Due to Choi's inventive contribution—no matter how small—he shared ownership of the entire patent with Yoon. As a co-owner, Choi was free to license the invention to U.S. Surgical. Yoon could not maintain the lawsuit against U.S. Surgical. Effectively, Yoon was deprived of the core patent right—the ability to exclude another from making, using, or selling the patented technology—because he omitted Choi, the co-inventor of some subject matter, from the patent. Yoon, of course, could have avoided this devastating consequence by requiring Choi, upon entering his employ, assign to Yoon the rights to all inventions arising from the collaboration.

III. INEQUITABLE CONDUCT

A. PURPOSE

Although just two entities—the applicant and the Patent Office—take part in prosecution of a patent application, the grant of a patent affects the public as a whole. And because patent prosecution is *ex parte*, the interested public—namely the applicant's competitors—has no input during the acquisition of the patent right. The Patent Office has no laboratories, no test facilities, no dedicated scientists, and no economists to evaluate the assertions of a patent applicant relating to the characteristics or commercial success of embodiments of the claimed subject matter. Absent compelling circumstances, such as a violation of immutable laws of physics giving rise to a rejection under § 101, the Patent Office does not challenge the veracity of a patent applicant's statements or declarations.

Because the system relies on the truthfulness of its participants, it imposes a duty of candor on the patent applicant. The applicant thus has a duty to disclose all material information to the patent examiner. This requirement manifests itself not in a statute-based condition for patentability, but in inequitable conduct—an equitable doctrine that carries many of the implications of a regulatory condition and that can be asserted later in defense to a charge of patent infringement. This duty of candor extends beyond the patent applicant or patentee and includes the prosecuting attorney, "because the knowledge and actions of [an] applicant's attorney are chargeable to [the] applicant." *FMC Corp. v. Manitowoc Co.*, 835 F.2d 1411, 1415 n.8 (Fed. Cir. 1987).

At one time, the prevalence of charges of inequitable conduct during litigation caused the Federal Circuit to lament that "the habit of charging inequitable conduct in almost every major patent case has become an absolute plague." *Burlington Indus., Inc. v. Dayco Corp.*, 849 F.2d 1418, 1422 (Fed. Cir. 1988). The plague continued through 2011—alleged infringers invariably sought out even the slenderest factual support for asserting inequitable conduct for strategic and tactical reasons.

The strategy is simple: a charge of inequitable conduct permits the alleged infringer to paint the patentee as unscrupulous and undeserving of its patent (thus offsetting to some degree the presumption of validity). An allegation of inequitable conduct also provides an opportunity to obtain discovery into otherwise privileged or immune documents (especially the prosecuting attorney's papers). Finally, the allegation creates satellite litigation focused on the patentee's conduct and credibility.

Due to the allure of even marginally justified claims of inequitable conduct, defendants often asserted this charge as a matter of course. For this reason, the Federal Circuit first attempted to curtail the doctrine by requiring proof of facts by clear and convincing evidence. This heightened burden of proof, however, did not quell the tide.

Realizing that inequitable conduct continued to metastasize and infect patent litigations and patent prosecution, the Federal Circuit revisited the equitable doctrine in *Therasense, Inc. v. Becton, Dickinson & Co.*, 649 F.3d 1276 (Fed. Cir. 2011) (en banc). The pre-*Therasense* standards for this doctrine "inadvertently led to many unintended consequences, among them, increased adjudication cost and complexity, reduced likelihood of settlement, burdened courts, strained PTO resources, increased PTO backlog, and impaired patent quality." *Therasense*, 649 F.3d at 1290. The Federal Circuit apparently cured the plague in *Therasense*, but it remains available in narrow circumstances.

Inequitable conduct renders an entire patent—not just the affected claims—unenforceable. *Kingsdown Med. Consultants, Ltd. v. Hollister Inc.*, 863 F.2d 867 (Fed. Cir. 1988). In fact, inequitable conduct occurring in the prosecution of one application, in certain circumstances, can even infect the entire family descending from that patent. *See, e.g.*, *Consolidated Aluminum Corp. v. Foseco Int'l Ltd.*, 910 F.2d 804, 812 (Fed. Cir. 1990); *but see Baxter Int'l, Inc. v. McGaw, Inc.*, 149 F.3d 1321, 1330–32 (Fed. Cir. 1998).

A patent applicant may "cure" any inequitable conduct, but only by expressly correcting the misrepresentation during prosecution. In such a case, however, there are three steps that the applicant must take:

> The first requirement to be met by an applicant . . . is that he expressly advise the PTO of [the misrepresentation], stating specifically wherein it resides. The second requirement is that, if the misrepresentation is of one or more facts, the PTO be advised what the actual facts are, the applicant making it clear that further examination in light thereof may be required if any PTO action has been based on the misrepresentation. Finally, on the basis of the new and factually accurate record, the applicant must establish patentability of the claimed subject matter.

Rohm & Haas Co. v. Crystal Chem. Co., 722 F.2d 1556, 1572 (Fed. Cir. 1983).

B. TEST FOR INEQUITABLE CONDUCT

Inequitable conduct combines two elements: false disclosure or withholding of material information and intent to deceive the Patent Office. These two prongs are factual and must be proven by clear and convincing evidence. *See, e.g.*, *Kingsdown*, 863 F.2d at 872. They must be proven separately, and a weak showing of materiality cannot be counter-balanced by a strong showing of intent.

The materiality prong sets forth a but-for test, meaning that the PTO would not have allowed the claim had it been aware of the withheld or false information. This requires an analysis similar to validity, but with an application of the pre-issuance burden of proof (i.e., a preponderance of the evidence) and an administrative claim construction (i.e., the broadest reasonable interpretation without a presumption of validity). As noted, affirmative acts of egregious misconduct, such as filing a false affidavit, are also material. Notably, affirmative acts need not satisfy the but-for standard; omissions like failure to disclose information must.

The intent prong requires proof, usually indirect circumstantial proof, of a specific intent to deceive the PTO. The specific intent to deceive, however, "must be the single most reasonable inference able to be drawn from the evidence." *Therasense*, 649 F.3d at 1291 (citation and quotation marks omitted). And the accused infringer must prove by clear and convincing evidence three separate things if alleging that undisclosed information is but-for material: (1) that the applicant knew of the information, (2) that the applicant knew the information was material, and (3) that the applicant made a deliberate decision to withhold the information. These things cannot be established based on the materiality of the information or testimony found to be lacking in credibility. *Am. Calcar, Inc. v. Am. Honda Motor Co.*, 651 F.3d 1318 (Fed. Cir. 2011).

1. Materiality

The traditional standard for materiality required a showing that "a reasonable examiner would have considered such prior art important in deciding whether to allow the parent application." *Driscoll v. Cebalo*, 731 F.2d 878, 884 (Fed. Cir. 1984). This standard arose in part from the administrative rule establishing the duty of candor then applicable for patent applicants. *See* 37 C.F.R. § 1.56(a) (1991). The Patent Office amended this rule in 1992, setting forth some more specific criteria for materiality. *See* 37 C.F.R. § 1.56(a). The pre-1992 Rule 56 and the current Rule 56 are not markedly different in effect. *See, e.g., Ulead Sys., Inc. v. Lex Computer & Mgmt. Corp.*, 351 F.3d 1139 (Fed. Cir. 2003). In any event, the PTO's rules do not set the standard for materiality. This judge-made, equitable doctrine is not a derivative of the administrative rules.

A patentee may oppose a finding of materiality by showing that a reference is cumulative, which would likely negate a determination that the omitted information is but-for material. A reference is cumulative if it repeats the disclosure of a subject already disclosed to the PTO. In fact, "a patentee has no obligation to disclose an otherwise material reference if the reference is cumulative or less material than those already before the examiner." *Halliburton Co. v. Schlumberger Tech. Corp.*, 925 F.2d 1435, 1440 (Fed. Cir. 1991).

Pre-*Therasense* decisions held that an affirmative statement (e.g., an affidavit) that misleads, distorts, or omits crucial facts can never be merely cumulative over other information. *Refac Int'l, Ltd. v. Lotus Dev. Corp.*, 81 F.3d 1576, 1583–84 (Fed. Cir. 1996). In holding statements in a patent's written description as material, the Federal Circuit clarified: "[A]ffirmative misrepresentations by the patentee, in contrast to misleading omissions, are more likely to be regarded as material." *Hoffman-La Roche, Inc. v. Promega Corp.*, 323 F.3d 1354, 1367 (Fed. Cir. 2003).

Most inequitable conduct cases have traditionally concerned acts or omissions during prosecution, but the doctrine applies as well to post-issuance activities that affect the patentability or enforceability of the patent. For instance, the duty of candor applies to statements in a petition for a certificate of correction. *Cf. Winbond Elecs. Corp. v. Int'l Trade Comm'n*, 262 F.3d 1363 (Fed. Cir. 2001).

2. Intent

Even in the face of material, undisclosed references, the patent is only unenforceable for inequitable conduct if the patentee also intended to mislead the Patent Office. The intent prong weighs the patentee's conduct in light of all evidence, including evidence of good faith, to assess the culpability of the non-disclosure (or affirmative disclosure). Like any other inquiry into subjective intent, a case rarely presents a "smoking gun," or direct evidence of intent to mislead. *See Ristvedt-Johnson, Inc. v. Brandt, Inc.*, 805 F. Supp. 549, 554–

55 (N.D. Ill. 1992). Instead a court must usually infer intent from circumstantial evidence.

As shown by *Kingsdown*, an error alone, even a very negligent error, is not sufficient intent. *Kingsdown*, 863 F.2d at 876. In a patent with many claims, the PTO examiner had rejected claim 50 as indefinite. The applicant then amended that defective claim. In an effort to obtain other claims, the applicant filed a continuation application. The applicant mistakenly included again the rejected—not the amended—claim with a new number, 43. The patent issued with the new claim that had been once rejected as indefinite.

On these facts, the trial court found inequitable conduct with intent shown by the prosecuting attorney's gross negligence. On appeal, the Federal Circuit noted that the record showed that the prosecuting attorney was unaware of the error until the litigation. Although refusing to condone inattention to detail, the court referred to the "relative ease with which others also overlooked the differences in the claims" as evidence of no deceptive intent. *Id.* at 873. The en banc court also clarified gross negligence cannot satisfy the deceptive intent requirement. Even this blatant error was not intent because "the involved conduct, viewed in light of all the evidence, including evidence indicative of good faith, must indicate sufficient culpability to require a finding of intent to deceive." *Id.* at 876.

Kingsdown also stands for another very interesting principle. There the applicant had intentionally drafted claims to read on the infringer's device that was already in the marketplace. Thus, the applicant crafted its continuation to capture a product already available to consumers. As long as the claims comply with all applicable rules and laws, the Federal Circuit explained, "there is nothing improper, illegal or inequitable in filing a patent application for the purpose of obtaining a right to exclude a known competitor's product from the market." *Id.* at 874. This aspect of the prosecution had no relevance to the inequitable conduct inquiry.

A violation of the duty of candor can have implications beyond rendering a patent unenforceable. In a concurring opinion, the late Judge Helen Nies explained that more culpable conduct can bring other severe consequences:

> [T]hree standards [govern the penalties for] misconduct by a patentee . . . (1) misconduct which makes a patent unenforceable (which we have termed "inequitable conduct"); (2) misconduct which is sufficient to make a case "exceptional" under 35 U.S.C. § 285 so as to warrant, in the discretion of the trial judge, an award of attorneys fees; and (3) misconduct which rises to the level of common law fraud and which will support an antitrust claim. As a litigant moves from a purely defensive position, to a recoupment request, to an affirmative claim for damages, it is reasonable to impose more stringent requirements.

Argus Chem. Corp. v. Fibre Glass-Evercoat Co., 812 F.2d 1381, 1387 (Fed. Cir. 1987) (Nies, J., additional views). In general, the culpable misconduct must be egregious to cause a fee award to lead to treble damages under antitrust law. *See Walker Process Equip., Inc. v. Food Mach. & Chem. Corp.*, 382 U.S. 172 (1965). The extreme forms of misconduct require more proof of culpability.

C. INTERNATIONAL TREATMENT

Foreign patent regimes do not rely on inequitable conduct to ensure candor during prosecution. Instead, these regimes rely on other mechanisms to elicit the best prior art and eliminate improper patents. For example, competitors may often oppose an application by submitting prior art during prosecution or may bring some form of "nullity" action to cancel an issued patent. A specialized patent tribunal, with some similarities to the PTO's administrative Patent Trial and Appeal Board, often hears and resolves these challenges to patent validity.

IV. DOUBLE PATENTING

A. PURPOSE

The patent statute only permits one patent for each invention:

> Whoever invents or discovers any new and useful process, machine, manufacture, or composition of matter, or any new and useful improvement thereof, may obtain *a patent* therefor, subject to the conditions and requirements of this title.

35 U.S.C. § 101 (emphasis added). An inventor may not file a second application claiming in another form the same invention. Although not perfectly clear in the statute's language, this intuitive requirement makes sense. Without a prohibition on double patenting, a patentee could extend an exclusive right beyond the statutory term by filing a series of patent applications on identical (or nearly identical) inventions. For instance, an unscrupulous applicant could game the system by repeatedly applying for a patent on the same invention within the one-year grace period. The double patenting prohibition thus preserves the limited patent term.

B. TWO TYPES

1. Same Invention or Statutory

Same invention double patenting—also called "statutory" double patenting due to its basis in the statute—applies when an applicant claims a single invention in two separate applications. Because the claim defines an invention, statutory double patenting occurs when the two applications share at least one claim of identical scope. As a procedural matter, a court applying this double patenting rule must first construe the applications' claims and then compare them. In making this comparison, the court must realize that variations in verbiage do not necessarily cause variations in claim scope. For example, changing "suitcase" to "portable, semi-rigid traveling bag" might not change the scope of the claimed subject matter.

The imprecision of claim construction makes application of the double patenting rule difficult. The predecessor to the Federal Circuit observed that a "good test, and probably the only objective test, for 'same invention,' is whether one of the claims could be literally infringed without literally infringing the other. If it could be, the claims do not define identically the same invention." *In re Vogel*, 422 F.2d 438, 441 (CCPA 1970). For example, in *Vogel*, the court noted the difference between claims related to sausage-making: "The patent claims are limited to pork. Appealed claims 7 and 10 are limited to meat, which is not the same thing. . . . Claim 11 is limited to beef. Beef is not the same thing as pork." *Id.* at 442. Because a sausage maker could infringe claims in the later application without also infringing claims in the issued patent, the applicant was not claiming the same invention.

But if an application or patent claims the same invention twice, the latter set of claims are invalid for statutory double patenting under § 101. Unlike the second type—"obviousness-type" double patenting—a terminal disclaimer cannot overcome same-invention double patenting.

2. "Obviousness-Type" or Non-Statutory

Because even a slight differential in claim scope avoids statutory double patenting, the Federal Circuit's predecessor created "obviousness-type" or non-statutory double patenting to close the loophole. This judge-made rule shares the same policy as statutory double patenting: an inventor may not unduly extend the term of his exclusive right by filing a series of applications claiming only marginally different subject matter.

The more accurate label for this doctrine is probably non-statutory double patenting because obviousness-type double patenting does not really entail an obviousness analysis under § 103. After all, obviousness compares the claimed invention with actual prior art references, whereas non-statutory double patenting compares the scope of a claim with the scope of an earlier claim. Obviousness also often requires evidence of a motivation to combine or modify the prior art, whereas non-statutory double patenting does not. Lastly, obviousness requires examination into secondary considerations tending to establish non-obviousness, whereas non-statutory double patenting does not. *Geneva Pharms., Inc. v. GlaxoSmithKline PLC*, 349 F.3d 1373, 1377 n.1 (Fed. Cir. 2003).

Although sharing the misleading "obviousness" moniker, obviousness-type double patenting shares more in common with statutory double patenting than with obviousness. The test for obviousness-type double patenting hinges on differences in the claim scope. Merely marginal, negligible variants do not qualify for a separate patent.

Non-statutory double patenting is thus largely an equitable judgment turning on the qualitative differences between two claims. In making this judgment, the application's disclosure does not apply beyond information relevant to construing its respective claim. Nonetheless a disclosed embodiment within the scope of a claim may assist in determining whether one claim is an obvious variant of another. *In re Vogel*, 422 F.2d 438, 442 (CCPA 1970).

For example, in *Vogel*, the court determined that claim 11, which recited beef not pork, was not an obvious variant due to the differences between beef and pork. The court, however, ruled that the claims reciting meat not pork were obvious variants because pork is a type of meat, and thus allowing a claim on meat "would therefore extend the time of monopoly as to the pork process." *Id.* at 442. Because no terminal disclaimer cured this instance of non-statutory double patenting, the claims reciting meat were invalid.

Where a second claim reads on an inherent, natural result of an earlier claim, the claims are not patentably distinct. In *Eli Lilly & Co. v. Barr Laboratories, Inc.*, 251 F.3d 955 (Fed. Cir. 2001), the court held that a claimed method using fluoxetine hydrochloride to block serotonin in brain neurons was invalid for non-statutory double patenting. An earlier patent had claimed a method of treating human anxiety by administering an effective amount of fluoxetine or a pharmaceutically acceptable salt thereof. And the record showed that administering fluoxetine inherently, inevitably, and necessarily blocks the uptake of serotonin, regardless of whether administered for the treatment of anxiety. So the earlier patent necessarily included the later method claim.

In contrast to the "one-way" test for obviousness-type double patenting set forth in *Vogel*, a "two-way" test may be appropriate in limited circumstances. For example, in *In re Braat*, 937 F.2d 589 (Fed. Cir. 1991), the court encountered commonly assigned inventions related to optical storage. Due to delay by the Patent Office, the later-filed application (with subject matter similar to the first-filed application) issued as a patent before the first-filed application. Although complementary, the first-filed application dominated the later-filed application—i.e., the later-filed application claimed a combination of the subject matter claimed in the first-filed application and additional, new subject matter. Due to the inequity of punishing an inventor for circumstances beyond his control, the court applied a "two-way" test: Each patent's claims must have been an obvious variant of the other patent to show non-statutory double patenting.

When the Patent Office does not cause the delay in the issuance of a second claim, a "two-way" test does not apply. Thus, for example, the "one-way" test applies where an applicant chooses to obtain or prosecute narrower claims before seeking broader coverage. *In re Goodman*, 11 F.3d 1046 (Fed. Cir. 1993).

A later-filed, later-issued, but earlier-expiring patent can serve as a reference patent (and thus a basis for invalidity) for another patent under the obviousness-type double patenting doctrine. *Gilead Scis., Inc. v. Natco Pharma Ltd.*, 753 F.3d 1208, 1211–12 (Fed. Cir. 2014). In *Gilead*, the patentee did not dispute that the claims of the asserted '483 patent—directed to antiviral compounds and methods of their use—were patentably indistinct from the similar claims of the '375 reference patent. Instead, the patentee argued that the '375 patent could not serve as a reference patent under the obviousness-type double patenting doctrine because, although it expired 22 months before the '483 patent, it was filed and issued *after* the '483 patent.

According to the patentee, the doctrine was designed to prevent the extensions of the patent term. Yet, in this case, the '375 patent in no way extended the term for the '483 patent. Despite this compelling argument, the Federal Circuit disagreed: "[T]he primary ill avoided by . . . the double patenting doctrine is restriction on the public's freedom to use the invention claimed in a patent and all obvious modifications of it after that patent *expired*." *Id.* at 1215.

A dissent, however, considered this new rule unwarranted, especially given that the two previously accepted policy rationales underlying the judicially-created doctrine were not applicable. In other words, this extension of the double patenting rule did not either (1) prevent an extension of patent term, or (2) avoid multiple infringement suits by different assignees asserting essentially the same patented invention. *Id.* at 1218 (Rader, J., dissenting).

C. TERMINAL DISCLAIMER

Importantly, an applicant may separately claim subject matter nearly identical to an earlier filing so long as it uses a terminal disclaimer to disclaim any patent term beyond the expiration of the first patent. A terminal disclaimer may overcome obviousness-type, but not same invention, double patenting. As amended in the Leahy-Smith America Invents Act, U.S. patent law authorizes this practice:

> Whenever a claim of a patent is invalid the remaining claims shall not thereby be rendered invalid. A patentee, whether of the whole or any sectional interest therein, may, on payment of the fee required by law, make disclaimer of any complete claim, stating therein the extent of his interest in such patent. Such disclaimer shall be in writing and recorded in the Patent and Trademark Office, and it shall thereafter be considered as part of the original patent to the extent of the interest possessed by the disclaimant and by those claiming under him.

35 U.S.C. § 253(a). Under a terminal disclaimer, the term of the obvious variant of the initial patent expires concurrently with the term of the initial patent. A terminal disclaimer, however, only remains effective if the patents remain commonly owned throughout their terms. 37 C.F.R. § 1.321(c).

The practical effect of non-statutory double patenting is likely to decrease with the change in patent term from 17 years from issuance to 20 years from the effective filing. Patent applications claiming priority to the same parent can obtain no longer term (absent a patent term adjustment under § 154(b)), even without a terminal disclaimer. Terminal disclaimers remain necessary to ensure common ownership of the later patent with the earlier one.

V. INTERNATIONAL PROSECUTION

To adequately protect an invention in the international marketplace, a patent attorney must work with foreign, as well as domestic, patent laws. Despite harmonizing efforts of some international agreements—such as the Paris Convention, the Patent Cooperation Treaty, and the World Trade Organization's TRIPS agreement—there are still significant differences in patent practice from one country to another. Chapter 17 will discuss the implication of these international agreements in domestic U.S. law.

VI. THE BAYH-DOLE ACT

The Bayh-Dole Act of 1980, relating to ownership of patents obtained using federal funding, deserves mention here. Before the Act, federal research funding contracts commonly required anyone who made a patentable invention using federal funding to assign the resulting patent(s) to the federal government. The Act reversed this policy. Specifically, it allows certain government contractors—namely universities, small businesses, and nonprofit organizations—to retain ownership of patents that arise from their research and development efforts made pursuant to their government contracts. *See* 35 U.S.C. § 202. In essence, universities gained the important ability to own and monetize their patented inventions, even though the inventions were discovered with federal funding. The Act thus encouraged economic activity as an antidote to the economic malaise that plagued the 1970s.

But a government contractor's right to own its patent is not absolute under the Act. The federal agency that funded the research retains a "nonexclusive, nontransferable, irrevocable, paid-up license" to practice the invention. *See* 35 U.S.C. § 202(c)(4). Further, in certain situations, government contractors may still have to assign their patents to the government—for example, where they lack a place of business in the U.S., where "exceptional circumstances" arise, or where the federal government's ownership of the invention is necessary to further national security goals. *See* 35 U.S.C. § 202(a).

Further, inventive government contractors' ownership of their federally-funded patents is subject to the federal government's so-called "march-in rights." Using these rights, the funding agency can require the contractor to license the invention to a third-party "applicant" "upon terms that are reasonable under the circumstances." 35 U.S.C. § 203. If the contractor refuses, then the agency itself can grant a license to the applicant. *Id.* It has recently been reported that, since 1980, no federal agency has ever exercised its march-in rights to license an applicant. John R. Thomas, *March-In*

Rights Under the Bayh-Dole Act 8 (2016). The National Institutes of Health (NIH) has apparently received a handful of march-in petitions by applicants, but has denied each one. *Id.* In any event, it remains a possibility.

In *Bd. of Trustees of Leland Stanford Junior Univ. v. Roche Molecular Sys., Inc.*, 563 U.S. 776 (2011), Court addressed whether the Bayh-Dole Act automatically vests ownership of a federally-funded patent with the government contractor. It held it does not. Dr. Mark Holodniy, a research fellow at Stanford University (a federal contractor), collaborated with Cetus (a small company) to develop Nobel Prize-winning technique for quantifying blood borne levels of HIV. When he joined Stanford in 1988, he signed a contract stating he "agree[d] to assign" any patent rights he might obtain from the project to Stanford. But meanwhile, he signed a parallel contract with Cetus stating that he "will assign and do[es] hereby assign" his patent rights to Cetus. Cetus was later acquired by Roche—a third-party whom Stanford sued for patent infringement. In litigation, Roche asserted the defense that it actually owned Stanford's patent-in-suit by virtue of Cetus's agreement with Dr. Holodniy. The controversy thus arose as to who owned the patent—Stanford, or Cetus.

The district court held that Dr. Holodniy's contracts purported to give Cetus full patent rights, and left Stanford with none. But the Bayh-Dole Act saved the day for Stanford. Under the Bayh-Dole Act, the court reasoned, Dr. Holodniy had no interest to assign to Cetus because the individual inventor may obtain title to a federally-funded invention *only after* the government and the contractor (here, Stanford) had declined title.

The Federal Circuit and Supreme Court disagreed. "Since 1790, the patent law has operated on the premise that rights in an invention belong to the inventor." *Stanford*, 563 U.S. at 780. And while the Bayh-Dole Act allows government contractors to *retain* title in a patent, it does not *vest* title with contractors. Instead, even after the Bayh-Dole Act, patent ownership initially vests with the inventors, who are free to assign as they wish. And here, Dr. Holodniy chose to assign his patent rights to Cetus, the small company, not Stanford, the federal contractor. In the end, Stanford was apparently left with nothing more than a claim against Dr. Holodniy for breach of his contract promising to assign his patents to Stanford.

CHAPTER 11

THE PATENT TRIAL AND APPEAL BOARD

I. INTRODUCTION

Congress's creation of the Patent Trial and Appeal Board ("PTAB")—an administrative adjudicatory body within the Patent Office—was a significant change to the U.S. patent system. Following a boom in patenting largely due to the proliferation of the internet, the PTAB was established as a way to solve the alleged problem of having "too much" intellectual property in circulation. (Opponents to this theory respond that there cannot be too much public disclosure of non-obviousness inventions.) In essence, the creation of the PTAB is an extension of the Patent Office's traditional powers to amend or alter patents that it has already examined and issued.

In the AIA, Congress re-named the Board of Patent Appeals and Interferences ("BPAI") as the PTAB, and gave it new responsibilities, including presiding over the new adjudicatory proceedings established by the AIA. The PTAB can be viewed as a hybrid of the former BPAI proceedings and federal district court validity litigation. This view emphasizes Congress's express intention to provide a cheaper, quicker alternative to district court litigation over patent validity.

The PTAB comprises "persons of competent legal knowledge and scientific ability." 35 U.S.C. § 6(a). Within just a few years after the enactment of the

AIA, the Board quickly grew from about 80 administrative law judges to nearly 300. Many of the new judges are experienced patent litigators, seeking to "go where the action is" in patent law.

II. PTAB PROCEEDINGS

Below is an introduction to each type of PTAB proceeding established by the AIA.

A. POST-GRANT REVIEW

Anyone other than the patent owner may petition the PTAB to institute a post-grant review (PGR) within nine months of the patent's issuance. The scope of PGRs is broad, as a petitioner can make any validity challenge.

PGRs are rarely used, as recent statistics show that PGRs make up only about 2% of the PTAB's docket. This reality is predictable. For one, the nine-month deadline for requesting PGR presents a significant challenge: a patent challenger must both actively monitor other patent owners and "pounce" immediately upon a threatening patent. Without such a diligent plan, the market often does not identify threatening patents until later in the patent term.

PGRs also carry a relatively significant risk that a petitioner will be estopped in later litigation from making invalidity arguments that it "reasonably could have" made, but did not, in the PGR. 35 U.S.C. § 325(e).

The PTAB institutes a PGR if the petition shows it is "more likely than not" that at least one challenged claim is unpatentable. 35 U.S.C. § 324. Notably, the same three-judge panel that makes this determination also ultimately issues the final written decision. This fact creates the interesting psychological phenomenon that, in order for a PTAB panel to uphold a patent's validity in a PGR, therefore, it must decide contrary to its own earlier conclusion that the challenged claims are "more likely than not" invalid. Some commentators suspect that this reality tends to skew outcomes towards findings of unpatentability to some extent.

PGRs may also be instituted if the petition raises a "novel or unsettled legal question that is important to other patents or patent applications." *Id.* At the time this edition is published, the authors are not aware of any instance where the PTAB instituted a PGR for this reason.

Below is a typical timeline of events that take place in PGRs:

Event	Deadline
PGR petition	9 months after patent issuance
Patent owner's preliminary response	3 months after petition

Institution decision	3 months after preliminary response to the petition
Patent owner's response and motion to amend claims	3 months after institution
Petitioner's reply	3 months after patent owner response
Patent owner's sur-reply	1 month after petitioner's reply
Hearing (if requested)	To be determined
Final written decision	Approximately one year after institution

Limited discovery is permitted in PGRs, in part to deter parties from filing baseless declarations. Discovery in PGRs is "limited to the evidence directly related to factual assertions advanced by either party in the proceeding." 35 U.S.C. § 326. According to PTO rules, "routine discovery" includes (1) production of any exhibit cited in a paper or testimony; (2) the cross-examination of the other side's declarants; and (3) relevant information that is inconsistent with a position advanced during the proceeding. 37 C.F.R. § 42.51. Additional discovery beyond that is only available upon a showing of "good cause." 37 C.F.R.

§ 42.224. The following factors are considered to determine "good cause":

- The moving party must provide a specific factual reason for expecting reasonably that the discovery will be useful, i.e., having substantive value;
- Asking for the other party's litigation positions and their underlying bases is insufficient to demonstrate good cause;
- A party should not seek information that reasonably be generated without a discovery request;
- Instructions and questions should be easily understandable; and
- A request must not be overly burdensome in terms of time, cost, or human resources.

Bloomberg Inc. v. Markets-Alert Pty Ltd., No. CBM2013-00005, 2013 WL 11311787 (PTAB May 29, 2013) (Paper 32) (precedential).

Hearings are optional and more closely resemble an appellate argument before the Federal Circuit than a district court trial. In typical PTAB hearings, counsel address the PTAB's questions, and witnesses do not testify.

The PTAB's final written decisions are appealable directly to the Federal Circuit. 35 U.S.C. § 329. But the PTAB's decisions on whether to institute a proceeding are *not* appealable—either as an interlocutory appeal immediately following the institution decision or after the final written decision is issued. *Cf. Cuozzo Speed Techs., LLC v. Lee*, 579 U.S. 261, 272–73 (2016).

B. INTER PARTES REVIEW

IPRs are the much more common PTAB proceeding. IPRs currently comprise over 90% of all PTAB cases. Congress intended IPRs to be a cheaper, quicker alternative to district court litigation—and in this regard IPRs have been successful. District court defendants have flocked to the PTAB for IPRs, often taking wind from the sails of district court litigation. Indeed, a district court's stay of a case pending an IPR (and subsequent appeal) often results in a two-or-more year hiatus before the case can continue towards the jury trial.

IPRs resemble PGRs, but have a few important differences. First is timing: IPRs follow PGRs chronologically. Anyone who is not the patent owner may request an IPR *after* the nine-month PGR window closes—or, if a PGR is instituted, after the PGR concludes. Another important difference is that IPR petitioners may only assert a small number of validity challenges, namely anticipation or obviousness in light of patents and printed publications. 35 U.S.C. § 311(b). These validity challenges are based on materials outside the patent itself. Other invalidity grounds—such as ineligible subject matter, lack of written description, non-enablement, and indefiniteness—often focus on the content of the patent, and are outside the scope of IPRs.

Further, because the available grounds for IPRs are fewer in number, it stands to reason that IPRs involve a reduced risk of estoppel—that is, a lower risk that a petitioner will later be barred from asserting invalidity grounds that it "raised or reasonably could have raised" in the IPR. 35 U.S.C. § 315(e). Given the narrow scope of IPRs, petitioners only risk estoppel as to §§ 102 and 103 arguments relying on patents and printed publications. All other invalidity arguments are preserved for the future.

The PTAB institutes an IPR not when the petition shows that a claim is "more likely than not" unpatentable, as in PGRs, but rather when it shows a "reasonable likelihood that the petitioner would prevail with respect to at least 1 of the claims challenged in the petition." 35 U.S.C. § 314. IPRs are thus ostensibly somewhat easier to institute than PGRs. And unlike PGRs, the PTAB cannot institute an IPR because the petition shows a "novel or unsettled legal question." *See id.*

According to recent PTO statistics, about 115 IPR petitions and a handful of PGR petitions are filed every month. On average the PTAB grants about 60% of all IPR petitions, which means that the PTAB conducts IPRs on about 65% of all challenged patents. Electrical and computer inventions are by far the most frequently challenged, as such petitions make up about 65% of all petitions. Mechanical and business method patents are in second place with 22%, and chemical and biopharma patents are challenged in about 13% of all petitions.

IPRs generally follow the same timeline as PGRs. *See supra*, § II(A).

Discovery in IPRs focuses on depositions scrutinizing declarations and relied-upon exhibits. Thus, like PGRs, guard against submission of baseless declarations. But in IPRs there is no express statutory requirement that discovery be "directly related to factual assertions" of the parties. Also, additional discovery in IPRs is harder to obtain than in PGRs: it is only available when "necessary in the interest of justice." 35 U.S.C. § 316(a)(5)(B). Factors nearly identical to the *Bloomberg* good-cause factors apply to determining whether additional discovery is necessary in the interest of justice. *Garmin Int'l, Inc. v. Cuozzo Speed Techs. LLC*, Case IPR2012-00001 (PTAB Mar. 5, 2013) (Paper 26) (precedential). One difference is that here the moving party "should already be in possession of evidence tending to show beyond speculation that in fact something useful will be uncovered."

The laws governing the PTAB and inter partes review have been the subject of significant controversy at the Supreme Court since their enactment. The Supreme Court has issued several decisions interpreting those laws. In *SAS Institute, Inc. v. Iancu*, 138 S. Ct. 1348 (2018), the Court held that, under § 318(a), the PTAB must address the patentability of all challenged claims in its final written decision, and therefore the PTAB may not institute IPR on only a subset of challenged claims. In *Thryv, Inc. v. Click-to-Call Technologies, LP*, 140 S. Ct. 1367 (2020), the Supreme Court held that, under § 314(d), the PTAB's institution decisions are non-appealable. This means that a party "a party generally cannot contend on appeal that the agency should have refused 'to institute an inter partes review,'" *id.* at 1373, and more particularly, a party may not argue that the PTAB should have denied institution on untimeliness grounds, *id.* at 1373–1374. Further, in *Return Mail, Inc. v. United States Postal Service*, 139 S. Ct. 1853 (2019), the Court held that a "person" permitted to petition for inter partes review under § 311(a) does not include federal agencies.

C. DERIVATION PROCEEDINGS

Derivations flow from Congress's decision to change the U.S. patent system from first-to-invent to first-inventor-to-file. In the former first-to-invent regime, the PTO conducted "interference proceedings" to determine the true first inventor of a patent claim. In interferences, competing inventors strove to prove the earliest date of invention using, for example, lab notebooks.

With the AIA, the identity of the first true inventor became less important. In general, patents would be awarded to the first applicant. But the AIA preserved a mechanism for awarding patents to later applicants in a certain situation—when the first-filer unfairly applies for a patent on an invention appropriated from another.

Derivation proceedings must be filed within a year after a patent claim is published. 37 C.F.R. § 42.403. A petitioner must show that it has at least one claim that is "substantially the same" as the respondent's claimed invention, and that (i) the claimed invention was derived from the petitioner, and (ii) the petitioner did not authorize the respondent's patent application. Generally, a petition will be deemed insufficient without significant corroborating evidence—such as affidavits explaining how the invention was derived from the petitioner, and detailing the respondent's lack of authorization.

D. REVIEW OF EXAMINER DECISIONS

The PTAB also continues to carry out several responsibilities of the former BPAI. These duties include reviewing examiners' rejections and reviewing examiners' decisions in *ex parte* reexaminations. These proceedings follow long-standing procedures allowing challenge to final rejection of a patent application or reexamination.

III. CONSTITUTIONALITY

The PTAB and its proceedings under the AIA have undergone multiple constitutional challenges at the Supreme Court since the AIA's enactment. For example, in *United States v. Arthrex, Inc.*, 141 S. Ct. 1970 (2021), the Court held that the powers granted to administrative patent judges (APJs) on the PTAB violate the Appointments Clause. This Clause requires that principal officers of the United States must be nominated by the President and confirmed by the Senate. The AIA ran afoul of this rule by insulating APJs' final decisions from review by the Director. To cure the problem, the Court held that those provisions are unenforceable insofar as they prevent the Director from reviewing the PTAB's final decisions. After *Arthrex*, the PTO created a procedure whereby a party could request the Director's review of a final written decision by the PTAB.

Litigants have also argued that the AIA's post-grant procedures are unconstitutional for other reasons. For example, some have objected to the first-to-file regime on the grounds that Art. I, § 8, cl. 8 expressly contemplates awarding patents to "inventors," not mere filers. Others contend that the PTAB violates the Separation of Powers by usurping the Judicial Branch's exclusive historical role of adjudicating "cases and controversies" over patents—traditionally deemed private property. Still others object that AIA abridges patent holders' right to a jury trial guaranteed by the Seventh Amendment.

The Supreme Court has seemed reluctant to address these issues, denying certiorari multiple times before finally take a case. The Supreme Court may have been prompted to address the issue by a split Federal Circuit decision, in which Judge Reyna bucked the trend of Supreme Court's certiorari denials and wrote a lengthy dissent to the court's denial of en banc rehearing on the AIA's constitutionality. *See Cascades Projection LLC v. Epson Am., Inc.*, 864 F.3d 1309 (Fed. Cir. 2017). This dissent enumerated cogent arguments in favor of the AIA's unconstitutionality, and concluded:

> The Board's cancellation of patents through inter partes review may be the type of agency

> activity that 'sap[s] the judicial power as it exists under the federal Constitution' and 'establish[es] a government of a bureaucratic character alien to our system.' Or, it may not. It is a question we should address.

Id. at 1326. The Supreme Court granted certiorari on the issue a month later.

Specifically, in *Oil States Energy Servs., LLC v. Greene's Energy Group, LLC*, 138 S. Ct. 1365 (2018), the Supreme Court held that IPR proceedings violate neither the separation of powers doctrine nor the 7th Amendment right to jury trial. Oil States sued Greene's Energy for infringing its patent on a way to protect well-head equipment used in fracking. Greene's Energy responded by petitioning the PTAB for an IPR, and the district court case and IPR proceeded for a time in parallel. The district court eventually issued its claim construction order, foreclosing one of Greene's Energy's invalidity arguments. But a few months later, the PTAB issued its final written decision in the IPR in which it found the challenged claims invalid based on the very same invalidity argument. Oil States appealed, arguing that under Article III to the Constitution the federal judiciary alone has the power to cancel an issued patent, not an executive administrative body like the PTAB.

The Supreme Court disagreed. A central issue was whether patent rights are "public rights" or "public rights." In general, private rights tend to involve liability of one person to another, and are reserved for the federal judiciary alone to adjudicate. *N.*

Pipeline Const. Co. v. Marathon Pipe Line Co., 458 U.S. 50, 70 (1982). Public rights, in contrast, typically arise between the government and citizens—and Congress has latitude to place an executive administrative agency in charge of administering and adjudicating them. *Id.* Before the *Oil States*, patent rights were believed by many to be a mixture—and even perhaps somewhat on the side of private rights. But the Court pronounced in *Oil States* that patent rights "fall squarely within the public-rights doctrine." *Oil States*, 138 S. Ct. 1373. As such, the PTO has broad authority under Article III to the Constitution to adjudicate and revoke issued patents. After all, according to the Court, IPRs "involve the same basic matter as the grant of a patent," and are merely a "second look at an earlier administrative grant of a patent." *Id.* at 1374. The mere fact that the patent-at-issue in an IPR has already issued "does not make a difference here." *Id.*

A potential upshot of *Oil States* is that the patent system could become more subject to the political winds—and conceivably change dramatically depending on who is in power. Justice Gorsuch's dissent frames the dispute in these terms. According to Justice Gorsuch, to strip patent litigants of the judiciary's guarded neutrality is to heighten the risk of injecting policy debates and preferences into the operation of the patent system.

Notably, the Court also expressly limited its decision to the Article III and 7th Amendment questions, and clarified that the Court had not foreclosed the possibility of challenging the PTAB's unpatentability decisions as Due Process violations or Takings.

IV. CLAIM CONSTRUCTION

Initially, the PTAB used the broadest reasonable interpretation ("BRI") standard of claim construction in IPRs, but this practice became the subject of controversy. Eventually, the PTAB switched to claim construction under *Phillips v. AWH Corp.*, 415 F.3d 1303, 1309 (Fed. Cir. 2005), where the decision maker ascertains how a person or ordinary skill in the art would have understood the claims at the time of filing.

Patent examiners have long given claims their "broadest reasonable interpretation" during patent prosecution and reexamination. The BRI standard places a thumb on the scale in favor of rejecting claims in close cases, and thus promotes higher quality of issued patent claims. This may seem unfair at first glance, but any such unfairness is mitigated by the applicant's opportunity to amend the claims to circumvent the asserted prior art.

Controversy arose because, although the PTAB gave claim terms their broadest reasonable interpretation in IPRs and PGRs, the statute does not give patent owners an absolute right to amend their claims; instead it merely "allow[s] the patent owner to move to amend" the patent by amending or canceling claims or proposing a reasonable number of substitute claims. *See* 35 U.S.C. §§ 316(a)(9), 326(a)(9). The PTO's rules, in turn, presumptively permit a patent owner to propose one substitute claim for each challenged claim. *See* 37 C.F.R. §§ 42.121, 42.221. These motions have enjoyed almost no success. According to recent data, the PTAB has granted about 1% of all motions to amend.

Some argued that one reason the PTAB has allowed so few amendments was its early practice of applying a presumption against amendments. Specifically, the PTAB placed the burden of proof (preponderance of evidence) on patent owners to prove that their proposed substitute claims overcame all the invalidity arguments raised by the petitioner. In a highly fractured opinion, the en banc Federal Circuit eschewed the PTAB's presumption and re-allocated the burden of proof to the petitioner—requiring the petitioner to show that the patent owner's proposed substitute claims are unpatentable in light of the entirety of the record. *See Aqua Prods., Inc. v. Matal*, 872 F.3d 1290, 1296 (Fed. Cir. 2017). *Aqua Products* was a highly anticipated decision that some believed would cause a "sea change" in favor of claim amendments at the PTAB. It does not appear, however, that *Aqua Products*' effect was quite that great.

In *Cuozzo Speed Technologies, LLC v. Lee*, 579 U.S. 261 (2016), the Supreme Court held that the PTO may apply the BRI claim construction standard in IPRs—even absent a robust right for the patent owner to amend. There, inventor Giuseppe Cuozzo obtained a patent on a speedometer that discovered the applicable speed limit on a certain stretch of road using GPS, and informed the driver of excessive speed. Garmin challenged the patent via IPR. Giving the claims their broadest reasonable interpretation, the PTAB concluded that they were obvious in light of prior art identified by Garmin.

Mr. Cuozzo appealed, arguing that the PTO lacked authority to prescribe use of BRI standard through regulation. *See* 37 C.F.R. § 42.100. The Federal Circuit held that Congress plainly allowed the PTO to adopt the BRI rule for IPRs under 35 U.S.C. § 316(a)(4): "the [PTO] Director shall prescribe regulations . . . establishing and governing inter partes review under this chapter."

The Supreme Court agreed. Applying *Chevron*, the Court first pointed out that a gap existed in the statute—it did not require the application of either the BRI standard or the *Phillips* standard for claim construction. And second, the Court concluded that the PTO's choice of the BRI standard was reasonable and thus deserved deference.

The Court specifically addressed Mr. Cuozzo's argument that it is unfair for the PTAB to use the BRI standard in IPRs without giving patent owners real opportunity to amend claims. "This process," it concluded, "is not as unfair as Cuozzo suggests." Without much elaboration, the Court stated the opportunity to move to amend in IPRs, combined with the opportunities to amend given to the patent applicant during the original prosecution, gave the patentee sufficient opportunity to amend.

A question in response to the Supreme Court's reasoning is—what if an invalidity ground is raised for the first time during a post-grant proceeding at the PTAB, and the PTAB denies the patent owner's motion to amend in light of the new challenge? There, the patent owner may have been denied a fair chance to amend—casting doubt on the propriety of using the BRI standard.

Eventually, the PTO changed its rules to require the PTAB to use the *Phillips* claim construction standard and thus interpret claims according to their actual, not broadest reasonable, interpretation as understood by a skilled artisan. But it remains possible that the PTO could revert to the BRI standard.

V. ESTOPPEL

In post-grant PTAB proceedings, the petitioner must carefully choose which invalidity arguments to assert. The reason is that a petitioner may later be estopped from asserting invalidity arguments—in either district court litigation or other PTO proceedings—that it could have made but did not. *See* 35 U.S.C. § 315(e); 35 U.S.C. § 325(e).

The scope of estoppel is generally commensurate with the scope of invalidity arguments that are available in the proceeding. Because PGRs offer any validity challenge, it stands to reason that by filing a PGR, a petitioner might risk waiving a wide array of invalidity arguments. By comparison, because IPRs permit validity challenges based only on anticipation and obviousness grounds in light of patents and printed publications, IPR petitioners risk estoppel only on those types of arguments in subsequent proceedings.

A wrinkle in estoppel rules was created by the PTO's now-defunct regulation giving the PTAB latitude to choose the scope of an IPR or PGR. Specifically, the PTAB could institute proceedings as to (i) "some or all" of the challenged claims, and (ii) "some or all" of the asserted unpatentability grounds. *See* 37 C.F.R. §§ 42.108, 42.208 (2016). This discretion gave rise to the question—would estoppel apply to grounds or claims that the petitioner raised in the petition, but for which the PTAB denied institution?

In *Shaw Indus. Grp., Inc. v. Automated Creel Sys., Inc.*, 817 F.3d 1293 (Fed. Cir. 2016), the Federal Circuit held that estoppel does not arise for claims or grounds on which the PTAB denied institution, and therefore such claims and grounds may be asserted again in later litigation. In *Shaw*, ACS owned the '360 patent on a "creel" system for supplying yarn and other stranded materials to a manufacturing process. Accused infringer Shaw sought an IPR challenging all claims based on fifteen grounds. The PTAB instituted for all challenged claims except claim 4, and only as to two out of 15 asserted unpatentability grounds.

Months later, Shaw requested a second IPR on claim 4 based on two unpatentability grounds—one on which the PTAB denied institution based on Shaw's previous petition, and one on which the PTAB granted institution. This time, the PTAB instituted IPR for these claims and grounds, and ultimately invalidated the claim.

Automated Steel appealed, arguing that the PTAB should not be allowed to deny institution to address an invalidity argument, and then later grant institution to hear that same argument. The Federal Circuit explained that estoppel can only apply to claims and unpatentability grounds that are asserted "during" the proceeding. *Shaw*, at 1300 (quoting 35 U.S.C. § 315(e)). And because at the institution stage no IPR or PGR has even begun, estoppel does not apply to un-instituted claims or unpatentability grounds.

More recently, in *SAS*, the Supreme Court solved this problem by holding that the PTAB may not partially institute, i.e., institute only on certain claims. 138 S. Ct. at 1352–53. Accordingly, the Federal Circuit later clarified that "estoppel applies not just to claims and grounds asserted in the petition and instituted for consideration by the Board, but to all grounds not stated in the petition but which reasonably could have been asserted against the claims included in the petition." *California Inst. of Tech. v. Broadcom Ltd.*, 25 F.4th 976, 991 (Fed. Cir. 2022). Applying this principle, the court in *Broadcom* held that the defendants were estopped from asserting certain prior art references in district court, because they were undisputedly aware of those references when they filed their IPR petitions but did not include the references in the petitions. *Id.* Following this case, petitioners would be prudent to assert all the strongest grounds that they are aware of in IPRs or else risk estoppel later.

The question of whether an unpatentability ground "could have been raised" has confounded the courts and remains an open question following *Broadcom*. Some courts have adopted the test of determining what a skilled prior art searcher would have discovered through a diligent search. *See, e.g.*, *Clearlamp, LLC v. LKQ Corp.*, No. 12 C 2533, 2016 WL 4734389, at *7–10 (N.D. Ill. Mar. 18, 2016). The Clearlamp court explained that "[o]ne way to show what a skilled search would have found would be (1) to identify the search string and search source that would identify the allegedly unavailable prior art, and (2) present evidence, likely expert testimony, why such a criterion would be part of a skilled searcher's diligent search." *Id.* This test appears to be gaining traction among district courts, *see, e.g.*, *Trustid, Inc. v. Next Caller Inc.*, No. 18-172 (MN), 2021 WL 3015280, at *1 (D. Del. July 6, 2021), but to date it has not been approved by the Federal Circuit.

VI. STAYS OF DISTRICT COURT LITIGATION

District courts' authority to stay litigation in favor of PTAB proceedings contribute to the far-reaching effects of the AIA. This authority introduces obstacles to patent owners seeking to enforce their patents, and on the other side of the coin, it gives defendants opportunities to delay and attack the patent-in-suit in a relatively inexpensive administrative proceeding.

Most of the time, a district court will stay litigation pending completion of a corresponding PTAB proceeding. In *Versata Software, Inc. v. Callidus Software, Inc.*, 771 F.3d 1368 (Fed. Cir. 2014), the Federal Circuit reversed a district court's discretionary decision not to stay the case. The court applied the four-factor statutory test for CBMs, which mirrors the applicable test for IPRs and PGRs.

1. Simplification of the issues. Even though Callidus only sought CBM review for a subset of the patent claims at issue, this factor weighed in favor of stay. "[A] proper simplification analysis would look to what would be resolved by CBM review versus what would remain." *Id.* at 1372. Thus, this factor does not require that the CBM encompass all the issues present in the district court case in order to favor stay.

2. Stage of the case. The district court erred first by considering the stage of the case at the expected time of the PTAB's decision. It is the time of filing the motion to stay that counts. Further, courts are permitted to wait until the PTAB decides to institute a proceeding before it decides to stay the case. But this factor generally only disfavors a stay if the district court case is very far advanced, i.e., close to trial.

3. Undue prejudice to non-moving party. Defendants are generally within their rights to request a PTAB proceeding. For this reason, merely requesting a CBM and filing a motion to stay does not, by itself, amount to improper gamesmanship. This factor is only likely to disfavor a stay if additional reasons are present—such as

frivolousness of the defendant's PTAB petition or motion to stay.

4. Burden of litigation. The district court found that Callidus's efforts to transfer the case to the PTAB increased litigation burdens, not decreased them. But this was error because the district court should not evaluate this factor using a "backward-looking lens." Instead, the district court should focus prospectively on the impact of a litigation stay. "When framed appropriately, it becomes clear that a stay will indeed reduce the future burdens of litigation."

Finding clear error in several respects, the Federal Circuit vacated the district court's decision denying stay and remanded with instructions to stay the case.

CHAPTER 12

CLAIMS

I. INTRODUCTION

A. CENTRAL LEGAL ELEMENT OF A PATENT

A patent is, quite simply, the right to exclude others from making, using, selling, offering to sell, or importing inventive technology. But where does that exclusive right begin and end? Before testing for either infringement or validity, the exclusive right requires first a definition of the boundaries of the invention. Claims, which define those boundaries, are therefore a patent's most critical component. In fact, the Federal Circuit has proclaimed, quoting the celebrated and late Judge Giles Rich: "the name of the game is the claim." *In re Hiniker Co.*, 150 F.3d 1362, 1369 (Fed. Cir. 1998). A common metaphor equates the claim with a fence around the inventor's property right.

In accordance with their importance, claims are undeniably the most difficult drafting assignment in patent law and maybe even the most difficult drafting task in all fields of law. *Topliff v. Topliff*, 145 U.S. 156 (1892). After all, claims must describe and define complex technical subject matter in terms broad enough to foresee and capture future related technology and at the same time narrow enough to avoid all past related technology. The drafter must foresee future technology and distinguish past technology.

Perhaps most difficult, the drafter must succinctly define something that has never existed before in language of the past. Yet, this legal document must reflect the understanding of a person with ordinary skill in the art, a decidedly scientific point of view. In short, claim drafting puts a premium on technical and legal skill alike, without which the value of the invention decreases dramatically.

Chapter 13 addresses the processes courts use to divine the meaning of claims—a deceptively challenging task on par with claim drafting. This chapter addresses general and specific claim formats in addition to discussing definiteness, another patentability requirement.

B. HISTORICAL DEVELOPMENT

The Patent Act has only required a specific claim for the past century and a half. The first Patent Act in 1793, 1 Stat. 318, merely required that an inventor describe the invention in the body of the specification, without delineating its outer bounds. The Act, however, had a similar, even if less exacting, requirement that the inventor provide "a written description of his invention, and of the manner of using, or process of compounding the same, in such full, clear, and exact terms, as to distinguish the same from all other things before known." *In re Barker*, 559 F.2d 588, 592 (CCPA 1977). This aspect of the disclosure—the closest ancestor of the modern claiming requirement—served a vital purpose:

> It is, therefore, for the purpose of warning an innocent purchaser, or other person using a

> machine, of his infringement of the patent; and at the same time, of taking from the inventor the means of practicing upon the credulity or the fears of other persons, by pretending that his invention is more than what it really is, or different from its ostensible objects, that the patentee is required to distinguish his invention in his specification.

Evans v. Eaton, 20 U.S. (7 Wheat.) 356, 433–34 (1822). This general description requirement of early U.S. patent law is often referred to as "central claiming."

Although the term "claim" first appeared in the Patent Act of 1836, Chap. 357, 5 Stat. 117, claims did not become a statutory requirement until the Patent Act of 1870, Chap. 230, § 26, 16 Stat. 198. Indeed, section 26 of that Act required that a patentee "shall particularly point out and distinctly claim the part, improvement, or combination which he claims as his invention or discovery." Since then, all patentees must conclude the specification with at least one peripheral claim defining the exclusive right. *See, e.g.*, *McClain v. Ortmayer*, 141 U.S. 419, 424 (1891) (explaining that a patent "apprise[s] the public of what is still open to them"). "The scope of letters-patent must be limited to the invention covered by the claim . . . ." *Yale Lock Mfg. Co. v. Greenleaf*, 117 U.S. 554, 559 (1886). This type of claiming is called "peripheral claiming" to distinguish it from its "central claiming" ancestor.

C. § 112

The 1952 Patent Act, as amended, sets out the standards for claims, in both form as well as substance. As stated by § 112, claims constitute a portion of the specification, even if practitioners colloquially refer to the written description as the sole constituent of the specification. *See In re Dossel*, 115 F.3d 942 (Fed. Cir. 1997). Section 112 describes the requirements of claims:

> (b) CONCLUSION.—The specification shall conclude with one or more claims particularly pointing out and distinctly claiming the subject matter which the inventor or a joint inventor regards as the invention.
>
> (c) FORM.—A claim may be written in independent or, if the nature of the case admits, in dependent or multiple dependent form.
>
> (d) REFERENCE IN DEPENDENT FORMS.—Subject to subsection (e), a claim in dependent form shall contain a reference to a claim previously set forth and then specify a further limitation of the subject matter claimed. A claim in dependent form shall be construed to incorporate by reference all the limitations of the claim to which it refers.
>
> (e) REFERENCE IN MULTIPLE DEPENDENT FORM.—A claim in multiple dependent form shall contain a reference, in the alternative only, to more than one claim previously set forth and then specify a further limitation of the subject matter claimed. A

> multiple dependent claim shall not serve as a basis for any other multiple dependent claim. A multiple dependent claim shall be construed to incorporate by reference all the limitations of the particular claim in relation to which it is being considered.
>
> (f) ELEMENT IN CLAIM FOR A COMBINATION.—An element in a claim for a combination may be expressed as a means or step for performing a specified function without the recital of structure, material, or acts in support thereof, and such claim shall be construed to cover the corresponding structure, material, or acts described in the specification and equivalents thereof.

35 U.S.C. § 112 (2012).

Subsection (b) sets forth the substantive requirement of claims: they must particularly point out and distinctly claim their subject matter. This definiteness requirement mandates that a patentee sufficiently notify the public (as well as the Patent Office) of the bounds of the invention.

The other subsections set forth acceptable forms for claims, e.g., permitting independent, dependent, and (in limited circumstances) multiple dependent claims. The last paragraph, subsection (f), authorizes the use of "means-plus-function" claims. Because this paragraph carries its own special rules (in some ways using features of central claiming in the modern era), skilled practitioners often advise sparing and careful use of this alternative claim format.

Although this chapter serves as an introduction to the basic rules of claims and their format, drafting and prosecuting claims of appropriate scope requires legal skills honed only with experience. Simply put, purely academic study cannot serve as a substitute for exposure to the idiosyncrasies of the Patent Office, the conventions of the patent bar, and the past judicial treatment of claim terms and formats.

II. PARTS OF A CLAIM

At their incipiency, patent practitioners drafted "omnibus" claims in which the patentees claimed the invention "substantially as described" in his description. These claims provided only nebulous boundaries and relied heavily on the drawings and description to define the scope of the invention. Modern practice, however, places a premium on precise claim structure and language.

A claim has three parts: a preamble, a transitional phrase, and a body. Although these parts have varying degrees of significance in each case, each serves a critical legal function. As the statute permits, a claim may depend from—that is, incorporate all the limitations of—another claim.

Consider these hypothetical claims:

What is claimed is:

> 1. A book for a collection of pictographs comprising a front cover and a plurality of slate pages.

> 2. A book for a collection of pictographs according to claim 1, wherein the front cover consists of granite.

In claim 1, the independent claim, the preamble is "[a] book for a collection of pictographs"; the transitional phrase uses the legal term of art, "comprising"; and the body of the claim is "a front cover and a plurality of slate pages." Claim 2 depends from claim 1, thus incorporating all the limitations of claim 1, and further defines the claimed book as having a front cover made from granite.

A. ONE-SENTENCE RULE

Patent Office guidance makes each claim the predicate of a single sentence that begins with one of the following phrases (or something similar): "I claim"; "The invention claimed is"; or "What is claimed is." Manual of Patent Examining Procedure § 608.01(m). Although not a statutory requirement, the single sentence convention falls within the Patent Office's discretion under § 112. *Fressola v. Manbeck*, 36 USPQ2d 1211 (D.D.C. 1995). The *Fressola* court, in fact, lauded the one-sentence rule:

> [T]he one-sentence rule has no impact on the clarity of claims and has fostered the efficient processing of several million patent applications . . . Indeed, the Court believes that the one-sentence rule may even advance these statutory goals by encouraging claims that are generally more succinct than multiple-sentence claims of the same scope.

Id. at 1213–14. And specifically with respect to the statute, the court explained:

> While the statutory language may give the applicant ultimate control over the *substance* of his claim, it does not appear to speak to matters of pure *form*, such as the number of sentences allowed per claim; in other words, since an applicant can . . . make exactly the same claim in one sentence as he could in multiple sentences, the uniform format prescribed by the one-sentence rule does not interfere with his ability to claim whatever he "regards as his invention."

Id. at 1214.

B. PREAMBLE

The preamble is the initial portion of a claim. The preamble generally states the intended purpose or use of the invention and places it in a general category or field of technology. As a practical benefit, the Patent Office uses this broad categorization in assigning the technology to an appropriate examining group.

A significant conundrum of claim drafting relates to the impact of a preamble on defining the claimed invention—i.e., whether the preamble substantively limits the claim scope. As discussed in Chapter 13, the preamble generally does not limit the invention, unless the specification indicates that the patent applicant included important defining portions of the claim in the preamble. *Catalina Mktg. Int'l, Inc. v.*

Coolsavings.com, Inc., 289 F.3d 801 (Fed. Cir. 2002). Thus, the hypothetical claim set forth above encompasses any book otherwise meeting the limitations, even a book containing words in lieu of pictographs. Pictographs will not limit the invention of a book with slate pages, absent additional facts and circumstances.

C. TRANSITIONAL PHRASE

The transitional phrase connects the preamble to the body of the claim. Beyond that utilitarian function, the transition is a legal term of art with great implications for the scope of the claim. In particular, the transitional phrase determines whether the group of claim elements that follows is "open" or "closed." An open claim reads on any subject matter containing the recited limitations, even if additional, unrecited elements are also present. A closed claim means that additional, unrecited elements remove the accused product or process from the scope of the claims. An experienced patent drafter will choose among the well-defined transitional phrases—"comprising," "consisting of," or "consisting essentially of"—to achieve readily discernible and, perhaps more importantly, intended claim scope.

"Comprising," the most common transition, signals an open claim. An open claim encompasses all subject matter that contains each and every limitation recited in the body of the claim. *See, e.g.*, *Genentech, Inc. v. Chiron Corp.*, 112 F.3d 495 (Fed. Cir. 1997). Additional features in the accused product or process do not avoid infringement. Consistent with this fundamental patent rule, structure claimed in the singular using the indefinite article "a" means "at least one" and encompasses a device with multiple structures. *See Baldwin Graphic Sys., Inc. v. Seibert, Inc.*, 512 F.3d 1338 (Fed. Cir. 2008). In the above example, this means that a book with a back cover is nonetheless within the scope of claim so long as it has a front cover and slate pages. As another example, a claim to a safety razor "comprising" "a first," "a second," and "a third" blade will cover a razor with four blades. *Gillette Co. v. Energizer Holdings, Inc.*, 405 F.3d 1367 (Fed. Cir. 2005).

"Consisting of," which is less common, is incontrovertibly closed to additional elements. Subject matter is within the scope of a claim reciting "consisting of" as the transitional phrase only if the subject matter contains precisely the identical limitations in the claim—no more and no less. *See* ("[A] drafter uses the phrase 'consisting of' to mean 'I claim what follows and nothing else.' "). This restrictive transitional phrase often appears in conjunction with other claims having open-ended transitional phrases.

A patent drafter may include a narrow "consisting of" claim to ensure that this claim does not ensnare prior art in a crowded field. To illustrate, a claim that recites, "A composition consisting of A and B," does not encompass a composition of A, B, and C. In the context of the safety razor case, if the claim had read "a razor consisting of first, second, and third blades," it would not have covered a four-bladed razor. Nevertheless, a "consisting of" claim may encompass a composition consisting of A and B packaged in a container D, because the container is an aspect unrelated to the claimed composition. *See Norian Corp. v. Stryker Corp.*, 363 F.3d 1321 (Fed. Cir. 2004).

Between "comprising" and "consisting of" is a hybrid transitional phrase, "consisting essentially of." This phrase also has an established legal meaning: the claim is open to additional elements so long as those additional elements "do not materially affect the basic and novel characteristics of the invention." *PPG Indus. v. Guardian Indus. Corp.*, 156 F.3d 1351, 1354 (Fed. Cir. 1998). This term of art has an unavoidable factual component—what effect is material? A wise drafter of a hybrid claim thus sets forth in the written description or prosecution history the structural characteristics of a material effect. *See, e.g., AK Steel Corp. v. Sollac*, 344 F.3d 1234 (Fed. Cir. 2003).

To illustrate, a claim that recites, "A composition consisting essentially of A and B," encompasses a composition of A, B, and C only if C does not materially affect the basic and novel characteristics of the composition. That is, the composition of A, B, and C must be—in effect—insignificantly different than a composition of A and B. Because of its limited openness, savvy patentees prefer "consisting essentially of" over "consisting of" in circumstances where "comprising" is undesirable or unavailable. In the context of the safety razor case, if the claim had read "a razor consisting essentially of first, second, and third blades," it would only cover a four-bladed razor if the fourth blade had no material effect on the razor's shaving performance—an unlikely prospect.

While a patentee may use other terminology for the transitional phrase, ill-defined legal terms risk imprecision. For example, some phrases are typically open-ended and thus synonyms for "comprising." For instance, "including," "containing," and "characterized by" are generally considered open-ended. But other phrases may have indeterminate legal implications. For instance, "having" may be open, *Crystal Semiconductor Corp. v. TriTech Microelectronics International, Inc.*, 246 F.3d 1336, 1348 (Fed. Cir. 2001), or closed, *Pieczenik v. Dyax Corp.*, 76 Fed. Appx. 293 (Fed. Cir. 2003), depending on the court's reading of the specification and other factors. Similarly, the transitional phrase "composed of" lacks a firm meaning, signaling a restricted claim on par with either "consisting of" or "consisting essentially of," depending on the circumstances of the case. *AFG Indus., Inc. v. Cardinal IG Co.*, 239 F.3d 1239, 1245 (Fed. Cir. 2001); *In re Bertsch*, 132 F.2d 1014, 1019–20 (CCPA 1942). Accordingly, patentees use transition phrases other than the established conventions at their own peril. *Cf. Cias, Inc. v. Alliance Gaming Corp.*, 504 F.3d 1356 (Fed. Cir. 2007) (ruling that "comprised of" has the same meaning as "comprising," but only after wasting resources with an appeal to determine the phrase's meaning). Unfamiliar terms invite unintended limits on claim scope.

D. BODY

The body must define the invention in clear and concise terms—and set forth the structural or functional relations amongst the features of the invention. For ease of understanding, claims often signal primary limitations by indenting as well as alphanumeric indexing—(a), (b), (c), (1), (2), (3), and so forth. These indentations or alphanumeric labels facilitate prosecution by focusing the examiner on the basic limitations. Indentations also provide the public a simple, step-wise roadmap to understand the scope of the claim. In the example above, the body of the claim could be rewritten more effectively:

> 1. A book for a collection of pictographs comprising:
>
> (a) a front cover; and
>
> (b) a plurality of slate pages.

To define functional relationships, a patentee may claim the interaction between elements. In the above claim, the patentee could claim the connection between elements (a) and (b): "wherein the front cover is disconnectably connected to the plurality of pages." This language means that the front cover can be connected to and disconnected from the slate pages.

The vocabulary of claims may seem somewhat anomalous. But claims are utilitarian prose, not literature. And while the meaning of terms necessarily depends on a complex variety of factors (as discussed in Chapter 13), patent drafters may consult resources to learn the meaning of certain terms in past instances. *See generally* Irwin M. Aisenberg, *Attorney's Dictionary of Patent Claims* (1985).

Although each claim has its own unique body to define the unique invention, a few general rules typically inform the claim drafting process. For example, a skilled drafter does not introduce nouns with definite articles, such as "the" or "said." Instead, an indefinite article, such as "a," "an," or "one," or another phrase like "a plurality of" or "multiple" will typically accompany the first appearance of a noun. After that introduction, claims typically use definite articles, i.e., "the," to refer to already-introduced claim elements. For example, the wherein clause in the last hypothetical claim uses the definite article, "the," to refer to the limitation, "front cover," which has already been introduced earlier in the claim. This rule is important because a claim term lacking antecedent basis—that is, a term first introduced by a definite article—can make the entire claim invalid for indefiniteness. *But see Energizer Holdings, Inc. v. Int'l Trade Comm'n*, 435 F.3d 1366 (Fed. Cir. 2006).

As mentioned before, a skillful drafter precisely outlines the invented subject matter to capture the correct scope of the invention (and its foreseeable variants) while avoiding prior art. The body of the claim reflects that skill. Again, resources can assist with claim drafting, *see, e.g.*, Robert C. Faber, *Faber on Mechanics of Patent Claim Drafting* (6th ed. 2010), but experience is still the best teacher.

E. INDEPENDENT AND DEPENDENT CLAIMS

The bulk of § 112—subparagraphs (c)–(e), i.e., paragraphs 3–5—sets rules for dependent claims. A dependent claim must reference an earlier claim and recite at least one additional limitation narrowing the claim scope. In the above example, claim 2 is a proper dependent claim: "2. A book for a collection of pictographs according to claim 1, wherein the front cover consists of granite." This reference thus incorporates all the limitations of claim 1 and adds the granite cover limitation.

Dependent claims can serve as bases for further dependent claims (called "multiple dependent claims"). Using the above example, a dependent claim 3 could read: "3. A book for a collection of pictographs according to claim 1 or 2 further comprising a back cover." Here, claim 3 is a multiple dependent claim.

But a multiple dependent claim cannot serve as a basis for a further multiple dependent claim. Thus, a multiple dependent claim referring back to claim 3 would be improper—for example: "4. A book for a collection of pictographs according to claim 1, 2, or 3, wherein the book has a mass no greater than 10 kilograms." Claim 4, a multiple dependent claim, cannot depend from claim 3, another multiple dependent claim.

Astute patent drafters include many dependent claims. Dependent claims are, by definition, more limited and specific than independent claims. These claims help the invention survive unforeseen invalidity attacks based on unknown prior art or inadequate disclosure. Broad independent claims are desirable to capture more infringing behavior, but are also more vulnerable to prior art. It makes sense, then, for a patentee to seek the broadest independent claims that the Patent Office will allow, but at the same time narrow the claimed invention in a series of dependent claims to capture the most valuable embodiments at the time of prosecution.

Put differently, claim drafters visualize claim scope as a pyramid. The broadest claim sits at the foundation of the claim pyramid and supports a series of sequentially narrower claims with the most preferred embodiment at the peak. The claims of intermediate scope capture a wider range of subject matter but reduce as well the risk of invalidation. For example, the following set of claims shows this narrowing culminating in two peaks, yet with varying degrees of intermediate claims:

1. A book for a collection of pictographs comprising a front cover and a plurality of slate pages.

2. A book for a collection of pictographs according to claim 1, wherein the front cover comprises a rock.

3. A book for a collection of pictographs according to claim 2, wherein the rock is an igneous rock.

4. A book for a collection of pictographs according to claim 3, wherein the igneous rock is granite.

> 5. A book for a collection of pictographs according to claim 2, wherein the rock is gneiss.

The foundation is claim 1, and the two pyramid peaks are claim 4 (granite) and claim 5 (gneiss). Claims 2 and 3 are of intermediate scope supporting claim 4.

Aside from narrowing claims to minimize the invalidity risk, a patentee may also use dependent claims to change the form of the claim. For instance, if claim 1 recites a complex chemical compound requiring a full page to depict all substitutable active groups, a patentee may reference that claim in a method of treatment claim, reciting "A method of treating hair loss comprising administering the compound of claim 1 to a mammal in need thereof."

III. SPECIAL CLAIM FORMATS

Although all claims must follow the one-sentence rule and typically contain a preamble, transitional phrase, and body, some claim formats deserve special attention. In particular this section examines the means-plus-function, product-by-process, Jepson, and Markush claim formats.

A means-plus-function claim, permitted by § 112, ¶ 6,[1] is a functional claim that recites a "means" for accomplishing a function as set forth in the specification. A product-by-process claim, as the name suggests, claims a product made from the process steps recited in the claim. A Jepson claim

---

[1] Old habits die hard, and it would not be surprising if many practitioners continue using the traditional shorthand with the paragraphing identifier.

recites a specific improvement over the prior art. Lastly, a claim with a Markush group recites alternatives cabined by a certain format.

A. MEANS-PLUS-FUNCTION

1. § 112, ¶ 6 (Now § 112, ¶ (f))

The Patent Act expressly authorizes a functional claim format: "An element in a claim for a combination may be expressed as a means or step for performing a specified function without the recital of structure, material, or acts in support thereof." 35 U.S.C. § 112(f). No other claim format gets an express statutory endorsement.

But this express endorsement does not come without a price. The second clause of the same paragraph instructs that a means-plus-function claim "shall be construed to cover the corresponding structure, material, or acts described in the specification and equivalents thereof." *Id.* In other words, the claim scope will depend on the content of the specification.

The history of functional claiming begins long before § 112 became part of Title 35 in 1952. One of the earliest and most famous patent cases in the United States involved a functional claim. In the seminal case of *O'Reilly v. Morse*, 56 U.S. (15 How.) 62 (1854), Samuel Morse claimed the "use of [electricity] . . . for marking or printing intelligible characters." With this language, Morse really sought approval of a single means claim—now clearly forbidden under § 112 which requires "that the enabling disclosure of the specification be commensurate in scope with the claim." *In re Hyatt*, 708 F.2d 712, 714 (Fed. Cir. 1983) (citing *O'Reilly*, 56 U.S. at 112).

At the one point that distinguished the invention from prior art, Morse used sweeping functional language that could encompass innumerable ways to use electricity to print letters. The Supreme Court rejected the claim because its breadth encompassed far more than the telegraph machine Morse had in fact invented. *See O'Reilly*, 56 U.S. at 112–13. As just one example, Morse's claim could cover a fax machine.

After the famous *O'Reilly* case, however, functional claims began to serve the important role of allowing claim drafters to encompass many potential prior art elements in a combination claim. Claim drafters could relate aspects of the claim to the other features in the invention. For instance, a functional claim element could be used to designate a connection between two important features in a combination A and B. In the prior art, there could be many ways to connect A to B. Clearly the drafter would not want to undertake the burden of writing a separate claim for each of hundreds of different ways to connect elements—glue, nails, screws, tape, and so forth. Instead the drafter could specify a "connecting means." The functional claim element thus provided efficiency by encompassing all prior art performing that function. Functional claims served this classical purpose for many years without difficulty.

Ninety years after *O'Reilly*, the Supreme Court confronted again the breadth of functional claiming. In 1946, the Supreme Court prohibited use of functional claims at the exact point of novelty in a combination claim. *See Halliburton Oil Well Cementing Co. v. Walker*, 329 U.S. 1 (1946). The Supreme Court foresaw that functional language could embrace every conceivable way of performing a function, thus claiming more than the inventor had invented or claiming subject matter already available to the public. To prevent "the broadness, ambiguity, and overhanging threat of the functional claim," the Supreme Court prohibited inventor Walker's functional claim.

Patent drafters perceived *Halliburton* as a threat to the classical use of functional claims to improve drafting efficiency. So a few years later, acknowledging this classical utility, Congress expressly wrote means-plus-function claims into the statute. "This new language permits a patent applicant to express an element in a combination claim as a means for performing a function. The applicant need not recite structure, material, or acts in the claim's means-plus-function limitation." *Valmont Indus., Inc. v. Reinke Mfg. Co.*, 983 F.2d 1039, 1042 (Fed. Cir. 1993).

In this respect, the 1952 Act overruled *Halliburton. See In re Donaldson Co.*, 16 F.3d 1189 (Fed. Cir. 1994) (en banc). At the same time, the new § 112 ensured, however, that this statutory claim format could not be abused to acquire over-broad coverage. The statute limited this type of claim to the structures disclosed in the specification and their equivalents. *See In re Fuetterer*, 319 F.2d 259 (CCPA 1963).

2. Practical Significance

A simple example from a real patent case reveals the implications of the functional claim. The case involved a patent on a method of displaying non-prescription eyeglasses on racks. *See Al-Site Corp. v. VSI Int'l, Inc.*, 174 F.3d 1308 (Fed. Cir. 1999). The invention placed the eyeglasses on a tag and suspended the tag from a rack. The tag was attached to eyeglasses with a loop that encircled the nose bridge of the glasses. The loop that held the glasses was closed with a "fastening means in engagement with said extension [of the tag] to maintain said loop closed."

Under the statute, this claim points to the specification for the structure corresponding to fastening function. At that point, the specification could list innumerable alternative ways to fasten the loop. In fact, the specification listed only two fastening means—buttons and rivets. The statute allows these embodiments and their equivalents. *See, e.g.*, *Versa Corp. v. Ag-Bag Int'l Ltd.*, 392 F.3d 1325 (Fed. Cir. 2004). This claim format thus provides a convenient way to claim all fastening structures (and their equivalents) that are known to the inventor and listed in the specification without reciting those structures in multiple claims.

For many years after enactment of the 1952 Act, functional claims received different treatment in administrative proceedings to acquire a patent than in litigation proceedings to enforce a patent. The PTO reasoned that claims should receive their "broadest reasonable interpretation" during prosecution (the standard process for evaluating claims at the PTO), *In re Prater*, 415 F.2d 1393, 1404–05 (CCPA 1969), and refused to narrow the claim according to the structure recited in the specification. The PTO read means-plus-function claims to cover all possible means for performing the recited function. Thus, the PTO rejected more functional claims than the language of § 112 required. Meanwhile, courts enforcing patents applied the statutory language, limiting functional claims to the disclosed structure and equivalents.

The Federal Circuit corrected this discrepancy in *In re Donaldson Co.*, 16 F.3d 1189 (Fed. Cir. 1994) (en banc). In simple terms, the invention was a dust collector with flexible, diaphragm-like walls. To clean the collector, the operator reversed the air pressure causing the walls to flex in the opposite direction and dislodge caked dust into a bin below. The application claimed: "means, responsive to pressure increases in said chamber caused by said cleaning means, for moving particulate matter in a downward direction." The PTO rejected this claim over the Swift prior art reference. Swift also cleaned dust collectors by reversing air pulses. In Swift, however, the dust collector walls were sloped, not flexible. The PTO nonetheless reasoned that sloped walls were a means responsive to air pressure for moving dust downward. The PTO refused to consult the structure in the specification which recited the flexible walls as the claimed means. Therefore, the PTO rejected the application as obvious in light of the prior art, particularly the Swift reference.

On appeal, the Federal Circuit, in very insistent tones, instructed the PTO to follow § 112, ¶ 6: "Per our holding, the 'broadest reasonable interpretation' that an examiner may give means-plus-function language is that statutorily mandated in paragraph six. Accordingly, the PTO may not disregard the structure disclosed in the specification corresponding to such language when rendering a patentability determination." *Donaldson*, 16 F.3d at 1194–95. Because the Swift reference did not teach or suggest flexible walls, the court reversed the PTO's obviousness determination.

The significance of § 112, ¶ 6, for the examination of, as well as the enforcement of, patents prompts the inevitable question: What precise set of words invokes the procedures and limitations of § 112? This question has troubled both examiners at the PTO and courts enforcing exclusive rights. Therefore, the Federal Circuit has devised some guidelines for determining that particular language in a claim invokes this unusual treatment:

> Specifically, if the word "means" appears in a claim element in combination with a function, it is presumed to be a means-plus-function element to which § 112, ¶ 6 applies. Nevertheless, according to its express terms, § 112, ¶ 6 governs only claim elements that do not recite sufficient structural limitations. Therefore, the presumption that § 112, ¶ 6

> applies is overcome if the claim itself recites sufficient structure or material for performing the claimed function.

Al-Site Corp. v. VSI Int'l, Inc., 174 F.3d 1308, 1318 (Fed. Cir. 1999) (citations omitted).[2] Thus, a claim including the word "means" is presumptively a means-plus-function claim.

The converse is slightly different. The absence of the claim term, "means," creates a presumption against the application of § 112, ¶ 6—but not a strong one. Specifically, the Federal Circuit has held that, in the absence of the term "means,"

> we will apply the presumption . . . without requiring any heightened evidentiary showing and expressly overrule the characterization of that presumption as "strong." . . . When a claim term lacks the word "means," the presumption can be overcome and § 112, para. 6 will apply if the challenger demonstrates that the claim term fails to 'recite sufficiently definite structure' or else recites 'function without reciting sufficient structure for performing that function.' "

Williamson v. Citrix Online, LLC, 792 F.3d 1339, 1349 (Fed. Cir. 2015)

The statute makes clear that a functional claim also encompasses equivalents to the structure

---

[2] The court's reference to step-plus-function claims is based on the statute, which recognizes such claims. Due to their infrequency, step-plus-function claims remain an enigma. *Cf. Seal-Flex, Inc. v. Athletic Track & Court Constr.*, 172 F.3d 836, 847–51 (Fed. Cir. 1999) (Rader, J., concurring).

disclosed in the specification. The definition of these structural equivalents is a question of fact. In *Al-Site*, for example, the patentee claimed a device for displaying a pair of eyeglasses on a rack that permits a customer to test the fit and look of the eyewear without removing the display hanger. 174 F.3d at 1315. As discussed earlier, the recited "fastening means" covered only certain mechanical structures—a rivet and a button—as the disclosed structure. In that case, the accused device used an adhesive to adjoin the loop securing the eyewear. Although mechanical fasteners might seem very different from chemical adhesives, the jury decided that trial record made adhesives equivalent to rivets and buttons. The Federal Circuit, applying the very deferential treatment accorded to jury verdicts, upheld the verdict of infringement.

The patentee must clearly link the structure in the specification to the functional claim language, or else risk invalidity for indefiniteness. "This duty to link or associate structure to function is the *quid pro quo* for the convenience of employing § 112, ¶ 6." *B. Braun Med., Inc. v. Abbott Labs.*, 124 F.3d 1419, 1424 (Fed. Cir. 1997). The failure to disclose the structure thus renders the claim indefinite. *See, e.g.*, *Budde v. Harley-Davidson, Inc.*, 250 F.3d 1369 (Fed. Cir. 2001). A specification cannot simply use a broad reference to known methods or known equipment. To satisfy the definiteness requirement, a means-plus-function element must refer to specific structure disclosed in the specification. *Biomedino, LLC v. Waters Techs. Corp.*, 490 F.3d 946 (Fed. Cir. 2007).

In a computer implemented invention, a functional limitation must recite as structure an algorithm that performed the function. For example, in *Aristocrat Technologies Australia Pty. Ltd. v. International Game Technology*, 521 F.3d 1328 (Fed. Cir. 2008), the court examined a claim reciting a "game control means" or a "control means." The patentee argued that the functions disclosed in the claim language "implicitly discloses an algorithm for the microprocessor." *Aristocrat*, 521 F.3d at 1334. The court rejected that argument, holding that a summary disclosure of "appropriate programming" did not satisfy the statutory requirements: "That description goes no farther than saying that the claimed functions are performed by a general purpose computer. The reference to 'appropriate programming' imposes no limitation whatever, as any general purpose computer must be programmed." *Id.* Accordingly, the court invalidated the claims because "the patent does not disclose the required algorithm or algorithms, and a person of ordinary skill in the art would not recognize the patent as disclosing any algorithm at all." *Id.* at 1337–38.

3. Equivalents Under § 112 and the Doctrine of Equivalents

The doctrine of equivalents, which prohibits infringers from using technology that is insubstantially different from the claimed invention (as discussed more fully in Chapter 14), and structural equivalents in the means-plus-function format are, unsurprisingly, closely related—but have some important differences. To begin with similarities between the related concepts, the doctrine of equivalents and means-plus-function equivalents both use a similar evaluation methodology. Both test for "insubstantial differences" between the claimed and accused products or processes for the doctrine of equivalents or between the structures in the specification and prior art structures (when the PTO examines for patentability) or accused structures (when a court tests for infringement) for § 112, ¶ 6. *See Valmont Indus., Inc. v. Reinke Mfg. Co.*, 983 F.2d 1039, 1043 (Fed. Cir. 1993).

In addition, both the doctrine and structural equivalents apply on an element-by-element basis for infringement. *See Warner-Jenkinson Co., Inc. v. Hilton Davis Chem. Co.*, 520 U.S. 17, 27–28 (1997). But this element-by-element application requires a clarification that initiates an examination of the differences.

An important difference between the related concepts involves the effect of prior art. The prior art constrains the range of permissible equivalents under the doctrine of equivalents. *See Wilson Sporting Goods Co. v. David Geoffrey & Assoc.*, 904 F.2d 677 (Fed. Cir. 1990). But this principle does not apply to equivalency under § 112, ¶ 6:

> Although under the doctrine of equivalents prior art restricts the extent to which patent protection can be equitably extended beyond the claims to cover an accused device, the policies underlying that concept are not served by

> restricting [§ 112, ¶ 6] claim *limitations* in the same manner. Claim limitations may, and often do, read on the prior art, particularly in combination patents.

Intel Corp. v. U.S. Int'l Trade Comm'n, 946 F.2d 821, 842 (Fed. Cir. 1991) (citations omitted).

A second difference relates to assessment of function. As discussed above, means-plus-function claims require identity of function, not simply the substantially similar function permitted under the doctrine of equivalents. *Chiuminatta Concrete Concepts, Inc. v. Cardinal Indus., Inc.*, 145 F.3d 1303, 1308 (Fed. Cir. 1998). Thus, while lack of an identical function prevents infringement of a means-plus-function claim term, it will not necessarily preclude infringement under the doctrine of equivalents.

The third, and most important, difference is the timing of the assessment of equivalence under the doctrine and under § 112. Section 112 specifies a procedure under which a "claim shall be construed." This difference flows from the elemental principle that a claim's meaning is set at the time of filing. *Phillips v. AWH Corp.*, 415 F.3d 1303 (Fed. Cir. 2005) (en banc). Thus, the literal meaning of a means-plus-function claim element must be set upon filing, meaning that any structural equivalents must be known and in place at the time of filing. Because claim scope may not vary after filing, structural equivalents would not include what the Supreme Court called "after-arising equivalents." These "after-arising equivalents" are substitutes for claim terms known to those of skill in the art that arise due to technological advances after patent filing.

In contrast, the inquiry for infringement under the doctrine of equivalents takes place at the time of infringement. *See Warner-Jenkinson*, 520 U.S. at 37. Thus, the doctrine of equivalents, unlike structural equivalents under § 112, ¶ 6, embraces "after-arising equivalents":

> One important difference between § 112, ¶ 6 and the doctrine of equivalents involves the timing of the separate analyses for an "insubstantial change." As this court has recently clarified, a structural equivalent under § 112 must have been available at the time of the [filing] of the claim. An equivalent structure or act under § 112 cannot embrace technology developed after the issuance of the patent because the literal meaning of a claim is fixed upon its issuance. An "after arising equivalent" infringes, if at all, under the doctrine of equivalents. . . Furthermore, under § 112, ¶ 6, the accused device must perform the identical function as recited in the claim element while the doctrine of equivalents may be satisfied when the function performed by the accused device is only substantially the same.

Al-Site, 174 F.3d at 1320–21 (citations omitted).

The eyeglasses case illustrates this difference. The patentee claimed "means for fastening" and described rivets and buttons in the specification. Suppose Velcro® fasteners were invented a few years after the patent issued. Would those Velcro fasteners literally infringe the "fastening means" language and thus qualify as structural equivalents? The Federal Circuit answered that question in *Al-Site*:

> A proposed equivalent must have arisen at a definite period in time, i.e., either before or after patent [filing]. If before, a § 112, ¶ 6 structural equivalents analysis applies and any analysis for equivalent structure under the doctrine of equivalents collapses into the § 112, ¶ 6 analysis. If after, a non-textual infringement analysis proceeds under the doctrine of equivalents.

Id. at 1320 n.2. Thus, the Velcro® would not literally infringe the means language—but it could infringe under the doctrine of equivalents. It will not infringe literally because the meaning of the claim is fixed from the time of filing and cannot embrace "after-arising technology." The doctrine of equivalents, however, can embrace "after-arising technology."

Another important difference between the doctrine of equivalents and structural equivalents under § 112 is the relevant structure (material or acts as well) to which equivalents apply. Section 112 refers to the structure in the specification, while the doctrine refers to the structure in the claims. In sum, the doctrine of equivalents and structural equivalents are related concepts, albeit with non-trivial differences in terms of timing, scope, and purpose.

4. International Treatment

The United States is unique in its treatment of functional claims. Until amendments in 1996, Japan often restricted functional claims to the specific exemplified embodiments. The prior statute required that claims set forth the indispensable features of the invention, but Article 36(5) now states: "The scope of claims as provided in paragraph (2) shall state a claim or claims and state for each claim all matters necessary to specify the invention for which the applicant requests the grant of a patent." The European Patent Office permits functional rather than structural claim limitations if the invention cannot be defined structurally without restricting the scope of the invention.

B. PRODUCT-BY-PROCESS

1. Purpose

Before the advent of sophisticated reverse engineering and analytical technology, product-by-process claims served an important function. In some circumstances, an inventor could create a product (usually a new molecular structure) without knowing its precise structure or characteristics. The inventor thus did not have any way to precisely claim the product's structure. In that instance, the law permitted the inventor to claim the product in the only way possible—by claiming the product according to the inventor's fabrication process.

In more modern practice, an inventor can practically always claim a product according to its structure. And a product claim is very strong and desirable because it protects that claimed structure however made or used. Thus, if another innovator makes the same product by a new process (even a more efficient process), the first inventor of the structure retains the exclusive right to that structure.

To illustrate with a hypothetical, an inventor could make an excellent new shoe polish out of a petroleum byproduct and obtain a product patent on the new entity. If another innovator finds a cheaper way to make the patented polish out of timber byproducts, the first inventor still has the exclusive right to the new product. The second innovator may obtain a patent on the timber fabrication process, but not a patent on the pre-existing structure.

Similarly, if another innovator finds a new use for the structure, the first inventor still has an exclusive right to the product for all of its uses, even those he did not invent himself. In our hypothetical, another innovator learns that the shoe polish composition grows hair when applied to human skin. Again, the second innovator gets a process patent on a method of using the old product (to grow hair), but the first inventor still has an exclusive right to the product for all of its uses. These blocking patents invariably induce their owners to cross license.

As noted earlier, a product patent is more valuable than a process patent because it gives the patentee an exclusive right to the new structure however made or used. A process claim, on the other hand, is traditionally weaker and narrower. A mere change in the order of the steps or slight alterations in starting materials or catalysts can constitute a new process (sometimes with more efficient results). Thus a process patent can often be circumvented with a new process to reach the same result, but a product patent is not so easily avoided.

Returning to the product-by-process format, this type of claim is a product claim. Therefore, it gives the patentee entitlement to the structure however made or used. Nonetheless the claim itself recites no structure but only a fabrication process. Thus, with a claim to a single process, the applicant has received exclusive rights to the product even if made by a variety of other methods. Accordingly, this claim form has created some difficulties for courts in determining its precise reach and scope. After all, this alternative product claim could cover that product without regard to its manufacture, even though the claim specifically recites a step-wise procedure. *See SmithKline Beecham Corp. v. Apotex Corp.*, 439 F.3d 1312 (Fed. Cir. 2006); *Scripps Clinic & Research Found. v. Genentech, Inc.*, 927 F.2d 1565 (Fed. Cir. 1991).

Construing a product-by-process claim in this manner, however, contradicts the historical justification for the claim format. *Abbott Labs. v. Sandoz, Inc.*, 566 F.3d 1282 (Fed. Cir. 2009) (en banc). Even in that earlier era, however, the Supreme Court had construed an early version of a product-by-process claim as limited to the claimed method: "Every patent for a product or composition of matter must identify it so that it can be recognized aside from the description of the process for making it, or else nothing can be held to infringe the patent which is not made by that process." *Cochrane v. Badische Anilin & Soda Fabrik*, 111 U.S. 293, 310 (1884). Thus, this precedent became the basis for the U.S. rule for these claims.

Even so, the product-by-process claim focuses on the product, not the process for making the product. And a claim to a known product cannot be made patentable solely because it is made by a different process. That is, "a product-by-process claim can be anticipated by a prior art product that does not adhere to the claim's process limitation." *Amgen Inc. v. F. Hoffman-La Roche Ltd.*, 580 F.3d 1340, 1370 (Fed. Cir. 2009). Yet infringement is treated differently, because "process terms in product-by-process claims serve as limitations in determining infringement." *Abbott Lab'ys*, 566 F.3d at 1293. This anomaly is a limited exception to the longstanding rule "[t]hat which infringes, if later, would anticipate, if earlier." *Peters v. Active Mfg. Co.*, 129 U.S. 530, 537 (1889).

2. International Treatment

The United States is not alone in recognizing product-by-process claims. For example, the Guidelines for Examination in the European Patent Office explain:

> Claims for products defined in terms of a process of manufacture are allowable only if the products as such fulfill the requirements for patentability, i.e. *inter alia* that they are new

> and inventive, and it is impossible to define the claimed product other than in terms of a process of manufacture. A product is not rendered novel merely by the fact that it is produced by means of a new process. The claim may for instance take the form "Product X obtainable by process Y". Irrespective of whether the term "obtainable", "obtained", "directly obtained" or an equivalent wording is used in the product-by-process claim, it is still directed to the product *per se* and confers absolute protection upon the product.

Part F, Chapter IV, Paragraph 4.12. Japanese law allows the use of product-by-process claims in limited circumstances. Examination Guidelines for Patent and Utility Model in Japan, Part I, Chap. 1, § 2.2.2.4. *See also Kirin Amgen v. Hoechst Marion Carousel Ltd.*, [2005] 1 All ER 667.

C. JEPSON

A Jepson claim expressly recites in the claim the prior art (usually in the preamble) and then specifies and claims an improvement on that prior art. *See* 37 C.F.R. § 1.75(e). For example, the following is a Jepson claim: "A book for a collection of pictographs comprising a front cover and a plurality of slate pages, *wherein the improvement* comprises the front cover consisting of granite." The italicized phrase, or the use of something similar, alerts the Patent Office and the public that the patentee admits everything preceding that phrase, that is, everything in the preamble, is prior art. 37 C.F.R. § 1.75(e)(3).

Once admitted, the preamble may form a basis of an obviousness rejection, even if it was erroneously designated prior art. *In re Fout*, 675 F.2d 297 (CCPA 1982); *but see Reading & Bates Constr. Co. v. Baker Energy Res. Corp.*, 748 F.2d 645 (Fed. Cir. 1984) (holding that an inventor's own work in the preamble of a Jepson claim may not be treated as an admission of prior art). Due to the perils of using this claim format, skilled patent drafters avoid it unless necessary to obtain a patent in a crowded field. In Europe, on the other hand, the EPO more often insists on the use of this format.

D. MARKUSH

Named for a onetime patent applicant, *see Ex Parte Markush*, 1925 C.D. 126 (Comm'r Pat. 1925), this format permits a patentee to aggregate substitutable limitations into a group and claim them in the alternative. The following is an example: "A book for a collection of pictographs comprising a front cover and a plurality of slate pages, wherein the front cover comprises a rock *selected from the group consisting of granite, sandstone, and gneiss.*" The italicized phrase is the Markush group. Thus, the claim encompasses front covers made from any of those rocks. That is, the claimed genus of rocks includes the species of granite, sandstone, and gneiss.

The only formatting requirement is that the group be closed—"consisting of" or a similarly closed term must introduce the group. The only substantive requirement is that the named species share a common property that explains their grouping.

Although not constrained to specific subject matter, Markush groups are commonplace in claiming a chemical invention. Within the chemical practice, a claim will often recite variables, such as R, R^1, X, X^1, or the like, which are later defined by Markush groups.

This claiming technique is not unique to the United States—in fact, German chemists and their patent agents initially used variables to tabulate similar compounds, and this practice, which later morphed into Markush groups, traveled stateside when these applications were translated and filed in the United States. In modern times, the European Patent Office permits these claims as well:

> Where a single claim defines (chemical or non-chemical) alternatives, e.g. it contains a so called "Markush grouping", the requirement of Rule 44(1) for same or corresponding special technical features is considered met if the alternatives are of a similar nature (see F-IV, 3.7).
>
> When the Markush grouping is for alternatives of chemical compounds, they should be regarded as being of a similar nature where:
>
> (i) all alternatives have a common property or activity, and
>
> (ii) a common structure is present, i.e. a significant structural element is shared by all of the alternatives, or all alternatives belong to a recognised class of chemical compounds in the art to which the invention pertains.

GUIDELINES FOR EXAMINATION IN THE EUROPEAN PATENT OFFICE, Part F, Chapter V, Paragraph 3.2.5. Similarly, Japan similarly allows the use of Markush claims in limited circumstances. *See* EXAMINATION GUIDELINES FOR PATENT AND UTILITY MODEL IN JAPAN, Part I, Chap. 1, §§ 2.2.2.3(4), 2.2.3.2(2).

IV. DEFINITENESS

A. TEST

The Patent Act requires that the "claims particularly point[] out and distinctly claim[] the subject matter which the inventor or a joint inventor regards as the invention." 35 U.S.C. § 112(b) (2012). The claims, which appear at the end of the specification, must define the invention. These "particular" and "distinct" boundaries notify the public and the Patent Office of the scope of the invention.

Definiteness thus focuses on "whether the claim meets the threshold requirements of clarity and precision, not whether more suitable language or modes of expression are available." Manual of Patent Examining Procedure § 2173.02. Accordingly, if the claims are too vague, indecipherable, or impenetrable, they do not meet a substantive requirement for patentability: definiteness.

The basic rule is that a person of ordinary skill in the art must be able to understand the claims when read in light of the specification. *Orthokinetics, Inc. v. Safety Travel Chairs, Inc.*, 806 F.2d 1565, 1576 (Fed. Cir. 1986). In *Orthokinetics*, the patentee claimed a collapsible wheelchair that could be inserted into a car. The trial court ruled that, as a matter of law, the claims were invalid as indefinite because the patentee did not specify the dimensions of the wheelchair necessary to fit different makes and models of cars. A Checkers cab or a Hummer certainly has a different geometry than a Volkswagen bug.

The Federal Circuit reversed, specifically noting that testimony showed that a person of ordinary skill in the art would understand and potentially adapt the claimed invention to fit vehicles of various sizes. This result makes sense because otherwise the applicant would have needed to draft a different claim for every type of automobile. As the court observed, the necessary variations to accommodate different automobile models would be easily obtained by one of ordinary skill in this art in light of the patent's disclosures. Of course, this particular invention also lies in a rather predictable field of technology.

The amount and quality of claim detail necessary to satisfy the definiteness requirement varies with the scope of the claims, the complexity of the subject matter, and the level of ordinary skill in the art. *Miles Lab'ys, Inc. v. Shandon Inc.*, 997 F.2d 870 (Fed. Cir. 1993). Courts examine and determine the scope of the claims as a matter of law, but review the other two definiteness variables as questions of fact. *See, e.g., BJ Servs. Co. v. Halliburton Energy Servs., Inc.*, 338 F.3d 1368 (Fed. Cir. 2003).

Nevertheless, "[i]ndefiniteness is also a legal determination arising out of the court's performance of its duty construing the claims." *Id.* at 1372. In fact, the Federal Circuit has commented that difficult questions of claim construction do not render claims indefinite:

> Under a broad concept of indefiniteness, all but the clearest claim construction issues could be regarded as giving rise to invalidating indefiniteness in the claims at issue. But we have not adopted that approach to the law of indefiniteness. We have not insisted that claims be plain on their face in order to avoid condemnation for indefiniteness; rather, what we have asked is that the claims be amenable to construction, however difficult that task may be. If a claim is insolubly ambiguous, and no narrowing construction can properly be adopted, we have held the claim indefinite.

Exxon Research & Eng'g Co. v. United States, 265 F.3d 1371, 1375 (Fed. Cir. 2001).

This passage uses two important phrases: "amenable to construction" and "insolubly ambiguous." The latter characterization seemed to require a near impossibility of discerning the meaning of the claims. The more reasonable reading of this entire passage, however, suggests that claims do not lack definiteness if its new terms allow a person of ordinary skill in the art to reasonably infer a meaning. *Bancorp Servs., L.L.C. v. Hartford Life Ins. Co.*, 359 F.3d 1367 (Fed. Cir. 2004).

In *Nautilus, Inc. v. Biosig Instruments, Inc.*, 572 U.S. 898, 2130 (2014), the Supreme Court changed the language of the indefiniteness standard with perhaps little impact on the substance of the rule. The Court rejected the Federal Circuit's formulation of the standard—namely that a claim is definite so long as it is not "insolubly ambiguous." *Nautilus*, 572 U.S. at 2124. In its place, the Supreme Court adopted a different phraseology: "a patent is invalid for indefiniteness if its claims, read in light of the specification delineating the patent, and the prosecution history, fail to inform, with reasonable certainty, those skilled in the art about the scope of the invention." *Id.*

At first glance, the Supreme Court's decision appears to lower the standard for indefiniteness. But despite the modification to the standard's language, the Federal Circuit on remand described the new test as a "familiar standard," and reached the same result as before. The Federal Circuit's formulation reflected the practical reality—unchanged by the Supreme Court—that an issued claim is presumed valid, even in the context of definiteness. *See* 35 U.S.C. § 282; *see also Exxon Research & Eng'g Co. v. United States*, 265 F.3d 1371, 1375 (Fed. Cir. 2001). Because the validity presumption remains in force, courts may still turn to claim construction to resolve potential ambiguities in claim language, as explicitly contemplated in the now-rejected standard—but now will simply be "steer[ing] by the bright star of 'reasonable certainty,' rather than the unreliable compass of 'insoluble ambiguity.'" *Biosig*

Instruments, Inc. v. Nautilus, Inc., 783 F.3d 1374, 1379 (Fed. Cir. 2015).

B. RELATIVE TERMINOLOGY & WORDS OF APPROXIMATION

The definiteness requirement also comes into play with claim terms like "substantially," "about," and "approximately." Wary of the strict limits of absolute specificity, patentees often define their inventions with relative terminology or words of approximation. In fact, a patentee is not required to recite patentable subject matter with mathematical precision. *Invitrogen Corp. v. Biocrest Mfg. L.P.*, 424 F.3d 1374 (Fed. Cir. 2005). The definiteness inquiry remains the same: if a person of ordinary skill in the art would understand (even with relative difficulty) the scope of the invention, relative claim terms such as "close proximity" are not indefinite. *Rosemount, Inc. v. Beckman Instruments, Inc.*, 727 F.2d 1540, 1547 (Fed. Cir. 1984). Persons having ordinary skill in the art often find sufficient guidance in the specification.

Nevertheless, words of approximation—pejoratively called "weasel words"—cause greater concern due to their ubiquity in claims. Their ubiquity, though, is tolerated when they accommodate minor variations within the scope of the invention in accordance with the exactness demanded by the technological field and by the prior art. *Andrew Corp. v. Gabriel Elecs., Inc.*, 847 F.2d 819 (Fed. Cir. 1988). For example, in *Verve, LLC v. Crane Cams, Inc.*, 311 F.3d 1116 (Fed. Cir. 2002), the court reversed a judgment that claims reciting "a substantially constant wall thickness" were indefinite because the trial court improperly failed to consider the understanding of a person of ordinary skill in the art.

Similarly, other words, such as "about" and "approximately," are permissible to provide some leeway in avoiding an unforgiving (and unnecessary) numerical limitation. In some circumstances, however, the claimed subject matter requires precision at odds with words of approximation, particularly where the prior art abuts against the imprecise limitation. *See Amgen, Inc. v. Chugai Pharm. Co.*, 927 F.2d 1200 (Fed. Cir. 1991). Thus, each circumstance must be evaluated on its own terms, even if words of degree or approximation often provide a discernible claim scope.

CHAPTER 13
CLAIM CONSTRUCTION

I. INTRODUCTION

When granted a patent, an inventor receives an official copy of the patent, complete with an elaborate cover having the seal of the United States Patent and Trademark Office. The patent also proclaims that the "requirements of law have been complied with, and it has been determined that a patent on the invention shall be granted under the law." This proclamation includes the promise that the inventor now possesses rights under the Patent Act. These rights, however, cannot extend beyond the scope of the patented invention. Thus, the key to patent rights (both infringement and validity) depends on the interpretation of the patent claims.

In this respect, the patent is like a deed to real property—it demarcates the limits of the property. *See, e.g., Motion Picture Patents Co. v. Universal Film Mfg. Co.*, 243 U.S. 502 (1917). A deed informs a prospective purchaser of the property's boundaries, which enables that purchaser to visit, survey, and assess the property before buying or renting. The deed also notifies potential trespassers of the boundaries of the property.

Similarly a patent contains signposts signaling the contours of the patentee's property: claims. A claim defines the patentee's property right. In one respect, however, claims differ from real property deeds. Deeds demarcate boundaries with mathematical precision down to the fraction of an inch. Patent claims, on the other hand, attempt to define new products or processes in old language—a task that defies precision. Interpretation of language defining new technology—a step removed from the drafting task—can be even more difficult.

The law professes to construe claims according to the understanding of a person of ordinary skill in the art at the time of invention. This simple rule hides the complexity of the process. Even this simple linguistic framework has two key aspects: a technological aspect and a temporal aspect. Each aspect presents a court with challenges in discerning claim meaning. With these governing aspects in mind, a court—the ultimate arbiter of claim meaning—will use various sources to construe a disputed claim:

- the claim language itself;
- the written description, also called the specification;
- the prosecution history, or the public record of the discourse with the Patent Office during acquisition of the patent;
- extrinsic sources such as dictionaries, treatises, and encyclopedias (preferably, but not always, technical); expert testimony; and prior art references (such as scientific articles).

In the search for the understanding of a skilled artisan at the time of invention, these sources vary in relative importance from one technology and patent to the next. Nevertheless, in an effort to impose some predictability on claim construction, courts (and most important, the Federal Circuit) have articulated a hierarchy among these sources preferring intrinsic evidence unique to the patent—that is, the claim language, the specification, and the prosecution history—over extrinsic evidence. In particular, courts express skepticism about expert testimony as a key to claim interpretation.

Claim construction becomes the primary issue in patent enforcement proceedings. Before determining whether an activity trespasses on the patented property, the court (or even an attorney offering an opinion on infringement) must set the boundaries of the exclusive right. Patent infringement receives detailed treatment in Chapter 14. Claim construction, however, is not only an infringement doctrine; it precedes almost every analysis in patent law.

For starters, the Patent Office must construe claims during the process of deciding whether a patent meets the substantive requirements for patentability. Indeed, the first step in any validity-related determination—regardless of whether during the prosecution or enforcement phase—is claim construction.

Claims also play a critical role in notifying the public, including a patentee's competitors and potential competitors, of the scope of the patentee's exclusive rights. As empirical evidence of claim construction's heightened importance, the Federal

Circuit has revisited the claim construction process en banc multiple times and produced scores upon scores of panel opinions as well.

In sum, any patent practitioner simply must acquire competence in accurately construing claim language. A prosecuting attorney must be able to choose language that effectively protects an invention. A litigating attorney must be able to craft winning interpretations and effective defenses. A counseling attorney must be able to evaluate the scope of patent rights and the implications of market activities on businesses. A transactional attorney must be able to formulate language that withstands litigation challenges in evaluating and forming license or cooperative research agreements between commercial entities. Claim construction is at the heart of every facet of patent work.

II. CLAIM CONSTRUCTION

As recently amended, the patent laws require that a patentee's or applicant's "specification shall conclude with one or more claims particularly pointing out and distinctly claiming the subject matter which the inventor or joint inventor regards as the invention." 35 U.S.C. § 112(a). As discussed in Chapter 12, claims appear at the end of a patent as sequentially numbered predicates that set forth the boundaries of an invention. The meaning of the words in a claim is a challenging inquiry rivaled in patent law only by the difficulty of an obviousness determination.

A. CHALLENGES OF CLAIM CONSTRUCTION

A patentee has only words and grammatical constructs to define a technological advance. Words, by their very nature as symbols, are fraught with ambiguity and multiple meanings. Philosophers have struggled for centuries with the implications of communication with symbols. Plato, in his famous *Allegory of the Cave*, pictured humanity as trapped in a cave watching shadows dance on the opposite wall cast by a fire that is out of sight. The shadows cast by the real figures moving around the fire are humanity's only (obviously imperfect) contact with reality. Thus, the symbols provide a common experience, but an experience potentially distant and distorted from reality. The allegory illustrates that each observer focuses on a different aspect of the dancing shadow and potentially derives a different meaning from the symbol. Words thus unite and divide humanity.

Similarly Ludwig Wittgenstein, perhaps the greatest philosopher of the 20th century, devoted his life to the mystery of meaning. He posited in his writings that meaning was a product of social conditioning and context. Every human learns the meaning of symbols, including words, from his own unique experience. Because each individual learns from distinct experiences and cultures, they are conditioned to perceive symbols differently. Even if symbols could precisely represent reality, each human would perceive them differently. Sadly Wittgenstein died in seclusion after retreating in despair over the impossibility of genuine human interaction and communication.

Returning from philosophy to patent law, words are necessarily vague at the margins. Sometimes, they are vague by design. Other times, through no fault of their user, words simply cannot convey the intended concept with accuracy. Open any dictionary. Almost every word has a plethora of definitions. Inversely, every thought, feeling, and description may be expressed with an almost infinite number of different word configurations. At this reality, the poet rejoices, but the patent lawyer shudders. These linguistic options impede precise meaning. For instance, in commenting on the process of statutory interpretation—an exercise corresponding in many respects with claim construction—Justice Frankfurter commented:

> [Words] are symbols of meaning. But unlike mathematical symbols, the phrasing of a document, especially a complicated enactment, seldom attains more than approximate precision. If individual words are inexact symbols, with shifting variables, their configuration can hardly achieve invariant meaning or assured definiteness.

Autogiro Co. of Am. v. United States, 384 F.2d 391, 396 (Ct. Cl. 1967) (quoting Frankfurter, *Some Reflections on the Reading of Statutes*, 47 COL. L. REV. 527, 528 (1947)).

The technological content of patent claims further complicates expression. The intricate moving parts of a carburetor, the complex reactions in a chemical process, or the topology of a computer chip do not find easy expression in words. As one court commented, "Things are not made for the sake of words, but words for things." *Autogiro*, 384 F.2d at 397. Moreover, by definition, the patent drafter describes something new, something never before described.

To compensate for this problem, courts allow inventors to invent new words or phrases for their claiming task. Thus, the inventor may define, either explicitly or implicitly through usage, claim terms in ways inconsistent with ordinary and customary meanings. Patentees may be their own lexicographers by changing the art-specific meaning of preexisting terms or by coining new ones. The flexibility to define and redefine terms, however, comes with its own set of problems. For example, what is the scope of the new definition? Will old words adequately convey a new meaning? When does an old symbol carry novel meaning and when does it simply carry its common meaning?

Despite the inherent imprecision of words, courts insist that a patent must give competitors notice of the scope of the exclusive right. Without proper notice, competitors cannot adjust their conduct to avoid infringement. A reasonable competitor should be able to make prudent commercial decisions after reading the patent. This notice imperative requires predictability, an objective at odds with the inherent inexactness of claim terms. The law nonetheless strives for this predictability by tying the meaning of the patentee's words to the understanding of one having ordinary skill in the art at the time of the invention.

B. CLAIM CONSTRUCTION IN THE FEDERAL CIRCUIT ERA: *MARKMAN*

The objective of the Federal Circuit's creation in 1982 was primarily to bring predictability and uniformity to patents. And as the court began fulfilling those goals, the amount of patent litigation markedly increased, including an increase in patent cases tried before a jury.

Lay juries typically displayed a limited ability to comprehend and resolve intricate scientific questions and interpret the technical terms of a patent. *See, e.g.*, *Markman v. Westview Instruments, Inc.*, 52 F.3d 967 (Fed. Cir. 1995) (en banc), *aff'd*, 517 U.S. 370 (1996) (jury misreads simple term "inventory" and trial judge overrules jury); *McGill Inc. v. John Zink Co.*, 736 F.2d 666 (Fed. Cir. 1984) (holding that the jury's interpretation of the term "recovered liquid hydrocarbon absorbent" was inconsistent with other claim language, the patent's specification and file history, and expert testimony).

The jury system's unbridled discretion in interpreting a patent's claims threatened to undo much of the predictability achieved through the unification of patent appeals into a single court. Recognizing the problem, the Federal Circuit attacked it head on. In one of its most important cases, the Federal Circuit withdrew claim construction from the jury. By making claim construction a question of law within the sole province of the trial judge, the Federal Circuit ruled that the Seventh Amendment did not require a jury trial on those issues.

In *Markman*, the Federal Circuit also took the opportunity to set forth its approach to construing claims. This approach endorsed a hierarchical analysis to resolve disputes over claim meaning. The court assigned the highest value, when construing a claim, to the language of the claim itself. Where the language and context of the claim itself adequately defines the invention, the patentee's chosen language governs.

The Federal Circuit also gave special priority to evidence from other sources intrinsic to the patent: the specification and the prosecution history. Nonetheless, the court stated that, absent an express definition, "[t]he written description part of the specification itself does not delimit the right to exclude [because] [t]hat is the function and purpose of claims." 52 F.3d at 980. Similarly, "[a]lthough the prosecution history can and should be used to understand the language used in the claims, it too cannot enlarge, diminish, or vary the limitations in the claims." *Id.* (quotation omitted).

The Federal Circuit appropriately emphasized the preeminence of the claims themselves. After all, these are the words the applicant chose and the PTO accepted as the limits of the exclusive right. Invariably, however, these terms may contain technical nuances not apparent on their face. For that reason, the court gave priority to the contemporaneous writings in the specification and prosecution history to provide the interpretation context.

For the same reason, the court acknowledged that extrinsic evidence derived from sources outside the patent and its prosecution history may on occasion have relevance. In particular, the court stated:

> Extrinsic evidence consists of all evidence external to the patent and prosecution history, including expert and inventor testimony, dictionaries, and learned treatises. This evidence may be helpful to explain scientific principles, the meaning of technical terms, and terms of art that appear in the patent and prosecution history. Extrinsic evidence may demonstrate the state of the prior art at the time of the invention. It is useful to show what was then old, to distinguish what was new, and to aid the court in the construction of the patent.

Markman, 52 F.3d at 980 (citation and quotation omitted). As a caution, however, the court advised that extrinsic evidence serves to help in "understanding of the patent, not for the purpose of varying or contradicting the terms of the claims." *Id.* at 981. And upon consideration of all the relevant evidence (intrinsic and extrinsic), the court will divine the meaning of the disputed terms as a matter of law.

The *Markman* case involved an invention to prevent the loss of clothing at the dry cleaners. The invention claimed an inventory control and reporting system. Upon receiving an item of clothing, the shopkeeper attached a bar code. Then as the clothing passes different points in the dry-cleaning process, a computer system reads the bar code and monitors its progress and position. The parties disputed the meaning of the claim term "inventory." The patentee wanted to read the term broadly to embrace dollars and invoices, so the claim would cover computer systems that monitor finances for the cleaner business. The defendant wanted to limit "inventory" to articles of clothing.

The jury found for the patentee, but the trial judge and the Federal Circuit read the specification and the prosecution history to limit "inventory" to articles of clothing. In reaching this conclusion, the Federal Circuit rejected the patentee's attempts to alter this meaning through self-serving inventor testimony or expert testimony. Instead the court rejected this evidence as testimony on the ultimate legal question reserved for the court.

The Supreme Court's *Markman* decision primarily focused on the role of the jury. The Seventh Amendment guarantees "the right to a trial by jury" in federal civil cases. U.S. CONST. amend. VII. Under Seventh Amendment jurisprudence, however, a right to a jury arises only for factual issues decided by a jury at common law in 1790—that is, at the date of the amendment's adoption. A review of patent adjudication before 1790 disclosed no analogue to modern claim construction. This result was not surprising, as patent claims first appeared in 1836 and did not gain their modern importance until 1870. Without a pre-1790 analogue, the Supreme Court resolved the Seventh Amendment issue on the basis of practical considerations: judges could do the job better than juries.

In removing claim construction from the jury, the Supreme Court did not agree with the Federal Circuit that the issue is purely legal. Instead, the Court acknowledged that claim construction involves the "mongrel practice" of deriving a legal conclusion after the consideration of factual evidence. In particular, the Court explained that the "fact/law distinction at times has turned on a determination that, as a matter of the sound administration of justice, one judicial actor is better positioned than another to decide the issue in question." *Markman v. Westview Instruments, Inc.*, 517 U.S. 370, 388 (1996) (quotation omitted). Accordingly, the Court opted for judicial claim constructions.

After the Supreme Court's decision, the Federal Circuit embarked on a plan to improve patent adjudication by removing claim construction from juries. But this advance brought a different form of procedural uncertainty. Adopting the fiction that claim construction does not involve fact finding, the Federal Circuit held shortly after *Markman* that it reviews claim construction *de novo*, without giving any deference to the district court judge. *Cybor Corp. v. FAS Techs., Inc.*, 138 F.3d 1448 (Fed. Cir. 1998) (en banc). In many cases, the patent trial became only an act of setting the stage for the main play at the appellate level. And frequent reversals of district court claim interpretations added to the uncertainty and cost of litigation.

Nearly 20 years later, the standard of review at the appellate level for claim construction returned to the Supreme Court. The Supreme Court did not sustain de novo review of claim meaning, but instead noted that *subsidiary* facts, like the meaning of technical terms or the understanding of skilled artisans, must be reviewed for clear error. *Teva Pharms. USA, Inc. v. Sandoz, Inc.*, 574 U.S. 318 (2015). This review standard applies most often when a trial court needs explanation beyond the specification to learn the meaning of a technical term at the time of invention.

Claim construction undeniably includes fact-based inquiries into the state of technology and technological expression at the time of invention. A dissent from a denial of a rehearing en banc calls the de novo standard a fallacy: "If . . . as part of claim construction, we must determine the nature of the invention described in the specification and ensure that the scope of the claims are limited only to the actual invention disclosed, we must acknowledge the factual underpinnings of this analysis and there should be deference." *Retractable Techs., Inc. v. Becton, Dickinson & Co.*, 659 F.3d 1369 (Fed. Cir. 2011) (Moore, J., dissenting). The ultimate claim construction standard examines the understanding of a person of ordinary skill in the art at the time of invention—another factual inquiry.

Often the Federal Circuit has reached a claim construction that neither party advocated for. *See, e.g., Exxon Chem. Patents, Inc. v. Lubrizol Corp.*, 64 F.3d 1553 (Fed. Cir. 1995). Still, the Federal Circuit insists that it "begin[s] with and carefully consider[s] the trial court's work." *Key Pharms. v. Hercon Labs. Corp.*, 161 F.3d 709, 713 (Fed. Cir. 1998). In other words, the appellate court is more inclined to affirm a thorough claim construction than a cursory one. In sum, even when the Federal Circuit reaches independent conclusions on claim meaning, the reasoning of the trial court holds persuasive value.

During the 17 years between *Cybor* and *Teva*, the Federal Circuit reviewed claim constructions without deference. To some degree, this continues even after *Teva* because the Circuit still decides if the district court's decisions are based on fact or law.

The era of de novo review fostered a significant debate about that standard's contribution to the Federal Circuit's high reversal rate in claim construction cases. Some assessed that reversal rate as ranging from approximately one-third to somewhere approaching one-half. *See* Christian Chu, *Empirical Analysis of the Federal Circuit's Claim Construction Trends*, 16 BERK. TECH. L. J. 1075 (2001); Kimberly Moore, *Are District Court Judges Equipped to Resolve Patent Cases?*, 15 HARV. J.L. TECH. 1 (2001). This high reversal rate, in turn, causes criticism that the parties in patent cases tend to discount the trial court's interpretation as merely the "first act" in a play that culminates at the Federal Circuit. *Cybor*, 138 F.3d at 1476 (Rader, J, dissenting). Thus, the non-deferential standard of review, in effect, "postpone[s] the point of certainty to the end of the litigation process, at which point, of course, every outcome is certain anyway." *Id.* Accordingly, this standard of review frustrates early certainty of claim meaning. On remand after reversal, the trial court faces the possibility of a costly second trial.

To avoid a retrial, district judges often strive to convert the *Markman* claim construction hearing into a mandatory summary judgment hearing. Usually this conversion works because the litigants desire early finality and the claim construction issue largely resolves infringement and validity. Indeed in the post-*Markman* era, most patent cases arrive at the Federal Circuit after a grant of summary judgment or the issuance of a consent judgment.

C. THE PROCESS AT THE TRIAL LEVEL

With claim construction in the hands of judges, each trial judge enjoys wide discretion to vary the process of holding a *Markman* hearing and construing the claim. Patent litigants must learn to tolerate the lack of uniformity in claim construction practices. The amount of discovery, the number of terms to be construed, the timing and length of the *Markman* hearing are all issues that vary from one judge to the next. *See, e.g., Sofamor Danek Group, Inc. v. DePuy-Motech, Inc.*, 74 F.3d 1216 (Fed. Cir. 1996). In fact, the trial court has no obligation to construe the claims before trial or even hear live testimony on claim meaning. Moreover, the district judge can and often does revisit the initial claim construction as additional facts or arguments come to light. *Utah Med. Prods., Inc. v. Graphic Controls Corp.*, 350 F.3d 1376 (Fed. Cir. 2003).

No party may immediately appeal an adverse claim construction as a matter of right. *Nystrom v. TREX Co.,* 339 F.3d 1347 (Fed. Cir. 2003). Instead, to reach the Federal Circuit for a "binding" claim construction, one of four scenarios must occur: the trial court must rule on all pending issues, either summarily or through a trial; the trial court must dismiss any pending claims without prejudice; the trial court must direct a judgment of fewer than all pending claims under Federal Rule of Civil Procedure 54(b); or the appellant must seek the trial court's and the appellate court's permission for an interlocutory appeal under 28 U.S.C. § 1292(c). The Federal Circuit has consistently declined to accept interlocutory appeals to review claim construction on a premature record. *See Bayer AG v. Biovail Corp.*, 279 F.3d 1340 (Fed. Cir. 2002).

D. SOURCES OF CLAIM MEANING

Acutely aware of growing dissatisfaction with its high reversal rate and the uncertainties of claim construction procedure, the Federal Circuit convened another en banc rehearing on the issue. *Phillips v. AWH Corp.*, 415 F.3d 1303 (Fed. Cir. 2005). *Phillips*, like *Markman*, involved quite simple technology. The invention claimed modular security walls that might be used for a prison. Because the internal support structures, or "baffles," touched only one side of the walls, these modular panels insulated against fire and noise. The patent also depicted these "baffles" at angles that would deflect bullets. Based on those depictions, the trial court (and the original Federal Circuit panel) limited the contested claim term "baffle" to an angled structure that would serve to deflect bullets. The accused structure had baffles disposed at right angles from the outer wall surfaces, thus reducing the chance that the baffle would serve the bullet deflection function.

The district court had entered summary judgment for the defendant, AWH, because Phillips could not prove infringement under a claim construction requiring baffles with acute or obtuse angles. The en banc court, however, declined to limit the broad term "baffle" to the projectile-deflecting embodiments in the specification.

The claim language recited "internal steel baffles extending inwardly." The en banc court placed the primary emphasis on the claim language itself that did not limit the baffles to any specific angled configuration. The court then relied on the intrinsic evidence to support that reading:

> The intrinsic evidence confirms that a person of skill in the art would understand that the term "baffles," as used in the '798 patent, would have that generic meaning. . . The fact that the written description of the '798 patent sets forth multiple objectives to be served by the baffles recited in the claims confirms that the term "baffles" should not be read restrictively to require that the baffles in each case serve all of the recited functions.

415 F.3d at 1325–27.

As in *Markman*, the Federal Circuit in *Phillips* reiterated its commitment to a hierarchy of evidentiary sources for claim construction. The claim language itself is preeminent in importance. Additional intrinsic evidence occupies the next level of importance. The court observed that the best context for the claim language comes from the patentee's own words and descriptions in the contemporaneous specification and prosecution history.

Finally, extrinsic evidence has a more limited role in the process. The court expressed wariness about the possibility of litigation-induced evidence in this category: "extrinsic evidence consisting of expert reports and testimony is generated at the time of and for the purpose of litigation and thus can suffer from bias." *Id.* at 1318. In claim construction proceedings, a court may pursue an iterative process that consults the intrinsic evidence then relevant extrinsic evidence then intrinsic evidence again, all the while focusing on the claim language. Again, the understanding of a person having ordinary skill in the art at the time of the invention provides the standard for the entire process.

1. The Claim Language

The court in *Phillips* restated the "bedrock principle of patent law that the claims of a patent define the invention." *Id.* at 1312 (citations omitted). Thus, the claim language governs the process of ascertaining the scope of the invention and not, for example, the patentee's commercial embodiment. *See Zenith Labs., Inc. v. Bristol-Myers Squibb Co.*, 19 F.3d 1418 (Fed. Cir. 1994). That is, "the claim construction inquiry, therefore, begins and ends in all cases with the actual words of the claim." *Renishaw PLC v. Marposs Societa' per Azioni*, 158 F.3d 1243, 1248 (Fed. Cir. 1998).

The Federal Circuit also expressed that "the words of a claim are generally given their ordinary and customary meaning." *Phillips*, 415 F.3d at 1312 (citations omitted); *see also Johnson Worldwide Assocs., Inc. v. Zebco Corp.*, 175 F.3d 985 (Fed. Cir. 1999) (discussing a "heavy presumption" that the claim terms receive their ordinary meaning). This shorthand, however, is not an invitation to divorce the terms from their proper technological and temporal context. The Federal Circuit has emphasized that the "customary meaning" refers to the customary meaning in the art. *Home Diagnostics, Inc. v. LifeScan, Inc.*, 381 F.3d 1352 (Fed. Cir. 2004). Different arts might have different customs:

> The word "normal" that appears in this case has a different "customary" meaning to a psychiatrist in a mental hospital (where "normal" refers to a sane mental state) than to a pharmacist seeking proper dosages (where "normal" doses would vary with body weight and other factors), than to a marriage counselor (where a "normal" marriage probably means an average marriage, i.e., one perpetually in danger of divorce), than to an oil well driller in a pump technology.

Ferguson Beauregard/Logic Controls, Div. of Dover Res., Inc. v. Mega Sys., LLC, 350 F.3d 1327, 1347–48 (Fed. Cir. 2003) (Rader, J., concurring). In sum, the meaning of a word varies according to its context and the technological understanding at the time of the invention.

The "ordinary and customary meaning" may guide claim construction "generally" and "frequently," *Phillips*, 415 F.3d at 1312, but the Federal Circuit has explained reasons to depart from this principle:

> First, the claim term will not receive its ordinary meaning if the patentee acted as his own lexicographer and clearly set forth a definition of the disputed claim term in either the specification or prosecution history. Second, a claim term will not carry its ordinary meaning if the intrinsic evidence shows that the patentee distinguished that term from prior art on the basis of a particular embodiment, expressly disclaimed subject matter, or described a particular embodiment as important to the invention.
>
> Third, . . . a claim term also will not have its ordinary meaning if the term chosen by the patentee so deprives the claim of clarity as to require resort to the other intrinsic evidence for a definite meaning. Last, as a matter of statutory authority, a claim term will cover nothing more than the corresponding structure or step disclosed in the specification, as well as equivalents thereto, if the patentee phrased the claim in step-or means-plus-function format.

CCS Fitness, Inc. v. Brunswick Corp., 288 F.3d 1359, 1366–67 (Fed. Cir. 2002) (citations and quotations omitted). In this list, the first two departure categories distill down to a single concept: Is there something in the specification or the prosecution history that would reasonably lead a person of ordinary skill in the art to believe that the patentee's words do not carry their customary meaning? These categories accordingly encompass express lexicography and express or implicit disclaimers. The third, somewhat amorphous, category relates to the ambiguity of the words present in the claim itself. The ordinary meaning must be clear and apparent to take effect. The fourth and final category acknowledges the statute. A means-plus-function claim is limited to the structure disclosed in the specification and the equivalents of that structure. *See* Chapter 12.

The "ordinary and customary meaning" principle carries a warning. Strict adherence to the words in the claim may result in a claim scope that the patentee did not intend at all. For example, in *Chef America, Inc. v. Lamb-Weston, Inc.*, 358 F.3d 1371 (Fed. Cir. 2004), the patentee claimed a process for making dough products with a light, flaky, and crispy texture when later heated in an oven or microwave. But the words of the claim recited a step of "heating the . . . dough *to* a temperature in the range of about 400°F to 850°F." *Id.* at 1372 (emphasis added). Thus, the claim recited a process that heated the dough itself to a temperature of at least 400°F. At that temperature, of course, the dough would become an unusable charcoal briquet.

No doubt the claim drafter meant that the dough ought to be baked in an oven *at* a temperature in the range of about 400°F to 850°F for a brief time. The claim did not, however, use the proper preposition. The Federal Circuit simply lacked the power to redraft the claims: "Even a nonsensical result does not require the court to redraft the claims of the . . . patent. . . . Where, as here, the claim is susceptible to only one reasonable construction, . . . we must construe the claims based on the patentee's version of the claim as he himself drafted it." *Id.* at 1374.

In reaching its conclusion, the *Chef America* court disregarded an affidavit reflecting the understanding of a person of ordinary skill in the art because that evidence did not show that the claim language had a different meaning. Instead that evidence merely confirmed that a person of ordinary skill in the art would have recognized that the claimed process was inoperable and that the patentee likely intended to use different words. That is, the testimony reinforced that the claim drafter committed an error, because "the only possible interpretation of the claim led to a nonsensical result." *Ortho-McNeil Pharm., Inc. v. Mylan Lab'ys, Inc.*, 520 F.3d 1358, 1363 (Fed. Cir. 2008). Still, an inventor must choose claim language with care because U.S. courts will not correct claim drafting errors.

2. The Specification

A claim is only one part of a patent. In the words of the Federal Circuit, "[t]he claims, of course, do not stand alone. Rather they are part of a fully integrated written instrument, consisting principally of a specification that concludes with the claims. For that reason, claims must be read in view of the specification of which they are a part." *Phillips*, 415 F.3d at 1315 (citations omitted). This pithy statement does not disclose the entire complicated relationship between the written description and the scope of the claims.

As a starting point, the specification provides the context for a proper understanding of the claims. After all, the specification is a contemporaneous document drafted to explain the invention. *See, e.g.*, *Vitronics Corp. v. Conceptronic, Inc.*, 90 F.3d 1576 (Fed. Cir. 1996). In *Phillips*, the Federal Circuit invoked a commentary from its predecessor, the Court of Claims, that characterized the specification " 'as a concordance for the claims,' based on the statutory requirement that the specification 'describe the manner and process of making and using' the patented invention." *Phillips*, 415 F.3d at 1315 (quoting *Autogiro Co. of Am. v. United States*, 384 F.2d 391, 397–98 (Ct. Cl. 1967)). By the same token, this strong language does not mean that the claimed invention is limited to any embodiment or embodiments described in the specification.

The claims, after all, define the invention. The specification has a different role, namely describing the fabrication and use of the invention. To fulfill its function, the specification need not describe every permutation or combination of the invention. The *Phillips* court itself did not limit the "baffle" claim to the angled embodiment prominently and repeatedly described in the specification. Instead, the Circuit applied the correct practice of examining the specification to determine whether, either implicitly or explicitly, the patentee had limited the scope of the claim language.

In general, the claimed invention is not limited to a preferred embodiment, even if the specification does not describe any other embodiment. For example, in *Teleflex, Inc. v. Ficosa North America Corp.*, 299 F.3d 1313 (Fed. Cir. 2002), the court rejected an argument that a claim reciting a clip—a component of a two-piece shift cable in an automobile—was limited to the sole embodiment disclosed in the specification. In examining the specification for any restriction on the broad ordinary meaning, the court explained that "the number of embodiments disclosed in the specification is not determinative of the meaning of disputed claim terms." *Id.* at 1327. Because the intrinsic record was devoid of any clear statements of manifest restriction, the court accorded "clip" its full range of meaning.

Indeed, "the specification need not present every embodiment or permutation of the invention and the claims are not limited to the preferred embodiment of the invention." *Netword, LLC v. Centraal Corp.*, 242 F.3d 1347, 1352 (Fed. Cir. 2001). That is, "limitations from the specification are not to be read into the claims," even though claims must be read in light of the specification. *Comark Commc'ns, Inc. v. Harris Corp.*, 156 F.3d 1182, 1186 (Fed. Cir. 1998). While numerous opinions echo that guideline, a complete picture of claim construction law suggests that the specification very often does impose constraints on claim scope.

When a patentee repeatedly emphasizes a feature or function of an invention, that emphasis often converts into a constraint on claim scope. For example, in *SciMed Life Systems, Inc. v. Advanced Cardiovascular Systems, Inc.*, 242 F.3d 1337 (Fed. Cir. 2001), the patents claimed balloon dilatation catheters for coronary angioplasty. Each claim recited a general "lumen" configuration. The specification reiterated over and over that the invention comprised only a coaxial—and not a side-by-side—lumen configuration:

> At various points, the common specification of the three patents indicates that the claimed invention uses coaxial, rather than side-by-side lumens, i.e., that the guide wire lumen is contained within the inflation lumen and that the inflation lumen is annular. Read together, these portions of the common specification lead to the inescapable conclusion that the references in the asserted claims to an inflation lumen "separate from" the guide wire lumen must be understood as referring to coaxial lumens, and thus that the asserted claims read only on catheters having coaxial lumens.

Id. at 1342. Thus, repetition and emphasis resulted in a limitation on the general claim term "lumen."

This case also illustrates another instance when specification descriptions will almost invariably limit broader claim terms, namely when the specification expressly defines the entire invention in terms of the narrower embodiment or configuration. In *SciMed*, the specification expressly defined "all embodiments of the present invention":

> It is difficult to imagine how the patents could have been clearer in making the point that the coaxial lumen configuration was a necessary element of every variant of the claimed invention. Moreover, there is no suggestion that the patentee made that statement unaware of the alternative dual lumen configuration, because earlier in the patent the patentee had distinguished the dual lumen configuration used in prior art devices as having disadvantages that the coaxial lumens used in the patented invention had overcome.

Id. at 1344.

The difficulty, however, arises when the specification repeatedly emphasizes a feature, but includes a statement or two endorsing a broader reading or when the specification does not explicitly apply a narrower description to the entire invention, but nonetheless suggests the narrower reading. For instance, in the case about safety razors, the specification described the claim in terms of a "three-bladed" configuration over 30 times. *Gillette Co. v. Energizer Holdings, Inc.*, 405 F.3d 1367 (Fed. Cir. 2005). Yet in one passage, the specification also referred to a "plurality of blades" that could encompass more than three blades. The Federal

Circuit, in that instance, relied on a broader reasonable reading of the claims themselves.

Nonetheless, repeated usage of a single term in accordance with a single meaning often indicates that that term has only that single meaning. That is, "when a patentee uses a claim term throughout the entire patent specification, in a manner consistent with only a single meaning, he has defined that term 'by implication.'" *Bell Atl. Network Servs., Inc. v. Covad Commc'ns Group, Inc.*, 262 F.3d 1258, 1271 (Fed. Cir. 2001). On the other hand, where the patentee varies the use of a claim term, that varied usage indicates that that term has a broader meaning encompassing at least all of those usages. *See, e.g.*, *Johnson Worldwide Assocs., Inc. v. Zebco Corp.*, 175 F.3d 985 (Fed. Cir. 1999).

In sum, the relationship between the specification and claim scope is very complex. The claims must be read "in view of the specification, of which they are a part," *Markman v. Westview Instruments, Inc.*, 52 F.3d 967, 979 (Fed. Cir. 1995) (en banc), but never to the point of "read[ing] a limitation from the specification into the claims." *Liebel-Flarsheim Company v. Medrad, Inc.*, 358 F.3d 898, 904 (Fed. Cir. 2004). The Federal Circuit has not been able to articulate a neutral principle that distinguishes clearly these potentially conflicting guidelines.

In *Liebel-Flarsheim*, the Federal Circuit expressed confidence that a careful reading of the claims from the vantage point of the skilled artisan would usually put the specification into its proper context. In general terms, a court must consult the specification during every claim construction, but the specification descriptions do not limit broader claim language, unless the specification clearly indicates, either expressly or implicitly, that the invention is narrower than the scope of the claim language.

3. The Prosecution History

As the third intrinsic source for claim meaning, the written record created during the administrative process culminating in the patent's grant—also known as the prosecution history or file wrapper—also forms an important source for claim meaning. As discussed in Chapter 2, the prosecution history contains the correspondence between the inventor and the Patent Office. In these back-and-forth negotiations, an examiner typically issues rejections or objections regarding the claims, and the applicant rebuts those rejections or objections by making legal or factual arguments, amending the claims, or both. This record becomes publicly available upon patent issuance. Therefore, applicants cannot argue before the Patent Office that claims are very narrow to avoid prior art and obtain allowance then later argue before a court that the claims are very broad to prove infringement. *See, e.g., Southwall Techs., Inc. v. Cardinal IG Co.*, 54 F.3d 1570 (Fed. Cir. 1995).

The Federal Circuit in *Phillips* endorsed prosecution history as part of the claim construction process: "In addition to consulting the specification, we have held that a court 'should also consider the patent's prosecution history, if it is in evidence.' " *Phillips*, 415 F.3d at 1317 (quoting *Markman*, 52

F.3d at 980). At the same time, the Circuit recognized the limitations of this claim construction tool: "Yet because the prosecution history represents an ongoing negotiation between the PTO and the applicant, rather than the final product of that negotiation, it often lacks the clarity of the specification and thus is less useful for claim construction purposes." *Id.* at 1317. The Circuit might have also observed that prosecution histories are often sketchy and incomplete.

The administrative record of allowance is not evidence of the patentee's subjective intent—intent is irrelevant. Instead, the prosecution history is an objective record that the public may rely upon when discerning the scope of the invention. *See Biogen, Inc. v. Berlex Lab'ys, Inc.*, 318 F.3d 1132 (Fed. Cir. 2003). Besides incompleteness, the administrative record includes many arguments and amendments that were not necessary to obtain allowance. *Elkay Mfg. Co. v. Ebco Mfg. Co.*, 192 F.3d 973 (Fed. Cir. 1999). Comments in the prosecution history of related applications—regardless of whether ancestors or descendants—also affect the scope of a patent. *See Microsoft Corp. v. Multi-Tech Sys., Inc.*, 357 F.3d 1340 (Fed. Cir. 2004).

A patent's prosecution history thus may inform the proper construction of a claim, although its importance—similar to the importance of the specification—varies according to the completeness and relevance of the record. If, for example, the patentee's statements are ambiguous, reasonably amenable to multiple interpretations, or at best inconclusive, the Federal Circuit will not rely on passing commentary to narrow the claims. *See* N. *Telecom Ltd. v. Samsung Elecs. Co.*, 215 F.3d 1281 (Fed. Cir. 2000). In addition, the case law holds that blatantly erroneous comments in the prosecution history do not restrict the meaning of the claims, so long as a person of ordinary skill in the art would readily identify the comments as mistaken. *See, e.g.*, *Biotec Biologische Naturverpackungen GmbH v. Biocorp, Inc.*, 249 F.3d 1341 (Fed. Cir. 2001).

Some prosecution histories may evince the applicant's unambiguous surrender of subject matter. In that case, the claim scope will be limited, even though the claim language may not also reflect that surrender of subject matter. For instance, in *Omega Engineering, Inc. v. Raytek Corp.*, 334 F.3d 1314 (Fed. Cir. 2003), the court considered whether the patentee made a "clear and unmistakable" disclaimer with respect to the term "to visibly outline." After considering the prosecution history in its entirety, the court determined that the patentee narrowed the meaning of the claim by repeatedly distinguishing the prior art: "Since the patentee offered a narrower construction of the verb 'to visibly outline' in the disputed function, it has clearly and unmistakably disclaimed the territory between the full ordinary meaning of the claim language and the asserted new meaning." *Id.* at 1327.

The applicant's characterization of the invention in the prosecution history can, as shown by *Omega*, narrow claim scope. In some instances, however, a patentee will attempt to manipulate the proceedings before the Patent Office in an attempt to alter the scope of the invention. Courts, though, are loath to accept a litigation-induced, self-serving attempt to modify the meaning of a term, particularly one that is inconsistent with the remainder of the intrinsic evidence. Where the specification defines a term (either implicitly or expressly), the prosecution history cannot broaden that definition. *Multiform Desiccants, Inc. v. Medzam, Ltd.*, 133 F.3d 1473 (Fed. Cir. 1998).

4. Extrinsic Evidence

Extrinsic evidence may also factor into the court's claim construction. Extrinsic evidence is, as its name suggests, any evidence external to the patent and the prosecution history—including, for example, dictionaries, treatises, encyclopedias, expert testimony, and prior art references. Although not forming a part of the public record, this category is important to frame the inquiry within its proper technological and temporal context. Extrinsic evidence can provide the background knowledge or understanding of a person or ordinary skill in the art at the time of the invention. *See, e.g.*, *Markman v. Westview Instruments, Inc.*, 52 F.3d 967 (Fed. Cir. 1995) (en banc).

In *Phillips*, the Federal Circuit "authorized district courts to rely on extrinsic evidence," 415 F.3d at 1317, but with considerable cautionary comments. For instance, extrinsic evidence, the court observed, "is less significant than the intrinsic record in determining the legally operative meaning of claim language." *Id.* (internal citation omitted). Thus, if an analysis of the intrinsic evidence yields an unambiguous definition for a disputed claim term, extrinsic evidence may not alter that definition. The primary role for extrinsic evidence, as suggested by the Federal Circuit, may lie in "educat[ing] the court regarding the field of the invention and . . . help[ing] the court determine what a person of ordinary skill in the art would understand the claim terms to mean." *Id.* at 1319.

The Federal Circuit also advises that extrinsic evidence "may be used only to help the court come to the proper understanding of the claims; it may not be used to vary or contradict the claim language." *Vitronics Corp. v. Conceptronic, Inc.*, 90 F.3d 1576, 1584 (Fed. Cir. 1996). Despite this somewhat restricted application, patent litigation often features considerable wrangling over extrinsic evidence. The cautions about this form of evidence require some additional examination of its various categories.

a) Dictionaries, Treatises, and Encyclopedias

At first blush, these publicly available resources might seem to provide an excellent objective source of claim meaning. After all, these resources are independent of influence from the pressures of litigation and may provide context for a claim's customary meaning in the art at the time of the invention. At one point, the Federal Circuit began to place heavy reliance on dictionary definitions:

> Dictionaries, encyclopedias and treatises . . . may be the most meaningful sources of

> information to aid judges in better understanding both the technology and the terminology used by those skilled in the art to describe the technology.

Texas Digital Sys., Inc. v. Telegenix, Inc., 308 F.3d 1193, 1202–03 (Fed. Cir. 2002). When this reliance on a form of extrinsic evidence began to trump intrinsic evidence, the Federal Circuit stepped in and offered a correction. This dictionary dalliance away from the importance of intrinsic evidence, therefore, was brief. The *Phillips* case was the vehicle to correct the line of cases that had given "greater emphasis to dictionary definitions" and a "less prominent role to the specification and the prosecution history." *Phillips*, 415 F.3d at 1319.

The Federal Circuit explained its reasons for skepticism about according dictionaries precedence over the specification:

> The main problem with elevating the dictionary to such prominence is that it focuses the inquiry on the abstract meaning of words rather than on the meaning of claim terms within the context of the patent. . . . [H]eavy reliance on the dictionary divorced from the intrinsic evidence risks transforming the meaning of the claim terms to the artisan into the meaning of the term in abstract, out of its particular context, which is the specification.

Id. at 1321. The Federal Circuit then proceeded to describe the potential problem in more specific terms:

> The problem is that if the district court starts with the broad dictionary definition in every case and fails to fully appreciate how the specification implicitly limits that definition, the error will systematically cause the construction of the claim to be unduly expansive.

Id. The en banc court also noted that dictionaries, even technical dictionaries, present multiple definitions. And different dictionaries and even different editions of the same dictionary can present further variance in term meaning, all divorced from the specific context of the patent.

After discounting these extrinsic sources, the Circuit nonetheless reaffirmed "the appropriate use of dictionaries." *Id.* at 1322. These sources are particularly useful to "assist in understanding the commonly understood meaning of words," as opposed to the technical usage of terms in the context of particular art at the particular time of invention. *Id.* In sum, these sources remain available, but in a more confined role.

b) Expert Testimony

Because claim construction requires the understanding of a person of ordinary skill in the art at the time of the invention, expert testimony may also provide context for construing claims. A technical expert may aid a court's understanding with respect to the state of the art, the disclosure of the prior art, or even the meaning of a claim term. Similarly, an inventor's testimony—even though from the perspective of a person having "extraordinary" skill in the art—may also have relevance for the meaning of a term in limited circumstances. Above all, however, a court must treat this evidence carefully to prevent any manipulation to expand claim scope beyond the reach specified in intrinsic evidence.

The Federal Circuit offered some guidance in *Phillips* on the role of expert testimony:

> [E]xpert reports and testimony [are] generated at the time of and for the purpose of litigation and thus can suffer from bias that is not present in intrinsic evidence. The effect of that bias can be exacerbated if the expert is not one of skill in the relevant art or if the expert's opinion is offered in a form that is not subject to cross-examination.

Id. at 1318. Thus, the trial court has, with expert testimony in particular, a "considerable task of filtering the useful extrinsic evidence from the fluff." *Id.*

This advice did not originate with *Phillips*; the Federal Circuit has consistently singled out expert testimony for careful scrutiny by district court judges. In a very influential case following *Markman*, the Circuit advised that expert testimony on the proper construction of a disputed claim term should "rarely, if ever, occur." *Vitronics Corp. v. Conceptronic, Inc.*, 90 F.3d 1576, 1585 (Fed. Cir. 1996). Later the Federal Circuit backed off that strong admonition to grant trial judges more discretion to take relevant evidence from experts, but retained its warnings about relying on experts to vary from the intrinsic record. *Pitney Bowes, Inc. v. Hewlett-Packard Co.*, 182 F.3d 1298, 1308–09 (Fed. Cir. 1999). In its proper context, the Federal Circuit itself has relied on expert testimony. For instance, expert testimony assisted recognition that the term "acid" in pharmacology (and not general chemistry) includes salts of that acid. *See, e.g., Merck & Co. v. Teva Pharms., USA, Inc.*, 347 F.3d 1367 (Fed. Cir. 2003).

Inventor testimony, a special form of expert testimony, intensifies the potential for non-credible testimony. After all, the inventor certainly has a stake in the outcome of the litigation. Nonetheless, the "inventor is a competent witness to explain the invention" as well as "background information, including explanation of the problems that existed at the time the invention was made and the inventor's solution to these problems." *Voice Techs Group, Inc. v. VMC Sys., Inc.*, 164 F.3d 605, 615 (Fed. Cir. 1999). In light of the potential for self-serving testimony, however, courts will typically only permit the inventor's testimony to restrict—and not expand—the meaning of a disputed claim term. *See, e.g., Jonsson v. Stanley Works*, 903 F.2d 812 (Fed. Cir. 1990).

c) Prior Art References and Scientific Articles

Less controversial than expert testimony and less frequently cited than dictionaries, prior art references and scientific articles may help establish the knowledge within the art at the time of invention, regardless of whether reported to the Patent Office during prosecution. *Arthur A. Collins, Inc. v. N. Telecom Ltd.*, 216 F.3d 1042 (Fed. Cir. 2000). In particular, prior art references may aid in the definition of a term beyond its normal function of protecting the public domain. In *Kumar v. Ovonic Battery Co.*, 351 F.3d 1364 (Fed. Cir. 2003), the court disregarded dictionary definitions in favor of a prior art definition extensively discussed during prosecution.

E. GUIDELINES FOR CLAIM CONSTRUCTION

Although loose language in case law occasionally recites "rules" for claim construction, the process is not amenable to rules. The so-called canons of claim construction are more accurately characterized as guidelines rather than immutable truths. *Renishaw PLC v. Marposs Societa' per Azioni*, 158 F.3d 1243 (Fed. Cir. 1998). A "rule" for one case may have no application in the next. Thus, a proper claim construction avoids rote regurgitation of "rules" without a thorough analysis based on the relevant evidence informing the most likely perception of a person of ordinary skill in the art at the time of the invention. Nevertheless, the following list attempts to organize the guiding principles from strongest to weakest:

1. The ordinary and customary meaning of claim language enjoys a heavy presumption of accuracy.

2. Where intrinsic evidence unambiguously delineates claim scope, it controls.

3. For intrinsic evidence, a claim term should be read with reference to the specification, but not to the extent of importing a limitation from the specification into the claim.

4. To determine ordinary meaning, a court may rely on general and technical dictionary definitions.

5. A claim, if possible, should be construed to encompass a disclosed embodiment of the invention, and a reading that excludes the preferred embodiment is rarely correct.

6. Claims may be construed to uphold their validity, but construction must precede a validity determination and should not prevent a clear interpretation that renders the claim invalid.

7. Claim differentiation, strongest for dependent claim relationships, may be overcome by intrinsic or even relevant extrinsic evidence.

8. Extrinsic evidence, though relevant, may not contradict intrinsic evidence.

The following graph effectively brings together many of these teachings:

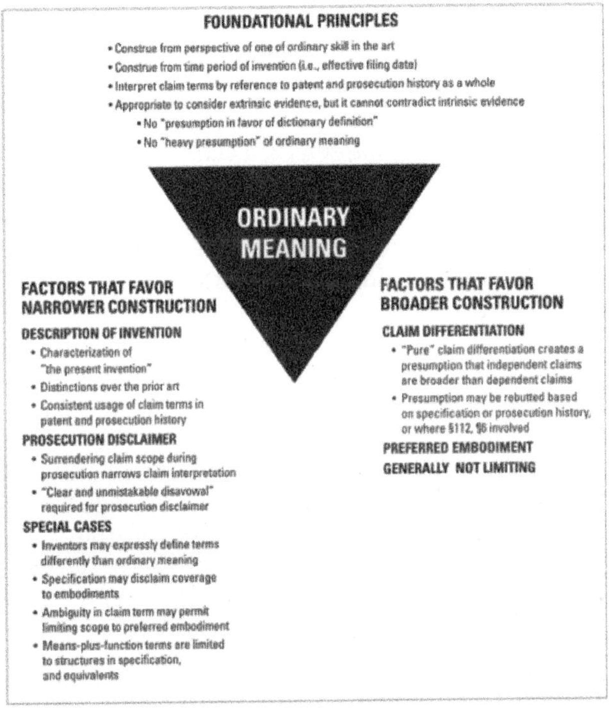

F. PRACTICAL PROBLEMS

The process of construing claims presents some recurrent difficulties. Some of these difficulties include whether a preamble limits the scope of the invention, whether construing a claim in light of the specification violates the prohibition against importing limitations from the specification, whether the accused device has a role in claim construction, and whether a claim construction may change within the same case.

1. Preamble

As discussed in Chapter 12, a claim's preamble has the purpose of setting forth the subject matter of the invention. Although a preamble may be simple like "a method," it may also recite more information like "a method for curing colon cancer." Courts often struggle to decide whether that additional information—often an intended use—limits the scope of the claim. The answer to that question usually hinges on the importance of the preamble information to give meaning to the rest of the claim. *Pitney Bowes, Inc. v. Hewlett-Packard Co.*, 182 F.3d 1298 (Fed. Cir. 1999). Stated differently, a preamble has the significance that the rest of the claim dictates. *Bell Commc'ns Research, Inc. v. Vitalink Commc'ns Corp.*, 55 F.3d 615 (Fed. Cir. 1995).

In *Catalina Marketing International, Inc. v. Coolsavings.com, Inc.*, 289 F.3d 801 (Fed. Cir. 2002), the Federal Circuit expounded on this general rule about the preamble as a limitation:

> For example, this court has held that Jepson[110] claiming generally indicates intent to use the preamble to define the claimed invention, thereby limiting claim scope. Additionally, dependence on a particular disputed preamble phrase for antecedent basis may limit claim

---

[110] A Jepson claim, a specific type of claim that recites an improvement, is examined more fully in Chapter 12.

scope because it indicates a reliance on both the preamble and claim body to define the claimed invention. Likewise, when the preamble is essential to understand limitations or terms in the claim body, the preamble limits claim scope.

Further, when reciting additional structure or steps underscored as important by the specification, the preamble may operate as a claim limitation.

Moreover, clear reliance on the preamble during prosecution to distinguish the claimed invention from the prior art transforms the preamble into a claim limitation because such reliance indicates use of the preamble to define, in part, the claimed invention. Without such reliance, however, a preamble generally is not limiting when the claim body describes a structurally complete invention such that deletion of the preamble phrase does not affect the structure or steps of the claimed invention. Thus, preamble language merely extolling benefits or features of the claimed invention does not limit the claim scope without clear reliance on those benefits or features as patentably significant.

Moreover, preambles describing the use of an invention generally do not limit the claims because the patentability of apparatus or composition claims depends on the claimed structure, not on the use or purpose of that structure.

Id. at 808–09 (cleaned up) (footnote added). Distilled down, this test depends on whether the intrinsic record elevates the preamble beyond a statement of intended or general use.

2. Construing Claims in Light of the Specification Versus Impermissibly Importing a Limitation from the Specification

As the Federal Circuit stresses, the written description is the "single best guide to the meaning of a disputed term." *Phillips*, 415 F.3d at 1315 (citation omitted). On the other hand, the claims and specification have different purposes in the patent document, and for that reason the specification cannot in all cases be coextensive with the scope of the claims. And, of course, an applicant may limit the scope of the invention expressly or implicitly through the written description. Claim construction practices have not effectively articulated an invariable rule for determining the specification's role—mere informant or scope constrainer. In fact, these competing roles are a microcosm for the larger issue of claim construction. *See, e.g.*, *Retractable Techs., Inc. v. Becton, Dickinson & Co.*, 653 F.3d 1296 (Fed. Cir. 2011).

The *Texas Digital* case placed undue emphasis on dictionaries to prevent the cardinal patent law "sin" of pulling a limitation from the specification into the claims. *See Phillips*, 415 F.3d at 1320. When the *Phillips* court undertook to restrict the application of dictionaries, it acknowledged this purpose of the dictionary cases and the difficult distinction between "using the specification to interpret the meaning of a claim and importing limitations from the specification into the claim." *Id.* at 1323. The Federal Circuit thought that the distinction was manageable "if the court's focus remains on understanding how a person of ordinary skill in the art would understand the claim terms." *Id.* "In particular," the court continued, "we have expressly rejected the contention that if a patent describes only a single embodiment, the claims of the patent must be construed as limited to that embodiment." *Id.* In another case, the Federal Circuit explained:

> [T]his court recognizes that it must interpret the claims in light of the specification, yet avoid impermissibly importing limitations from the specification. That balance turns on how the specification characterizes the claimed invention. In this respect, this court looks to whether the specification refers to a limitation only as a part of less than all possible embodiments or whether the specification read as a whole suggests that the very character of the invention requires the limitation be a part of every embodiment. For example, it is impermissible to read the one and only disclosed embodiment into a claim without other indicia that the patentee so intended to limit the invention. On the other hand, where the specification makes clear at various points that the claimed invention is narrower than the claim language might imply, it is entirely permissible and proper to limit the claims.

Alloc, Inc. v. Int'l Trade Comm'n, 342 F.3d 1361, 1370 (Fed. Cir. 2003) (cleaned up).

3. Construing Claims to the Extent Necessary Versus Construing Claims in Light of the Accused Device

A court should construe only those claim terms "in controversy, and only to the extent necessary to resolve the controversy." *Vivid Techs., Inc. v. Am. Sci. & Eng'g, Inc.*, 200 F.3d 795, 803 (Fed. Cir. 1999). This sensible statement stems from the nature of our judicial system, which only resolves actual controversies. A problem, however, arises with respect to determining the claim terms "in controversy." To frame the dispute, a court usually needs some information about the accused device.

Nonetheless, the law ignores the accused device once the parties identify the disputed terms. In this way, the law ensures that the second step of infringement (comparing the accused device to the properly construed claims) remains separate from the first (construing the claims). Indeed, "claims are not construed 'to cover' or 'not to cover' the accused device. That would make infringement a matter of judicial whim. It is only *after* the claims have been *construed without reference to the accused device* that the claims, as so construed, are applied to the accused device to determine infringement." *SRI Int'l v. Matsushita Elec. Corp. of Am.*, 775 F.2d 1107, 1118 (Fed. Cir. 1985) (en banc). The court may not construe the claims with an eye to the outcome.

Beyond that proscription on result-oriented claim construction, however, the trial court retains broad discretion to consult the accused product or process for the context of the dispute. The Federal Circuit explained:

> The rule [against construing a claim with reference to the accused device], however, does not forbid awareness of the accused product or process to supply the parameters and scope of the infringement analysis, including its claim construction component. In other words, the "reference" rule accepted in *Pall Corp.*, *Multiform Desiccants*, and *Scripps Clinic* does not forbid any glimpse of the accused product or process during or before claim construction. In light of these principles, if the litigants cannot themselves inform a trial court of the specific issues presented by the infringement inquiry—that is, issues of the breadth of the claim construction analysis and the most useful terms to facilitate that defining process—then a trial court may refer to the accused product or process for that context during the process.

Wilson Sporting Goods Co. v. Hillerich & Bradsby, 442 F.3d 1322, 1326–27 (Fed. Cir. 2006).

4. Evolving Claim Construction

On occasion, litigants will seek—and the trial court may issue—a ruling on claim construction before all issues in the case have crystallized. A court must often construe the claims to resolve a preliminary injunction issue. To prevail on a motion for preliminary relief, the patentee must show a reasonable likelihood of success on the merits, which in turn requires proof of likely infringement. At this preliminary stage, the full issues of claim construction are not fully developed. The discovery process may be just underway. In this setting, the district court's claim construction is tentative. The law, in fact, does not prohibit a trial court from "engag[ing] in a rolling claim construction, in which the court revisits and alters its interpretation of the claim terms as its understanding of the technology evolves." *Jack Guttman, Inc. v. Kopykake Enters., Inc.*, 302 F.3d 1352, 1361 (Fed. Cir. 2002).

The Federal Circuit has itself construed the same claim differently between an initial appeal on a preliminary injunction and an appeal on the final judgment. *CVI/Beta Ventures, Inc. v. Tura LP*, 112 F.3d 1146, 1160 n.7 (Fed. Cir. 1997) (commenting that "unlike the earlier appeal, this appeal required us to construe the asserted claims based upon the final and complete record in the case"). A trial court has the discretion to revisit or reconsider an earlier claim construction ruling, even if not initially issued in connection with a preliminary injunction. For example, in *Utah Medical Products, Inc. v. Graphic Controls Corp.*, 350 F.3d 1376 (Fed. Cir. 2003), the court upheld a claim construction that was modified in light of additional arguments misreading the first attempt at construing the claims. The appellate court, in fact, commended the trial court's correction: "Recognizing the shortcomings of its original attempt to define the scope of the claims, the district court admirably amended its construction to supply a better definition before trial." *Id.* at 1382.

G. CLAIM CONSTRUCTION AT THE PATENT OFFICE

While the same sources of claim meaning affect the meaning of claims during prosecution before the Patent Office, the pre-issuance standard for claim construction features a slightly different perspective than enforcement proceedings. In simple terms, claim construction during enforcement requires firm and discernible boundaries on the exclusive right. During prosecution, on the other hand, the process of setting claim scope is still underway. That process often requires the applicant to amend or modify the definition of the invention.

During prosecution, therefore, the Patent Office accords claims their "broadest reasonable interpretation consistent with the specification" and the understanding of one of ordinary skill in the art at the time of prosecution. *In re Bond*, 910 F.2d 831, 833 (Fed. Cir. 1990) (citation omitted). This standard expands claim scope to minimize the likelihood that the claims will acquire an undeserved breadth. And "[c]onstruing claims broadly during prosecution is not unfair to the applicant . . . because the applicant has the opportunity to amend the claims to obtain more precise claim coverage." *In re Am. Acad. of Sci. Tech Ctr.*, 367 F.3d 1359, 1364 (Fed. Cir. 2004). Accordingly, any ambiguity in the scope of the claims results in an expanded, not constricted, interpretation during prosecution.

CHAPTER 14
INFRINGEMENT

I. INTRODUCTION

Anyone who makes, uses, sells, offers to sell, or imports a patented invention (without the owner's consent) infringes. Infringement falls in two general categories: direct and indirect. Direct infringement further subdivides into literal infringement and non-textual infringement under the doctrine of equivalents. Direct infringement depends primarily on the construction of the claims. Any product or process that includes each and every limitation directly infringes that claim.

Indirect infringement, also called vicarious infringement, subdivides into contributory infringement and inducement. These subcategories hold accountable individuals who supply a component of the invention or direct another's infringement.

Aside from these fundamental categories, the patent statute creates a few special categories of infringement. For example, a unique enforcement scheme governs generic pharmaceuticals seeking approval from the Food and Drug Administration. The statute also extends infringement to extraterritorial activities in some specific situations. Similarly, the statute forbids importation of a product made from a patented process outside the United States.

Lastly, in some special circumstances, courts excuse actions that might otherwise be infringing. A patentee may have—even unintentionally—granted the alleged infringer an implied license or exhausted his patent rights by already selling the invention. Moreover, a party has the right to repair a licensed good, but not to the extent of remaking it entirely (reconstruction). Any party, furthermore, may use a patent for idle curiosity without fear of infringing.

II. LITERAL INFRINGEMENT

The right to exclude extends beyond the traditional categories of "making, using, or selling." In whole, § 271(a) provides: "Except as otherwise provided in this title, whoever without authority makes, uses, offers to sell, or sells any patented invention, within the United States or imports into the United States any patented invention during the term of the patent therefor, infringes the patent." This section sets forth a patentee's core rights.

Infringement entails a two-step analysis: first, the court construes the claims; and second, the finder of fact compares those construed claims to the accused product or process. *See, e.g.*, *Markman v. Westview Instruments, Inc.*, 52 F.3d 967, 976 (Fed. Cir. 1995) (en banc). The first step, claim construction, dominates the inquiry. Once the scope of the exclusive right is known, the second step is often a foregone conclusion. Thus, the prior chapter on claim construction was really an analysis of the requirements for literal infringement which vary from patent to patent and claim to claim.

Only the patentee may make, use, sell, offer for sale, or import patented subject matter. Without a license, any others simply infringe. Notably, an "offer for sale" infringes only if the sale will occur before expiration of the patent. 35 U.S.C § 271(i). With that sole exception, these rights are straightforward, even if nuanced. For example, the sale of equipment for performing a process is not a sale of the process itself. *Joy Techs., Inc. v. Flakt, Inc.*, 6 F.3d 770, 773 (Fed. Cir. 1993). This provision's complexity, furthermore, lurks in requirements created by case law, such as territorial restrictions or other unstated exceptions.

An example, discussed further in § V below, is the doctrine of "divided" or "joint" infringement. Infringement generally requires proof that a single actor performed all steps of a claimed method. A single actor may be liable for infringement, however, under agency principles if it controls or directs another party to perform the patented steps. *Limelight Networks, Inc. v. Akamai Techs., Inc.*, 572 U.S. 915 (2014).

III. THE DOCTRINE OF EQUIVALENTS—NON-TEXTUAL INFRINGEMENT

A. PURPOSE

In sharp contrast with the simple two-step process for literal infringement, the doctrine of equivalents (DOE) extends the exclusive right beyond the literal scope of the claims. An entity may infringe a patent even though its accused product or process practices subject matter outside the literal scope of the claims.

Counterintuitive at first blush, judicial opinions strive to justify this judge-made doctrine. For instance, courts have postulated that strict adherence to literal claim scope would diminish the value of patents and foster "unscrupulous copyists":

> [T]o permit imitation of a patented invention which does not copy every literal detail would be to convert the protection of the patent grant into a hollow and useless thing. Such a limitation would leave room for—indeed encourage—the unscrupulous copyist to make unimportant and insubstantial changes and substitutions in the patent which, though adding nothing, would be enough to take the copied matter outside the claim, and hence outside the reach of law.

Graver Tank & Mfg. Co. v. Linde Air Prods. Co., 339 U.S. 605, 607 (1950).

This "unscrupulous copyist" justification, however, cannot carry the entire weight of the DOE. In the first place, the DOE applies even in cases of inadvertent use of the invention. Thus, the doctrine is not limited to intentional infringement, let alone "unscrupulous copying" (whatever that means). This justification supplies no neutral standard for distinguishing between designing around (evading the claims by designing an improvement for one or more features of the invention—a laudatory form of "copying" encouraged by the patent system) and infringing behavior. The "unscrupulous copyist" justification also has other weaknesses.

Courts have also justified the DOE by saying it ameliorates the inherent difficulties of defining an inventive idea in words. In fact, the Supreme Court commented:

> Unfortunately, the nature of language makes it impossible to capture the essence of a thing in a patent application. . . . The language in the patent claims may not capture every nuance of the invention or describe with complete precision the range of its novelty.

Festo Corp. v. Shoketsu Kinzoku Kogyo Kabushiki Co., 535 U.S. 722, 731 (2002). Again this justification cannot alone support the DOE. Patent law already has several rules to accommodate the purely linguistic impediments in claim drafting. For instance, the drafter has the option to coin new terms under the lexicographer rule. The patent owner may even use reissue proceedings and continuation practices to rewrite unintentionally narrow claims.

With these tools to assist in fashioning claim language, this justification poses another question: Should the DOE rescue a claim drafting mistake? Claim drafting and correction tools should allow a careful claim drafter to clothe the invention adequately in language. Thus, when literal language does not capture a variant that the drafter should have foreseen and covered, should the DOE be available to compensate for the drafter's error? The straightforward answer is probably not, but courts have on occasion allowed the DOE to compensate for claiming insufficiencies. *See, e.g., Primos, Inc. v.*

Hunter's Specialties, Inc., 451 F.3d 841 (Fed. Cir. 2006).

Lastly, the doctrine accommodates the enforcement of the patent against after-arising technology—that is, subject matter that was unknowable at the time the patent issued. *Sage Prods., Inc. v. Devon Indus., Inc.*, 126 F.3d 1420 (Fed. Cir. 1997). A dissent-in-part from the Federal Circuit's subsequently overruled en banc *Festo* opinion explains this justification:

> Without a doctrine of equivalents, any claim drafted in current technological terms could be easily circumvented after the advent of an advance in technology. A claim using the terms "anode" and "cathode" from tube technology would lack the "collectors" and "emitters" of transistor technology that emerged in 1948. Thus, without a doctrine of equivalents, infringers in 1949 would have unfettered license to appropriate all patented technology using the out-dated terms "cathode" and "anode."

Festo Corp. v. Shoketsu Kinzoku Kogyo Kabushiki Co., 234 F.3d 558, 619 (Fed. Cir. 2000) (en banc) (Rader, J., concurring-in-part, dissenting-in-part). This objective test grounded in foreseeability places a premium on drafting patent applications describing and claiming all subject matter known to a person of ordinary skill in the art. But even here, the application of the DOE is not restricted solely to unforeseeable technology.

B. TEST(S)

Although the DOE attempts to mitigate the unfairness of holding a patentee to the precisely defined limitations in the claims, the doctrine might, if taken to an extreme, endanger the notice function of claims. A competitor should be able to recognize—and thus reasonably rely upon—the boundaries of a patent. Thus the vague and unspecified scope of non-textual infringement would unnecessarily restrict legitimate innovation and competition. For this reason, courts have sought over time to define the DOE restrictively. At present, courts use two phraseologies to capture the same, amorphous idea: function-way-result and insubstantial differences.

The Supreme Court, for example, used the function-way-result test in *Graver Tank*: "[A] patentee may invoke this doctrine to proceed against the producer of a device if it performs substantially the same function in substantially the same way to obtain the same result." 339 U.S. at 608 (quotations omitted). The Court further explained that "if two devices do the same work in substantially the same way, and accomplish substantially the same result, they are the same, even though they differ in name, form or shape." *Id.* (citation omitted). In addition, the Court noted that although not a formulaic inquiry, the doctrine may depend on whether a person of ordinary skill in the art would recognize the interchangeability between the claimed subject matter and the alleged equivalent. This factual determination can be informed by any number of evidentiary sources, including expert testimony, articles, texts, and treatises, and prior art. Based on this test, the *Graver Tank* Court held that silicates of manganese were equivalent to the silicates of alkaline earth metals (such as magnesium) recited in the claimed welding composition.

The Federal Circuit had fashioned another test, the insubstantial differences analysis. *Hilton Davis Chem. Co. v. Warner-Jenkinson Co.*, 62 F.3d 1512 (Fed. Cir. 1995) (en banc). The Supreme Court accepted both semantic formulations of the test:

> In our view, the particular linguistic framework used is less important than whether the test is probative of the essential inquiry: Does the accused product or process contain elements identical or equivalent to each claimed element of the patented invention? Different linguistic frameworks may be more suitable to different cases, depending on their particular facts.

Warner-Jenkinson Co. v. Hilton Davis Chem. Co., 520 U.S. 17, 40 (1997). And the alternative insubstantial differences test captures the same concept, fittingly, where the inflexibility of language impedes the determination at hand. In *Warner-Jenkinson*, for example, the Court remanded for a determination whether a purification process operated at a pH of 5.0 is insubstantially different from a nearly identical process operated at a pH of 6.0.

C. LIMITATIONS

Courts, in particular the Federal Circuit, recognized, however, the impossibility of defining amorphous terms like "insubstantial" or even "equivalent." These formulations are always a matter of degree. Yet, without some definition, the DOE would threaten the notice function of claims. Because a confining definition proved elusive, the Federal Circuit adopted confining limitations on the DOE. If it could not define the doctrine, it would confine it.

The most frequent confining rules are prosecution history estoppel and the all-elements rule. The Federal Circuit has also acknowledged that the scope and content of the prior art as well as the scope and content of the patentee's disclosure may limit the reach of the DOE.

1. Prosecution History Estoppel

Just as a claim amendment or argument informs the proper construction of a claim, an amendment or statement during prosecution may inform, and often defeat, a claim of equivalency.[1] Prosecution history estoppel thus "preclud[es] a patentee from regaining, through litigation, coverage of subject matter relinquished during prosecution of the application for the patent." *Wang Labs., Inc. v. Mitsubishi Elecs. Am., Inc.*, 103 F.3d 1571, 1577–78 (Fed. Cir. 1997). Notably, a patentee relinquishes subject matter in a narrowing amendment "when either (1) a preexisting claim limitation is narrowed by amendment or (2) a

---

[1] Prosecution disclaimer when construing claims differs in name from prosecution history estoppel when confining equivalents. Nonetheless the same standard applies to both doctrines for using prosecution history to limit claim coverage. *See Omega Eng'g, Inc. v. Raytek Corp.*, 334 F.3d 1314, 1326 n.1 (Fed. Cir. 2003).

new claim limitation is added by amendment." *Honeywell Int'l Inc. v. Hamilton Sundstrand Corp.*, 370 F.3d 1131, 1140 (Fed. Cir. 2004). Although on its face relatively straightforward, the legal framework complicates this intuitive concept.

In *Warner-Jenkinson*, the Court introduced the foundation of a series of steps for analyzing whether an applicant amended a claim for a reason related to patentability, thus invoking prosecution history estoppel. The Court explained that a patentee has the burden of establishing the reason for amendment and that, in the absence of a justification, the presumption arose that the reason was related to patentability. This presumption generated great debate, which the Supreme Court revisited five years later in *Festo Corp. v. Shoketsu Kinzoku Kogyo Kabushiki Co.*, 535 U.S. 722 (2002). In that case, the Court set forth three categories that rebut the presumption of prosecution history estoppel once a claim has been narrowed:

> The equivalent may have been unforeseeable at the time of the [amendment]; the rationale underlying the amendment may bear no more than a tangential relation to the equivalent in question; or there may be some other reason suggesting that the patentee could not reasonably be expected to have described the insubstantial substitute in question.

Id. at 740–41.

While the three rebuttal criteria—foreseeability, tangentiality, and some other reason—are unsettled, the Court did provide some guidance. For example, foreseeability imposes on claim drafters the duty to expressly claim technology that was foreseeable at the time of the amendment. The DOE cannot reach foreseeable technology. Foreseeability is an objective criterion driven by the knowledge of a person of ordinary skill in the art at the time of the amendment, a fact-based inquiry. *Smithkline Beecham Corp. v. Excel Pharms., Inc.*, 356 F.3d 1357 (Fed. Cir. 2004). The foreseeability principle (perhaps the best justification for the DOE overall) originated from the effort to reconcile the preeminent notice function of claims with the protective function of the doctrine of equivalents. The reconciling principle is simple: the doctrine of equivalents does not capture subject matter that the patent drafter reasonably could have foreseen during the application process and included in the claims. *Johnson & Johnston Assoc. Inc. v. R.E. Service Co., Inc.*, 285 F.3d 1046, 1056 (Fed. Cir. 2002) (Rader, J., concurring).

Tangentiality refers to amendments that do not pertain or relate to the disputed element in the accused device. *Primos, Inc. v. Hunter's Specialties, Inc.*, 451 F.3d 841 (Fed. Cir. 2006). This is a very narrow category. *Festo*, 344 F.3d at 1369–70. This vague tangentiality factor runs counter to principles of public notice that enable designing around.

The last category is a catch-all and, as such, has a narrow applicability, such as where the limitations of language prevent drafting a claim to include the equivalent subject matter. *Amgen Inc. v. Hoechst Marion Roussel, Inc.*, 457 F.3d 1293 (Fed. Cir. 2006).

2. All-Elements Rule

Even if accompanied by a less complicated framework, the all-elements rule provides another potent restraint on the reach of the DOE. In emphasizing the vitality of the all-elements rule, the Supreme Court noted:

> Each element contained in a patent claim is deemed material to defining the scope of the patented invention, and thus the doctrine of equivalents must be applied to individual elements of the claim, not to the invention as a whole. It is important to ensure that the application of the [DOE], even as to an individual element, is not allowed such broad play as to effectively eliminate that element in its entirety.

Warner-Jenkinson, 520 U.S. at 29. This restraint—that is, application of equivalency on a limitation-by-limitation basis—is firmly entrenched in case law. After all, if a device wholly lacks a claim element, it could not infringe under the DOE without vitiating that part of the claim. *See, e.g.*, *Pennwalt Corp. v. Durand-Wayland, Inc.*, 833 F.2d 931, 935 (Fed. Cir. 1987) (en banc).

The all-elements rule, however, contains an inherent inconsistency. On the one hand, the DOE applies to find infringement when the claim does not literally cover the accused process or product, i.e., when a claim limitation is literally missing. On the other hand, the all-elements rule limitation precludes application of the DOE when a claim limitation is literally missing. No neutral standard determines when a missing limitation compels infringement under the DOE or precludes the DOE under the all-elements rule.

As a matter of practice, the all-elements rule probably applies when the court decides that the missing element creates a substantial (rather than insubstantial) difference from the literal claim language. The all-elements rule in reality just reapplies the test for the DOE itself. Thus, the all-elements rule may in fact just be a way that the Federal Circuit can reach a determination of equivalency (usually a matter of fact for the jury) as a question of law for the court.

The case of *Corning Glass Works v. Sumitomo Electric U.S.A., Inc.*, 868 F.2d 1251 (Fed. Cir. 1989), illustrates the difficulty of deciding when a missing claim limitation invokes the DOE or precludes the DOE under the all-elements rule. In that case, the patent claimed a fiber optic cable with inner core layer and an outer cladding around the core. The claim called for doping the core to make its index of refraction greater than the index of refraction for the outer cladding. Because the core has a different refractive index, light would follow the course of the cable. This important invention was the advent of fiber optics.

The accused device did not, however, positively dope the core as required in the claims; rather, it negatively doped the cladding. The result was the same: the differences in the indices of refraction caused the light to follow the cable. The Federal Circuit could easily determine that the assertion of the DOE ignored the express claim limitation requiring a doped core. On the other hand, the Federal Circuit could also easily determine that the DOE applied to overcome an insubstantial difference despite the missing limitation.

In holding that the doped core layer limitation was not vitiated, the Federal Circuit remarked that it "has not set out in its precedent a definitive formula for determining equivalency between a required limitation or combination of limitations and what has been allegedly substituted therefor in the accused device. Nor do we propose to adopt one here." *Corning Glass*, 868 F.2d at 1260.

3. Prior Art

Another intuitive limitation on the DOE prevents the doctrine from extending the exclusive right to encompass the prior art. A court may not permit a patentee to prevent another from using subject matter that belongs to the public. This subject matter, of course, includes not only anticipatory subject matter but also obvious subject matter. That is, an equivalent cannot solely comprise unpatentable subject matter. Accordingly, this analytical construct requires not only a hypothetical claim but also a hypothetical validity analysis.

The court in *Wilson Sporting Goods Co. v. David Geoffrey & Associates*, 904 F.2d 677 (Fed. Cir. 1990), applied this analytical construct to prohibit the scope of enforcement from reaching the accused golf balls. The patent at issue claimed a golf ball with a particular configuration of dimples that divided the surface area of the ball into 80 triangles. These 80 triangles defined six equatorial circumferences—that is, intersecting circles that each passed around the widest portion of the ball. These "great" circles each defined an axis of symmetry, along which there were no dimples. The prior art contained balls also having six great circles, although these great circles had dimples intersecting them. In holding that the accused golf balls were not equivalents, the court explained:

> Whether prior art restricts the range of equivalents of what is literally claimed can be a difficult question to answer. To simplify analysis and bring the issue onto familiar turf, it may be helpful to conceptualize the limitation on the scope of equivalents by visualizing a *hypothetical* patent claim, sufficient in scope to *literally* cover the accused product. The pertinent question then becomes whether that hypothetical claim could have been allowed by the PTO over the prior art. If not, then it would be improper to permit the patentee to obtain that coverage in an infringement suit under the doctrine of equivalents. If the hypothetical claim could have been allowed, then *prior art* is not a bar to infringement under the doctrine of equivalents.

Id. at 684.

With that framework in hand, the court held that because the accused balls would have been obvious in light of the prior art, they did not infringe under the DOE. Although not mandatory in every case, this framework can be helpful in some instances to limit the range of equivalents. Indeed, it prevents a patentee from gaining through equivalency subject matter that could not have been gained during prosecution. *See Key Mfg. Group, Inc. v. Microdot, Inc.*, 925 F.2d 1444 (Fed. Cir. 1991).

The hypothetical claim analysis, however, is itself not unbounded. A patentee may not use it to narrow a claim in some aspects while at the same time broadening it in other aspects. A "hypothetical claim analysis is not an opportunity to freely redraft granted claims," because "[t]hat opportunity existed in the PTO, where the submitted claims were examined for patentability." *Streamfeeder, LLC v. Sure-Feed Sys., Inc.*, 175 F.3d 974, 983 (Fed. Cir. 1999).

4. Public Dedication

In certain circumstances, a patentee loses the opportunity to assert the DOE because of failure to draft claims to encompass equivalent subject matter. Although this evokes unforeseeability as a requirement for infringement by equivalency, the public dedication limitation requires something more specific: a manifest showing of the patentee's knowledge of an equivalent. In particular, a patentee who discloses an alternative embodiment in the specification, yet fails to claim it, dedicates that subject matter to the public.

In *Johnson & Johnston Associates Inc. v. R.E. Service Co.*, 285 F.3d 1046 (Fed. Cir. 2002) (en banc), the Federal Circuit determined that a patentee could not assert that claims reciting an aluminum device covered a steel device as an equivalent because the specification expressly mentioned, but did not claim, the stainless steel embodiment. But the patentee, the court clarified, was not without recourse:

> A patentee who inadvertently fails to claim disclosed subject matter, however, is not left without remedy. Within two years from the grant of the original patent, a patentee may file a reissue application and attempt to enlarge the scope of the original claims to include the disclosed but previously unclaimed subject matter. 35 U.S.C. § 251. In addition, a patentee can file a separate application claiming the disclosed subject matter under 35 U.S.C. § 120. Notably, Johnston took advantage of the latter of the two options by filing two continuation applications that literally claim the relevant subject matter.

Id. at 1055.

D. MEANS-PLUS-FUNCTION CLAIMS

As discussed in Chapter 12, a patent claim in means-plus-function format covers literally the corresponding structure in the specification as well as that structure's equivalents. This statutory clause incorporates insubstantially different subject matter into the literal scope of the claim. *See, e.g.*, *Al-Site Corp. v. VSI Int'l, Inc.*, 174 F.3d 1308 (Fed. Cir. 1999).

Does this mean that a structural equivalent (a literal part of the claim) could itself have an equivalent under the DOE, thus creating an equivalent of an equivalent? No. The time frame of application of these various tests for equivalents precludes an equivalent of an equivalent. Because the meaning of claim language must be established at the time of filing (otherwise it is invalid for indefiniteness), a means-plus-function claim only includes those structural equivalents known at the time of filing. An equivalent under the DOE, on the other hand, applies to subject matter (usually unforeseeable) that arises after the patent's issuance, i.e., at the time of infringement. *See, e.g.*, *Chiuminatta Concrete Concepts, Inc. v. Cardinal Indus., Inc.*, 145 F.3d 1303, 1310 (Fed. Cir. 1998). Thus, a proposed equivalent will either arise before filing and fall under the statutory framework or arise after filing and invoke the DOE. *Al-Site*, 174 F.3d at 1320 n.2.

E. REVERSE DOCTRINE OF EQUIVALENTS

Just as the DOE provides a patentee with exclusive rights over subject matter outside the literal claim scope, it may provide an infringer with an additional defense to literal infringement. Literally infringing activities may be outside the scope of enforcement. The reverse DOE applies "where a device is so far changed in principle from a patented article that it performs the same or similar function in a substantially different way, but nevertheless falls within the literal words of the claim." *Graver Tank & Mfg. Co. v. Linde Air Prods. Co.*, 339 U.S. 605, 608–09 (1950). While this equitable doctrine exists, courts have serious doubts about its continued viability, and the Federal Circuit has noted that it has never affirmed a finding of non-infringement under the doctrine. *See, e.g.*, *Roche Palo Alto LLC v. Apotex, Inc.*, 531 F.3d 1372, 1378 (Fed. Cir. 2008).

IV. INDIRECT INFRINGEMENT

The patent statute sets forth two primary categories of vicarious infringement. The first, inducement of infringement, arises under § 271(b):

> Whoever actively induces infringement of a patent shall be liable as an infringer.

The second, contributory infringement, arises from the next subsection, § 271(c):

> Whoever offers to sell or sells within the United States or imports into the United States a component of a patented machine, manufacture, combination, or composition, or a material or apparatus for use in practicing a patented process, constituting a material part of the invention, knowing the same to be especially made or especially adapted for use in an infringement of such patent, and not a staple article or commodity of commerce suitable for

> substantial noninfringing use, shall be liable as a contributory infringer.

Although different, these types of indirect infringement complement one another. A contributory infringer, for example, also induces infringement. Both types share three elements:

1. The indirect infringer acted knowingly or intentionally in either inducing infringement or selling a material component that has no substantial noninfringing uses;

2. The indirect infringer's actions culminated in another's direct infringement; and

3. The indirect infringer's actions took place during the patent's term.

See, e.g., *Hewlett-Packard Co. v. Bausch & Lomb Inc.*, 909 F.2d 1464, 1469 (Fed. Cir. 1990). Although direct infringement is an obvious prerequisite, the focus must remain on what the allegedly indirect infringer did and when he did it. *See, e.g.*, *Standard Oil Co. v. Nippon Shokubai Kagaku Kogyo Co.*, 754 F.2d 345 (Fed. Cir. 1985).

Inducement of infringement and contributory infringement, however, are not the same. Inducement more flexibly encompasses a greater number of situations, including those that involve subject matter with non-infringing as well as infringing uses or that involve encouragement of the use of certain subject matter.

A. INDUCEMENT OF INFRINGEMENT

Although the statute does not explicitly set forth that inducement requires knowledge, judicial gloss has firmly entrenched this requirement. To begin with, the alleged indirect infringer "must have actual or constructive knowledge of the patent." *Insituform Techs., Inc. v. Cat Contracting, Inc.*, 161 F.3d 688, 695 (Fed. Cir. 1998). In addition to that knowledge, the patentee must show that the alleged indirect infringer had knowledge that the induced acts constituted patent infringement. *Global-Tech Appliances, Inc. v. SEB S.A.*, 563 U.S. 754, 766 (2011).

The Federal Circuit has clarified that the indirect infringer's intent must be specific—that is, an intent (knowing of the patent) to cause the infringement. *DSU Med. Corp. v. JMS Co.*, 471 F.3d 1293, 1305 (Fed. Cir. 2006) (en banc in relevant part). Specifically, the Federal Circuit overruled the general intent standard for inducement in *Hewlett-Packard Co. v. Bausch & Lomb Inc.*, 909 F.2d 1464, 1469 (Fed. Cir. 1990) (holding that "proof of actual intent to cause the acts which constitute the infringement is a necessary prerequisite to finding active inducement"). Instead, the en banc court endorsed the specific standard of intent in *Manville Sales Corp. v. Paramount Systems, Inc.*, 917 F.2d 544, 553 (Fed. Cir. 1990) (holding that the alleged indirect infringer must "possess[ ] specific intent to encourage another's infringement" and that "the alleged infringer's actions induced infringement acts *and* that he knew or should have known his actions would induce actual infringements").

This requisite intent or knowledge manifests itself in various circumstances, all of which require facilitating, encouraging, or aiding another's infringement. For example, a sale of an infringing business may in some circumstances indirectly infringe. *Compare Water Techs. Corp. v. Calco, Ltd.*, 850 F.2d 660 (Fed. Cir. 1988) *with Hewlett-Packard Co. v. Bausch & Lomb, Inc.*, 909 F.2d 1464 (Fed. Cir. 1990). Similarly, instructing another—for example, by providing directions on how to infringe a method claim—would also suffice. *See, e.g., Warner-Lambert Co. v. Apotex Corp.*, 316 F.3d 1348 (Fed. Cir. 2003). And not infrequently, a company's officers or directors may incur personal liability for inducing the company's infringement, at least in limited circumstances. *See, e.g., Sensonics, Inc. v. Aerosonic Corp.*, 81 F.3d 1566 (Fed. Cir. 1996).

In *Global-Tech*, the Supreme Court clarified that the intent necessary under § 271(b) can be satisfied by "willful blindness" consistent with general principles. A willfully blind defendant is one who meets two requirements. First, the defendant subjectively believes that there is a high probability that a fact (e.g., infringement) exists. And second, the defendant takes deliberate steps to avoid learning that fact. The Supreme Court contrasted a willfully blind defendant with those who are reckless or negligent: "By contrast, a reckless defendant is one who merely knows of a substantial and unjustified risk of such wrongdoing, and a negligent defendant is one who should have known of a similar risk but, in fact, did not." *Global-Tech*, 563 U.S. at 770 (citations omitted).

The Supreme Court also clarified, in a subsequent case, that an accused infringer's belief of the asserted patent's invalidity is not a defense to inducement. *Commil USA, LLC v. Cisco Sys., Inc.*, 575 U.S. 632, 1928 (2015). The district court had denied defendant Cisco the opportunity to present evidence of its belief of the asserted patent's invalidity in order to negate plaintiff Commil's allegations of induced infringement. The Federal Circuit reversed this decision: "It is axiomatic that one cannot infringe an invalid patent," and thus a genuine belief of invalidity could preclude the required finding that the defendant believed its actions caused infringement. *Commil USA, LLC v. Cisco Sys., Inc.*, 720 F.3d 1361, 1368 (Fed. Cir. 2013), But the Supreme Court sided with the district court: "The scienter element for induced infringement concerns infringement; that is a different issue than validity." *Commil*, 575 U.S. at 1928.

B. CONTRIBUTORY INFRINGEMENT

Although requiring knowledge of the patent, contributory infringement applies in narrower circumstances than inducement. In particular, this remedy requires a sale, offer for sale, or importation of only a portion of the patented invention in addition to a lack of substantial non-infringing uses for that component. A contributory infringer must know of the patent and provide another with a non-staple component (that is, a component whose only use is in a patented combination). *See, e.g.*, *Aro Mfg. Co. v. Convertible Top Replacement Co.*, 377 U.S. 476 (1964); *Dawson Chem. Co. v. Rohm & Haas Co.*, 448 U.S. 176 (1980).

Notably, the patent statute exempts from contributory infringement certain activities, when done by the patentee, that could otherwise amount to misuse under § 271(d). *See* Chapter 15. Specifically, a patentee may, without misusing his patent rights, "(1) derive[ ] revenue from acts which if performed by another without his consent would constitute contributory infringement of the patent [and] (2) license[ ] or authorize[ ] another to perform acts which if performed without his consent would constitute contributory infringement of the patent." 35 U.S.C. § 271(d). Counterintuitively then, contributory infringement is relevant to determining permissible uses of patent rights.

V. "JOINT" OR "DIVIDED" INFRINGEMENT

The actions of multiple parties may sometimes combine to collectively meet the steps of a method claim. This doctrine closes a perceived loophole that would allow a defendant to escape infringement liability where, for example, its customer performs one (or a minimal number) of the claimed method steps. Under a divided or joint infringement theory, the defendant may be held liable where the customer's performance of the step is attributable to the defendant. *See Muniauction, Inc. v. Thomson Corp.*, 532 F.3d 1318, 1329 (Fed. Cir. 2008).

In *Muniauction*, the patent covered methods for conducting municipal bond auctions online over a web browser. The step of inputting bids was performed by the bidder using the browser, not the accused auctioneer. Yet the patent owner, Muniauction, argued that Thompson should nonetheless be liable for direct infringement under § 271(a) because Thompson instructed its customers on how to input bids and controlled bidders' access to its system.

The Federal Circuit explained that cases involving attribution fall on a spectrum. On one end, a party is liable for "directing or controlling" another's actions. On the other end, mere arms-length cooperation between separate entities will not give rise to direct infringement by a single entity. The court concluded that Thompson's relationship with bidders fell on the arms-length end of the spectrum, and so Thompson was not liable for direct infringement under § 271(a).

The Federal Circuit adopted a different rule in the context of indirect infringement—until the Supreme Court rejected it. *Limelight Networks, Inc. v. Akamai Techs., Inc.*, 572 U.S. 915, 2117 (2014). The *Limelight* case clarified divided infringement principles over the course of several important decisions in succession.

Limelight's patent covered a method for delivering electronic data using a content delivery network. The method included the step of "tagging," or designating certain components of a file for storage on a server. The accused infringer Akamai maintained servers, but its customers performed the "tagging" step.

Limelight sued for induced infringement under § 271(b).

The en banc Federal Circuit fashioned a unique rule for divided infringement: an accused infringer is liable for inducement if it performs some of the claimed method steps and induces another to perform the remaining steps. It thus eliminated the requirement for a single direct infringer.

The Supreme Court reversed, holding that direct infringement under § 271(a) by a single entity is a requirement for indirect infringement under § 271(b). But apparently recognizing the need to close the loophole for clever defendants who shift one claimed method step onto their customers, the Court hinted that the Federal Circuit should address this issue by clarifying when "attribution" of a customer's actions to an accused infringer is permissible.

On remand again, the en banc Federal Circuit formulated the rules of attribution this way:

> We will hold an entity responsible for others' performance of method steps in two sets of circumstances: (1) where that entity directs or controls others' performance, and (2) where the actors form a joint enterprise . . . . [A]n actor is liable for infringement under § 271(a) if it acts through an agent (applying traditional agency principles) or contracts with another to perform one or more steps of a claimed method . . . . [L]iability under § 271(a) can also be found when an alleged infringer conditions participation in an activity or receipt of a benefit upon

> performance of a step or steps of a patented method and establishes the manner or timing of that performance. . . . Alternatively, . . . [a] joint enterprise requires proof of four elements:
>
> (1) an agreement, express or implied, among the members of the group;
>
> (2) a common purpose to be carried out by the group;
>
> (3) a community of pecuniary interest in that purpose, among the members; and
>
> (4) an equal right to a voice in the direction of the enterprise, which gives an equal right of control.

Akamai Techs., Inc. v. Limelight Networks, Inc., 797 F.3d 1020, 1022–23 (Fed. Cir. 2015).

Under this rubric, the Federal Circuit re-instated the jury's infringement verdict. "Limelight conditions its customers' use of its content delivery network upon its customers' performance of the tagging and serving steps, and . . . establishes the manner or timing of its customers' performance." *Id.* at 1024.

VI. TERRITORIAL SCOPE

As a general matter, the right to exclude granted by a United States patent may only proscribe activities within U.S. borders. That is, domestic patent law cannot reach purely extraterritorial activities. *See, e.g.*, *Waymark Corp. v. Porta Sys. Corp.*, 245 F.3d 1364 (Fed. Cir. 2001). The globalization of markets and the ease of transferring portions of an enterprise abroad, however, have influenced this general rule.

In a famous case, the Federal Circuit had to determine if an "electronic mail system" with one component located in Canada (the BlackBerry® system) infringed a domestic patent as a "use" under § 271(a). The court decided that the "control and beneficial use" of the patented system occurred within the borders of the United States. Therefore, even though one claimed feature lay outside U.S. borders, the court upheld the jury verdict of infringement. *NTP, Inc. v. Research in Motion, Ltd.*, 418 F.3d 1282 (Fed. Cir. 2005).

Another section of the patent statute has also expanded the reach of domestic patent law. Before 1984, an entity could manufacture and export the unassembled components of a patented combination without infringing. In *Deepsouth Packing Co. v. Laitram Corp.*, 406 U.S. 518 (1972), for example, the Court permitted the defendant to continue manufacturing all the components of a patented shrimp peeler domestically and ship them—unassembled, of course—abroad for assembly and usage. In the words of the Supreme Court, "[t]he statute makes it clear that it is not an infringement to make or use a patented product outside of the United States." *Id.* at 527. Section 271(f)—enacted in 1984—partially overruled this decision.

Further, before 1988, the extraterritorial manufacture of a good followed by importation of that good would not infringe a patent reading on that product. That is, method patents could not prevent processes performed abroad, even if the product of that process later entered the United States. *See, e.g.*, *United States v. Studiengesellschaft Kohle, m.b.H*, 670 F.2d 1122 (D.C. Cir. 1981). Section 271(g) changed this rule, albeit with important exceptions.

A. EXPORTING COMPONENTS OF A PATENTED COMBINATION

In ordinary circumstances, a party supplying patented components along with instructions for their combination incurs liability for inducing infringement or contributory infringement under either § 271(b) or (c). But where the assembly of the components occurs outside the United States, there can be no direct infringement and thus no indirect infringement. When *Deepsouth* affirmed this principle, it opened a loophole for infringement. A potential infringer needed only to move the final assembly step abroad to avoid liability. A 1984 enactment closed the loophole:

> (1) Whoever without authority supplies or causes to be supplied in or from the United States all or a substantial portion of the components of a patented invention, where such components are uncombined in whole or in part, in such manner as to actively induce the combination of such components outside of the United States in a manner that would infringe the patent if such combination occurred within the United States, shall be liable as an infringer.
>
> (2) Whoever without authority supplies or causes to be supplied in or from the United

> States any component of a patented invention that is especially made or especially adapted for use in the invention and not a staple article or commodity of commerce suitable for substantial noninfringing use, where such component is uncombined in whole or in part, knowing that such component is so made or adapted and intending that such component will be combined outside of the United States in a manner that would infringe the patent if such combination occurred within the United States, shall be liable as an infringer.

35 U.S.C. § 271(f). This subsection gave rise to a question of the scope of a patent owner's extraterritorial rights when applied to software. In particular, does an entity that "supplies" a component abroad incur liability for copies made from that component in the foreign country?

The Supreme Court addressed this question in *Microsoft Corp. v. AT & T Corp.*, 550 U.S. 437 (2007). There, Microsoft included infringing voice recognition software in its software package. Microsoft then put this software on a master "golden" disk and sent it abroad. Once abroad, Microsoft affiliates copied the master program onto thousands of other computers. A district court imposed liability on Microsoft under § 271(f) for all of those copies even though made abroad. After the Federal Circuit upheld that judgment because "the act of copying was subsumed in the act of 'supplying,'" the Supreme Court reversed.

The Supreme Court instead determined that the statutory term "supplying" does not mean that Microsoft is liable in the U.S. for copying that occurs abroad. Instead the Supreme Court reiterated the territorial limitation on infringement: "As a principle of general application, moreover, we have stated that courts should assume that legislators take account of the legitimate sovereign interests of other nations when they write American laws. . . . Foreign conduct is generally the domain of foreign law, and in the area here involved, in particular, foreign law may embody different policy judgments about the relative rights of inventors, competitors, and the public in patented inventions." *Microsoft*, 550 U.S. at 455 (quotations and citations omitted). Indeed, the Court firmly explained: "In short, foreign law alone, not United States law, currently governs the manufacture and sale of components of patented inventions in foreign countries. If AT & T desires to prevent copying in foreign countries, its remedy today lies in obtaining and enforcing foreign patents." *Id.* at 456.

Interestingly, § 271(f) does not apply to methods, and it can only—by its own terms—apply to tangible things that have "components." *Cardiac Pacemakers, Inc. v. St. Jude Med., Inc.*, 576 F.3d 1348 (Fed. Cir. 2009) (en banc).

B. IMPORTATION OF GOODS MANUFACTURED BY A PATENTED PROCESS

In limited circumstances, a product made by a patented process extraterritorially infringes a United States patent. The statute, in particular, provides:

> Whoever without authority imports into the United States or offers to sell, sells, or uses within the United States a product which is made by a process patented in the United States shall be liable as an infringer, if the importation, offer to sell, sale, or use of the product occurs during the term of such process patent. In an action for infringement of a process patent, no remedy may be granted for infringement on account of the noncommercial use or retail sale of a product unless there is no adequate remedy under this title for infringement on account of the importation or other use, offer to sell, or sale of that product. A product which is made by a patented process will, for purposes of this title, not be considered to be so made after—
>
> (1) it is materially changed by subsequent processes; or
>
> (2) it becomes a trivial and nonessential component of another product.

35 U.S.C. § 271(g). As a starting point, the imported physical article must have been produced by a patented process. Mere information generated by a patented process does not fall within the scope of the 1988 Act. *See Bayer AG v. Housey Pharms., Inc.*, 340

F.3d 1367 (Fed. Cir. 2003). The statute exempts any product "materially changed" after the patented process and any product that is only a "trivial and nonessential component" of another product.

In the important pharmaceutical field, for instance, an importer can escape liability by either importing intermediates that need more processing before the market or that become insignificant components of a larger product. In one case, the Federal Circuit assessed the material change exception based on "the substantiality of the change between the product of the patented process and the product that is being imported." *Eli Lilly & Co. v. Am. Cyanamid Co.*, 82 F.3d 1568, 1573 (Fed. Cir. 1996).

VII. INTERNATIONAL TRADE COMMISSION

While most patentees enforce their patents in federal court, the international marketplace has given considerable importance to another remedy: exclusion at the U.S. border. Often a patentee has the option of enforcing their patents by asking the International Trade Commission (ITC) to investigate an unfair act under 19 U.S.C. § 1337, commonly known as Section 337.

The primary advantages of an ITC action include (i) faster resolution—it typically takes just over one year until the final determination issues (a distinct advantage for a petitioner who can prepare its case for months before placing the respondent under the pressure of time limits by filing a complaint)—and (ii) administrative law judges who are familiar with patent disputes. In addition, an ITC investigation does not preclude a patentee from concurrently filing a suit in district court over the same allegedly infringing acts. Thus, although an ITC action cannot award damages, it does not preclude a concurrent damages action in federal court. *Cf. In re Princo Corp.*, 478 F.3d 1345 (Fed. Cir. 2007).

Although these investigations are similar to cases brought in district court, they have important differences, for example, with respect to the parties involved, the elements for proof, and the available relief. For example, an ITC staff attorney represents the public in most investigations, thus interjecting a third entity into the proceedings.

The statute provides in part:

> (1) Subject to paragraph (2), the following are unlawful, and when found by the Commission to exist shall be dealt with, in addition to any other provision of law, as provided in this section: . . .
>
> (B) The importation into the United States, the sale for importation, or the sale within the United States after importation by the owner, importer, or consignee, of articles that—
>
> (i) infringe a valid and enforceable United States patent . . . ; or
>
> (ii) are made, produced, processed, or mined under, or by means of, a process covered by the claims of a valid and enforceable United States patent.

19 U.S.C. § 1337(a). Accordingly, an ITC action requires an importation (or sale for importation or sale after importation) of either an infringing good or a good produced, processed, or mined by a patented process. Although mimicking some provisions of 35 U.S.C. § 271, the infringement analyses are not identical. For example, the two statutory exceptions available in district court under § 271(g)—material change as well as trivial and nonessential component—are not available defenses for respondents before the ITC. *Kinik Co. v. Int'l Trade Comm'n*, 362 F.3d 1359 (Fed. Cir. 2004).

Beyond proving infringement, a patentee filing a complaint with the ITC must prove that a domestic industry exists or is in the process of being established. The statute, in particular, states:

> (2) Subparagraph[ ] (B) . . . of paragraph (1) appl[ies] only if an industry in the United States, relating to the articles protected by the patent . . . concerned, exists or is in the process of being established.
>
> (3) For purposes of paragraph (2), an industry in the United States shall be considered to exist if there is in the United States, with respect to the articles protected by the patent . . . concerned—
>
> > (A) significant investment in plant and equipment;
> >
> > (B) significant employment of labor or capital; or

> (C) substantial investment in its exploitation, including engineering, research and development, or licensing.

19 U.S.C. § 1337(a). Proving domestic industry has two prongs, both of which must occur in the United States. The first prong is technical: the patent must read on goods of either the patentee or a licensee. *Cf.*, *Corning Glass Works v. U.S. Int'l Trade Comm'n*, 799 F.2d 1559 (Fed. Cir. 1986). And the second prong is economic: the patentee must have significant investment in plant and equipment, significant employment of labor or capital, or substantial investment in the patent's exploitation. Notably, the patentee no longer needs to prove that the domestic industry is injured or threatened by the importation of infringing goods (or goods made by an infringing process). 19 U.S.C. § 1337(a)(1)(A); Pub. L. No. 100–418, 102 Stat. 1107 (1988).

Once a patentee prevails before the ITC, it may seek both a cease-and-desist order and an exclusion order, which the ITC may award after considering the public interest. A cease-and-desist order halts the sale and distribution of already-imported infringing goods, and an exclusion order directs U.S. Customs and Border Protection to halt the importation of the infringing goods. 19 U.S.C. §§ 1337(d) & (f). An exclusion order can be limited (i.e., tailored to particular infringing entities) or general, depending on the type and scope of violation. Notably, these are purely equitable remedies. A prevailing patentee may only seek monetary damages in federal court.

Certain Electronic Devices, Including Wireless Communication Devices, Portable Music and Data Processing Devices, and Tablet Computers, No. 337-TA-794, serves as an interesting example of an ITC case. Samsung filed a complaint with the ITC seeking the exclusion of Apple's iPhone and iPad products from entry into the country. It argued that those accused products infringed its patents covering 3G wireless communication technology. The Administrative Law Judge decided in an initial determination that the accused products did not infringe. As is customary, the Commission reviewed the ALJ's decision. It solicited comments and input from the public, and received numerous written submissions from a variety of electronics companies attempting to sway the Commission's high-stakes decision. Ultimately, the Commission decided that one of the asserted patents was, in fact, infringed by Apple's products, and so the Commission entered a limited exclusion order that barred Apple's accused products from entry into the country.

But the story did not end there. In a rare (almost unheard of) procedural twist, President Obama intervened by vetoing the Commission's final determination within the 60-day presidential review period that follows each ITC proceeding. Of course, the decision received highly polarized responses—some praised the President's decision as a victory for consumers, while others decried his decision as undercutting the patent right.

VIII. EXCEPTIONS TO INFRINGEMENT

By tautology, authorized uses or sales of patented subject matter do not infringe. An express license authorizes use of the patented invention within the terms of the license. Each license agreement is a unique document tailored to the particular rights the patentee wishes to convey to the licensee. *See, e.g.*, *Intergraph Corp. v. Intel Corp.*, 241 F.3d 1353 (Fed. Cir. 2001).

In some cases, courts will imply a license as a matter of law to achieve some greater public objective. Beyond implied licenses, courts have also created some doctrines, like the first sale doctrine—sometimes called exhaustion—or the repair/reconstruction doctrine to authorize use of patented technology without liability. Furthermore, the activities of the infringer may be so minor or without commercial significance to except them from infringement. The patent statute also carves out particular behavior relating to pharmaceuticals.

A. IMPLIED LICENSES, FIRST SALE & EXHAUSTION, AND REPAIR & RECONSTRUCTION

Exhaustion bars enforcement of a patent where the patentee (or his licensee) has already made an unrestricted sale of the patented article and reaped the reward of the exclusive right. *Intel Corp. v. ULSI Sys. Tech., Inc.*, 995 F.2d 1566 (Fed. Cir. 1993). The patentee exhausts his patent rights—to both the article as well as the methods of using the article—

with the first authorized sale. *Quanta Computer, Inc. v. LG Elecs., Inc.*, 553 U.S. 617 (2008).

The patent exhaustion rule stems from common law principles against restraints on alienation, which protect a property buyer from the seller's efforts to limit how the buyer can dispose of the property. Another rationale for the exhaustion doctrine is that the patentee, upon selling the product covered by the patent, is deemed to have received his full reward for the invention. It is assumed that the patentee took advantage of the right to exclude others and charge a higher price, to some degree, for the patented product. Having received this reward (whose availability ends when the term expires), the patentee is not permitted to recover another reward from downstream purchasers.

In *Quanta,* the Supreme Court affirmed that method claims are equally exhausted by the sale of claims to tangible articles. The Court also held that the sale of device that substantially embodies a patent prevents a patentee from using patent rights to control post-sale uses and downstream sales of the device. The Court also explained that multiple patent rights may be exhausted by a single sale: "The sale of a device that practices patent A does not, by virtue of practicing patent A, exhaust patent B. But if the device practices patent A *while substantially embodying* patent B, its relationship to patent A does not prevent exhaustion of patent B." *Quanta,* 553 U.S. at 634.

The Supreme Court expanded the patent exhaustion doctrine in two important respects in

Impression Products, Inc. v. Lexmark Int'l, Inc., 581 U.S. 360 (2017). There, patentee Lexmark manufactured and sold its patented printer toner cartridges. For certain cartridges, Lexmark discounted the purchase price by 20% in exchange for buyers' contractual commitment to return the cartridges to Lexmark rather than refurbish and re-sell them. Lexmark made some of these conditional sales in the U.S., and some in foreign countries at lower prices than in the U.S. (given that the patent did not operate overseas).

Meanwhile, defendant Impression Products—a third-party who had no contract with Lexmark—began obtaining, refurbishing, and reselling Lexmark's toner cartridges. Lexmark alleged that Impression Products infringed by either selling the refurbished cartridges directly in the U.S., or selling them overseas and then importing them.

The Court first held that Lexmark's single-use restriction contained in its conditional sale contracts may have been enforceable under contract law (against Lexmark's own customers), but they did not reserve patent rights that would support a patent infringement action against Impression Products. "[E]ven when a patentee sells an item under an express restriction, the patentee does not retain patent rights in that product." *Id.* at 1532–33. In making this decision, the Supreme Court essentially directed the would-be plaintiff to contract law, rather than patent law, to support its claim. There remains concern, however, that contract law will not adequately substitute for patent law in the context of conditional sales. Perhaps most illustrative of this concern is that Lexmark never could have sued Impression Products on a breach of contract claim in the first place because the parties had no contract.

Next, the Court held that Lexmark's U.S. patent rights were exhausted even when it sold its toner cartridges overseas. Lexmark's fundamental concern was that it would be unfair for Lexmark to be required to sell its toner cartridges overseas at lower prices (due to U.S. patent's lack of exclusionary power overseas), only for its competitors to re-import those goods and undercut even Lexmark's U.S. market. Lexmark argued that, merely by selling its products at lower prices overseas where no U.S. patent has force, Lexmark had not received the financial reward promised by its U.S. patent. And thus the "reward" rationale that typically supports exhaustion was not applicable. But the Supreme Court rejected this argument:

> The patentee may not be able to command the same amount for its products abroad as it does in the United States. But the Patent Act does not guarantee a particular price, much less the price from selling to American consumers. Instead, the right to exclude just ensures that the patentee receives one reward—of whatever amount the patentee deems to be "satisfactory compensation" for every item that passes outside the scope of the patent monopoly.

Id. at 1528 (citation omitted).

While this holding seems tidy in that it maintains consistency between copyright and patent law and between foreign and domestic business, it signals to international companies that the undercutting of the U.S. market through products already sold overseas at lower prices is simply a reality they must live with, a risk of doing business both in the U.S. and abroad. From a humanitarian perspective, the holding may regretfully disincentivize companies from selling beneficial products (such as life-saving pharmaceuticals) to poor countries at prices that are market-appropriate, i.e., lower than those charged in the U.S.

While, under *Impression Products*, contractual restrictions on downstream use of patented products are only a matter of contract law, not patent law, there remains a related and viable patent doctrine dating back to at least the early 1880s that may be used to restrict downstream usage of products. Under the repair-reconstruction doctrine, a purchaser of a patented good has the right to repair it without incurring liability for infringement. But if the repairs are too extensive—that is, if the repairs entirely reconstruct the patented invention—the owner has in fact infringed. Despite the inherent difficulty in dividing permissible repair from impermissible reconstruction, case law has outlined guiding principles.

If, for example, a patented item is entirely spent during use, rebuilding the item constitutes an impermissible reconstruction. But if, on the other hand, a patented item contains a replaceable part, replacing that part constitutes permissible repair, irrespective of whether the part is worn out. *Husky Injection Molding Sys., Ltd. v. R & D Tool & Eng'g Co.*, 291 F.3d 780 (Fed. Cir. 2002). In theory at least, the distinction between reconstruction and repair might depend on an analysis of the predictable life span of a patented invention. Repair would ensure the invention reaches its full useful life, while reconstruction might inordinately double or triple that predictable life. No court has adopted this formulation, however. Instead, articulating a universally applicable distinction between reconstructing a spent part and repairing a replaceable part has proven elusive in practice, and the determination is necessarily fact-dependent.

B. EXPERIMENTAL USE

Despite the unqualified statutory language that unauthorized uses of patented technology constitute infringement, courts have excepted *de minimis* as well as experimental uses from infringement. A *de minimis* use occurs when there is merely a nominal infringement for which insignificant damages would arise. *See Deuterium Corp. v. United States*, 19 Cl. Ct. 624 (1990). An experimental use, however, occurs when there is a non-commercial evaluation of patented subject matter. In 1813, for example, Justice Story commented that "it could never have been the intention of the legislature to punish a man, who constructed such a machine merely for philosophical experiments, or for the purpose of ascertaining the sufficiency of the machine to produce its effects." *Whittemore v. Cutter*, 29 F.Cas. 1120, 1121 (C.C. Mass. 1813) (No. 17,600).

This common-law experimental use exception operates to protect alleged infringers in only the narrowest of circumstances—where the infringer acted "for amusement, to satisfy idle curiosity, or for strictly philosophical inquiry" without "definite, cognizable, and not insubstantial commercial purposes." *Embrex, Inc. v. Serv. Eng'g Corp.*, 216 F.3d 1343, 1349 (Fed. Cir. 2000). Even academic institutions engaged in research—irrespective of whether that research has a practical, real-world application—do not fall under the experimental use exception:

> Our precedent clearly does not immunize use that is in any way commercial in nature. Similarly, our precedent does not immunize any conduct that is in keeping with the alleged infringer's legitimate business, regardless of commercial implications. For example, major research universities . . . often sanction and fund research projects with arguably no commercial application whatsoever. However, these projects unmistakably further the institution's legitimate business objectives, including educating and enlightening students and faculty participating in these projects. These projects also serve, for example, to increase the status of the institution and lure lucrative research grants, students and faculty.

Madey v. Duke Univ., 307 F.3d 1351, 1362 (Fed. Cir. 2002).

Perhaps the most significant case under this doctrine refused to protect a generic drug manufacturer that tested a patented pharmaceutical prior to the patent's expiration, even if those tests are necessary to obtain government approval. *See Roche Prods., Inc. v. Bolar Pharm. Co.*, 733 F.2d 858 (Fed. Cir. 1984). This decision resulted in a *de facto* extension of patent term because a generic manufacturer may not begin proving the safety and efficacy of the drug until after the patent expires.

To eliminate this practical extension of patent rights, a new comprehensive law overruled *Roche* and dramatically altered the relationship between research-based and generic pharmaceutical companies. *See* Drug Price Competition and Patent Term Restoration Act of 1984, Pub. L No. 98–417, 98 Stat. 1585. This Act, commonly known as the Hatch-Waxman Act, provided in part:

> It shall not be an act of infringement to make, use, offer to sell, or sell within the United States or import into the United States a patented invention . . . solely for uses reasonably related to the development and submission of information under a Federal law which regulates the manufacture, use, or sale of drugs or veterinary biological products.

35 U.S.C. § 271(e)(1).

Although only referencing drugs on its face, this provision also applies to experimentation with medical devices for submission of information showing safety and efficacy under the same statutory scheme that regulates the safety and efficacy of drugs. *Eli Lilly & Co. v. Medtronic, Inc.*, 496 U.S. 661 (1990). The Supreme Court has clarified that this provision has a very broad scope. Any research activity that may have even a remote link, this is, "uses reasonably related" to submissions for government approval, are exempt from infringement. Thus, pre-clinical investigations and tests not even necessarily linked to a particular pharmaceutical composition may escape infringement liability. *Merck KGaA v. Integra Lifesciences I, Ltd.*, 545 U.S. 193 (2005).

IX. "ARTIFICIAL" INFRINGEMENT UNDER § 271(e)(2)

Like most patent law doctrines, infringement is by and large universally applicable across technological boundaries, with one notable exception. As an integral part of the Hatch-Waxman Act, which codified the experimental use exception for the development of generic drugs under § 271(e)(1) as mentioned above, patents relating to pharmaceuticals receive special treatment under the patent statute.

While infringement under the Hatch-Waxman Act is discussed in detail in Chapter 19, it suffices to say here that this non-exclusive infringement—meaning that pharmaceutical-related patents may nonetheless be enforced under other subsections of § 271—relates to a generic manufacturer's submission of an Abbreviated New Drug Application (ANDA) that asserts bioequivalence to a previously approved drug. *See* 21 U.S.C. § 355(j)(2). In the most frequently litigated circumstance, the ANDA filer will also make a "paragraph IV" certification that any patent reading on the approved drug "is invalid or will not be infringed by the manufacture, use, or sale of the new drug." 21 U.S.C. § 355(j)(2)(A)(vii)(IV). Indeed, the mere act of filing that ANDA is an infringement:

> It shall be an act of infringement to submit—
>
> (A) an application under section 505(j) of the Federal Food, Drug, and Cosmetic Act or described in section 505(b)(2) of such Act for a drug claimed in a patent or the use of which is claimed in a patent, . . . if the purpose of such submission is to obtain approval under such Act to engage in the commercial manufacture, use, or sale of a drug . . . claimed in a patent or the use of which is claimed in a patent before the expiration of such patent.

35 U.S.C. § 271(e)(2).

X. INFRINGEMENT ABROAD

Currently, individual European countries issue patents, as does the European Patent Office. Notably, a single EPO patent may be enforced in each nation individually. In other words, the single patent is treated as multiple national patents. *See* European Patent Convention, Article 64(1). Indeed, "[a]ny infringement of a European patent shall be dealt with by national law." Article 64(3). For the most part, this does not cause problems, as most European nations have substantially harmonized patent laws.

Claim construction, however, is not uniform throughout the member countries—which should come as no surprise given the inherently problematic nature of the inquiry. Germany and the United Kingdom, for example, construe claims broadly and narrowly, respectively. Due to this difference in claim interpretation, the European Patent Convention purports to set forth a proper methodology: "The extent of the protection conferred by a European patent or a European patent application shall be determined by the terms of the claims. Nevertheless, the description and drawings shall be used to interpret the claims." Article 69(1). Given the laconic nature of this methodology, the Protocol on the Interpretation of Article 69 provides additional guidance:

> Article 69 should not be interpreted as meaning that the extent of the protection conferred by a European patent is to be understood as that defined by the strict, literal meaning of the wording used in the claims, the description and drawings being employed only for the purpose of resolving an ambiguity found in the claims. Nor should it be taken to mean that the claims serve only as a guideline and that the actual protection conferred may extend to what, from a consideration of the description and drawings by a person skilled in the art, the patent proprietor has contemplated. On the contrary, it is to be interpreted as defining a position between these

> extremes which combines a fair protection for the patent proprietor with a reasonable degree of legal certainty for third parties.

Even though this purports to set forth a uniform standard, individual countries still have varying practices. Interestingly, each country may nonetheless achieve similar results through the doctrine of equivalents. Of course, this generalization, too, has difficulties because the United Kingdom professes to have no DOE. *Kirin-Amgen Inc. v Hoechst Marion Roussel Ltd.*, [2004] UKHL 46. Instead the United Kingdom employs a "purposive construction" doctrine that may occasionally recast claims to achieve the overarching purpose (as divined by the judges) of the invention.

The advent of the Unified Patent Court, which will likely take place as this edition goes to print, will bring about a streamlined system in which a single patent may be enforced in multiple European countries.

CHAPTER 15
ADDITIONAL DEFENSES

I. INTRODUCTION

Aside from defenses of noninfringement, failure to comply with the patentability requirements in §§ 101, 102, 103, and 112, inequitable conduct, and double patenting (all in prior chapters), additional defenses—primarily equitable in nature—may also preclude a patentee from successfully enforcing a patent. These additional defenses—which include laches, estoppel, a peculiar type of implied license called a "shop right," misuse, temporary presence in the United States, and first inventorship—do not affect the patent's validity; rather, they affect whether the patent may be asserted against a particular party (with the exception of prosecution laches and patent misuse, which preclude enforcement against all parties). When successfully established, these defenses provide something akin to a limited license to practice the patentee's invention.

Courts and parties often address laches and estoppel concurrently, even though they entail different (yet nonetheless related) concepts. Even though they are not unique to patent law, patent-specific cases have recurring fact patterns that have generated a notable body of case law. Although infrequently occurring and heavily fact-dependent, these doctrines are well-defined.

The next three defenses, which are unique to patent law, occur with even less frequency than laches and estoppel. The first, "shop rights," is firmly entrenched with a lengthy history, but is rare in the modern corporate environment. An employer obtains a "shop right" to practice an invention that its employee created while in its employ. But this implied license is only the default rule, and employers may enter into contracts with their employees and independent contractors regarding ownership of inventions.

Next, the temporary presence defense under 35 U.S.C. § 272 excuses any transitory infringement by foreign-based vessels and vehicles engaged in international commerce. Under § 272, the temporary presence of a vessel, aircraft, or vehicle within the territory of the United States does not constitute infringement so long as it is limited solely to the operation of that craft and not sold, offered for sale, or involved in the manufacture of anything sold or exported from the United States.

Lastly, the first inventor defense under 35 U.S.C. § 273 was substantially expanded as a part of the Leahy-Smith America Invents Act (AIA). This defense permits a prior, good-faith user of potentially infringing subject matter to continue using that method. In this respect, the defense is akin to prior invention under first-to-invent's § 102(g), with a critical distinction being that a prior user need not have publicly disclosed the subject matter to evade liability for infringement. Many foreign jurisdictions have similar prior-user provisions as well.

The final defense addressed by this chapter is patent misuse, which borrows antitrust principles to preclude a patentee from enforcing his patent rights under some licensing agreements that extend beyond the literal terms of the exclusive right. Initially this doctrine was a defense limited to contributory infringers who sold unpatented components that were part of a patented combination or process. The defense originally belonged only to a narrow class of defendants. But the defense outgrew those confines. Now any defendant, regardless of whether it is merely a contributory infringer, may render a patent unenforceable for patent misuse. Still this remedy is rare.

II. LACHES AND ESTOPPEL

Even though not specifically identified in 35 U.S.C. § 282 as defenses to patent infringement, accused infringers may invoke laches or estoppel to avoid a judgment of liability. Laches resolves the inequity of a patentee attempting to enforce his patent rights too late. Estoppel, on the other hand, resolves the inequity of a patentee attempting to enforce his patent rights after inducing the defendant to reasonably believe that the patentee would not sue. Notably, the trial court has broad discretion to apply these defenses according to the equities of the situation.

In *A.C. Aukerman Co. v. R. L. Chaides Construction Co.*, 960 F.2d 1020 (Fed. Cir. 1992), the Federal Circuit addressed these equitable defenses en banc, distinguishing them and setting forth their necessary elements of proof. The court, however, cautioned that the elements of these defenses are not immutable rules but guiding principles.

A. LACHES

The *Aukerman* court reaffirmed that two traditional elements apply in patent cases. The first element requires the alleged infringer to prove that the patentee's delay in bringing suit was unreasonable and inexcusable. This period of delay begins at the time the patentee knew or should have known of the allegedly infringing activities and ends when the patentee brings suit, although the clock cannot start before the asserted patent issues. Any mitigating circumstances justifying the delay—for example, other litigation, negotiations with the defendant, poverty or illness, a national emergency, the extent of infringement and its evolution over the period of delay, or an ownership dispute—may influence the determination of inexcusability.

On the question of reasonable time delays, the laches defense only applies in cases where a delay lasts longer than six years. *SCA Hygiene Prods. Aktiebolag v. First Quality Baby Prods., LLC*, 580 U.S. 328 (2017). In *SCA Hygiene*, the Supreme Court clarified that laches—as an equitable tool against untimely claims—is subordinate to Congress's express judgment that a patent owner may recover for infringement so long as its delay in filing suit is six years or less. *See* 35 U.S.C. § 286; *SCA Hygiene*, at 961.

The second element requires the alleged infringer to prove a material prejudice caused by that delay. Such prejudice is typically available in two flavors: economic and evidentiary. Economic prejudice is not solely a question of the amount of damages that a defendant would pay if found to be infringing; instead, economic prejudice requires a detrimental change in the economic position of the defendant over the period of delay, such as the loss of monetary investments or incurrence of excessive damages. For instance, economic prejudice may occur where an infringer would have had an opportunity to switch to a non-infringing product had the patentee not been dilatory in asserting his patent.

While economic prejudice is difficult to describe in the abstract because it attempts to prevent an excessive (and avoidable) punishment caused by the delay, evidentiary prejudice is much more straightforward. The defendant suffers evidentiary prejudice where the delay severely inhibits its ability to proffer a full and fair defense. That usually means the loss of critical records or documents, important witnesses, or simply diminished recollection of witnesses. The unobtainable evidence must significantly impede the court's ability to determine crucial facts in dispute, making the litigation intractable or perhaps even futile.

If a defendant successfully proves that the patentee's delay was unreasonable and that material prejudice resulted from that delay, the defendant escapes liability only for conduct before the filing date of the litigation. Once the patentee files suit, that date triggers prospective liability even where laches precludes a defendant's liability for past infringement. Thus a patentee could still seek an injunction on continued infringement.

B. EQUITABLE ESTOPPEL

Similar to laches, the *Aukerman* court clarified the three-pronged test for equitable estoppel. First, the patentee must have misled the defendant into reasonably believing that the patentee does not intend to enforce its patent against that defendant. Unlike laches, delay is not essential to a successful invocation of estoppel, even if a relevant fact or circumstance. Rather, the first prong requires that a patentee's conduct must support an inference that the patentee did not intend to assert an infringement claim against the alleged infringer. In most instances, this means that the alleged infringer has specific knowledge of the patent—an unnecessary requirement for laches.

The alleged infringer typically knows (or has a reasonable belief) that the patentee knew of the allegedly infringing acts for an unduly long period of time. Frequently this occurs where the patentee notifies the defendant of the alleged infringement, lulls the alleged infringer into an expectation that the threat has lapsed, then springs into action once again to enforce the patent. But beyond affirmative conduct, a patentee's inaction coupled with a special relationship to the defendant may satisfy this first element. The instances of acquiescence or abandonment, however, are far less common than the cases involving affirmative misrepresentations.

The second element of estoppel requires the defendant to prove reliance on the patentee's misleading conduct. As the *Aukerman* court explained:

> Reliance is not the same as prejudice or harm, although frequently confused. An infringer can build a plant being entirely unaware of the patent. . . . To show reliance, the infringer must have had a relationship or communication with the plaintiff which lulls the infringer into a sense of security in going ahead with building the plant.

960 F.2d at 1043. Thus, the defendant must take an action—such as building a new facility, promoting and advertising accused products, or hiring additional employees—based on its reasonable belief that the patentee would not in fact assert the patent.

The third prong of equitable estoppel is similar to the second element of laches, namely, the defendant must suffer material prejudice. Again this prejudice may be either economic or evidentiary. Where the defendant has reasonably relied on the patentee's non-enforcement conduct, economic prejudice becomes easy to prove. Building a new facility or hiring additional employees, for example, would likely suffice.

If a defendant proves these factors and the court rules that it would be inequitable to allow the patentee to press the patent infringement claim any further, the patentee's entire claim is barred. Unlike laches, a successful estoppel defense excuses past, present, and future behavior from liability.

C. PROSECUTION LACHES

In addition to a delay in filing a suit for infringement, a patentee may forfeit rights to an invention as a result of a delay in prosecuting the applications that matured into the patent. *Woodbridge v. United States*, 263 U.S. 50 (1923); *Webster Elec. Co. v. Splitdorf Elec. Co.*, 264 U.S. 463 (1924). Although prosecution laches was recognized long ago, for many years it remained a forgotten defense to the problem of so-called "submarine patents." Although a patent's term now expires 20 years after the earliest effective filing date, it once expired 17 years after the date of issuance. Under that regime, an inventor could file an application to obtain an early date of priority, then, through the use of continuing applications permitted by the Patent Office's rules, prolong prosecution until the inventive technology matured in the marketplace.

The cunning inventor would then amend the claims to cover products already on the market and sue the competition. *See, e.g., State Indus., Inc. v. A.O. Smith Corp.*, 751 F.2d 1226 (Fed. Cir. 1985). The previously secret application—remember that the Patent Office began publishing pending applications for applications filed only after the American Inventors Protection Act of 1999—would "surface" as an issued patent only after the market had committed to the patented technology. Faced with the prospect of protracted and expensive litigation, the (now-beguiled) competitors often would simply license the submarine patent. And even if the application became a public document through issuance of a patent, continuations remained available for claims that avoided double patenting (either due to a mistake by the PTO or the operation of 35 U.S.C. § 121).

In 2002, however, the Federal Circuit reaffirmed the availability of prosecution laches as a defense, even if it provided no guidance on its application. *Symbol Techs., Inc. v. Lemelson Med., Educ. & Research Found.*, 277 F.3d 1361 (Fed. Cir. 2002). Instead, the court affirmatively ruled that laches may preclude enforcement of patent claims that issued after an unreasonable and unexplained delay in prosecution. This delay could occur even though the applicant complied with pertinent statutes and rules.

In a subsequent case involving an appeal from the Patent Office, an applicant was barred from obtaining claims to an invention due to an unreasonably long eight-year prosecution process. *In re Bogese*, 303 F.3d 1362 (Fed. Cir. 2002). In filing a series of twelve continuation applications, the applicant, in particular, neither amended the pending claims nor addressed the outstanding rejections. The applicability of prosecution laches will, of course, winnow in light of the 20-years-from-filing term for patents as well as other Patent Office rules governing continuing prosecution, such as requests for continued examination under 37 C.F.R. § 1.114.

A recent case, *Hyatt v. Hirshfeld*, 998 F.3d 1347 (Fed. Cir. 2021), may have prompted some uptick in the use of the prosecution laches defense, but the facts of that case are rather unique. There, the PTO asserted the prosecution laches defense in Mr. Hyatt's district court lawsuit to obtain a patent under § 145. Mr. Hyatt, one of the biggest filers of submarine patents, had created a large web of decades-old applications by claiming priority to numerous earlier applications with overlapping disclosures. To further complicate matters, Mr. Hyatt's numerous applications had long and essentially identical claims. The PTO had enormous difficulty administering his applications and, indeed, could not even determine the priority date to begin the prior art searching process in many cases. The PTO adopted special procedures and established an art unit dedicated to administering Mr. Hyatt's applications. Under these circumstances, the *Hyatt* court vacated the district court's grant of summary judgment of no prosecution laches, explaining that Mr. Hyatt's "clear abuse of the patent system" triggered the defense.

D. LICENSEE ESTOPPEL

Although not directly related to patent enforcement, the related area of enforcing licenses on patents features another equitable doctrine, the doctrine of licensee estoppel. At one time, patentees often insisted on a clause in license agreements that prevented the licensee from challenging the validity or enforceability of the patent. *See, e.g.*, *Automatic Radio Mfg. Co. v. Hazeltine Research, Inc.*, 339 U.S. 827 (1950). These provisions could insulate weak, or even invalid, patents from attack. The Supreme Court, therefore, stepped in and ended that practice.

In *Lear, Inc. v. Adkins*, 395 U.S. 653 (1969), the Court held that the public's interest in freely accessing ideas that belong in the public domain outweighed the interest in binding a party to a contractual promise not to sue. At the crux of its opinion, the Court explained: "Licensees may often be the only individuals with enough economic incentive to challenge the patentability of an inventor's discovery. If they are muzzled, the public may continually be required to pay tribute to would-be monopolists without need or justification." *Id.* at 670.

Although the reasoning of *Lear* would appear sweeping, its reach has been more limited. For example, a party entering into a consent decree in settlement of ongoing patent litigation that acknowledges the validity of a patent may not later challenge that patent's validity, due in part to res judicata, finality of judgments, and the public's interest in encouraging settlements of patent litigation. *Foster v. Hallco Mfg. Co.*, 947 F.2d 469 (Fed. Cir. 1991); *see also Hemstreet v. Spiegel, Inc.*, 851 F.2d 348 (Fed. Cir. 1988).

The Supreme Court, however, reinvigorated the *Lear* doctrine in *MedImmune, Inc. v. Genentech, Inc.*, 549 U.S. 118 (2007). In that case, MedImmune promised to pay royalties to Genentech under a license agreement. At some point, however, MedImmune started to believe that the licensed patent was invalid and unenforceable and notified Genentech that it would be paying the contractual royalties "under protest and with reservation of all of its rights." 549 U.S. at 122. Thereafter, MedImmune filed a suit under the Declaratory Judgment Act, all the while continuing to fulfill its obligations under the agreement. Without expressly discussing the precise contours of *Lear*, the Court held that there was a sufficient case or controversy to permit licensee to sue without surrendering the benefits of the license:

> To begin with, it is not clear where the prohibition against challenging the validity of the patents is to be found. It can hardly be implied from the mere promise to pay royalties on patents "which have neither expired nor been held invalid by a court or other body of competent jurisdiction from which no appeal has been or may be taken," App. 399. *Promising to pay royalties on patents that have not been held invalid does not amount to a promise not to seek a holding of their invalidity.*

Id. at 134–35 (emphasis added). Earlier, the Supreme Court had similarly hinted that the *Lear* doctrine does not apply to a non-repudiating licensee: "We express no opinion on whether a *nonrepudiating licensee* is similarly relieved of its contract obligation during a successful challenge to a patent's validity—that is, on the applicability of licensee estoppel under these circumstances." *Id.* at 124. Therefore, while these circumstances may create a justiciable dispute, the parties may take that possibility into account in drafting and negotiating the license agreement.

Perhaps more importantly (and despite not being fully before the Court in the case), a footnote in *MedImmune* swept away well-established jurisprudence regarding the requisite showing to establish jurisdiction under the Declaratory Judgment Act. *Id.* at 133 n.11. Following that footnote, the Federal Circuit ruled that any time a patentee offers to license its patent in light of specific, identified acts, there is a justiciable case or controversy giving rise to declaratory judgment jurisdiction. *SanDisk Corp. v. STMicroelectronics, Inc.*, 480 F.3d 1372 (Fed. Cir. 2007).

E. ASSIGNOR ESTOPPEL

The *Lear* doctrine prohibits, in limited circumstances, a patentee from assigning the entire risk of an invalid patent to a licensee. That is, a license clause cannot prevent a licensee from challenging the validity of a licensed patent (absent additional circumstances). Assume, however, that the roles are reversed, and a patentee assigns his patent to an assignee. May the assignor—who received at least a modicum of consideration in return for the assignment—later attempt to invalidate the assigned patent? The Federal Circuit in *Diamond Scientific Co. v. Ambico, Inc.*, answered that question in the negative, because assignor estoppel "prevents one who has assigned the rights to a patent (or patent application) from later contending that what was assigned is a nullity." 848 F.2d 1220, 1224 (Fed. Cir. 1988).

This equitable doctrine, the court went on to clarify, is rooted in the fundamental notion of fair dealing: "[I]t is the implicit representation by the assignor that the patent rights that he is assigning (presumably for value) are not worthless that sets the assignor apart from the rest of the world and can deprive him of the ability to challenge later the validity of the patent. To allow the assignor to make that representation at the time of the assignment (to his advantage) and later to repudiate it (again to his advantage) could work an injustice against the assignee." *Id.*

III. SHOP RIGHTS

Corporations often undertake inventive research. A rational corporation, of course, willingly invests in research so long as it will profit from that research. To ensure that it owns the fruit of its employees' labor, a company oftentimes requires its employees to assign all rights to any inventions conceived during their employment. *See Univ. of W. Va. v. VanVoorhies*, 342 F.3d 1290 (Fed. Cir. 2003). Cases involving the shop rights doctrine, however, arise because an employer has not placed such a condition in their employment contracts. Then, upon issuance of a patent, the inventor/employee may even seek to enforce the exclusive right against his employer. The law provides that employer with limited rights to practice that invention, when the facts and circumstances surrounding the development of the invention equitably justify the employer's continued use of the invention.

For example, in *McElmurry v. Arkansas Power & Light Co.*, 995 F.2d 1576 (Fed. Cir. 1993), Arkansas Power & Light (AP & L) hired the inventor of the patent at issue, Bowman, as a consultant at one of AP & L's power plants. While a consultant, Bowman invented an improved method of measuring the level of fly ash in a hopper. AP & L eventually installed, at its own expense, this fly ash measurement system in all of its power plant hoppers. Bowman also assisted with the installation of the system at a different facility (again at AP & L's expense), but not before he filed an application that eventually matured into a patent on the system. When AP & L installed the system on more hoppers without Bowman's assistance, the patent holder filed suit. The power company raised the shop rights doctrine as its defense.

The Federal Circuit emphasized the fact-specific and equitable nature of the shop right rule. The court thus adopted certain factors to evaluate the overall circumstances: whether the employer financed the employee's invention by providing wages, materials, tools, and working space; the contractual nature of the relationship between the employer and employee; whether the employee consented to the employer's use of the invention; and whether the employee induced, acquiesced in, or assisted in the use of the invention. Because the events compelled the conclusion that the employer retained rights to

Bowman's invention, AP & L was not liable for the use of the invention.

Although common law principles of equity may create domestic shop rights, other jurisdictions have addressed employer-employee ownership and use rights by statute. For example, German law provides for mandatory compensation for inventions created through employment. Under the German Employed Inventor's Rights Law, an employer may only obtain rights to "tied" inventions, which result from the employee's assignments or the activities of the employer. For such "tied" inventions, the employee may demand reasonable compensation from the employer. By way of contrast, "free" inventions may not be used by the employer absent permission of the employee. German law disallows an employee from contracting away his right to compensation for any "tied" inventions.

IV. TEMPORARY PRESENCE IN THE UNITED STATES

An infrequently applied, yet longstanding principle, relates to the non-infringement of shippers and transporters engaged in international commerce. *See Brown v. Duchesne*, 60 U.S. (19 How.) 183 (1856). Enacted in part to implement the Paris Convention, the Patent Act currently provides:

> The use of any invention in any vessel, aircraft or vehicle of any country which affords similar privileges to vessels, aircraft or vehicles of the United States, entering the United States temporarily or accidentally, shall not constitute

> infringement of any patent, if the invention is used exclusively for the needs of the vessel, aircraft or vehicle and is not offered for sale or sold in or used for the manufacture of anything to be sold in or exported from the United States.

35 U.S.C. § 272. The key to this provision is that the entry of the foreign vessel, aircraft, or vehicle must be "temporary."

In one case, *National Steel Car, Ltd. v. Canadian Pacific Railway, Ltd.*, 357 F.3d 1319 (Fed. Cir. 2004), the Federal Circuit held that railway cars for hauling lumber from Canada that would be physically present in the United States for over 50 percent of their useful lifespans fell within the exception of § 272 and thus did not infringe. In particular, the court explained that "a vehicle entering the United States 'temporarily' [is] a vehicle entering the United States for a limited period of time for the sole purpose of engaging in international commerce." *Id.* at 1329.

V. FIRST INVENTOR DEFENSE

As a part of the AIA, Congress created essentially an entirely new defense based on prior use. As amended, § 273 states, in part:

> (a) IN GENERAL.—A person shall be entitled to a defense under section 282(b) with respect to subject matter consisting of a process, or consisting of a machine, manufacture, or composition of matter used in a manufacturing or other commercial process, that would

otherwise infringe a claimed invention being asserted against the person if—

(1) such person, acting in good faith, commercially used the subject matter in the United States, either in connection with an internal commercial use or an actual arm's length sale or other arm's length commercial transfer of a useful end result of such commercial use; and

(2) such commercial use occurred at least 1 year before the earlier of either—

(A) the effective filing date of the claimed invention; or

(B) the date on which the claimed invention was disclosed to the public in a manner that qualified for the exception from prior art under section 102(b).

(b) BURDEN OF PROOF.—A person asserting a defense under this section shall have the burden of establishing the defense by clear and convincing evidence.

This defense is personal to the user and non-transferable. It neither creates a license nor enables exhaustion to downstream parties. And it does not invalidate the patent; it merely excludes the activities from liability.

VI. PATENT MISUSE

Patent law and antitrust law both govern aspects of innovation, competition, and commerce. *Atari*

Games Corp. v. Nintendo of Am., Inc., 897 F.2d 1572 (Fed. Cir. 1990). At one of their intersections lies a defense available to any accused infringer: if a patentee misuses its patent rights by violating antitrust-like principles, that patentee may not assert its patent against any party. The violation need not rise to a full-fledged antitrust violation, even if most successful invocations of the misuse defense double as antitrust violations.

This defense is particularly peculiar because it excuses potentially infringing behavior even if the victim of the patentee's misuse is a third party wholly distinct from the infringer. That is, this doctrine releases a wrongdoer (the infringer) and permits ongoing harm (infringement) because the victim (the patentee) may have wronged an unrelated third party through anticompetitive activity. Just like every other equitable defense, misuse is heavily fact dependent, hinging on the totality of circumstances that excuse the patentee's seemingly anticompetitive behavior. The statute and precedent, as clarified by the executive branch of the federal government, have severely limited its application to only a few, select instances.

The defense of patent misuse arose in a series of cases where the patent owner alleged contributory infringement by a manufacturer of unpatented components that were nonetheless covered by a patent license agreement. In these early cases, the party accused of contributory infringement raised this defense to escape infringement for sales of "unpatented" articles for use with a patented invention. *Motion Picture Patents Co. v. Universal Film Mfg. Co.*, 243 U.S. 502 (1917); *Mercoid Corp. v. Mid-Continent Inv. Co.*, 320 U.S. 661 (1944); *Mercoid Corp. v. Minneapolis-Honeywell Regulator Co.*, 320 U.S. 680 (1944).

But the Supreme Court expanded the equitable defense's reach beyond those confines in *Morton Salt Co. v. G.S. Suppiger Co.*, 314 U.S. 488 (1942). There the patented technology related to a machine that regulated the amount of salt deposited automatically into canned goods. Both the patentee and accused infringer made salt-deposition machines as well as the salt tablets themselves, although the Court noted that the competition in the sale of salt tablets was irrelevant. Rather than selling its patented machines, the patentee leased them on the condition that the lessees only purchase and use the patentee's salt tablets.

The Court saw this agreement as a restraint on trade of an unpatented article, the salt tablets. In other words, the patent owner was using its patent to anticompetitively govern unpatented products. In expanding patent misuse's application to noncompetitors, the Court explained: "It is the adverse effect upon the public interest of a successful infringement suit, in conjunction with the patentee's course of conduct, which disqualifies him to maintain the suit, regardless of whether the particular defendant has suffered misuse of the patent." *Id.* at 494. Under American law, it is highly unusual to allow a party completely unaffected by the alleged wrong to invoke that injustice as an equitable defense.

In 1952, Congress enacted 35 U.S.C. § 271(d)(1) through (3), and later added (4) and (5), so that the statute now carves out five separate behaviors that do not constitute patent misuse. Specifically, a patentee may:

> (1) derive[ ] revenue from acts which if performed by another without his consent would constitute contributory infringement of the patent;
>
> (2) license[ ] or authorize[ ] another to perform acts which if performed by another without his consent would constitute contributory infringement of the patent;
>
> (3) [seek] to enforce his patent rights against infringement or contributory infringement;
>
> (4) refuse[ ] to license or use any rights to the patent; or
>
> (5) condition[ ] the license of any rights to the patent or the sale of the patented product on the acquisition of a license to rights in another patent or purchase of a separate product, unless, in view of the circumstances, the patent owner has market power in the relevant market for the patent or patented product on which the license or sale is conditioned.

35 U.S.C § 271(d). Therefore, a patentee who refuses to license others to sell a non-staple article (i.e., an article whose only uses infringe) and insists that

customers purchase a non-staple good from him is not misusing his patent. *Dawson Chem. Co. v. Rohm & Haas Co.*, 448 U.S. 176 (1980).

The Federal Circuit now requires some anticompetitive effect, even if not rising to an antitrust violation, for a misuse violation. In fact, current law appears to have cabined patent misuse to two limited instances: using the market power generated by a patent to restrain competition in an unpatented field and extending the term of a patent beyond its statutory term. *See, e.g.*, *B. Braun Med., Inc. v. Abbott Labs.*, 124 F.3d 1419 (Fed. Cir. 1997). In this context, it is important to note that a patent alone, though sometimes characterized as a "monopoly," does not create market power. *Illinois Tool Works Inc. v. Indep. Ink, Inc.*, 547 U.S. 28, 46 (2006).

More recent patent misuse cases from the Federal Circuit continue to cabin the doctrine as well. *U.S. Philips Corp. v. Int'l Trade Comm'n*, 424 F.3d 1179 (Fed. Cir. 2005). For example, the Federal Circuit affirmed the ability of a patentee to selectively license its patents. *Princo Corp. v. Int'l Trade Comm'n*, 616 F.3d 1318 (Fed. Cir. 2010) (en banc).

CHAPTER 16
REMEDIES

Once a court has determined that an enforceable patent claim is not invalid and infringed, the patentee is entitled to remedies under two statutory provisions: 35 U.S.C. §§ 283 & 284. At its very essence, the patent right naturally implies injunctive relief. In many instances, the most attractive or beneficial remedy for infringement is to make that infringer stop the infringing activity. The authority for granting injunctions, § 283, states:

> The several courts having jurisdiction of cases under this title may grant injunctions in accordance with the principles of equity to prevent the violation of any right secured by patent, on such terms as the court deems reasonable.

A patentee may also recover monetary compensation for the infringing activity. In one sense, damages measure the value of the invention. The authority for granting damages, § 284, states:

> Upon finding for the claimant the court shall award the claimant damages adequate to compensate for the infringement, but in no event less than a reasonable royalty for the use made of the invention by the infringer, together with interest and costs as fixed by the court.

Remedies theories significantly influence substantive patent law. The availability and amount of damages inform not only an applicant's claiming strategy but also the administrative practices of the Patent and Trademark Office. Remedies also flesh out the interaction of patent law and other areas that regulate competition between corporations, such as antitrust and unfair competition.

I. INJUNCTIONS

An injunction is a critical part of patent law. In fact, one of the earliest pronouncements of the Federal Circuit related to its importance:

> The very nature of the patent right is the right to exclude others. Once the patentee's patents have been held to be valid and infringed, he should be entitled to the full enjoyment and protection of his patent rights. The infringer should not be allowed to continue his infringement in the face of such a holding. A court should not be reluctant to use its equity powers once a party has so clearly established his patent rights.

Smith Int'l, Inc. v. Hughes Tool Co., 718 F.2d 1573, 1581 (Fed. Cir. 1983). As the court recognized, injunctive relief is oftentimes a more valuable remedy than monetary relief. A patentee's first-mover advantage or, perhaps more importantly, its market share are often more valuable than past damages. Both of them require a remedy that "removes the trespasser" from the property right.

Foreign patent systems, particularly those emanating from the civil law tradition, reflect this truth: injunctive relief often is the only practical infringement remedy available. Thus, in many countries, an injunction is practically the only remedy.

Injunctive relief is available at three stages of litigation: preliminary to adjudication, accompanying a final judgment, and subsequent to enforcement of the injunction via contempt proceedings. Although permanent injunctions are available to patentees once a court rules that the accused party infringed a valid and enforceable patent, litigation often spans a couple of years (or even the better part of a decade in some cases). Accordingly, a preliminary injunction can, in some situations, have tremendous value, particularly where the true damage caused by infringement would be difficult to assess.

Before the Federal Circuit, patentees often faced formidable obstacles in obtaining preliminary injunctive relief. The equitable factors for injunctive relief were particularly hard to satisfy in patent cases. To begin with, injunctive relief required a showing of a likelihood of success in proving both validity and infringement at trial. With uncertain and factually intensive patentability standards, the likelihood of sustaining a patent's validity was a difficult burden. In fact, a prior judgment of validity seemed to be the sole way of proving likely validity. And of course, proof of likely infringement posed similar obstacles.

Further, equity required no adequate legal remedy before imposing a preliminary injunction. Because damages would be available as a legal remedy, a patentee could almost never leap this hurdle. In its early case law, the Federal Circuit, however, reduced these obstacles substantially.

In *H.H. Robertson, Co. v. United Steel Deck, Inc.*, 820 F.2d 384 (Fed. Cir. 1987), the court reaffirmed that preliminary injunctions were available in patent cases, and the standards were neither higher nor lower than in other areas of the law. Rather, the four-factored test is the same: (1) a reasonable likelihood of success on the merits; (2) irreparable harm to the patentee without a preliminary injunction; (3) a balance of the parties' relative hardships; and (4) the public interest.

With respect to the first equitable factor, the patentee bears the burden of proving validity and infringement, keeping in mind the burdens and presumptions at trial. The Federal Circuit emphasized, for instance, that the patent enjoys a presumption of validity, which may only be overcome by clear and convincing evidence. Even so, the alleged infringer need only show a substantial question about the patent's validity.

On the second factor, irreparable harm—sometimes rephrased as a lack of an adequate remedy at law—the patentee enjoys a presumption of harm upon a showing of a likelihood of success on the merits. This presumption arises from the finite term of a patent, which of course runs as the litigation proceeds. The Federal Circuit observed that damage therefore necessarily results from a delay in excluding infringing goods from the marketplace. Importantly, this presumption is not irrebuttable, and the alleged infringer may still show a lack of irreparable harm by certain activities of the patentee, such as licensing.

Even with irreparable harm, a court must still examine the third and fourth factors—the relative hardships between the patentee and infringer and the public interest. The fourth factor comes into play most frequently with respect to public health and safety concerns, such as cutting off the sole source of a life-saving technology. Although a lack of either a likely success on the merits or irreparable harm to the patentee in the absence of an injunction mandates a denial of a motion for a preliminary injunction, a court must consider all four factors.

Even if a court does not preliminarily enjoin the infringer's activities while the litigation is pending, it may permanently enjoin the infringer upon a final judgment of infringement. The Supreme Court overturned the commonsense principle that the remedy for an exclusive right is to "remove the trespasser." Instead, in *eBay, Inc. v. MercExchange, L.L.C.*, 547 U.S. 388 (2006), the Court seemed to decide that the trespasser may continue to reside in your back yard upon payment of some rent.

Prior to *eBay,* the Federal Circuit favored a permanent injunction upon a judgment of infringement as a general rule. That general rule disappeared in the face of an era of concern about "patent trolls." In fact, MercExchange, the patent owner, had some of the characteristics attributed to "trolls," such as a predominant licensing practice and no production of the patented invention. The

Supreme Court interpreted the language of § 283 (above) and emphasized that the use of the term "may" makes an injunction optional under the standard four-factor equity test even after a finding of willful infringement.

The more interesting aspect of the Supreme Court's decision was the competing concurrences. Three justices, including Chief Justice Roberts, wrote that "a page of history is worth a volume of logic," apparently advocating a continued adherence to a general rule in favor of removing trespassers after a finding of infringement. Three other justices, including Justice Kennedy, wrote that a segment of the patent "industry" (apparently a reference to trolls) warrants a change in the past permanent injunction rules. As an aside, there is no consensus on the characteristics of a "patent troll." Most would agree, for instance, that a university (which never practices its many contributions to technology) is not a troll. In any event, *eBay* will require additional proof justifying a permanent injunction even after a finding of infringement.

The irony is that the Court's reliance on "may" to make an exclusionary remedy suspect overlooks the real purpose of the non-mandatory verb. The "may" was necessarily present in the statute to guard against the rare instance when enforcing a patent could endanger public health and safety. The public interest factor had always been part of the equitable test for an injunction. Even under the general presumption in favor of "removing trespassers," threats to public health would likely defeat a permanent injunction.

The most famous case on this principle, even if nearly a century old, is *City of Milwaukee v. Activated Sludge, Inc.*, 69 F.2d 577 (7th Cir. 1934). In that case, the appellate court vacated a permanent injunction that would have prevented the city of Milwaukee from using an infringing system of sewage treatment. If enjoined, the city would have dumped its sewage into Lake Michigan. Accordingly, an injunction would have caused great harm to the public health and welfare without a substantial benefit to the patentee, who did not practice the claimed invention. To prevent this kind of threat, the statute used the term "may" to grant discretion to protect public health and safety. Sadly, without comment on this reason for the conditional language, the Supreme Court in *eBay* made injunctions difficult for entire classes of patent owners based on their characteristics rather than their conduct. After a permanent injunction issues, parties occasionally dispute the precise contours of its scope. For the most part, such a dispute arises when the patentee brings a contempt proceeding based on a reengineered product that is similar, though not identical, to the original infringing product. The infringer naturally asserts that the differences take the modified good outside the scope of the patent (and thus of the injunction), while the patentee asserts the opposite. *Tivo Inc. v. EchoStar Corp.*, 646 F.3d 869 (Fed. Cir. 2011) (en banc). Alternatively, the patentee could bring a separate infringement action.

II. DAMAGES

Although equitable relief can hold tremendous value for the patentee, legal relief is also essential to compensate for infringement. The statute instructs that a court must "award the claimant damages adequate to compensate for the infringement." 35 U.S.C. § 284. These damages qualify as "but-for" remedies, because a court attempts to reconstruct the pecuniary benefit that the patentee would have obtained without infringement.

A court has wide discretion to use any economically viable theory to achieve these compensatory damages. A patentee is not subject to a one-size-fits-all theory of damages. The only mandatory part of the equation is that the award cannot be "less than a reasonable royalty." Typically damages not classified as a reasonable royalty fall under the rubric of lost profits, which although usually more lucrative are also more speculative and more difficult to prove.

A. LOST PROFITS

The lost profits method of damages calculation attempts to restore to the patentee the profits lost due to sales diverted to the infringer. To acquire lost profits damages, a patentee must first show that the infringement caused the profit loss. The "but-for" causation test requires the patentee to show that it would have made each of the infringer's sales if infringement had not occurred.

With Chief Judge Markey of the Court of Customs and Patent Appeals as author, the Sixth Circuit set forth a key test for showing causation. This lost profits test, occasionally called the DAMP test or the *Panduit* test, relies on four factors:

> To obtain as damages the profits on sales he would have made absent the infringement, i.e., the sales made by the infringer, a patent owner must prove: (1) demand for the patented product, (2) absence of acceptable noninfringing substitutes, (3) his manufacturing and marketing capability to exploit the demand, and (4) the amount of the profit he would have made.

Panduit Corp. v. Stahlin Bros. Fibre Works, Inc., 575 F.2d 1152, 1156 (6th Cir. 1978). This test operates most reliably in a two-supplier market, where the patentee and the infringer are the only players. In that setting, the DAMP test implements the presumption that the patentee would have made every sale that the infringer made. *See, e.g., Kaufman Co. v. Lantech, Inc.*, 926 F.2d 1136 (Fed. Cir. 1991); *Micro Chem., Inc. v. Lextron, Inc.*, 318 F.3d 1119 (Fed. Cir. 2003).

The DAMP test, of course, still requires identification of the relevant market, which excludes alternatives to the patented product that have significantly different prices or characteristics. In economic terms, this identification roughly equates to differentiating the perfect from the imperfect substitutes for the patented good. After defining the market and showing only two suppliers, the patentee need only show that it had the capability to produce and market the additional infringing goods at a profit.

Importantly, because market conditions often vary widely, courts have not exclusively employed the *Panduit* test for proving lost profits. Other complimentary theories have emerged as ways to compensate the patentee for profits lost due to the infringement. For example, the leading Federal Circuit case on proof of lost profits, *Rite-Hite Corp. v. Kelley Co.*, 56 F.3d 1538 (Fed. Cir. 1995) (en banc), held that a patentee may sometimes recover lost profits for product sales in direct competition with the infringing goods, even though those products are not even covered by the patent. The product replaced by the infringer's goods need not itself be patented. Rather, the product need only be in direct competition with the infringing goods. The key is that the infringer's product must substitute for the patentee's product. If the patentee can show that consumers would have bought its product if the infringing product were not on the market (even if the goods are different in some respects), the patentee can recover the profits it would have foreseeably made on the sales that instead went to the infringer. *See, e.g., King Instruments Corp. v. Perego*, 65 F.3d 941 (Fed. Cir. 1995).

Permitting recovery of lost profits on competitive goods eliminates the need for a second "reverse" infringement investigation into whether the patentee's goods embody the claimed invention. Furthermore, permitting recovery even where the patentee does not commercialize the claimed invention eliminates a potential for inadequate compensation—and a windfall to the infringer.

Similarly, the Federal Circuit has expanded the DAMP test to allow recovery of lost profits in a market with many competing products. *See State Indus., Inc. v. Mor-Flo Industries, Inc.*, 883 F.2d 1573 (Fed. Cir. 1989). With many substitutes in the market, the patentee has great difficulty showing it would have made each of the infringer's sales. Nonetheless, under a market share approach, the patentee can recover lost profits according to its proportional share of the market. The market share rule, in a commonsense fashion, divvies up the customers that bought the infringing good amongst the non-infringing substitutes and the patentee according to their market share. Of course, these non-infringing substitutes must still be sufficiently similar in price and characteristics to qualify as substitutes in the same market.

In *BIC Leisure Products, Inc. v. Windsurfing International, Inc.*, 1 F.3d 1214 (Fed. Cir. 1993), for instance, the patentee had exclusive rights to sailboard technology that encompassed both large, expensive sailboards and small, inexpensive funboards. The claim thus embraced at least two separate markets. The patentee, Windsurfing International, a manufacturer of large sailboards, could not show that it would have made each of the infringer's sales because BIC sold only funboards.

To illustrate the market share methodology, imagine the same sailboard market but now the infringing good A, the third-party good B, and the patentee good C are all large, interchangeable sailboards with comparable prices (usually the ultimate measure of substitutability and market definition). Assuming that goods A, B, and C each enjoy 33$^{1}/_{3}$% of the market, the market share rule would split the sales of A evenly between the third party and the patentee. The patentee would thus receive lost profits calculated on 50% of the infringing sales. Thus, the two-supplier market rule can be understood as a simplification of the more generally applicable market share rule. That is, imagine a market comprising infringing good A and patentee good B. No matter the market share of each good, the patentee will always capture the sales of infringing good A, thus receiving lost profits based on 100% of the infringing sales.

Of course, the infringer may always attempt to rebut the second prong of the DAMP test by showing the availability of a non-infringing substitute. In *Panduit*, the court reasoned that a "product lacking the advantages of that patented can hardly be termed a substitute 'acceptable' to the customer who wants those advantages." 575 F.2d at 1162. This phrase emphasizes that the claimed invention will rarely have substitutes unless they encompass all the same advantages. This articulation of the test for non-infringing substitutes is rather strict. The marketplace, on the other hand, very often supplies several substitutes for every product—each with its own advantages and tradeoffs. Thus, as the emphasis in damages law has shifted towards a compensation model, the requirements for "non-infringing substitutes" have reflected economic reasoning.

In *Grain Processing Corp. v. American Maize-Products*, 185 F.3d 1341 (Fed. Cir. 1999), for example, the court held that a product not under production or on sale anywhere can serve as a non-infringing substitute. In that case, the accused infringer could have easily made and sold the substitute but had instead sold the cheaper infringing product. The Federal Circuit, however, recognized that in the absence of infringement, the infringer would have simply and easily switched to the alternative:

> Reconstructing the market, by definition a hypothetical enterprise, requires the patentee to project economic results that did not occur. To prevent the hypothetical from lapsing into pure speculation, this court requires sound economic proof of the nature of the market and likely outcomes with infringement factored out of the economic picture.
>
> By the same token, a fair and accurate reconstruction of the "but for" market must also take into account, where relevant, alternative actions the infringer foreseeably would have undertaken had he not infringed. Without the infringing product, a rational would-be infringer is likely to offer an acceptable noninfringing alternative, if available, to compete with the patent owner rather than leave the market altogether. . . . Thus, an accurate reconstruction of the hypothetical "but for" market takes into account any alternatives available to the infringer.

Grain Processing, 185 F.3d at 1350–51. In the *Grain Processing* market, the alternative was not even on the market at the time of infringement, but it was widely known and easily adopted when the judgement occurred.

In a subsequent case, *Micro Chemical, Inc. v. Lextron, Inc.*, 318 F.3d 1119 (Fed. Cir. 2003), however, the Federal Circuit clarified and limited the *Grain Processing* holding. In that later case, the court emphasized that the non-infringing substitute must be readily available, meaning easy access to equipment, know-how, and experience for the substitution. In *Micro Chemical,* a development period of four months coupled with multiple design changes showed that the purported substitute was not readily available.

Based on these cases, the Federal Circuit seems to have directed damages proof towards a unified theory of lost profits. Under this unified theory, entitlement to lost profits would entail four steps. First, the patentee would define the relevant marketplace to include the infringing good and its consumer-recognized substitutes, taking into consideration varying prices and characteristics. The analysis continues to the remaining steps only if the patentee sells a substitute for the infringing good, even if that substitute does not embody the invention.

Second, the patentee would determine a presumptive market share of the patentee's goods without infringement—that is, a hypothetical reconstruction of the relevant market based solely on market shares of non-infringing goods. *See, e.g.*,

Ericsson, Inc. v. Harris Corp., 352 F.3d 1369 (Fed. Cir. 2003). Third, the infringer would rebut or reduce (perhaps to zero) this market share, either by demonstrating that the infringing good and the patentee's good are imperfect substitutes, *see King Instruments Corp. v. Perego*, 65 F.3d 941 (Fed. Cir. 1995), or by demonstrating that non-infringing alternatives were readily available, even if not on the market, *see Micro Chemical, Inc. v. Lextron, Inc.*, 318 F.3d 1119 (Fed. Cir. 2003).

Fourth, the patentee's lost profits would equal the profit margin indicated by an economic analysis of the likely price in the post-reduction market multiplied by the number of infringing sales. At this point, the model probably requires some economic expertise to determine the elasticity of demand (the market's sensitivity to price changes). This model would apply as well to a market with multiple infringing goods competing with many patentee and third-party goods.

B. PRICE EROSION

A patentee may use theories other than lost profits to obtain full compensation for the infringement. Price erosion damages—a close relative to lost profits—attempt to correct for the cross-elasticity of demand between the infringing good and the patentee's good. That is, if an infringing good is a reasonable substitute for the patentee's good, the price of the infringing good will likely depress the price of the patentee's good.

An infringer may often enter the patentee's market at a lower price. After all, the infringer has far less research and development costs, not to mention the comparative ease of entering a developed market. The cheaper infringing good will likely force the patentee to reduce prices to retain sales. Thus, the patentee would not only lose sales to the infringer but also earn fewer profits due to the depressed price. Price erosion thus assumes that, without infringing competition, the patentee could have sustained a higher price and allows damages to compensate for the difference.

Once again, proof of price erosion requires some economic sophistication:

> Moreover, in a credible economic analysis, the patentee cannot show entitlement to a higher price divorced from the effect of that higher price on demand for the product. In other words, the patentee must also present evidence of the (presumably reduced) amount of product the patentee would have sold at the higher price. . . "[B]ut for" infringement, Crystal would have tried to charge at least 89 cents more per CODEC.
>
> * * *
>
> Nor did Crystal make any estimates as to the number of sales it would have lost or kept had it increased its prices by 89 cents per unit. Thus, Crystal did not make a showing of "but for" causation of price erosion.

* * *

> Without economic evidence of the resulting market for higher priced CODECs, Crystal cannot have both lost profits and price erosion damages on each of those lost sales. The district court correctly denied Crystal's price erosion damages for lack of adequate record support.

Crystal Semiconductor Corp. v. TriTech Microelectronics Int'l Inc., 246 F.3d 1336, 1359–60 (Fed. Cir. 2001). This case illustrates as well the need for economic proof of hypothetical markets in a damages calculus.

C. REASONABLE ROYALTY

As a fallback position, a patentee may seek damages that amount to a reasonable royalty. Thus, a patentee may try to prove that it deserves lost profits for each of the infringer's sales. If unable to show it would have made each of those sales, the patentee still receives reasonable royalties on each of the infringer's uncompensated sales. Courts define a reasonable royalty as the amount likely to have come from a hypothetical negotiation between a willing patentee and infringer at the time infringement began.

The best way to prove this hypothetical negotiation amount is to produce evidence of licenses the patentee in fact entered with other parties similarly situated to the infringer. But even if the patentee has not licensed the patent, established royalty rates on comparable patents can ground this hypothetical analysis in economic reality. *Mahurkar v. C.R. Bard, Inc.*, 79 F.3d 1572 (Fed. Cir. 1996). Importantly, however, a hypothetical reasonable royalty may exceed an established royalty in many cases, such as when widespread infringement artificially depressed the value of the license. *Nickson Indus., Inc. v. Rol Mfg. Co.*, 847 F.2d 795 (Fed. Cir. 1988).

Courts often use a multi-factored list—often called the *Georgia-Pacific* factors—to guide the hypothetical negotiation and prevent it from lapsing into unconstrained speculation. These *G-P* factors really present three valuation theories: cash-based, cost-based, and market-based.

The cash-based theory of valuation seeks the cash or rental value of the technology. Several of the *G-P* factors based on licensing values support this theory. For instance, those factors include:

1. The royalties received by the patentee for the licensing of the patent in suit, proving or tending to prove an established royalty.

2. The rates paid by the licensee for the use of other patents comparable to the patent in suit.

6. The effect of selling the patented specialty in promoting sales of other products of the licensee; the existing value of the invention to the licensor as a generator of sales of his non-patented items; and the extent of such derivative or convoyed sales.

The cost-based valuation theory examines the technical advantages of the technology. This theory often turns on the cost to replace the patented technology with the closest substitute (usually the prior art). Thus this theory incorporates at least the following technical *G-P* factor:

> 9. The utility and advantages of the patent property over the old modes or devices, if any, that had been used for working out similar results.

The market-based theory analyses the demand in the marketplace created by the patent's advances over prior art. The market-based factors under *G-P* include:

> 8. The established profitability of the product made under the patent; its commercial success; and its current popularity.
>
> 13. The portion of the realizable profit that should be credited to the invention as distinguished from non-patented elements, the manufacturing process, business risks, or significant features or improvements added by the infringer.

Finally, the *G-P* factors also include some procedural suggestions for setting the proper reasonable royalty:

> 15. The amount that a licensor (such as the patentee) and a licensee (such as the infringer) would have agreed upon (at the time the infringement began) if both had been reasonably and voluntarily trying to reach an agreement; that is, the amount which a prudent licensee—

> who desired, as a business proposition, to obtain a license to manufacture and sell a particular article embodying the patented invention—would have been willing to pay as a royalty and yet be able to make a reasonable profit and which amount would have been acceptable by a prudent patentee who was willing to grant a license.

Georgia-Pacific Corp. v. United States Plywood Corp., 318 F. Supp. 1116, 1120 (S.D.N.Y. 1970), *modified* 446 F.2d 295 (2d Cir. 1971); *see also SmithKline Diagnostics, Inc. v. Helena Labs. Corp.*, 926 F.2d 1161 (Fed. Cir. 1991).

There are no shortcuts to this analysis. A failure to recreate the hypothetical negotiation within the confines of the particular case is fundamentally flawed. *Uniloc USA, Inc. v. Microsoft Corp.*, 632 F.3d 1292 (Fed. Cir. 2011). Moreover, these various valuation theories generally require a combination of technical and economic skill to isolate and evaluate the various influences on royalty rates.

Because a reasonable royalty serves as a floor for the damage award and because lost profits are typically larger than reasonable royalties, patentees often seek to maximize the damage award by splitting it between the two. For example, imagine an evenly divided market of perfect substitutes, with five goods—infringing good A, third-party goods B, C, and D, and patentee good E—each enjoying a 20% market share. Under the market share rule, 25% of the infringing sales would be captured by the patentee, who would thus be entitled to recover lost profits on that portion. The patentee would therefore be entitled to a reasonable royalty on the sales of A comprising the market share captured by goods not made by the patentee: 75%. Assume further that the patentee's profit margin is approximately equal to the infringer's profit margin (which is typically true in a competitive market). In this situation, the size of the award for a reasonable royalty would likely be roughly equivalent to the size of the award for lost profits.

D. THE ENTIRE MARKET VALUE RULE

The "entire market value rule" has two manifestations: convoyed sales and royalty base valuation. Under convoyed sales, as suggested in the *Georgia-Pacific* factors, a patentee may recover lost profits for unpatented components that it would have sold without infringement. To use a simple illustration, if the patented technology were a new kind of tennis racquet frame, the patentee might also seek damages for strings and racquet covers—items sold along with the invention, so long as the demand for the racquet drove the sales of the strings and not *vice versa*.

In *Rite-Hite*, the Federal Circuit explained:

> When a patentee seeks damages on unpatented components sold with a patented apparatus, courts have applied a formulation known as the "entire market value rule" to determine whether such components should be included in the damage computation, whether for reasonable royalty purposes, or for lost profits purposes.

> Early cases invoking the entire market value rule required that for a patentee owning an "improvement patent" to recover damages calculated on sales of a larger machine incorporating that improvement, the patentee was required to show that the entire value of the whole machine, as a marketable article, was "properly and legally attributable" to the patented feature . . . We have held that the entire market value rule permits recovery of damages based on the value of a patentee's entire apparatus containing several features when the patent-related feature is the "basis for customer demand."
>
> The entire market value rule has typically been applied to include in the compensation base unpatented components of a device when the unpatented and patented components are physically part of the same machine. The rule has been extended to allow inclusion of physically separate unpatented components normally sold with the patented components. However, in such cases, the unpatented and patented components together were considered to be components of a single assembly or parts of a complete machine, or they together constituted a functional unit.

Rite-Hite, 56 F.3d at 1549–50. Thus, under the Federal Circuit rule for convoyed sales, the unpatented component must form a functional unit with the patented device. A more economically and legally sound method might consider the foreseeability of the convoyed sale as the Federal Circuit set the test for "but for" profits on unpainted components. Instead the court erected a functionality test that may preclude recovery of many sales that the market would show are genuinely convoyed with the patented goods.

In the tennis racquet illustration, this rule could permit the patentee to recover the profits on strings, because they function as a single unit with the racquet (and the racquet drove sales). The racquet cover, however, might not qualify under the rule because the cover has little to do with striking a tennis ball. As a theoretical matter as this illustration shows, the "functional unit" test seems at odds with the rest of the *Rite-Hite* reasoning that allowed lost profits based on the reasonable expectation that the patentee would have made the sale "but for" infringement. Foreign courts often follow this sounder economic reasoning. *See, e.g., Gerber Garment Tech. Inc. v. Lectra Sys. Ltd.,* [1995] RPC 383.

The entire market value rule also has a wider, and potentially more troublesome, application. It can also operate to expand the royalty base part of the reasonable royalty calculation. Courts have postulated that reasonable royalties are calculated by multiplying the royalty base (generally the covered product) times the royalty rate (the rental value of the technology). *See, e.g., Lucent Techs., Inc. v. Gateway, Inc.,* 580 F.3d 1301, 1339 (Fed. Cir. 2009). Invoking the entire market value rule, a patentee may wish to expand the base to include an entire expensive product even though the invention is confined to a small component, thus inflating the royalty.

To qualify a large product as the royalty base for a patent on a smaller component, the patentee must show that the infringing component creates the demand and the value of the entirety of the larger royalty base. *Uniloc USA, Inc. v. Microsoft Corp.*, 632 F.3d 1292 (Fed. Cir. 2011). In one rare case involving hybrid automobile engines, the patentee was able to make that showing. *Paice LLC v. Toyota Motor Corp.*, 609 F. Supp. 2d 620, 630 (E.D. Tex. 2009).

In a classic case involving the use of the rule to inflate the base, *Cornell Univ. v. Hewlett-Packard Co.*, 609 F. Supp. 2d 279 (N.D.N.Y. 2009), the court determined that the patented feature—i.e., the infringing component—did not create the basis for the customer demand for the entire device with its vast number of non-infringing components. The invention was an important advance that enabled a computer to do multiple calculations in a single clock cycle. Thus, the invention improved a critical part of a computer chip. Cornell wished to use Hewlett-Packard's largest server (a product valued at half a million dollars and used to run entire train systems or defense applications) as the royalty base.

Instead the court used a "smallest salable unit" test to tie the royalty base to the cost of the chip, a tiny fraction of the cost of the large server. *Cornell*, at 283. The Federal Circuit later opined that the entire market value "rule" was really an "exception" for the few times when an invention drives demand for a larger product. *LaserDynamics, Inc. v. Quanta Computer, Inc.*, 694 F.3d 51, 67 (Fed. Cir. 2012). The Circuit also adopted the "smallest salable unit" test for such circumstances. *Id.*

E. MARKING

Even though infringement is a strict liability tort, the statute places a key limitation on recovery for past infringement. In particular, a patentee must provide notice of its patent rights by marking its product. The marking provision, § 287(a), states:

> Patentees, and persons making, offering for sale, or selling within the United States any patented article for or under them, or importing any patented article into the United States, may give notice to the public that the same is patented, either by fixing thereon the word "patent" or the abbreviation "pat.", together with the number of the patent, or by fixing thereon the word 'patent' or the abbreviation 'pat.' together with an address of a posting on the Internet, accessible to the public without charge for accessing the address, that associates the patented article with the number of the patent, or when, from the character of the article, this can not be done, by fixing to it, or to the package wherein one or more of them is contained, a label containing a like notice. In the event of failure so to mark, no damages shall be recovered by the patentee in any action for infringement, except on proof that the infringer was notified of the infringement and continued to infringe thereafter, in which

> event damages may be recovered only for infringement occurring after such notice. Filing of an action for infringement shall constitute such notice.

Oftentimes, a patentee does not itself make, offer for sale, sell, or import a product embodying the invention and instead chooses to license the patent. In such a case, the marking statute still applies—the statute recites "for or under"—and precludes a damage award to the patentee, unless its licensees mark the patented goods. *Amsted Indus. Inc. v. Buckeye Steel Castings Co.*, 24 F.3d 178 (Fed. Cir. 1994).

Without adequate marking, the statute precludes recovery of any damages until actual notice to the infringer. This actual notice requires an affirmative act by the patentee which informs the infringer of the infringement. *Dunlap v. Schofield*, 152 U.S. 244 (1894). This means that the notice cannot merely advise the infringer of the patent's existence or ownership; rather, the patentee must identify the allegedly infringing device with a specific charge of infringement. The focus is on the patentee's actions. It is irrelevant that the infringer knew of the infringement independent of the actual notice from the patentee. While a generalized notification does not suffice, filing an infringement lawsuit satisfies the requirement. In any event, without the constructive notice supplied by marking a patented article with the patent number, the patentee may not recover any damages before giving the infringer actual notice.

A party, however, cannot mark an article without a good-faith belief that the patent actually covers the article. In fact, 35 U.S.C. § 292 allows a private party who has suffered a competitive injury to sue for false marking. Alternatively, the United States may bring an action against entities who mark an article with a patent number "with the intent of counterfeiting or imitating the mark of the patentee, or of deceiving the public." The recent AIA, however, removed from the statute a right for a third party to sue for false marking. America Invents Act, sec. 16, 125 Stat. 329 (2011).

Not all patents claim products or devices, of course. In cases where the patent claims only a method, the patentee has nothing physical or tangible to mark. In such a case, the marking statute does not apply; the patentee may recover damages without supplying actual notice to the infringer. But where the patent claims (and the patentee asserts) both product and process claims, the law has reached varied results. On the one hand, in *American Medical Systems, Inc. v. Medical Engineering Corp.*, 6 F.3d 1523, 1538 (Fed. Cir. 1993), the court reasoned:

> The purpose behind the marking statute is to encourage the patentee to give notice to the public of the patent. The reason that the marking statute does not apply to method claims is that, ordinarily, where the patent claims are directed to only a method or process there is nothing to mark. Where the patent contains both apparatus and method claims, however, to the extent that there is a tangible item to mark

> by which notice of the asserted method claims can be given, a party is obliged to do so if it intends to avail itself of the constructive notice provisions of section 287(a).

On the other hand, in *Hanson v. Alpine Valley Ski Area, Inc.*, 718 F.2d 1075 (Fed. Cir. 1983), and *Crystal Semiconductor Corp. v. TriTech Microelectronics Int'l, Inc.*, 246 F.3d 1336 (Fed. Cir. 2001), the court sustained damages on an unmarked process when the patentee could have marked an apparatus that performed the process. If a patentee does not assert apparatus claims and only asserts method claims (even where the patent contains apparatus and method claims), there is no requirement to mark under § 287(a).

III. WILLFUL INFRINGEMENT: ENHANCED DAMAGES AND ATTORNEY FEES

No matter the size of the compensatory award and no matter whether the patentee establishes it by lost profits, a reasonable royalty, or a combination of both, the statute allows a court to enhance the damages as well as award attorney fees to the prevailing party. Enhanced damages are authorized by § 284:

> [T]he court may increase the damages up to three times the amount found or assessed.

Attorney fees are authorized by § 285:

> The court in exceptional cases may award reasonable attorney fees to the prevailing party.

Under these sections, the court has discretion to treble the damages and to award attorney fees in cases of "willful infringement." Under § 285, the court has additional discretion to award attorney fees in cases of bad faith litigation or inequitable conduct. Nevertheless, willful infringement forms a substantial portion of the case law on enhanced damages.

A. ATTORNEY FEES

Congress enacted the provision allowing prevailing parties to obtain attorney fees awards in 1946. *See* 35 U.S.C. § 70 (1946). Since then courts viewed attorney fees awards not as penalties for losing a patent infringement suit, but rather as only appropriate in extraordinary cases involving bad faith or culpable behavior. Generally court assessed attorney fees awards based on a totality of circumstances. *Octane Fitness, LLC v. ICON Health & Fitness, Inc.*, 572 U.S. 545, 1756 (2014).

In *Brooks Furniture Mfg., Inc. v. Dutailier Int'l, Inc.*, 393 F.3d 1378 (Fed. Cir. 2005), the Federal Circuit raised the bar for fee awards. Under that case, attorney fees were allowed in two scenarios: litigation misconduct, or rare instances when (1) the litigation is brought in subjective bad faith, and (2) the litigation is objectively baseless. *Brooks*, at 1381 (citing *Professional Real Estate Investors v. Columbia Pictures Industries*, 508 U.S. 49, 60–61 (1993)). *Brooks Furniture* also required proof of attorney fees entitlement to meet the standard of clear and convincing evidence. *Id.* at 1382.

In *Octane Fitness*, the Supreme Court rejected *Brooks* on both counts. It criticized the Federal Circuit's attorney fees standard as too "rigid and mechanical" and lacking support in the statutory text. 572 U.S. at 1755. The Court instead gave district courts more discretion—and perhaps less guidance—and explained that an "exceptional" case under § 285 is "simply one that stands out from others" in terms of both substantive litigation positions as well as litigation conduct. *Id.* at 1756. The Court also lowered the evidentiary standard from clear and convincing evidence to a preponderance of evidence.

On the day *Octane Fitness* issued, the Supreme Court also decided *Highmark Inc. v. Allcare Health Mgmt. Sys., Inc.*, 572 U.S. 559 (2014). In *Highmark* the Supreme Court further cemented district courts' discretion to grant attorney fees awards. It rejected the Federal Circuit's *de novo* review standard for attorney fees awards, and instead held that such awards were reviewable for abuse of discretion. The combination of *Octane Fitness* and *Highmark*, in theory, raised the likelihood of successful attorney fees motions.

B. ENHANCED DAMAGES

Two years later in *Halo Electronics, Inc. v. Pulse Electronics, Inc.*, 579 U.S. 93 (2016) (discussed below), the Supreme Court made a similar transformation in enhanced damages under § 284, lowering the standard and giving district courts additional discretion.

In general, much like a reasonable royalty, willfulness requires an assessment of the totality of the circumstances surrounding the infringement. These factors traditionally include:

1. Whether the infringer deliberately copied the ideas or design of another.

2. Whether the infringer, when he knew of the other's patent protection, investigated the scope of the patent and formed a good-faith belief that it was invalid or that it was not infringed.

3. The infringer's behavior as a party to the litigation.

4. The infringer's size and financial condition.

5. The closeness of the case.

6. The duration of the defendant's misconduct.

7. Remedial action by the defendant.

8. The defendant's motivation for harm.

9. Whether the defendant attempted to conceal its misconduct.

See Read Corp. v. Portec, Inc., 970 F.2d 816 (Fed. Cir. 1992). The fact-finder, often the jury, determines willfulness. But even if the jury concludes that the infringer acted willfully, the court retains the discretion to both decline to award enhanced damages and to set the level of the enhancement (up to three times).

The *Read* factors compelled putative infringers to obtain opinion letters to satisfy the duty to avoid infringing another's patent rights. Although providing a steady source of employment, that compulsion became problematic during a trial on infringement. For example, the opinion letter might provide opposing counsel insight into the infringer's litigation strategy, might make the opinion drafter a witness (thus disqualifying her and possibly her firm), might force waiver of the attorney-client privilege, might compel disclosure of the putative infringer's trade secrets, and most importantly might impair the opinion drafter's ability to provide an alleged infringer with a full and frank assessment of the chances of avoiding liability.

To resolve some of these concerns, the Federal Circuit addressed the friction between the attorney-client privilege and the necessity of opinion letters to avoid willful infringement. *See, e.g.*, *Knorr-Bremse Systeme fuer Nutzfahrzeuge Gmbh v. Dana Corp.*, 383 F.3d 1337 (Fed. Cir. 2004). The Patent Act, to some degree, incorporated the Circuit's efforts: "The failure of an infringer to obtain the advice of counsel with respect to any allegedly infringed patent, or the failure of the infringer to present such advice to the court or jury, may not be used to prove that the accused infringer willfully infringed the patent or that the infringer intended to induce infringement of the patent." 35 U.S.C. § 298.

Ultimately the Federal Circuit tried to put an end to the friction with *In re Seagate*, 497 F.3d 1360 (Fed. Cir. 2007) (en banc). *Seagate* caused a sea change in the law of willfulness. Instead of the long-standing duty of due care to avoid infringement, the court substituted a test of objective recklessness for willfulness. While *Seagate* seemed to address well the strategic use of willfulness, the Supreme Court rejected this test in favor of a less "rigid," more "holistic" standard. *See Halo Elecs., Inc. v. Pulse Elecs., Inc.*, 579 U.S. 93 (2016).

In *Halo*, the Court made three re-adjustments to the willfulness standard. First, it rejected the objective recklessness element of *Seagate*, and instead held that willfulness under § 284 hinges on the *subjective* knowledge of the infringer at the time of infringement. The Supreme Court here expressed concern that the objective recklessness requirement had the unintended consequence of giving a pass to purposeful infringers simply because of their trial attorneys' ability to make convincing non-infringement arguments *ex post facto*. Second, it replaced the Federal Circuit's clear-and-convincing standard of proof with the preponderance-of-evidence standard, noting that § 284 did not explicitly require a heightened evidentiary burden. Finally, it rejected the Federal Circuit's tri-partite review standard, under which (1) objective recklessness was reviewed *de novo*; (2) subjective knowledge was reviewed for substantial evidence; and (3) the ultimate decision on enhanced damages was reviewed for an abuse of discretion. Instead the Supreme Court adopted the abuse of discretion standard alone for § 285 enhanced damages determinations ensuring that district court decisions on willfulness can rarely be overturned on appeal.

IV. INTERNATIONAL REMEDIES

Preliminary and permanent injunctions are typically available in legal regimes outside the United States. In fact, in some jurisdictions—particularly those emanating from a civil law tradition—injunctions often are the sole practical remedy available. Preliminary injunctions take many forms. Some, such as Italian precautionary measures and Austrian interim injunctions, are roughly analogous to United States preliminary injunctions. Others are different, such as *ex parte* orders like the British "Anton Piller" order and the French saisie-contrefaçon. Such orders do not aim to allow patentees to confiscate infringing technologies, but are in a sense a form of discovery, allowing patentees to establish the origin and extent of the infringement.

The effectiveness of such proceedings varies considerably. In Japan, a patentee's application for a preliminary injunction occurs in a separate proceeding from the primary lawsuit, although the same judges may decide both matters. Because the duration of the preliminary injunction suit may not be considerably shorter than that of the primary suit, experienced litigants often do not seek a preliminary injunction at all. In contrast, the most potent preliminary measure is the Dutch *kort geding*, or short proceeding, which typically only lasts weeks between the initiation of the proceeding and written opinion.

Aside from equitable relief, foreign jurisdictions also award damages to compensate for infringement, moving towards a greater acceptance of a reconstruction of the but-for world, similar to the United States methodologies. *See Gerber Garment Tech. Inc. v. Lectra Sys. Ltd.*, [1995] RPC 383. In Japan, for example, remedies such as lost profits are now available in contrast to the historically limited monetary relief. China, which for years relied almost exclusively on statutory damages that have no relation to the value of the technology, has begun to seek compensatory remedies, including disgorgement of infringer's profits. *See Uncle Martian case.* Similarly, the scope and size of potential damage awards in Germany has seemed to increase, allowing damages to be determined under more generous unfair competition principles. In another recent and consequential development, the UK Supreme Court has decided that it had the authority to set a global fair, reasonable, and non-discriminatory (FRAND) license rate for standard-essential patents—not just a rate that applies to the geographic territory within its jurisdiction. *Unwired Planet Int'l Ltd. v. Huawei Techs. (UK) Co. Ltd.* [2020] UKSC 37. It remains to be seen whether and to what extent other courts around the world choose exercise the same power. For now, the UK has become a go-to forum for obtaining a world-wide rate for standard-essential patents.

CHAPTER 17

INTERNATIONAL PATENT LAW

I. MAJOR INTERNATIONAL AGREEMENTS

This Nutshell focuses primarily on the patent laws of the United States, but draws upon experience of other national patent systems as well. This comparative approach applies with particular force for patents because technology, of course, knows no borders. Adequate protection for inventions in an international market will require protection in many different nations. Normally the reach of patent law in each individual nation extends only to acts carried out in the territory of that state. As a general rule each nation has its own laws and institutions to enforce patents. This general rule, however, turns out to be only approximately true as further explained in Chapter 14.

To obtain adequate protection for inventions in a global market, inventors must seek patent protection beyond their own national boundaries. Due to different filing requirements for patent applications including critical timing issues, protection in many nations presents significant burdens. The international community drafted the first great commercial treaty, now known colloquially as the Paris Convention, to alleviate this burden. The latest version of this treaty occurred in Stockholm in 1967. The World Intellectual Property Organization (WIPO) explains the intricacies of this international treaty on its website: https://www.wipo.int/treaties/en/ip/paris/.

A. PARIS CONVENTION

The Paris Convention, administered by WIPO, contains three notable principles that bind all signatories: national treatment; patent independence; and international priority. Because over 150 countries are now signatories to the Paris Convention, these principles are nearly universal. The first, national treatment, requires that a signatory refrain from discriminating against foreign inventors. Foreign inventors may not be treated any different than domestic inventors. Paris Convention, Art. 2.

Patent independence, the second principle, ensures that each patent functions independent of its foreign counterparts. Art. 4bis. For example, a domestic patent expires on its own terms without regard to the status of counterpart patents in other nations, thus permitting a patentee to allow individual patents to lapse or expire without relinquishing counterpart patent rights in other jurisdictions. At the same time, however, the independence principle requires an inventor to enforce each patent individually in each country, which raises the specter of inconsistent judgments of claim scope and validity.

Finally, the most important principle, international priority, protects an inventor's priority dates when filing patents in different nations. Art 4.

The first three paragraphs of Article 4 create this protection:

> A.—
>
> (1) Any person who has duly filed an application for a patent, or for the registration of a utility model, or of an industrial design, or of a trademark, in one of the countries of the Union, or his successor in title, shall enjoy, for the purpose of filing in the other countries, a right of priority during the periods hereinafter fixed.
>
> (2) Any filing that is equivalent to a regular national filing under the domestic legislation of any country of the Union or under bilateral or multilateral treaties concluded between countries of the Union shall be recognized as giving rise to the right of priority. . .
>
> B.—
>
> Consequently, any subsequent filing in any of the other countries of the Union before the expiration of the periods referred to above shall not be invalidated by reason of any acts accomplished in the interval . . .
>
> C.—
>
> (1) The periods of priority referred to above shall be twelve months for patents and utility models, and six months for industrial designs and trademarks.

> (2) These periods shall start from the date of filing of the first application; the day of filing shall not be included in the period. . . .

In its most fundamental aspect, the Paris Convention permits an inventor to secure a priority date by filing an application in any member country (typically, the inventor's home country). With that initial filing, the inventor then has up to one year to file an application on the same subject matter in any other member country. If filed in any member country within the year, the initial filing date becomes the effective filing date for priority. An applicant for a United States patent may take advantage of this procedure, which is authorized by Article 4 of the Paris Convention, under 35 U.S.C. § 119, which states:

> (a) An application for patent for an invention filed in this country by any person who has, or whose legal representatives or assigns have, previously regularly filed an application for a patent for the same invention in a foreign country which affords similar privileges in the case of applications filed in the United States or to citizens of the United States, or in a WTO member country, *shall have the same effect* as the same application would have if filed in this country on the date on which the application for patent for the same invention was first filed in such foreign country, if the application in this country is filed within twelve months from the earliest date on which such foreign application was filed.

Section 119 requires a few critical elements: (1) both the foreign and domestic applications must have a common owner; (2) both the foreign and domestic applications must claim the same invention; (3) the foreign application must be for a patent; (4) the foreign application must have been in a country that provides reciprocal rights to United States' citizens or in a country that is a WTO member; (5) the domestic filing must come within one year of the foreign filing; and (6) the statutory bars under first-to-invent's § 102(b) remain in effect.

Of these, most problems involve verifying that the foreign application describes the same invention claimed in the domestic application. For example, in *In re Gosteli*, 872 F.2d 1008 (Fed. Cir. 1989), the court refused to grant priority under § 119 to a patent application filed in Luxembourg. The United States application was rejected in light of a patent filed in the United States after the Luxembourg application. This prior art anticipated the claimed genus because it disclosed a species within that scope. If the applicant could claim priority back to its Luxembourg filing, of course, the reference would not be prior art. Unfortunately when transferring the Luxembourg application to the United States, the applicant supplemented the United States application with additional disclosure not appearing in the prior foreign application. Thus, the United States application claimed that broader subject matter or new matter with respect to the Luxembourg filing.

The court first explained that the written description requirement under § 112, which is described in Chapter 9, applied to a claim to priority under § 119, much like a claim to a priority of a domestic application under § 120. Under that new matter doctrine, the foreign application must evince possession of the subject matter claimed in the domestic application. Because the Luxembourg filing did not sufficiently describe the claimed genus, the broad claims could not claim priority back to the foreign filing and thus were invalid for anticipation.

Gosteli was decided in 1989. The court based its judgment on the principle that the Paris Convention only protects the same invention taught in the foreign application. "Same Invention," G2/98, 2001 Official Journal EPO 413. However, since 1995 foreign acts themselves can be used to show prior invention by the inventor, and hence arguably the intermediate reference in *Gosteli* could have been eliminated using a Rule 131 affidavit antedating the reference. *See* Chapter 7.

Notably, claiming priority to a foreign application under § 119 to avoid an intervening reference does not alter the date of a domestic patent for prior art purposes. Under the pre-Leahy-Smith America Invents Act (AIA) regime, the date of a domestic patent for prior art was the domestic filing date, not the foreign priority date. *In re Hilmer*, 359 F.2d 859 (CCPA 1966); *In re Hilmer*, 424 F.2d 1108 (CCPA 1970). In *Hilmer*, the PTO conducted an interference between Hilmer and Habicht over their claims to the same invention. Because of an earlier filing date in the U.S., Habicht prevailed. Hilmer did not give up, but drafted a new set of claims that were slightly different from the interference count. The PTO examiner imposed a rejection based on Habicht, and Hilmer responded that its priority date related back to a prior German filing that antedated the Habicht filing in the U.S. The PTO sought to rely on Habicht's filing date in Switzerland that was prior to Hilmer's German filing.

The Court of Customs and Patent Appeals, however, denied the PTO that earlier filing date in Switzerland as the basis for the prior art. Although § 119 purports to give the foreign filing the "same effect" as a domestic filing, the CCPA declared that this provision is only a defensive provision, meaning it only permits a claim of priority to preserve the validity of a claimed invention. The CCPA prevented the PTO from using § 119 to give the Habicht reference the offensive capability to act as prior art beyond its U.S. filing date. The CCPA relied on the language of first-to-invent's § 102(e) that limited this prior art category to filings "in the United States."

This anomaly has been eliminated by the AIA's revisions to § 102. The AIA's § 102(a)(2) looks to the "effective filing date" of a potential prior art reference. And as defined in § 100(i), the earliest "effective filing date" expressly includes foreign priority documents and priority claims filed under § 119, among others:

> (1) The term 'effective filing date' for a claimed invention in a patent or application for patent means—

(A) if subparagraph (B) does not apply, the actual filing date of the patent or the application for the patent containing a claim to the invention; or

(B) the filing date of the earliest application for which the patent or application is entitled, as to such invention, to a right of priority under section 119, 365(a), 365(b), 386(a), or 386(b) or to the benefit of an earlier filing date under section 120, 121, 365(c), or 386(c).

The patent laws of most other countries permit rejection of an application on the basis of another unpublished application from an earlier Paris Convention application. However, such unpublished applications can usually only apply for novelty rejections, not obviousness or inventive step rejections.

B. PATENT COOPERATION TREATY

By its own terms, the Paris Convention is not an exclusive agreement. In fact, the PCT complements the Paris Convention. Without the PCT, international applicants would have to file an application in each separate country within a year of their first national filing. With the PCT in place, those applicants can instead file a single PCT application. The PCT filing, in turn, designates additional nations where the applicant intends to seek patent rights. At its most basic, the PCT defers nation-by-nation prosecution—also known as entry into the "national phase"—until many months after the priority date. With these additional months, a patent applicant can defer the costs of international prosecution, which can be substantial with translation and foreign counsel fees.

To take advantage of the fee-deferring and time-shifting effect, an applicant files a PCT application with a PCT "Receiving Office." The application automatically publishes 18 months after the earliest priority date, which may be the filing date of an application to which the PCT application claims priority. The Receiving Office also automatically performs a prior art search and issues a perfunctory search report without substantive examination. A PCT applicant, however, may request (for an additional fee) a preliminary examination of the claims. This request is also called a "demand" for preliminary examination. Even though this may superficially seem like substantive examination, the preliminary examination report is in fact a non-binding opinion on the patentability of the claimed invention.

In essence, the PCT facilitates a patent filing system, not a patent granting system. The PCT does not create an "international patent" of any kind. To get patents, applicants still need to apply to each national office. Under the Paris Convention alone, a patent applicant would need to file those multiple applications in other nations within 12 months of the first filing. That process would entail multiple different formality requirements, translations, amendment and publication procedures, and fees. This timeline illustrates the traditional Paris Convention filing system:

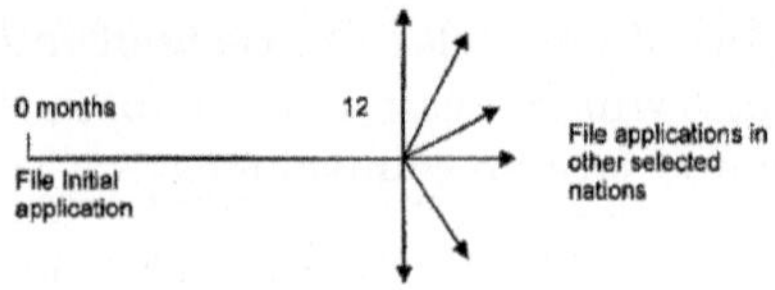

Under the PCT system, the applicant can file a single international application which can then undergo a single preliminary examination. This filing process permits the applicant to postpone entry into multiple nations for up to 30 months from the original filing. The following illustration shows the contrast from the traditional Paris Convention system and highlights the advantages of the PCT filing system. As this shows, the applicant can amend a single application in response to prior art and likely streamline the process of acquiring a patent from the various national patent offices at the end of 30 months:

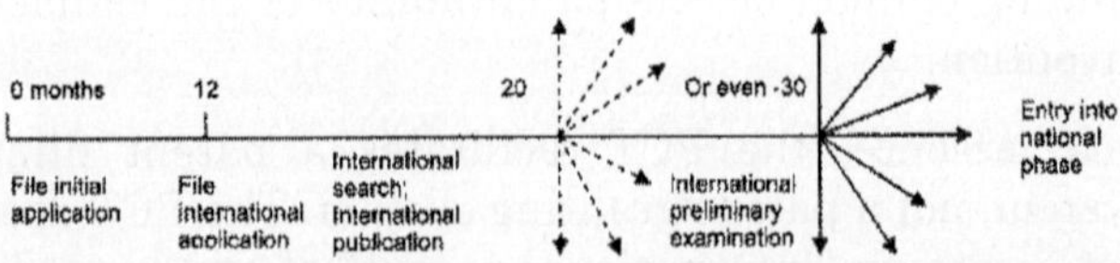

In sum, the PCT can reduce the burden and expense of seeking worldwide protection for an invention. In the long run, the PCT affords extra time beyond the 12 months granted by the Paris Convention. This additional delay in prosecution often gives time for an accurate evaluation of the value of the patent rights eventually obtained. The extra time may also allow applicants to identify potential licensees or other parties interested in the technology before incurring filing fees and costs at the national phase.

C. REGIONAL AGREEMENTS

1. European Patent Convention and the European Union

In Europe, a patent applicant has the option of filing a single application for multinational rights and prosecuting that single application in pursuit of a single patent under the European Patent Convention (EPC). The EPC establishes a single office—the European Patent Office (EPO)—for substantive examination and also creates a single period of opposition (9 months) before an application matures into a patent. The inventor, however, must enforce the single EPC patent on a country-by-country basis. Hence, the process of obtaining a patent in Europe is complex. Each country that has joined the EPC maintains its own local patent system, but also acknowledges patents obtained through the EPO.

Members of the European Union have retained the power to make patent law for themselves subject to the powers granted to European Union institutions to create patent laws for the entire Union. Thus, when the EPO institutions reach a consensus, those rules bind the signatories. Under this procedure, the Union created the biotechnology directive, an order from the European Commission to each of the member states to conform their patent law to those requirements. The European Commission itself enforces the directive to ensure that each signatory complies. The Commission has attempted to create a uniform rule for software patents, but has not as yet been able to enact either a software directive or regulation. The current status of the efforts of the Commission in the field of patents appears on its industrial property website: https://ec.europa.eu/growth/industry/strategy/intellectual-property_en.

Europe is also on the brink of achieving an important break-through in patent enforcement. Following to a degree the experience of the U.S. with the creation of the Federal Circuit, the European Union has agreed to establish a Unified Patent Court (UPC). The new UPC will receive appeals from national courts which will conduct patent trials. Those appeals will go to either London (for chemical and bio-pharmaceutical cases), Paris (for electronics and related technology) or Munich (for mechanical and other technology).

The UPC is expected to be established in late 2022 or early 2023, according to recent reports. The UPC will include a Court of First Instance and a Court of Appeal. The Court of First Instance will have a central division (located in Paris but having sections in London and Munich), as well as local and regional divisions. A contracting state can set up its own local divisions, or it may team up with a neighbor and establish a regional division spanning both countries.

Establishing a Europe-wide court naturally raises disagreements on what language that will be used. The UPC Agreement of 2012 recites rules that reflect the signatories' compromises on language. In general, local Courts of First Instance may use an official language of the signatory country hosting the proceeding. Art. 49(1) (available at https://www.unified-patent-court.org/sites/default/files/upc-agreement.pdf). In the case of a regional division spanning multiple countries, the countries within the region can together designate an official language for the region. As a default, a Court of First Impression may use English, French, or German—the three official languages of the European Patent Office. Art. 49(2). As yet another choice, it can use the language in which the patent was granted, so long as the panel of judges approves. Art. 49(3). In turn, the Court of Appeal will generally use the language of used by the Court of First Instance. Art. 50(1).

2. TRIPS and Bilateral Free Trade Agreements

The World Trade Organization assumed a leadership role in harmonizing intellectual property rights under its TRIPS—Trade-Related Aspects of Intellectual Property—agreement. TRIPS harmonizes international regimes by establishing minimum legal standards for patentable subject matter, patentability, infringement, enforcement, patent terms, compulsory licensing, and more. In one important respect, TRIPS is not just an ordinary treaty that relies on each signatory to implement and enforce its provisions. Instead the TRIPS agreement includes a method for determining violations and an enforcement system to impose trade sanctions on any country found to violate its provisions. This agreement revolutionized the treatment of intellectual property in signatory countries, particularly those countries with weak protections for intellectual property. For example, to comply with the terms of this agreement, India enacted laws that made pharmaceutical compositions eligible for patenting.

TRIPS is a landmark treaty for many reasons, but one section is of particular importance. Part III of the agreement sets minimum standards for enforcement of the rights of individual owners of intellectual property. This unique part requires nations to provide "fair and equitable" enforcement procedures, TRIPS, Art. 41.2. The agreement requires decisions "preferably in writing" and "without undue delay." TRIPS Art. 41.3. The agreement also mandates some form of discovery. In fact, Article 43 empowers judges to "order that this evidence be provided by the opposing party, subject to . . . protection of confidential information." TRIPS, Art. 43.1. The agreement also provides injunctions, TRIPS, Art. 44, adequate damages, TRIPS Art. 45, and powers to seize goods to prevent infringing goods from entering the market or to preserve evidence. TRIPS, Art. 50. Thus, TRIPS has set standards for the performance of judicial officers in nations wishing to join the WTO.

TRIPS also set minimum standards for patent protection in WTO nations. Thus, those nations must offer patents, "whether products or processes, in all fields of technology." TRIPS, Art. 27.1. Article 27 also establishes three substantive criteria for patentability: novelty, inventive step (or obviousness), and industrial application (or utility).

Another important provision of TRIPS governs compulsory licensing. Compulsory licensing is the disfavored process wherein a government forces a patent owner to license its technology. Article 31 of TRIPS limits that practice. Perhaps the most important limit is that a patent owner has a right to "adequate compensation" for any technology subject to the government-compelled license. TRIPS, Art. 31(h).

Many nations have responded to the challenges of enforcing IP rights by creating special courts with the expertise to handle these complex adjudications. TRIPS, by its terms, does not require these special courts. TRIPS, Art. 41.5. Nonetheless Japan, China, Thailand, Korea, and many European nations (e.g., U.K., Germany), to name just a few, have created special IP courts. Some of these nations, like Japan and China, have special IP courts at both the trial and appellate levels. Others, like the U.K., have special IP courts only at the trial level. Then, of course, the U.S. is the prime example of a system with judges having IP expertise only at the appellate phase. These courts of expertise testify to the importance of intellectual property in the modern world economy.

In addition to the landmark multinational TRIPS agreement, numerous free trade agreements (often bilateral agreements between the U.S. and Jordan or Korea or another nation) contain provisions ensuring adequate patent protections. Some of these treaties go beyond TRIPS to provide "TRIPS plus" requirements. Again, these treaties encourage compliance with the threat of trade sanctions for violations.

II. INTERNATIONAL ENFORCEMENT

Patents are generally territorial, meaning each state enforces its own patents in its own territory. However, occasionally the patent laws of one state take into account activities in another state. For example courts in both the U.S. and the U.K. have enforced patents against systems that used computers located in another state. *NTP, Inc. v. Research In Motion, Ltd.*, 418 F.3d 1282 (Fed. Cir. 2005); *Menashe Bus. Mercantile Ltd. v. William Hill Org. Ltd*, [2003] 1 All E.R. 279. Moreover as discussed in Chapter 14, the U.S. has a special provision that covers some foreign acts, 35 U.S.C. § 271(f).

Finally, to streamline the process of enforcing patents in several nations, litigants have occasionally asked a court in one nation to consider a claim of patent infringement that took place in another state. That request asks the court to apply under conflict of law principles the law of the nation in which the infringement occurred. In the United States, for instance, the Federal Circuit has declined invitations to use supplemental jurisdiction to consider foreign infringement under foreign law. *Mars Inc. v. Kabushiki-Kaisha Nippon Conlux*, 24 F.3d 1368 (Fed. Cir. 1994); *Voda v. Cordis Corp.*, 476 F.3d 887 (Fed. Cir. 2007).

CHAPTER 18
DESIGN PATENTS

I. INTRODUCTION

Design patents protect ornamental features on a functional product. Because protective only of shapes, configurations, and visual appearance, designs were once widely regarded as second-class in the U.S. patent system. Then the market began to illustrate that attractive features often sell a product as well as its technical advantages. Some markets, like furniture or jewelry, recognized the value of designs ahead of other markets, like high-end electronics. As computers began to compete for market share, leading producers recognized that vital graphic user interfaces (GUIs) were more associated with appearance than functionality.

Design protection matured into a vital form of intellectual property with the recognition of its value in high-stakes litigation. Most importantly, in 2012, Apple won a $1 billion jury verdict against Samsung for design patent infringement—one of the largest patent verdicts in history. *See Apple Inc. v. Samsung Elecs. Co.*, 735 F.3d 1352, 1355 (Fed. Cir. 2013) (mentioning that the award was subsequently reduced).

The market also came to realize that design patents have several advantages for market protection. In the first place, they are inexpensive and generally easy to obtain. Unlike copyright infringement, proving design patent infringement does not require a showing that the defendant accessed and copied the claimed design. And unlike trademark infringement, design infringement does not require proving consumer confusion or "secondary meaning" (generally, proof that the mark denotes a source in trademark law parlance). In sum, designs have become an essential element of a comprehensive product and market protection strategy.

II. CLAIMING A DESIGN

Unlike a utility patent, a design patent claims a "new, original and ornamental design for an article of manufacture." 35 U.S.C. § 171. Design patents can relate to almost any product with visual appeal—automobile parts, toys, clothing, electronics, office supplies, computer icons, footwear, and even multi-colored toothpaste. For example, the first U.S. design patent (issued in 1842) covered a font design.

Design patent specifications consist primarily of drawings that depict the shape or surface decoration of a particular product. A design patent application, by rule, only has a single claim (37 C.F.R. § 1.153). This practical rule suggests that careful claiming will seek protection of distinct features as well as a product's overall appearance. Designs on related articles remain distinct (and the subject of a separate application) if they have different shapes and appearances. For example, two lamps with different decorative surface depictions must be claimed separately. On the other hand, if the two lamps have only minimal configuration differences, they may qualify as a single design concept and appear in a single application.

While an application may include a preamble (usually denoting the owner) or title (a few words naming the product), the primary part of the design patent application is its drawings. Unlike a utility application, where the claim sets forth the scope of the invention in a lengthy single written sentence, the design "claim" is a set of drawings. To capture the overall visual appearance of the design, the "description" generally includes multiple drawings from different angles—front, side, top, bottom and more.

An applicant may claim a design as an entire article, as only a part of an article, or as only a surface ornamentation on an article. The key to these different claiming forms are the broken lines. The broken lines in a design drawing are not claimed and have no legal importance except to supply the context and placement of the claimed ornamental feature. Thus, a design on a mere surface ornamentation must show its attachment to an article with the article shown in broken lines.

To illustrate these rules, the *Apple v. Samsung* case serves an excellent example. Apple's patent claimed distinct features as well as its overall iPhone design. Thus, Samsung could not rely on the fact that its product was different from broken-line features shown in Apple's patent. The solid claimed lines were the same and showed Samsung's infringement:

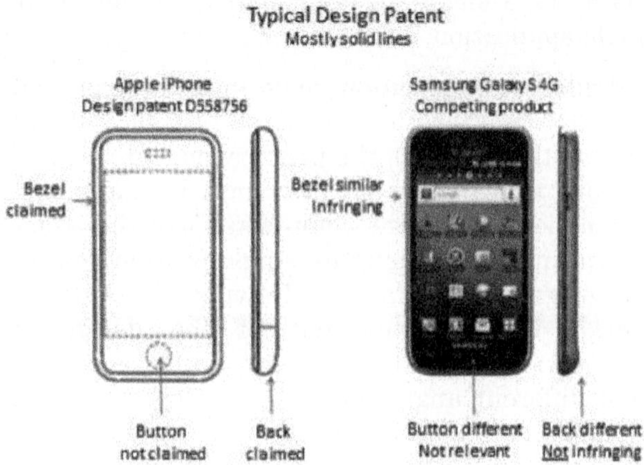

III. VALIDITY

At the outset, a design patent does not protect utility. After all, a "utility patent" protects the uses and functions of a product. *See* 35 U.S.C. § 101. A "design patent," on the other hand protects the way the appearance of a product, the ways it looks, not works. *See* 35 U.S.C. § 171. An applicant can get both utility and design patents on the same product if it possesses both inventive utility as well as ornamentally. At the same time, a product's function primarily dictates its design, that article lacks ornamentality and is not proper statutory subject matter under 35 U.S.C. § 171.

Like a utility patent, design patents are subject to validity challenges. *High Point Design LLC v. Buyers Direct, Inc.*, 730 F.3d 1301 (Fed. Cir. 1301), illustrates the two primary validity issues for designs—obviousness and functionality. Buyer's Direct, Inc. ("BDI") obtained the '183 design patent on slippers that it marketed as Snoozies®.

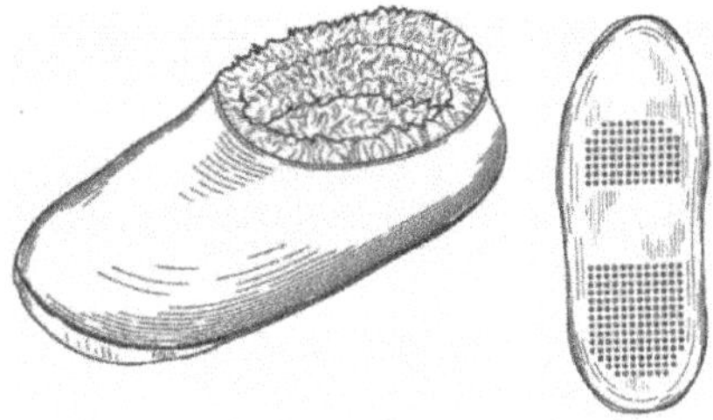

FIG. 1 FIG. 7

BDI's competitor High Point sold similar slippers called the Fuzzy Babba® slippers. During litigation, High Point argued the '183 patent was obvious in light of prior art slippers made by Woolrich (an example is shown below).

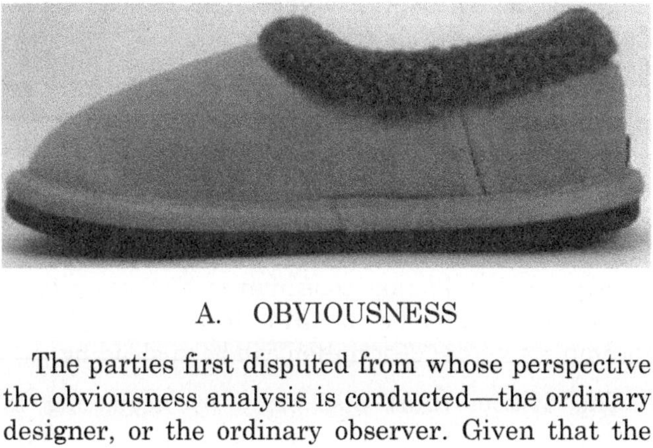

A. OBVIOUSNESS

The parties first disputed from whose perspective the obviousness analysis is conducted—the ordinary designer, or the ordinary observer. Given that the ordinary designer would be expected to have more familiarity with the design choices and greater attention to detail, using the ordinary designer may tend to make it more difficult to prove obviousness. The Federal Circuit concluded that obviousness is determined from the vantage point of the ordinary designer.

The court then reviewed the district court's two-step obviousness analysis under *Durling v. Spectrum Furniture Co.*, 101 F.3d 100, 103 (Fed. Cir. 1996). Under *Durling*, the court must first find a single reference whose design characteristics are basically the same as the claimed design. This step itself has two sub-steps: (i) discern the correct visual impression created by the patented design as a whole, and (ii) determine whether there is a single reference that creates "basically the same" visual impression. Second, once the primary reference is found, other references may be used to modify it to create a design that has the same overall visual appearance as the claimed design.

The Federal Circuit held that the district court erred in its *Durling* analysis in several respects. First, it erred in its translation of the pictorial design into a verbal description. "On remand," the court explained, "the district court should add sufficient detail to its verbal description of the claimed design to evoke a visual image consonant with that design." *High Point*, 730 F.3d at 1314. In other words, an incomplete verbal description can be misleading.

The district court also erred by neglecting to perform a side-by-side comparison and fully articulate its reasoning on whether any single prior art reference created "basically the same" visual impression as the claimed design. The Federal Circuit expressed strong doubts that summary judgment was appropriate in this case, and suggested that the issue should instead go to trial: "[T]here appear to be genuine issues of material fact as to whether the Woolrich Prior Art are, in fact, proper primary references." *Id.*

The district made a third error by glossing over BDI's proffered evidence of secondary considerations of non-obviousness, including evidence of commercial success and copying. Evidence of secondary considerations in design patent cases "must always when present be considered en route to a determination of obviousness." *Id.* at 1315. With each of the above corrections to the district court's obviousness decision, the Federal Circuit remanded to the district court.

B. FUNCTIONALITY

The court in *High Point* also addressed the separate validity issue of functionality. A design patent is invalid if the claimed design is "primarily functional." Functionality has a high standard—the claimed design must be "dictated by" the utilitarian purpose of the article. Generally speaking, therefore, if any artistic skill was used in making the design, the functionality doctrine should not bar patentability.

Several factors are used to determine whether a claimed design is "dictated by function":

1. Whether the protected design represents the best design;

2. Whether alternative designs would adversely affect the utility of the specified article;

3. Whether there are any concomitant utility patents;

4. Whether the advertising touts particular features of the design as having specific utility; and

5. Whether there are any elements in the design or an overall appearance clearly not dictated by function.

Id. In this case, the trial court applied the wrong test for functionality: it overlooked whether the claimed design was "dictated by function," and instead wrongly considered whether the primary design features *can perform functions*.

For example, the fact that the slipper "covers the whole foot" does not mean the design is purely functional—and in fact it says nothing about what design options were available and selected. Likewise, the fact that the claimed slippers had a fuzzy interior did not support the district court's finding that the precise type of fuzzy interior chosen by the inventor was dictated by function. The variety and number of ways to perform a specific function thus can inform the determination of whether a design is "primarily functional."

IV. INFRINGEMENT

In 2008, the Federal Circuit clarified the test for design patent infringement in *Egyptian Goddess, Inc. v. Swisa, Inc.*, 543 F.3d 665 (Fed. Cir. 2008). In particular, the court repudiated its earlier "point of novelty" infringement test. Under that test, an accused product did not infringe unless it incorporated the so-called the "points of novelty" that distinguished the patented design from prior art designs. Instead the court reestablished the "ordinary observer" test as the standard for infringement.

Egyptian Goddess owned the '389 design patent covering a nail buffer in the shape of a rectangular tube. The claimed design had buffer surfaces on only *three* out of four sides. In contrast, the defendant, Swisa, sold a similar-looking, four-sided buffer, but which included buffer surfaces on *all four* sides.

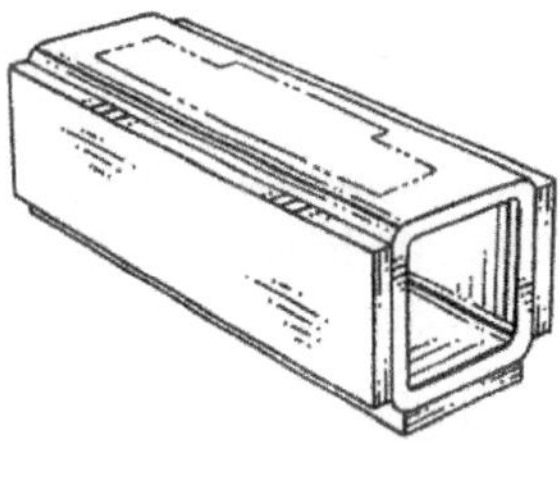

The district court granted summary judgment of non-infringement. Citing Federal Circuit precedent, it explained that design patent infringement requires both (1) substantial similarity of the designs in the eyes of an ordinary observer ("ordinary observer"

test), and (2) that the accused design contain substantially the same points of novelty that distinguished the patent from the prior art ("point of novelty" test).

On the point of novelty prong, the district court compared the '389 patent design to a prior art nail buffer resembling a triangular tube with buffer surfaces on each of three sides. The point of novelty, the court concluded, was thus the fourth bare side which transformed the '389 patent design from a triangular tube to a rectangular tube. And because Swisa's buffer lacked the fourth bare side—but instead had a fourth buffer side—the "point of novelty" requirement was not met.

The Federal Circuit questioned the soundness of the "point of novelty" test. The legal starting point, it explained, is *Gorham v. White*, 14 Wall. 511, 529 (1871), in which the Supreme Court first articulated the standard for design patent infringement:

> [I]f, in the eye of an ordinary observer, giving such attention as a purchaser usually gives, two designs are substantially the same, if the resemblance is such as to deceive such an observer, inducing him to purchase one supposing it to be the other, the first one patented is infringed by other.

Importantly, the Supreme Court's test made no mention of so-called "points of novelty"; rather it only formulated what became called the "ordinary observer" test (corresponding to the first prong of the

Federal Circuit's pre-*Eqyptian Goddess* infringement standard).

Over 100 years after *Gorham*, the point-of-novelty test made its first appearance in Federal Circuit jurisprudence in *Litton Systems, Inc. v. Whirlpool Corp.*, 728 F.2d 1423 (Fed. Cir. 1984). In *Litton*, the Federal Circuit relied on a then-40-year-old 8th Circuit case to hold that similarity under the ordinary observer test was not enough to establish patent infringement. Instead, "no matter how similar two items look, the accused device must appropriate the novelty in the patented device which distinguishes it from the prior art." *Litton*, at 1444 (citing *Sears, Roebuck & Co. v. Talge*, 140 F.2d 395, 396 (8th Cir. 1944)). The point-of-novelty test gained acceptance following *Litton*. But it was always unclear whether the point-of-novelty test was a separate test from the ordinary observer test or whether the two tests were actually conjunctive prongs of a single test.

Compounding the confusion was the difficulty of applying the point-of-novelty test. A more novel design often encompassed more points of novelty. In such cases, the infringement determination inevitably became a morass of arguments about which new feature was the true, or most important, point of novelty. This practice often resulted in assigning exaggerated importance to small differences between the claimed design and the accused design—and tended to discourage comparing the designs based on their overall visual impression.

The Federal Circuit offered a unique solution to the confusion:

> We think, however, that *Litton* and the predecessor cases on which it relied are more properly read as applying a version of the ordinary observer test in which the ordinary observer is deemed to view the differences between the patented design and the accused product in the context of the prior art.

Egyptian Goddess, 543 F.3d at 676. It thus clarified that the ordinary observer test must be applied through the eyes of an observer who is familiar with the prior art.

In practice, *Egyptian Goddess* has led courts to use a three-way comparison to decide infringement—namely between the most pertinent prior art, the claimed design, and the accused product. This comparison is a useful tool to frame the issue correctly and ascertain whether an accused design is truly a "copy" of the patented design.

It may help to consider an example. Hypothetically a design patent could cover the ornamental design of an electric toothbrush. In this hypothetical, (i) the prior art consists only of conventional, non-electric toothbrushes with thin, plastic handles, and (ii) the accused product is an electric toothbrush largely resembling the claimed design. In this case, infringement seems likely because the accused product is much closer to the claimed design than the prior art.

Using the same example, now assume that the prior art consisted of numerous electric toothbrushes of all shapes and sizes—many of which closely resemble the claimed design. Because the accused product now resembles the prior art as well as the claimed design, the question becomes more complicated. The likelihood of infringement has declined. The inquiry now focuses on minor differences between the designs—and the products' "overall" appearances may not be viewed as substantially similar in context of the prior art.

In *Arminak and Associates, Inc. v. Saint-Gobain Calmar, Inc.*, 501 F.3d 1314 (Fed. Cir. 2007), the court took a closer look at who is the ordinary observer—a retail customer at the point of sale, or rather an industrial or commercial buyer in the middle of the distribution chain. Arminak owned two patents on ornamental designs for "trigger shrouds" for household cleaning solution spray bottles.

FIG. 1

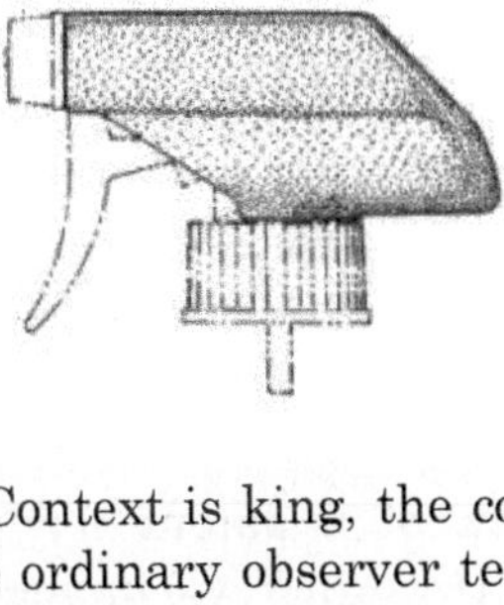

FIG. 1

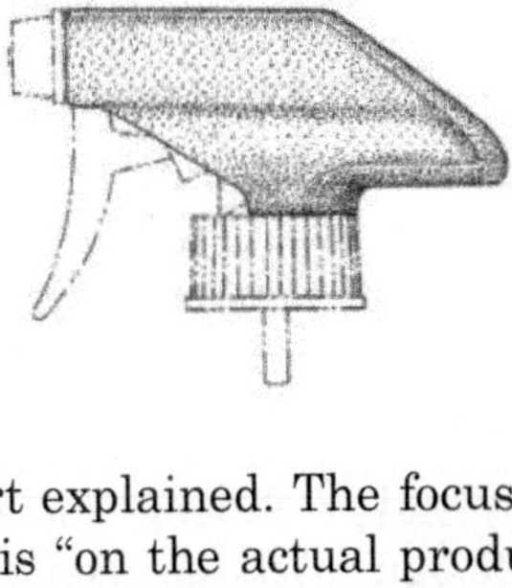

Context is king, the court explained. The focus of the ordinary observer test is "on the actual product that is presented for purchase, and the ordinary purchase of *that* product." *Arminak*, at 1322 (quotations and citations omitted) (emphasis in original). Prior cases thus revealed that an ordinary observer could be anyone among a long list of people: visitors to trade shows, truck drivers and truck fleet operators, commercial purchasers of lingerie hangers, and medical equipment distributors. The ordinary purchaser was not always the "end-user."

The Court held that the ordinary observer, under the facts of *Arminak*, was the commercial buyer in the chain of distribution. These companies bought individual components of bottles—caps, spray tubes, labels, trigger sprayer, and liquid—and assembled them for sale to retailers. Unfortunately for Arminak, the patent owner, commercial buyers were highly attentive to the features of the trigger shrouds to ensure that the right trigger shrouds were attached to the right bottles. They "wouldn't be fooled for a second" by the accused infringing shrouds. Identifying the correct "ordinary observer" therefore was an important step in affirming the district court's conclusion of non-infringement.

V. DAMAGES

The types of damages available for design patent infringement include lost profits, reasonable royalty, and—the most attractive—infringer's profits. 35 U.S.C. § 289 provides for the infringer's profits remedy:

> Whoever during the term of a patent for a design, without license of the owner, (1) applies the patented design, or any colorable imitation

> thereof, to any article of manufacture for the purpose of sale, or (2) sells or exposes for sale any article of manufacture to which such design or colorable imitation has been applied shall be liable to the owner to the extent of his total profit, but not less than $250, recoverable in any United States district court having jurisdiction of the parties.

At first blush, this provision seems astonishing: a plaintiff can recover the infringer's "total profit" earned by selling an infringing "article of manufacture." That is a more powerful remedy than is often available in utility patent infringement cases.

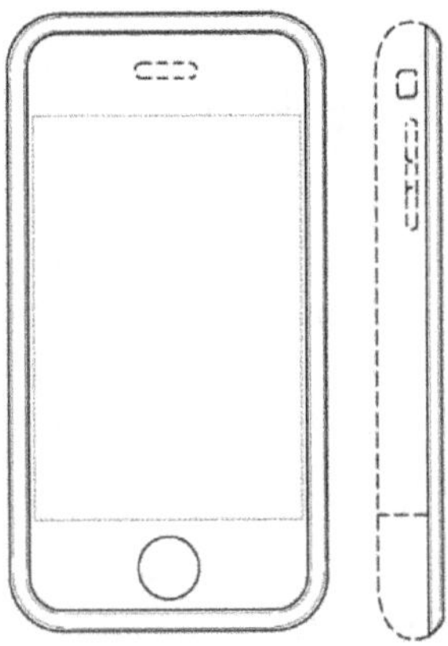

But in *Samsung Elecs. Co. v. Apple Inc.*, 580 U.S. 53 (2016), the Supreme Court limited § 289 by requiring apportionment of the infringer's total profits to reflect only the feature(s) of the accused product covered by the design patent. Apple had originally won an eye-popping $1 billion award for design patents covering the iPhone, but by the time the case reached the Supreme Court it had been whittled to a still eye-popping $399 million. One example design is shown below.

The Federal Circuit affirmed the $399 million award. It rejected Samsung's argument that the "article of manufacture" referred to in § 289 should be limited to the screen or phone cover and should not be interpreted instead to encompass the entire phone. The court reasoned that "the article of manufacture" referred to Samsung's smartphones in their totality because their screens and outer shells were not sold separately from their "innards."

The Supreme Court reversed on the question of what the term "article of manufacture" in § 289 meant in context of a multicomponent product. It concluded that the plain language of "article of manufacture" could refer to *either* a product sold to a consumer *or* a component of that product. "Thus, reading 'article of manufacture' in § 289 to cover only an end product sold to a consumer gives too narrow a meaning to the phrase." *Samsung*, 580 U.S. at 436. The Court expressly declined to decide the ultimate issues in the case—whether, for each design patent at issue, the relevant "article of manufacture" referred to a complete smartphone or only a component. It therefore would be up to the lower courts to articulate more granular guiding principles for determining whether an accused product in its entirety is an "article of manufacture" subject to damages awards equaling the defendant's "total profits" for that product—or instead merely a component, worthy of some smaller damages amount.

CHAPTER 19

THE HATCH-WAXMAN ACT

I. INTRODUCTION

The Food and Drug Administration (FDA) was formed in 1906 to enhance public health by regulating food production and pharmaceuticals, among other things. The FDA and patent law coexisted for many decades prior to the early 1980's, when Congress perceived the need to encourage the manufacturing and distribution of generic pharmaceuticals.

The Drug Price Competition and Patent Term Restoration Act, commonly known as the Hatch-Waxman Act, struck a "balance between two potentially competing policy interests—inducing pioneering development of pharmaceutical formulations . . . and facilitating efficient transition to a market with low-cost, generic copies of those pioneering inventions at the close of a patent term." *Novo Nordisk A/S v. Caraco Pharm. Labs., Ltd.*, 601 F.3d 1359 (Fed. Cir. 2010). According to this balance, the branded drug companies got three primary benefits: 1) a patent term extension of up to 5 years to compensate for FDA or USPTO delays; 2) an automatic 30-month stay on issuance of any generic during challenges to a patent's validity; and 3) a 5-year period of data exclusivity under FDA laws and rules delaying a generic from relying on the branded company's clinical studies to acquire FDA approval.

The generic companies also received three primary benefits: 1) the Abbreviated New Drug Application (ANDA), which permitted generic companies to rely on branded drug companies' clinical studies upon a showing of bioequivalence with the patented drug and expiration of the data exclusivity period; 2) exemption from infringement for showing bioequivalence before patent expiration; 3) a validity challenge to the branded drugs' patents without risking prohibitive damages that includes a 180-day period of exclusivity for the first ANDA filer.

Both NDA (new drug application) owners and ANDA owners (generic applicants) alike benefited from an Orange Book which listed patents associated with innovative new drugs. Under Hatch-Waxman patent linkage, the NDA owners knew that the Orange Book listing would prevent FDA approval of a generic as long as a valid patent appeared in the Book. The ANDA owners knew exactly which patents to challenge under the Hatch-Waxman invalidity procedure.

The core benefits for both innovators and generics show that, before patent linkage, FDA's process created two mirror-image distortions to pharmaceutical patent terms. On the one hand, the FDA's requirements took time away from patent terms on the front end. The patent term clock would often consume up to 7 years while patentees sought FDA approval to market a drug.

On the other hand, FDA procedures artificially extended patent terms because generic drug makers had to wait until a patent expired before they could even begin the lengthy drug approval process. Importantly, the Federal Circuit had ruled that generics could not avoid infringement if they experimented on an innovative drug for administrative approval purposes before patent expiration. *See Roche Prod., Inc. v. Bolar Pharm. Co.*, 733 F.2d 858 (Fed. Cir. 1984) (using pharmaceutical drugs to perform testing required by the FDA did not fall within the "experimental use" exception to patent infringement). The *Bolar* decision in April 1984 gave both generics and innovators an incentive to agree to patent linkage.

In September 1984, a few months after *Bolar*, Congress enacted the Hatch-Waxman Act. The Hatch-Waxman Act is an intricate formula linking FDA approval for safety and efficacy with USPTO approval for innovation. But at its core, the Act reflects a trade-off to fix, for both sides, the twin patent term distortions. Patentees received a term extension in 35 U.S.C. § 156; generic drug makers obtained an exemption to the *Bolar* rule in 35 U.S.C. § 271(e)(1)—the "safe harbor."

II. THE ANDA PROCESS

The process to acquire FDA approval to market a drug begins with filing an NDA. The NDA sets in motion the process to establish the new chemical entity's safety and efficacy. NDAs are costly, take multiple years to complete, and have a number of parts. For example, NDAs must include data collected from four phases of testing: (a) the preclinical stage, in vitro and animal testing; (b) clinical trial phase I, testing on a small number of humans to determine general safety and side effects; (c) clinical phase II, testing on a larger number of humans for preliminary data on efficacy in treating a particular disease; and (d) clinical phase III, testing on thousands of patients, whose results can be reliably extrapolated to the general population. An NDA must also include physical samples and full disclosures of the drug's composition, methods of manufacture, labeling, and any patents covering the drug. If the FDA approves the NDA, then the patents purportedly covering the drug are listed in a publication called the *Approved Drug Products with Therapeutic Equivalence Evaluations* (known as the "Orange Book").

However, the Hatch-Waxman Act significantly streamlines the approval process for generic drug makers. The law permits them to file ANDAs, in which they rely on the NDAs already submitted by brand-name pharmaceutical companies and simply prove "bioequivalence," i.e., that the drug they seek to market is the same drug that has already been approved.

But filing an ANDA comes with a cost—a generic drug maker must make a certification as to each patent that is identified in the Orange Book as covering the approved drug. Specifically, the applicant must certify either that (I) no such patent information has been submitted to the FDA; (II) the patent is expired; (III) the patent is set to expire on a certain date; or (IV) the patent is invalid, unenforceable, or will not be infringed by the manufacture, use, or sale of the new generic drug. These certifications are commonly referred to as Paragraph I, II, III, and IV certifications.

The different certifications have distinct consequences. ANDAs with Paragraphs I or II certifications may be approved without further delay. Because a Paragraph III certification is effectively a certification that the generic drug will not be marketed until after patent expiration, an ANDA with such a certification will not be approved until after patent expiration.

But filing a Paragraph IV certification—which is an artificial act of infringement under the statute, *Caraco Pharm. Labs., Ltd. v. Forest Labs., Inc.*, 527 F.3d 1278, 1283 (Fed. Cir. 2008) (citing 35 U.S.C. § 271(e)(2)), triggers a series of events. Specifically, the ANDA applicant must give the patentee notice of the Paragraph IV certification, as well as detailed bases for the belief that the patent is invalid, unenforceable, or not infringed. Once the patentee receives this notice, it has 45 days to sue the ANDA applicant for infringement—or else the ANDA may be approved immediately. 21 U.S.C. § 355(j)(5)(B)(iii). If the patentee sues within the 45-day time limit, approval is postponed until the earliest of (i) the patent's expiration, (ii) a judgment of invalidity or unenforceability, or (iii) 30 months after the patentee's receipt of notice—but if a party to the suit "fail[s] to reasonably cooperate in expediting the action," then the court may order a longer or shorter stay on approval, as appropriate under the circumstances. *Id.* This 30-month stay both protects the NDA owner and allows time for the court to consider the invalidity contentions at the heart of the new lawsuit. The patentee is given the first opportunity to file suit because declaratory judgment actions by the ANDA applicant are prohibited within the 45-day period.

Meanwhile, the first ANDA filer gets a significant prize for venturing to challenge the validity of the NDA drug: 180 days of generic exclusivity. Thus, the first generic applicant to file an ANDA under Paragraph IV certification gains 180 days of marketing exclusivity, meaning the FDA does not approve another ANDA for that period. This valuable benefit incentivizes generic companies to be the first to file a paragraph IV ANDA. In sum, the ANDA filer gets to challenge the patent validity without risking damages.

The following chart traces these procedures:

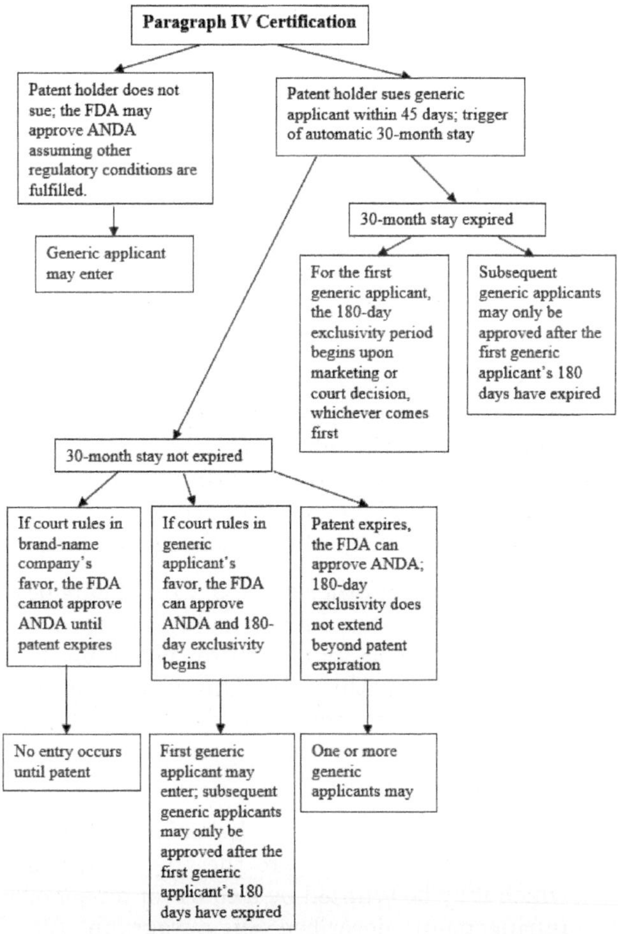

Notably, when the patentee establishes artificial infringement, it does not receive the full range of remedies available for other types of infringement. Instead, the statute provides:

> For an act of infringement described in paragraph (2)—
>
> (A) the court shall order the effective date of any approval of the drug or veterinary biological product involved in the infringement to be a date which is not earlier than the date of the expiration of the patent which has been infringed,
>
> (B) injunctive relief may be granted against an infringer to prevent the commercial manufacture, use, offer to sell, or sale within the United States or importation into the United States of an approved drug, veterinary biological product, or biological product, [and]
>
> (C) damages or other monetary relief may be awarded against an infringer only if there has been commercial manufacture, use, offer to sell, or sale within the United States or importation into the United States of an approved drug, veterinary biological product, or biological product . . . .
>
> The remedies prescribed by subparagraphs (A), (B), [and] (C) . . . are the only remedies which may be granted by a court for an act of infringement described in paragraph (2), except that a court may award attorney fees under section 285.

35 U.S.C. § 271(e)(4). Thus, the patentee may not receive monetary damages (unless the infringer has made the generic drug available to the public). Injunctive relief, which takes the form of both enjoining commercial activity as well as enjoining the approval of the ANDA, constitutes the primary award. In some circumstances—for instance, where there is litigation misconduct including vexatious or unjustified litigation or frivolous filings—attorney fees may be awarded. *Yamanouchi Pharm. Co. v. Danbury Pharmacal, Inc.*, 231 F.3d 1339 (Fed. Cir. 2000). The artificial act of infringement, however, cannot constitute willful infringement. *Glaxo Group Ltd. v. Apotex, Inc.*, 376 F.3d 1339 (Fed. Cir. 2004). In sum, the Hatch-Waxman Act encourages litigation as a public policy tool to encourage early challenges to the validity of pharmaceutical patents.

III. THE SAFE HARBOR UNDER § 271(e)(1)

35 U.S.C. § 271(e)(1) provides generic drug makers a safe harbor for making, using, selling, or offering to sell patented pharmaceutical inventions in the United States, so long as those activities are "reasonably related" to obtaining FDA approval. The types of activities that fall within the safe harbor have been the subject of controversy.

The Federal Circuit explored the boundaries of the safe harbor in *Classen Immunotherapies, Inc. v. Biogen IDEC*, 659 F.3d 1057 (Fed. Cir. 2011), and concluded that the safe harbor encompasses pre-marketing experimentation undertaken in the course of obtaining FDA marketing approval of generic drugs. Classen argued that Biogen and GlaxoSmithKline infringed by participating in studies designed to evaluate potential associations between childhood vaccinations and type I diabetes. In defense, Biogen and GlaxoSmithKline contended that § 271(e)(1) shielded them from infringement liability. The studies at issue, however, yielded information that would be submitted as a matter of course to FDA as part of a program monitoring the drug. In short, Biogen and GlaxoSmithKline were not in a "phase of research" that could possibly lead to marketing approval. And because the safe harbor provision was "directed to pre-marketing approval of generic counterparts before patent expiration," the safe harbor did not apply.

The following year, a different panel of the Federal Circuit expanded the *Bolar* exemption, arguably misconstruing *Classen* in the process. *See Momenta Pharm., Inc. v. Amphastar Pharm., Inc.*, 686 F.3d 1348 (Fed. Cir. 2012). At issue was the highly successful drug enoxaparin, a heterogeneous mixture of variable-length polysaccharide chains that made up the naturally occurring polymer heparin. Enoxaparin was used as an anti-coagulant to prevent harmful blood clots and yielded over $1 billion per year in sales revenue. Momenta asserted that Amphastar infringed by quality control testing its generic version of enoxaparin.

Amphastar planned to submit its quality control test results to the FDA on an ongoing basis to *sustain* (not *obtain*) the FDA's marketing approval of the generic drug. Amphastar argued that its quality control testing was shielded by § 271(e)(1). The Federal Circuit agreed, narrowly construing its *Classen* holding that "§ 271(e)(1) does not apply to information that may be routinely reported to the FDA, long after marketing approval has been obtained." Specifically, the court held that Amphastar's infringing quality control testing did not qualify as "routine," but instead was required by the FDA for continued marketing approval. A vigorous dissent, relying on extensive legislative history from the Hatch-Waxman Act, continued to support *Classen's* holding that the § 271(e)(1) safe harbor encompasses *pre-approval* experimental activities—not Amphastar's experimentation for post-approval purposes.

IV. THE ORANGE BOOK

As mentioned briefly above, the FDA publishes a list of all approved drugs in a publication called the *Approved Drug Products with Therapeutic Equivalence Evaluations* (i.e., the "Orange Book" because of the print version's orange cover). *See* Orange Book: Approved Drug Products With Therapeutic Equivalence Evaluations (available at https://www.accessdata.fda.gov/scripts/cder/ob/).

While the Orange Book is useful for pharmacists because it contains drugs' equivalence evaluations, it is also an important tool for resolving pharmaceutical patent disputes. The Orange Book lists all patents that a brand-name drug maker (the NDA holder) identifies as covering a drug. *See* 21 U.S.C. § 355(b)(1). Many issues arise with respect to the

Orange Book, including the eligibility of patents for inclusion in the Orange Book, the timing of patent listings, and even the mechanism for resolving disputes over Orange Book patent listings.

aaiPharma Inc. v. Thompson, 296 F.3d 227 (Fed. Cir. 2002), illustrates some challenges in ensuring the accuracy and completeness of the Orange Book. aaiPharma obtained the '853 patent on a polymorphic variant of the active ingredient in Prozac®, made by Eli Lilly. Because only the NDA holder (here Lilly) can add a patent to the Orange Book, aaiPharma asked Lilly to do so. After all, inclusion of the '853 patent in the Orange Book would give aaiPharma significant benefits—namely, in the event a generic drug maker filed an ANDA corresponding to the '853 patent, aaiPharma could preserve its market exclusivity for 30 months by filing an infringement suit and thereby triggering a stay of approval. But Lilly declined.

aaiPharma complained to the FDA, contending the FDA had the duty to ensure that the Orange Book was complete and accurate. But this argument conflicted with the FDA's own regulations, which gave the FDA a ministerial role, not the role of Orange Book arbiter. The FDA took the only action prescribed by its regulations—it sent a letter requesting that Lilly add the '853 patent to the Orange Book. But Lilly still declined. So aaiPharma filed suit against the FDA, alleging that the FDA's failure to ensure the accuracy of the Orange Book's patent listings violated the Administrative Procedure Act (APA).

The Federal Circuit explained that an NDA holder can indeed abuse the Orange Book in two ways. It can add patents to the Orange Book that do not actually cover a drug—thereby giving it the opportunity to trigger a 30-month stay of ANDA approvals that it does not deserve through litigation. It can also improperly refuse to add a third-party's patent to the Orange Book, depriving the third-party of the 30-month stay to which it is rightfully entitled. Both abuses are serious.

But, the Circuit explained, there is no remedy in the law for these potential abuses. The court in *Andrx Pharm., Inc. v. Biovail Corp.*, 276 F.3d 1368 (Fed. Cir. 2002), had held that a generic drug maker cannot sue an NDA holder for declaratory or injunctive relief requiring the NDA to de-list a patent from the Orange Book. It follows, the court explained in *aaiPharma,* that a third-party likewise cannot sue to force an NDA holder to list a patent in the Orange Book.

Nor is there a remedy at the FDA. aaiPharma argued that, when someone complains that the Orange Book patent listings are inaccurate, the FDA must do more than simply ask the NDA holder about it and accept whatever it says. This level of "ministeriality" improperly delegates the FDA's statutory duties to NDA holders.

The Federal Circuit rejected this argument. Using a Chevron analysis, the court first determined that Congress has not clearly expressed its intent regarding the FDA's role in correcting the Orange Book's patent listings. In the second Chevron step, the court concluded that the FDA's regulation establishing the ministerial nature of its role with respect to the Orange Book's patent listings was a reasonable interpretation of the statute. The court therefore concluded that the FDA is not obligated to adjudicate disputes regarding the correctness of the Orange Book's patent listings; rather it only has to ensure either that some patents are listed or there is no patent to list.

The court also punted the problem to Congress. "We conclude that until Congress takes further action to address the enforcement gap in Hatch Waxman's patent listing provisions, the FDA may persist in its purely ministerial approach to the Orange Book listing process." *aaiPharma*, 296 F.3d at 243.

In 2003, a year after *aaiPharma*, the FDA promulgated regulations clarifying what patents should be listed on the Orange Book—namely patents covering active ingredients, formulations and compositions, and methods of use. However, patents merely pertaining to processes, packaging, metabolites, and intermediates must not be listed on the Orange Book.

That same year, Congress amended the Hatch-Waxman Act to allow generic drug makers, if sued for infringement for filing an ANDA, to bring a counterclaim to de-list the asserted patent from Orange Book. *See* 21 U.S.C. §§ 355(j)(5)(C)(ii), 355(c)(3)(D)(ii).

V. DECLARATORY JUDGMENT JURISDICTION

The Hatch-Waxman Act incentivizes quick resolution of patent disputes by granting the NDA holder a 30-month stay of ANDA approval for filing an infringement suit based on an ANDA's Paragraph IV certification. But in some cases, an NDA holder may not wish to file suit. Although it may seem odd at first, generic drug makers are often displeased with this scenario because they might prefer not to commit further resources to manufacturing with patent issues lurking. In such situations, an ANDA applicant may wish to initiate the suit on its own based on declaratory judgment jurisdiction.

As discussed earlier, the Supreme Court has addressed the declaratory judgment standard in the patent context in *MedImmune, Inc. v. Genentech, Inc.*, 549 U.S. 118 (2007). The Court held that a patent licensee need not terminate a license—and therefore risk treble damages for willful infringement later—before filing a declaratory judgment suit. The accused infringer paid the patent owner the royalties it demanded, and *then* filed suit for declaratory judgment of non-infringement. Apart from the fact that the licensee had actually paid the royalty, there was no dispute that declaratory judgment jurisdiction would have been proper. The question was thus whether paying a royalty extinguishes declaratory judgment jurisdiction, or instead whether a "case or controversy" can exist even when a licensee has not yet repudiated and breached a licensee agreement.

The Court recited the expansive standard it had previously adopted: "whether the facts alleged, under all the circumstances, show that there is a substantial controversy, between parties having adverse legal interests, of sufficient immediacy and reality to warrant the issuance of a declaratory judgment." *MedImmune*, 549 U.S. at 127. This standard may be met, the Court concluded, even where the licensee has not repudiated the license.

Later that year, in *Teva Pharmaceuticals USA, Inc. v. Novartis Pharmaceuticals Corp.*, 482 F.3d 1330 (Fed. Cir. 2007), the Federal Circuit applied *MedImmune* in the Hatch-Waxman context. The NDA holder, Novartis, listed five drugs in the Orange Book as covering the drug Famvir®, a herpes drug. But when Teva filed an ANDA application for approval to market its generic version, Novartis filed an infringement suit only as to a single patent—the '937 patent covering Famvir's active ingredient. In response, Teva filed a declaratory judgment action as to the remaining four method patents out of a desire for "patent certainty."

Still pre-*MedImmune*, the district court applied the Federal Circuit's narrower, pre-*MedImmune* "reasonable apprehension of suit" test and dismissed Teva's claims for lack of declaratory judgment jurisdiction. This relatively high standard had required (1) an explicit threat or other action by the patentee that created a reasonable apprehension of suit, and (2) present activity—or concrete steps taken with intent to conduct such activity—by the accused infringer that could constitute infringement.

Applying the intervening *MedImmune* decision, the Federal Circuit reversed. Novartis argued that the four non-asserted method patents were "an entirely different controversy" than the '937 patent on the active ingredient. But the court disagreed. While Novartis's and Teva's suits were different "cases," they stemmed from the same controversy created when Novartis listed all five patents in the Orange Book.

Moreover, Teva infringed by submitting Paragraph IV certifications for all five patents. *See* 35 U.S.C. § 271(e). This solution was consistent with Congress's objectives to resolve patent disputes under the Hatch-Waxman Act as quickly as possible. It also prevented the NDA holder from gaming the system by obtaining the 30-month stay while also keeping significant patent questions unresolved to the detriment of the generic drug company. Under "all the circumstances," the court concluded, the declaratory judgment jurisdiction standard was met even for Novartis's four non-asserted method patents.

VI. AUTHORIZED GENERICS

Sometimes NDA holders market their drugs both as brand-name drugs *and* separately as generic drugs at reduced prices (called "authorized" or "flanking" generics). A brand-name company may elect to pursue this strategy to maximize profits, or it may use this procedure as leverage to induce a settlement with the generic. Under this approach, the NDA holder could license a generic company to make the drug as part of a settlement agreement. Marketing authorized generics can be an effective strategy to dominate the market.

This practice has proven controversial, however, because an authorized generic commonly diminishes the value of the 180-day generic market exclusivity belonging to the first generic drug maker to file a Paragraph IV certification. *See* 21 U.S.C. § 355(j)(5)(B)(iv). This exclusivity period prohibits competition from later ANDA filers and can be understood as a reward to the first ANDA filer for quickly opening itself up to litigation. The reward thus promotes the speedy resolution of pharmaceutical patent disputes.

But NDA holders themselves are not prohibited from competing in the generic market during the 180-day period, and so they may market both the higher-priced, brand-name drug *and* the lower-priced generic drug at the same time. In such cases, the reward to the first Paragraph IV filer is undoubtedly diminished, and to some extent so is the general incentive for drug makers to quickly file Paragraph IV certifications.

This controversy came to a head in *Mylan Pharmaceuticals, Inc. v. U.S. Food and Drug Administration*, 454 F.3d 270 (4th Cir. 2006). Proctor & Gamble (P&G) obtained an NDA for its brand-name drug, Macrobid®, an antibacterial drug. Just as Mylan (the first ANDA filer) began its 180-day generic market exclusivity period, a third-party began selling its own generic under a license from P&G. Not pleased, Mylan petitioned the FDA to issue a ruling prohibiting the third-party and P&G from competing in the generic market during Mylan's 180-day exclusivity period. And when the FDA denied Mylan's petition, Mylan sued the FDA for violation of the APA.

The dispute at the Fourth Circuit was whether FDA had the statutory power to exclude authorized generics from the market during the first ANDA filer's 180-day exclusivity period. The court held it did not. Mylan made an ultimately unsuccessful statutory interpretation argument: although the statutory text plainly did not prohibit authorized generics from entering the market during the 180-day period, the court should nevertheless set aside the plain language in favor of Congress's supposed intent to give the first ANDA filer 180 days of absolute generic market exclusivity.

The court reasoned that, while Congress did seek to protect the interests of generic drug companies in enacting the Hatch-Waxman Act, Mylan had ignored the countervailing interests of NDA holders that Congress also sought to protect. And nothing in the statute restricted the right of NDA holders to grant licenses to third-parties.

VII. PATENT LINKAGE ABROAD

An important recent development is China's enactment of its own patent linkage system. Article 76 of China's Fourth Amendment of Patent Law (effective June 1, 2021) establishes a dual-track dispute resolution system during the marketing approval process for generic drugs—similar in many ways to the United States' Hatch-Waxman Act. The system involves the use of the China Patent Information Registration Platform for Marketed Drugs ("CPIRPMD"), which corresponds to the United States' Orange Book. Brand companies are to register patents in the CPIRPMD, and generic companies must submit a declaration asserting one of four statuses of listed patents in order to obtain marketing approval: (I) no patent listed, (II) the patents are expired, licensed, or have been declared invalid, (III) the generic drug will not be marketed until expiration, or (IV) the generic drug does not practice the patents or the patents will be declared invalid. If a brand company receives a Type IV declaration, it may choose whether to litigate in the Beijing Intellectual Property Court or the National Medical Products Administration. This development is an important step forward for all stakeholders in the Chinese pharmaceutical market.

INDEX

References are to Pages